WONDROUS DIFFERENCE

FILM AND CULTURE
John Belton, Editor

Film and Culture
A SERIES OF COLUMBIA UNIVERSITY PRESS
Edited by John Belton

What Made Pistachio Nuts?
Henry Jenkins

Showstoppers: Busby Berkeley and the Tradition of Spectacle
Martin Rubin

Projections of War: Hollywood, American Culture, and World War II
Thomas Doherty

Laughing Screaming: Modern Hollywood Horror and Comedy
William Paul

Laughing Hysterically: American Screen Comedy of the 1950s
Ed Sikov

Primitive Passions: Visuality, Sexuality, Ethnography,
and Contemporary Chinese Cinema
Rey Chow

The Cinema of Max Ophuls: Magisterial Vision and the Figure of Woman
Susan M. White

Black Women as Cultural Readers
Jacqueline Bobo

Picturing Japaneseness: Monumental Style, National Identity, Japanese Film
Darrell William Davis

Attack of the Leading Ladies:
Gender, Sexuality, and Spectatorship in Classic Horror Cinema
Rhona J. Berenstein

WONDROUS

Difference

CINEMA, ANTHROPOLOGY,

& TURN-OF-THE-CENTURY

VISUAL CULTURE

Alison Griffiths

COLUMBIA UNIVERSITY PRESS   NEW YORK

Columbia University Press
Publishers Since 1893
New York   Chichester, West Sussex
Copyright © 2002 Columbia University Press
All rights reserved

Library of Congress Cataloging-in-Publication Data
Griffiths, Alison, 1963–
Wondrous Difference : cinema, anthropology, and turn-of-the-century visual culture /
Alison Griffiths.
p. cm.
Includes bibliographical references and index.
ISBN 0-231-11696-9 (alk. paper) — ISBN 0-231-11697-7 (pbk : alk. paper)
1. Motion pictures in ethnology—History.   2. Indigenous peoples in motion pictures—History.
3. Ethnological museums and collections—History.   I. Title.
GN347 .G73 2002
305.8—dc21   2001047227

∞
Columbia University Press books are printed on permanent and durable acid-free paper.

Printed in the United States of America

c 10 9 8 7 6 5 4 3 2 1
p 10 9 8 7 6 5 4 3 2 1

Columbia University Press wishes to express its appreciation

for assistance given by the Drown Fund of Baruch College

toward the cost of publishing this book.

For Valerie Griffiths and in memory of my father,
Thomas Henry Griffiths

Contents

Acknowledgments

WERE THERE ethnographic films before Robert Flaherty's *Nanook of the North*? This book began with this question some ten years ago, when I first attempted to marry my interests in early cinema and ethnographic film. Struck by the dearth of material on ethnographic filmmaking from the early cinema period, I soon realized that the terrain I was entering, while intellectually stimulating, was amorphous and potentially boundless. In my pursuit of precinematic antecedents and intellectual and institutional horizons for ethnographic film, cinema sometimes seemed like a vanishing point on an ever-receding landscape; by the time I completed three chapters of the dissertation, none of them directly addressing film, I began to have serious doubts about my approach. However, I came to believe that the questions these precinematic chapters addressed were vital in appreciating the intersections between cinema, anthropology, and turn-of-the-century visual culture. With support from faculty from both cinema studies and anthropology at New York University, including Antonia Lant (my adviser), Faye Ginsburg (whose intellectual rigor and unstinting generosity left an indelible mark on this book), Robert Stam, Richard Allen, and Fred Myers, I was encouraged to take on what turned out to be an immensely rewarding topic, one marked by moments of both intellectual exhilaration and self-doubt.

Years later, several people played pivotal roles in converting the dissertation into the present book, including David and Judith MacDougall, who vitalized some of my research questions during the latter stages of research and writing, and reviewers Richard Abel, Dana Polan, and Jay Ruby (along with an anonymous reader for Columbia University Press), who offered sound advice about revising the manuscript. In the book's final stages, Tom Gunning's careful and rigorous reading of the manuscript helped me make important adjustments in argument and tone. I am grateful to John Belton, too, for his critical input and thoughtful response to issues both large and small.

Two fellowships—a Graduate School of Arts and Sciences Dean's Dissertation Fellowship from NYU and a Charlotte Newcomb Dissertation Fellowship—afforded me the luxury of devoting all my energy to writing and revising. At Baruch College of the City University of New York, I have been fortunate in receiving unstinting support from Robert Myers, my Department Chair, as well as from Dean Alexander Logue and Provost Myrna Chase. Archivists in both England and the United States showed great ingenuity in tracking down sometimes obscure materials, and I would like to thank the following individuals for their patience and professionalism: in the U.K., Alison Strauss and Luke McKernan at the National Film and Television Archive, Roger Smither at the Film Division of the Imperial War Museum, Godfrey Waller in the manuscripts division of Cambridge University Library, Anita Herle at the Cambridge University Museum of Archaeology and Anthropology, Elizabeth Edwards at the Pitt Rivers Museum in Oxford, and Chris Wright at the Royal Anthropological Institute.

In the United States I would like to acknowledge the aid of curators and staff members at the American Museum of Natural History (AMNH), which became my second home during an intense period of research in both the special collections division of the library and the anthropology department. This book is indebted to the institution in a great many ways, and even when visiting the Museum with my family today, I find myself drifting toward the elevators leading to the fourth floor library. Several individuals at the AMNH are owed special thanks, including Barbara Mathé, Mark Katzman, Belinda Kaye, Elaine Charnov, and Joel Sweimler, who first brought to my attention scrapbooks containing a wealth of information on the history of film exhibition at the Museum. In Washington, D.C., Rosemary Hanes at the Library of Congress, Jake Homiak and his staff at the Human Studies Film Archive at the Smithsonian Institution, and Paula Fleming, archivist at the National Anthropological Archives helped me track down elusive film and print resources. Charles Silver at the Museum of Modern Art Film Study Center, Deborah Wythe at the Art Reference Library at the Brooklyn Museum of Art, and the interlibrary loan departments at the libraries of New York University and Baruch College of the City University of New York made life easier for me in the painstaking print research; I am sure they must have been relieved to see the back of me once the bulk of my research was over. My research assistants, John Zhang and Simone Senhouse-Gorham, played important roles in the final stages of manuscript preparation, and at Columbia University Press, my editor, Jennifer Crewe, and copyeditor, Roy Thomas, were a delight to work with. The following colleagues, family members, and friends have all been influential and may detect their presence in the book in some shape or form: Giorgio Bertellini, David Birdsell, Stephen Bottomore, Iris Cahn, Scott Curtis, Nurgul Ebril, Sara Friendly, John Fullerton, Jean Gallagher, Marie Gillespie, Beth Griffiths, Jim Griffiths, Nigel Griffiths, Anna Grimshaw, Alex Keller, Brian Larkin, James Latham, Scott MacDonald, Toby Miller, Margaret Montalbano, Amanda Roderick, Cindy Rosenthal, Karen Schwartzman, Bill Simon, Deborah Snyder, and Paul Willemen.

This book would not have been possible without Val Griffiths, whose courage, passion for knowledge, and gutsy outlook on life was just what I needed in our lengthy phone calls; she deserves the dedication a thousand times over. My biggest debt, however, is to William Boddy, who has influenced this book in so many ways that it is hard to know where to begin. Finally, writing and rewriting wouldn't have been half as much fun without the involvement of Evan Thomas and Tess Margaret, who brought fresh perspectives and a good deal else to bear along the way.

CREDITS: Portions of this book have appeared in different form in the following publications (cited chronologically):

" 'Journeys for Those Who Cannot Travel': Promenade Cinema and the Museum Life Group," *Wide Angle* 18.3 (July 1996): 53–84;

"Science and Spectacle: Native American Representation in Early Cinema," in Elizabeth Bird, ed., *Dressing in Feathers: The Construction of the Indian in American Popular Culture*, 79–95 (Boulder, Colo.: Westview, 1996);

"Knowledge and Visuality in Turn-of-the-Century Anthropology: The Early Ethnographic Cinema of Alfred Cort Haddon and Walter Baldwin Spencer," *Visual Anthropology Review* 12.2 (Fall-Winter 1996–97): 18–43;

" 'To Disappoint the Ravages of Time': Precinematic Ethnography at the American Museum of Natural History," in Claire Dupré la Tour, André Gaudreault, and Roberta Pearson, eds., *Cinema at the Turn of the Century*, 107–12 (Quebec and Switzerland: Éditions Payot Lausanne/Éditions Nota Bene, 1999);

" 'To the World the World We Show': Early Travelogues as Filmed Ethnography," *Film History* 11.3 (September 1999): 282–307;

" 'We Partake, as it Were, of His Life': The Status of the Visual in Early Ethnographic Film," in John Fullerton and Astrid Söderbergh-Widding, eds., *Moving Images: From Edison to the Webcam*, 91–110. Sydney: John Libbey, 1999.

and " 'Yes in Truth All the World Was There': World's Fairs and the Social Horizon of Early Ethnographic Film," *Living Pictures* 1.1 (July 2001): 58–77.

Illustrations

Introduction

ALBERT ECKHOUT'S 1641 painting of West Indian Tarairiu Indians on the cover of this book may seem an unlikely introduction to a work addressing cinema, anthropology, and visual culture at the beginning of the twentieth century. Predating the emergence of cinema by some two hundred and fifty years, the painting is rooted in a social world far removed from that of early cinema's era of late colonialism, urbanization, and industrialization. But if this seventeenth-century painting and early cinema share little in terms of their contexts and material base, each powerfully evokes the ambivalent emotional register of "wondrous difference" which marked the historically disparate efforts of western painters, photographers, and filmmakers to visually evoke the encounter with the ethnographic Other.[1]

"Wondrous difference" suggests the sense of both amazement and unease which have long inflected the reception of a wide range of images, moving and still, depicting distant and exotic peoples for popular audiences in the West. Paintings like Eckhout's established a tradition for representing native identities, encapsulating the ambivalence at the heart of visual representations of cultural Otherness. In a manner we will encounter in several early ethnographic photographs and films, Eckhout's iconography of savagery (nudity, spears, decorative feathers, animated dancing) is tempered by a suggestion of the subjective complexities of the people shown, including their awareness of the act of their inscription (three of the dancers seem to return the gaze of the painting's viewer), in the representation of the dancing as a social performance witnessed (and commented upon) by female tribe members, and in the vibrancy and animation of the image itself.

xix

That this ambivalence toward the ethnographic Other is visibly inscribed in a painting from the mid-seventeenth century should come as no surprise given the long tradition of image-making devoted to the representation of native peoples.[2] As I argue in the first part of this book, ethnographic cinema emerged not from a single site but from a confluence of discursive practices and image-making techniques that were remodeled to fit with cinema's institutional and ontological forms. Eckhout's painting is testimony to an enduring Western fascination with representing native peoples, a fascination conventionalized through the tropes of performance (as we shall see, dance quickly became a staple of ethnographic film), exotic mise-en-scène, and the spectacle of nudity. Our own ambivalent reaction to Eckhout's representation of the Tarairiu Indians is itself evoked in the image; while we don't identify, exactly, with the whispering women, our gaze is certainly partially mediated through their presence within the frame, and the muscular bodies of the nude dancers suggest the libidinal appeal of such representations. The sense of "wondrous difference" evoked by Eckhout's treatment of the bodies and rituals of the exotic Other can be found today when we view *National Geographic* programs on public television, turn our cable remote to the Discovery Channel, or attend the Margaret Mead Film and Video Festival, held annually at the American Museum of Natural History (AMNH) in New York City.

However, for the anthropological community over the past one hundred years, negotiating the paradoxical valences of "wondrous difference" has been a persistent intellectual and ethical challenge, implicit in the perennial debates over which representational forms are best suited for the dissemination of ethnographic knowledge. Visuality has been a double-edged sword for anthropologists, and a majority of anthropologists has always seemed more comfortable working with written forms of ethnographic data collection, resisting the use of imaging technologies in fieldwork. As late as 1960, pioneering visual anthropologist Margaret Mead urged her colleagues to make greater use of the technologies of the still camera, audiotape recorder, and motion picture camera in her speech as outgoing president of the American Anthropological Association. According to some observers, the reaction among Mead's professional audience was decidedly mixed. Her appeals were greeted with "restless stirrings and angry murmurs . . . as these notebook-oriented scholars expressed their irritation at this revolutionary suggestion."[3]

In some respects, however, it is hardly surprising that Mead's colleagues should have balked at the idea of using tape recorders and motion picture cameras in the field; beyond Mead's and Gregory Bateson's[4] own pathbreaking forays into ethnographic film and the isolated projects undertaken by Jean Rouch in France[5] and at the Institute für den Wissenschaftlichen Film (IWF) in Germany, there had been little intellectual or professional support for ethnographic filmmaking before 1960, and visual anthropology as a whole occupied a precarious position within the larger discipline.[6] The often prohibitive cost of film equipment and stock within the modest budgets of most fieldwork expeditions, together with the lack of training in cinematography and editing, put off all but the most intrepid of would-be ethnographic filmmakers. Furthermore, the association of motion pictures with cheap entertainment continued to discourage its use as a scientific apparatus. Exasperated by the antipathy of most of her fellow anthropologists toward film, all Mead could do was pursue her own ambitious program of ethnographic filmmaking and, where appropriate, gently chide her colleagues. But even if anthropologists had been able to overcome their technical inexperience, ignore cinema's ancestral ties to the fairground, and generate sufficient funds to buy a camera and film supplies, they were still left with the problem of what to do with the footage they recorded in the field. Would it function primarily as a visual supplement to written field notes, or would it impinge in more direct ways upon anthropological theory by being used not only as an extension of the eye, to paraphrase ethnographic filmmaker and theorist David MacDougall, but as an extension of the mind, a way of furthering conceptual understanding of indigenous cultures?[7] Should the unedited footage be made available merely to a small group of specialized researchers, or should it be edited to produce a work of interest to commercial distributors for theatrical audiences? Anthropologists also worried about controlling the exhibition context of their films. What effect would the screening venue have upon the film's reception, the credibility of the anthropologist-filmmaker, and the reputation of the institution hosting the event?

To a large extent, these questions have continued to vex visual anthropologists since Mead's address to her colleagues some forty years ago. If fist-sized digital cameras connected to laptop computers for editing in the field have revised traditional practices of cross-cultural image-making, anthropologists are nevertheless still left with the question of how to give their films the widest possible exposure and utility. Museums of natural history, especially the AMNH, have been important institutions in bringing the work of an international group of ethnographic filmmakers to the public, and are pivotal sites of investigation in this book. And yet, as I argue in chapter 6, cinema has always been something of an interloper in the twentieth-century museum, finding a niche market with IMAX attractions, but always remaining marginal in other exhibits. For example, a series of films programmed to accompany the popular 1999 AMNH exhibit "Epidemic" was poorly attended, despite the success of the temporary exhibition. It may be that the viewing conditions necessary for cinema somehow undercut the modes of ambulatory and distracted spectating found in the museum, and that, aside from ethnographic film festivals and giant-screen formats such as IMAX, people don't normally associate cinema viewing with going to a museum.

The challenge of defining cinema's place within museums of natural history has been framed by the perceived need for maintaining the proper scientific tenor in museum exhibits and public lectures. This problem has preoccupied museum curators since the late nineteenth century, perhaps at no time more clearly than at present, as museums compete with IMAX-equipped commercial multiplexes and entertainment complexes for urban audiences. As the first chapter of this book demonstrates, preserving a balance between civic mission and economic market has never been easy for museum administrators. While contemporary museums appropriate the protocols and values of the business world into their operations, retail and leisure complexes look to museums for tips on how to integrate media into their commercial displays. Today, retail stores with interactive kiosks increasingly resemble museums, and museums, with their flight simulators, prominently displayed corporate underwriting, and extensive retail operations, seem to blur into contemporary theme parks. The fate of the traditional public space of the museum seems increasingly under fire on a number of fronts, including from companies such as Discovery Zone, a Chicago-based firm which offers for-profit play centers for children.[8]

In many ways, the museum has been the central staging ground for debates over cinema, anthropology, and visual culture for much of the twentieth century; more than any other cultural site, the museum has been responsible for representing anthropology's public face, for giving audiences an opportunity to learn about its findings, methods, and predispositions. At the same time, putting the discipline of anthropology itself, as well as its objects of study, on display in the new institutional setting of the museum and world's fair provoked anxieties among anthropologists. Using world's fairs and expositions as training grounds for display methods and curatorial practices that would be taken up by museums, anthropologists looked to the rich and often frenetic visual culture of the nineteenth century for tips on making the discipline of anthropology accessible to the masses. At the same time, the immensely popular world's fairs in turn-of-the-century America informed the viewing experiences of museumgoers and early cinema audiences.

Turn-of-the-century museum curators were as conscious of institutional demands to make the museum experience interesting, even pleasurable, as their counterparts are today; for both generations, the central challenge lay in striking the proper balance between popular appeal and scientific rigor. For museum administrators at the beginning of the twentieth century, it was important to differentiate their culturally exalted institutions from the extremely popular, if culturally disparaged, commercial dime museum. Writing in the *Architectural Record* in 1900, L. A. Gratacap viewed the relationship between higher and lower forms of museological display in uncomplicated terms: "The Popular [*sic*] system of the scientific Museum is the system of the Dime Museum greatly elevated, dignified, and replenished with culture."[9] H. C. Bumpus spoke on behalf of several museum professionals when he voiced concern about the cluttered, disorganized, and inaccessible displays filling the vast majority of turn-of-the-century museums: "For purposes of popular exhibition and profitable instruction we no longer seek the exhaustive collections of 'every known species'; we look askance at extraordinary and monstrous types; we view with some misgivings the elaborately technical schemes of classification . . . and we become thoughtful when we witness the visitor's vacuity of expression as he passes before cases devoted to the phylogeny of the arachnids."[10] Bumpus's disapproval of the freak-show display of "extraordinary and monstrous types" was echoed by other professional curators at the beginning of the twentieth century. Frank Woolnough declared in the British *Museums Journal* in 1904 that "the old curiosity shop days of the museum are over. The misguided lamb with two heads, and the pig with two tails, are relegated to a back closet, if they have not already found a resting place in the sphere of the dust-bin. There is so much that is beautiful in nature to preserve that we have neither time, space, nor inclination to perpetuate her freaks and errors."[11] However, while some critics bemoaned the sensationalist leanings of turn-of-the-century popular museums, others worried that more officially sanctioned museums discouraged visitors with their overly scholarly preoccupations; for example, turn-of-the-century National Museum president George Browne Goode himself expressed this ambivalence when he criticized museums for being "both vulgar sideshows and elitist enclaves."[12]

With exhibit sponsorship arrangements between corporate enterprises and museums increasingly the norm in the beginning of the twenty-first century, Goode's concern seems as relevant today as over a century ago. In order to boost attendance at natural history museums, many institutions now feel the need for blockbuster shows, such as the 1994 AMNH "Jurassic Park" exhibition, inspired by the eponymous Steven Spielberg movie. The consideration of how temporary exhibits may piggy-back with a Hollywood blockbuster or other commercial artifacts is not unusual in exhibition design. Furthermore, the installation of an IMAX screen as an attendance booster and significant source of supplementary revenue is increasingly the norm.[13] But if the "Jurassic Park" exhibit was hugely successful in terms of attendance, it was nevertheless criticized by some members of the AMNH curatorial staff for what they saw as its crass commercialism. Elaine Charnov, director of the Margaret Mead Festival at the AMNH, for example, viewed the sponsored exhibit as an example of what she terms the "Disneyfication of culture institutions," as market forces seek a home within institutions of public culture.[14]

Traditional exhibits and annual events at museums of natural history thus compete with high-profile, high-profit, attractions such as IMAX, which, while popular with museumgoers, serve to blur the line between science and entertainment. Indeed, the case of IMAX screens within contemporary museums of natural history resonates with the concerns of AMNH president Henry Fairfield Osborn at the turn of the century about the dubious scientific value of film screenings at the Museum. Competing with Sony's commercial IMAX multiplex some ten blocks away, AMNH administrators promote IMAX as an educational experience in much the same way as their predecessors responsible for programming film at the AMNH ninety years before struggled to purge early cinema's associations with cheap and popular entertainment through rigorous supervision of film exhibition.

In light of such perennial institutional tensions, it should come as little surprise that anthropologists have been interested in (and perplexed by) the legibility of the photographic and cinematic sign as ethnographic evidence for most of the past century.[15] Beyond anxieties over cinema's roots in popular spectacle and the real difficulties in using motion pictures in the field, this ambivalence toward cinema also relates to a series of paradigmatic shifts within early twentieth-century anthropology, including the waning of social evolutionism and the emergence of the Malinowskian model of extended fieldwork. To put it simply, the kinds of questions that anthropologists were increasingly interested in pursuing in their fieldwork steered them away from visual forms of data collection in favor of the production of written texts. The rise of structural functionalism within British anthropology and of cultural relativism within American anthropology at the beginning of the twentieth century provoked new skepticism about claims for photography's scientific value.[16] As C. A. Bayly has argued, modern anthropology "saw the displacement of the desire for certainty on the part of the investigator from tangible outward physical features in favour of a system of knowledge whose reliability was vouchsafed by the writer's familiarity through direct contact with his subjects."[17] Visual media were increasingly judged ill-equipped to meet anthropology's changing methodological, theoretical, and institutional protocols. The elevated status of the anthropological monograph, which aimed to convey information not available through the mere examination of visible evidence, marginalized photography and film within ethnography, further discouraging anthropologists from adding mechanical recordings to their arsenal of fieldwork techniques. For most ethnographers, anthropology's faith in the written word closed the door to exploring cinema's potential as an ethnographic tool.[18]

This does not mean that twentieth-century anthropologists suddenly stopped taking photographs altogether or abandoned all attempts at using film to record native cultures. Rather, anthropology's emerging theoretical premises and goals placed new demands upon ethnographic data collection, demands ill-suited to the media of photography and film.[19] As anthropologists devoted more attention to aspects of culture that could *not* be rendered visually, they turned to their notebooks rather than their cameras. Consequently, by the mid-teens, photography was regarded by most anthropologists as "marginal in the process of explanation," capable of recording surface, not depth, successful at conveying information about indigenous technology but not about important matters of social structure and cultural beliefs.[20] While the anthropometric photograph of the naked native body before a grid background had served as a classificatory index for mid-nineteenth-century evolutionist theories of human development, the project of using the more recent technology of motion pictures to a similar end was considered irrelevant to anthropology's new challenge of representing the more subtle and complex questions of cultural patterns and belief systems.[21]

These paradigmatic shifts within anthropology left cinema somewhat adrift by the teens and twenties, forcing ethnographic film to continuously reinvent itself for much of the first half of the twentieth century. In 1955, for example, physical anthropologist Anthony Michaelis made a case for cinema's utility within anthropometric research, arguing that a great many "dynamic morphological characters" could be quantitatively recorded and analyzed providing the researcher developed a standardized experimental procedure.[22] Seemingly unaware of the work done by such distant predecessors as the French physician Félix-Louis Regnault,[23] who chronophotographed Senegalese men and women at the 1895 Exposition Ethnographique de l'Afrique Occidentale in Paris, Michaelis made a case for the utility of cinema within physical anthropology as if for the first time.[24]

An examination of the vibrant visual culture of the late nineteenth century can thus tell us a great deal about the roots of anthropology's ambivalent relationship to cinema. While contemporary ethnographic films are largely produced for nontheatrical markets, such as public television and specialized film festivals, ethnographic filmmaking before 1915 formed part of the visual lexicon of mainstream American popular culture. For example, it was not unusual for nickelodeon audiences to view a film of "Life in Japan" on the same bill as a melodrama or slapstick comedy.[25] This is not to suggest that today's audiences are any less interested in images of exotic peoples than they were a hundred years ago; on the contrary, one only has to look at contemporary advertisements from global computing firms such as IBM or producers of "lifestyle" products such as mineral water to see how intensively images of native peoples are used in marketing (the spate of ads featuring native peoples prior to and during the Olympics every four years suggests how discourses of exoticism, the "global village," and technology's supposed ability to break down social, cultural, and linguistic divides have become part of the marketing zeitgeist). Nevertheless, images of native peoples occupied a different place in the social imaginary of nineteenth-century and early twentieth-century Americans than they do today; in a period of imperial expansion, new touristic mobility, and urban and industrial change, Americans were coming into contact with native peoples (and their images on the screen) in unprecedented ways.

Exploring how early twentieth-century Americans encountered images of native peoples is one of the major goals of this book. By plugging gaps in our understanding of the complex relationships between cinema, anthropology, and turn-of-the-century visual culture, this book contextualizes early ethnographic film within the shifting intellectual milieu of the young discipline of anthropology and the vibrant arena of popular entertainment. Moreover, through excavating what Jonathan Crary calls the "visible tracks" left by a historical observer—tracks that cannot be identified in relation to images alone, but must be located in "other, grayer practices and discourses"—this book offers a more nuanced understanding of how images of native peoples produced in the context of the museum, world's fair, photograph, and motion picture were consumed by Western audiences.[26]

This book examines the visual culture of late nineteenth-century and early twentieth-century America—in particular, films with ethnographic content made between 1894 and 1915, although the final chapter also looks at the filmmaking of anthropologists working between 1925 and 1930. In some respects, the first two decades after cinema's invention are ethnographic film's "golden years" in terms of the sheer number of films produced and innovations in style and content. This era is certainly more dynamic than the interwar years, which, despite an increase in anthropological "single concept" films (those documenting ceremonies, native industries, and social customs distributed for university classroom use), remained dominated by ethnographic spectaculars that interpolated actuality footage into adventure-filled narratives. While films of the classical Hollywood era such as *Chang* (Merian C. Cooper and Ernest B. Schoedsack, 1927), *Congorilla* (Martin and Osa Johnson,

1932), and *King Kong* (Cooper and Schoedsack, 1933) contain scenes of ethnographic interest, such elements were subordinated to the narrative conventions of classical Hollywood filmmaking. But even before these examples, the vast majority of films representing native peoples were produced by commercial manufacturers, not anthropologists.

Notwithstanding the research into early nonfiction film and the travelogue by Fatimah Tobing Rony[27] and Jennifer Peterson,[28] actualities have generally attracted little scholarly attention compared to the fictional film.[29] In contrast to most fictional films, it is often difficult to identify the provenance of early actualities—where, why, and by whom a film was shot—contributing to their marginalization within the scholarly universe of early cinema texts. For anthropologists, this lack of specific information about the nature and context of the cinematic encounter severely limits the value of these films as ethnographic evidence. There is also the problem of how to respond to films that seem to be as much about the pleasures of looking as they are about anthropological explication; as Tom Gunning has argued, the "most characteristic quality of a 'view' [his term for early nonfiction film] lies in the way it mimes the act of looking and observing. In other words, we don't just experience a 'view' film as a presentation of a place, an event, or a process, but also as the mimesis of the act of observing."[30] The challenge for critics is to be sensitive to the distinct levels of signification operating in these films, including their overt aestheticism (hand-tinting, for example), their obsession with the corporeal, and their reflexivity (variously seen in a subject's return gaze, the movements of an on-screen individual who appears to be directing the profilmic action, and the occasional glimpses of the motion picture apparatus). This polysemic quality has no doubt daunted early cinema scholars who, like anthropologists, are also frustrated by the historical indeterminacy surrounding many of these filmic artifacts. At the Nederlands Filmmuseum Archive's Third Early Cinema Workshop, "The Eye of the Beholder" in 1998, for example, it was pointed out that such commonplace contemporary terms as "the colonial gaze" and "Western-looking regimes" can attribute too much power to the motion picture camera, while the axiomatic status of such terms can discourage film scholars from considering alternative ways of reading the films.[31] In the absence of precise information about a film's conditions of production and the negotiations between native peoples and filmmaker, our only entry points into the ethnographic meaning of a film are based upon information gleaned from promotional materials, critical reports, and from the surviving print itself, including the demeanor of the filmed subjects, the degree of apparent staging, and the position of the camera as an index of social relations. However, recognizing that textual clues and trade press descriptions cannot substitute for firsthand accounts of such cross-cultural encounters (which will themselves be inflected with subjective biases), we must proceed with caution in proposing monolithic models for the power relations inscribed in these films.[32]

The term *ethnographic film*[33] in this book refers principally to actuality films featuring native peoples that were produced by anthropologists, commercial, and amateur filmmakers alike.[34] While I have concentrated almost exclusively on films featuring native peoples, this is not to suggest that the term ethnographic film excludes motion pictures made about Euro-American cultures and subcultures; to restrict ethnographic film to only those films made about indigenous peoples would be to perpetuate a fallacious and largely repudiated view of ethnographic filmmaking. At the same time, my own task has been driven more by the debates generated in sites where cinema and anthropology clashed with popular culture, rather than an exhaustive account of the early years of ethnographic filmmaking, and I make no claims for having surveyed the vast corpus of ethnographic films made between 1894 and 1915.[35] Likewise, this book makes no attempt to exhaustively log all the textual correspondences between precinematic and cinematic forms of ethnographic representation; while I do explore the theoretical consequences of such central motifs of ethnographic signification such as dance, anthropometric poses, and the return gaze, I leave the task of untangling the myriad links between precinematic forms of ethnographic representation and cinema to others. As a discursive category, ethnographic film refers less to a set of unified significatory practices or to the anthropological method of intensive fieldwork than to the looking relations between the initiator of the gaze and the recipient. Indeed, the term *ethnographic film* was not widely employed until after World War II). In this light, ethnographic film should be seen as a generalized and dispersed set of practices, a way of using the cinematic medium to express ideas about racial and cultural difference, rather than as an autonomous and institutionalized film genre.[36]

This book adopts a multiperspectival approach to the study of cinema, anthropology, and turn-of-the-century visual culture. My use of diachronic case studies across disciplinary and geographical boundaries—a method analogous to the syncopated structure of the ethnographic travel lecture—is intended to suggest the quality and substance of the often fierce debates that cut across the heterogeneous forms of ethnographic filmmaking. The border crossings of the book's organization also parallel the global trafficking of nineteenth-century visual culture; just as photographs of native peoples circulated globally as *cartes-de-visites*, stereographs, and illustrations, so too did motion pictures of exotic cultures and subject peoples find their way into turn-of-the-century store-front theaters, dime museums, circus tents, lecture halls, churches, and parlors.[37]

Early films offering ethnographic knowledge or spectacle can be read simultaneously on several registers: as aesthetic objects; as fleeting, scopophilic gazes upon objectified men, women, and children; as historical artifacts; as colonialist propaganda; as the raw material of anthropological research; and as justifications for social policy. Assessing the tensions among these distinct registers and the extent to which each was privileged or suppressed in the context of exhibition suggests how these films operated in relation to dominant ideological beliefs about "primitivism" and subject peoples. The conditions of classification of ethnographic film must therefore be fluid enough to accommodate a discourse of ethnography that deviates from traditional notions of what constitutes ethnographic film (and from anthropological uses of the term *ethnography* to refer to a long-term, detailed study of a culture), especially those definitions premised on a too-ready distinction between "science" and "art." While sensitive to the quite distinct production contexts of various forms of early ethnographic filmmaking, I am more concerned with tracing the ways in which larger cultural assumptions about race and ethnicity were normalized within the textual and ideological tissue of scientific and popular visual culture than in joining the contemporary semantic battles over the constitution of the ethnographic film canon.

Rather than rely on a priori taxonomies for assessing whether or not films shot by nonanthropologists can be read ethnographically, I am more interested in posing the question historically by investigating the ways in which these films were promoted and understood ethnographically by their audiences and how they circulated within nineteenth-century visual culture. This entails moving beyond traditional questions of cinematic authorship in favor of the consideration of the exhibition contexts of early ethnographic film, since it is often at the level of reception that these films acquire their "ethnographic" meanings. It seems futile to impose contemporary notions of authorship of ethnographic filmmaking as currently practiced within the academy to a time when both cinema and anthropology embodied quite different regimes of knowledge, sight, and accreditation. Instead, ethnographic authority itself needs to be understood historically, since the ethnographic meanings these early films provided for their diverse audiences depended as much on the films' promotional and exhibition contexts as on their authors' qualifications or affiliations, their profilmic settings, their cinematic styles, or their ethnographic subjects.

Whether a specific film was shot by an anthropologist may have been less significant in constituting its ethnographic status at the turn of the century than many other extratextual features. As we shall see, the same ethnographic footage may have meant quite different things to different audiences, depending on whether they viewed it in the socially sanctioned spaces of the AMNH or the New York Explorers Club as opposed to a crowded nickelodeon in a working-class neighborhood. In the case of films exhibited simultaneously in both high-cultural and popular venues, such as millionaire-adventurer Paul Rainey's 1912 *African Hunt*, which appeared at both the AMNH and at the Lyceum Theater in New York City, the textual meanings attributed to the film were subject to constant renegotiation by audiences (and exhibitors), depending on the cultural profile of the screening site. It is only by analyzing what Gunning calls "the untidy processes of production and reception," that we can better grasp how these films came to mean what they did for turn-of-the-century audiences.[38]

This book draws upon the sedimented layers of evidence attesting to the enormous popularity of ethnographic films during the silent cinema period, in the form of film posters, reviews, published articles, internal memoranda, and private correspondence; it also addresses the institutional contexts responsible for nurturing the very idea of an ethnographic cinema. The challenge lies in finding the right hermeneutic tools for assessing the impact of early ethnographic cinema on a range of interpretive communities, including audiences hungry for the latest images of exotic peoples, anthropologists considering cinema's utility as a possible fieldwork aid, and museum curators attempting to maintain the proper balance between public entertainment and civic education. While there are scattered surviving documents from filmmakers and museum administrators testifying to a film's intended pedagogical or institutional role, there is little recorded discussion of the precise meanings constructed by early audiences. Having said this, traces of the aftershocks produced by certain ethnographic films can still be found in published reviews and in discussions at public institutions such as the AMNH, where internal memoranda and correspondence between guest lecturers and museum curators suggest some of the anxieties engendered by cinema as a new visual medium.

This book is organized into three parts. Part I examines some of the key informing contexts for cinema and anthropology in the late nineteenth century: the museum of natural history, the world's fair living village, and photography, and how each catered to the scopic drives and market forces of a burgeoning popular culture. The first three chapters also take up how the young discipline of anthropology represented itself in these sites, and how these representations affected the eventual place of cinema in the discipline. Chapter 1 focuses on the museum of natural history, since it was in the museum, I argue, that the protocols of viewing associated with ethnographic film were thoroughly rehearsed. The museum life group offered visitors a protocinematic experience, a form of "promenade cinema" whose modes of spectating were in many ways analogous to those of early ethnographic film. But in their attention to illusionistic detail, these hyperrealist displays threatened to undermine the very object lessons they were designed to impart, privileging spectacle over cognitive understanding and visceral thrill over intellectual engagement. We move in chapter 2 to turn-of-the-century world's fairs and expositions, where debates over the content, location, and visual appeal of reconstructed indigenous villages foreshadowed the uneasy status of ethnographic film within anthropology. Ethnographic villages commodified anthropology in ways similar to cinema, nominating film as a partial successor to the native village as the site for a spectacle of cultural difference. In its mechanical means of reproduction, cinema made selling cultural difference at once cheaper, more transportable, and more profitable. Chapter 3 analyzes some of the truth-claims made on behalf of photography within nineteenth-century anthropology, for it is only by understanding the reasons behind photography's rise and fall within the discipline that we can appreciate cinema's subsequent marginal role within anthropological investigation. This chapter also considers how nineteenth-century anthropologists grappled with the wider epistemological problems of visual evidence, a question that continues to provoke debate in the field.

If part I of the book is concerned with cinema and anthropology's complex interactions with late nineteenth-century visual culture, part II considers some of the earliest uses of the motion picture camera to record native peoples. Chapter 4 explores the photographic and cinematic work of two seminal figures in the prehistory of visual anthropology—Alfred Cort Haddon and his films of Mer (Murray) Islanders and Australian Aborigines in the Torres Strait in 1898, and Walter Baldwin Spencer and his films of the Arrernte people of Central Australia in 1901. After an account of the logistical and interpersonal challenges Haddon and Spencer faced in the field, this chapter investigates the intellectual and institutional frameworks for early twentieth-century anthropologists working with photography, film, and sound recording.[39] It also explores how some of the earliest films shot within an anthropological context were exhibited before general audiences and how they were promoted simultaneously as visual illustrations of anthropology's intellectual concerns *and* as popular entertainment.

Pursuing the popular curiosity surrounding images of native peoples in the late nineteenth century, chapter 5 examines some of the earliest ethnographic films shot by commercial filmmakers, including Thomas Edison's 1894 kinetoscopes of Buffalo Bill's Indians; travel films produced by such itinerant lecturers as Burton Holmes, Lyman H. Howe, and Frederick Monsen; commercial ethnographic films produced by Pathé and Kalem; and the ethnographic filmmaking of Joseph K. Dixon and Edward S. Curtis. Investigating how a discourse of ethnography was exploited in the promotional rhetoric of the early commercial travel film, this chapter focuses on three enduring tropes: ethnographic reconstruction, native dance, and the effects of the return gaze on the circuit of meaning within and beyond the cinematic frame. This chapter also considers how these early commercial films were discursively constructed as colonialist propaganda in the trade and popular press through their portrayal of both distant locales and cultural groups emigrating to the United States.

Part III of the book concentrates on the complex outcomes following the emergence of ethnographic film in popular culture and anthropological research in the first decade of the twentieth century. I argue in this final section that ethnographic film was by no means an integrated representational practice by the end of the early cinema period in 1908, exemplified in the contentious nature of the exchanges between curators at the AMNH following the Museum's first film screening in 1908. Chapter 6 considers ways in which film generated institutional anxieties both similar to and different from those engendered by the museum life group. For example, cinema's incorporation into the various educational and public programs at the AMNH sparked new concerns, including the degree of control curators and lecturers could exert over *moving*, as opposed to still, images and the task of maintaining the proper scientific tenor within film-lecture demonstrations.

Chapter 7 analyzes the filmmaking efforts and published writings of five early twentieth-century anthropologists, suggesting the interpenetration of the scientific and the popular in early ethnographic film and the difficulty of separating purely anthropological uses of the motion picture camera from commercial endeavors. The writings of anthropologists Frederick Starr, Pliny Goddard, M. W. Hilton-Simpson, J. A. Haeseler, and Franz Boas reveal a great deal about how ethnographic film was positioned within the still-evolving discipline of anthropology, and are significant both for the clarity with which they defined their object and for the ambitious scope of some of their proposals. If these writings indicate a lack of a consensus among anthropologists about exactly how cinema should be used within the discipline in the 1920s, they nevertheless include some remarkable proposals for how cinema might work hand in hand with Hollywood production studios to create anthropologically informed films for popular audiences.

The book concludes by assessing the current state of thinking on anthropology and visuality and the manner in which archival footage of native peoples has been recirculated in contemporary ethnographic film practice. In looking back upon the complex determinants of anthropology's ties to cinema and visual culture, this final chapter asks us to reconsider how early ethnographic films now gathering dust in dispersed archives may once again be at the forefront of debates about the continuing legacies of colonialism and the modern viewing subject.

WONDROUS DIFFERENCE

PART I

PRECINEMA &
ETHNOGRAPHIC
REPRESENTATION

1

Life Groups and the Modern Museum Spectator

An ideal museum is a mute school, a speechless university, a voiceless pulpit . . . every
specimen, every exhibition, every well-arranged hall speaks for itself. In this sense,
in its appeal to the eye, in its journeys for those who can not travel, the museum is
not the rival, but the helpful ally of all the spoken methods of instruction
within its own walls and throughout the great city [New York City].
— HENRY FAIRFIELD OSBORN (1910)[1]

Then, like the savage, they would probably go to museums from sheer curiosity and though
conscious of nothing but large buildings with fine promenades for wet days, with spacious
cases filled with fearful and wonderful objects, and illuminated by dazzling electric lights,
might not learn something, and who knows, contrive in time to get civilized.
— HUNTLEY CARTER (1907)[2]

ONE OF THE most productive sites for historical and theoretical investigation
of the precinematic roots of American ethnographic film is the nineteenth-
century museum of natural history, an institution that offered a veritable catalogue of popular figurations of the ethnographic Other. Organizers of this
public space attempted to negotiate, often in ambivalent and contradictory
ways, the competing interests of paternalistic economic and cultural elites, the
new and assertive academic discipline of anthropology, and the vast urban
working- and middle-class populations in search of amusement and
edification. In their efforts to reconcile the conflicting demands of scientific
seriousness with those of popular spectacle, the nineteenth-century museum
became the staging ground for heated debates over the appropriateness of
different modes of ethnographic representation. These debates, I argue, strikingly prefigure some of the disputes accompanying the use of film as an eth-

nographic tool, since film's origins in both scientific and popular culture echo the admixture of enlightenment and spectacle found in museum displays. By excavating the responses of museum curators and anthropologists to contextualized life groups and habitat groups, we can piece together a more complex portrait of how ethnographic cinema came about at the end of the nineteenth century, since these representational forms not only sparked professional debates similar to those that would accompany the subsequent introduction of film into the museum but also prefigured some of cinema's phenomenological features.

But there's another reason for beginning this book with a case study on museum groups: as direct inheritors of popularized modes of representing scientific knowledge that had first appeared at the Crystal Palace Exposition of 1851, tableaux groups were emblematic of attempts by curators to modernize and popularize museums, to make science and natural history more accessible to the masses through visual spectacle.[3] Symptomatic perhaps of how the visual rhetoric of advertising — eye-catching displays and easily assimilable visual messages — crept quietly into museum design, the life group offers us compelling evidence of how new modes of visual consumption associated with world's fairs, department stores, and popular amusements left their mark on museum exhibitry. But while museum groups had a great deal in common with the window displays of department stores and thus looked forward to a time when the benchmark of a successful exhibit was its degree of visual appeal, they also looked back to an earlier time when dioramas, *tableaux vivant*, and waxworks were popular forms of ethnographic exposition and public attraction. Museum groups served to boost attendance at museums of natural history, attracting visitors from lower socioeconomic backgrounds who might not otherwise step foot into a musty museum. Debates around museum groups installed at the American Museum of Natural History (AMNH) and elsewhere thus reveal a great deal about how a vibrant and chaotic visual culture both supported and challenged the emerging discipline of anthropology and how that discipline responded to the conflicting needs of scientific rigor and popular amusement. The AMNH was not only attracting a broader audience through its increasingly popularized programs but was constructing a new kind of museum spectator, a spectator trained in the viewing protocols of a rapidly changing urban culture that privileged new forms of seeing. But as museums discovered, there was a great deal more at stake in this endeavor than initially met the eye. That life groups ignited such passionate discussion among curators is symptomatic of deeper-seated anxieties about modern visual culture, anxieties that will become increasingly apparent as we move from the museum to the world's fair, where so many of these representational techniques were developed and deployed. Let us begin, then, with an analysis of how the AMNH attempted to organize the museum experience for its visitors, before examining the habitat and life group as vivid examples of popular culture taking a privileged seat alongside science.

Rational Amusement for the Masses: Attracting the Modern Spectator

Like many prominent nineteenth-century cultural institutions, the American Museum of Natural History in New York City conceived of its mission in broad philosophical terms, moving beyond the display of scientific artifacts to embrace a nobler purpose, namely, a desire to furnish the museum visitor with a uniquely civilizing experience that would bolster the quality of the nation's citizenry. As a philanthropic institution supported by the city's economic elite, the AMNH was an important arbiter of public taste and scientific education in late nineteenth-century New York City and beyond, operating with the explicit goal of bringing scientific rationality and enlightenment to the city's new industrial and immigrant working class. The Museum's mission to offer citizens of New York City a form of recreation that was both elevating and educational was frequently reiterated in the institution's publication, the *American Museum Journal*, and in the Museum's annual reports.[4] In 1907, for example, anthropologist Franz Boas argued that the Museum should compete aggressively with New York City's other, less socially uplifting, amusements:[5]

The value of the Museum as a resort for popular entertainment must not be underrated, particularly in a large city, where every opportunity that is given to the people to employ their leisure time in healthy and stimulating surroundings should be developed, where every attraction that counteracts the influence of the saloon and of the race-track is of great social importance.[6]

The Museum's efforts to divert visitors from New York City's less salubrious sites (including vaudeville houses, nickelodeons, and amusement parks such as Coney Island, Dreamland, and Luna Park) were noted as late as 1917 by AMNH director Frederic A. Lucas, who admitted that "when we are competing with every form of amusement in the city it is harder to get an audience."[7]

The perceived deleterious effects of competing working-class entertainments spurred the efforts of AMNH administrators and others to broaden the Museum's audience; museum officials and other members of the city's social elite frequently expressed concern over the effects of immigration, urban crowding, and the putative decline of the cultural and moral standards of city residents. Writing in the *North American Review* in 1903, Brooklyn Institute of Arts and Sciences (BIAS) curator Alfred Goldsborough Mayer argued that to ensure that public institutions functioned as effective civilizing and nationalizing instruments, they "should take great care that the influence which they exert shall refine the thought and elevate the ideals of that foreign element which is soon to exert a great and all too little known influence upon our national destiny."[8] The BIAS dedicated itself to the task of counteracting the potentially threatening effect of mass immigration on received notions of American identity through its presentation of a version of American history that supported traditional social beliefs. This ideological effort, like that of other civic, cultural, and educational institutions, was in part a response to emerging forms of mass entertainment (such as moving pictures) that had strong ties to immigrant groups and neighborhoods in New York City. In the midst of the Museum's ongoing battle for patronage waged against its established leisure-time competitors in the form of saloons, vaudeville houses, and amusement parks, the proliferating nickelodeons posed a new threat to the AMNH's mission of civic uplift because of cinema's special appeal to working-class and immigrant audiences.[9] In this context of civic uplift and ideological inculcation, visual media were seen as especially relevant for the museum's efforts to appeal to a metropolitan working class. They would compete with less salubrious forms of entertainment and perhaps encourage visitors to become members for the first time.

The AMNH was established in 1869 in the Arsenal Building on the east side of Central Park (fig. 1.1) and moved to its permanent home on West 77th Street in 1877, where the Bickmore Wing, named for the Museum's founder Albert S. Bickmore, first opened to the public.[10] The AMNH was one of the three

FIG. 1.1 Reception Day at the American Museum of Natural History's Arsenal Building on the Fifth Avenue side of Central Park. From *Frank Leslie's Illustrated Weekly*, June 5, 1875. (Neg. no. 324745. Courtesy Dept. of Library Services, AMNH)

major American ethnographic institutions at the turn of the century (along with Harvard's Peabody Museum in Cambridge and the Smithsonian Institution in Washington D.C.),[11] and occupied a prominent position in the development of museum and academic anthropology in the United States, in part through the work of Boas, who was on its staff between 1900 and 1905.[12] According to AMNH president Morris K. Jesup in 1892, the Museum strove to offer the masses a "home where they may find recreation, entertainment and education which serves to elevate and ennoble their life and character."[13] Conscious of its reputation and mandate to serve the citizenry of New York City, the Museum sought to provide its members and the general public alike with an opportunity for what Jesup termed "rational amusement" in the form of respectable recreational pursuits.[14]

FIG. 1.2 AMNH guard in the Ethnological Hall, 1900. (Neg. no. 42643. *Photo:* Orchard. Courtesy Dept. of Library Services, AMNH)

opposite
FIG. 1.3 Undated engraving of AMNH by E. J. Meeker from *Frank Leslie's Illustrated Weekly,* c. 1870s. (Neg. no. 324746. Courtesy Dept. of Library Services, AMNH)

Like the operators of amusement parks and international expositions, the administrators of the AMNH sought to control certain aspects of the visitor's physical movement through the Museum, achieving this through both overt and covert means (the AMNH guard's uniform in figure 1.2 is a visual reminder to the visitor that proper protocols of behavior would be enforced); as cultural theorist Tony Bennett explains, "the museum's new field of representations, as well as functioning semiotically, provided a performative environment in which new forms of conduct and behavior could be shaped and practiced."[15] The AMNH was typical of other turn-of-the-century museums of natural history in striving to become an exemplary and emulative public space, a "palace," Bennett argues, in which "mimetic practices . . . [for] improving tastes, values and norms of conduct were to be more broadly diffused through society."[16] For one turn-of-the-century critic, the goal of the natural history museum should not be to "turn every member of the gaping crowd into a doctor of science, but to awaken their imagination and interest, and to give to a street-bred folk some feeling for the nature it has well-nigh forgotten."[17] The AMNH shared this didactic role with other emerging private and public institutions, such as the department store. In such public

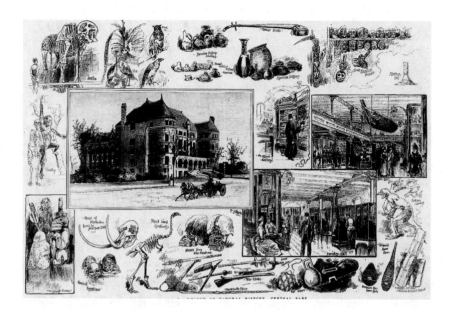

spaces, Bennett argues, behavioral norms were enforced in unobtrusive and self-perpetuating ways in order to consolidate the social learning taking place via other cultural sites, such as public parks, zoos, and libraries.[18] The regulated commingling of social classes was part of the museum's covert curriculum; as a German curator remarked in 1903, museums were "certainly places in which good manners may well be taught."[19] Museum officials believed that normative patterns of social behavior, including dress, decorum, and comportment, would be appropriated by working-class spectators through emulation; seeing middle-class spectators walking through the halls was sufficient to promote normative behavior (fig. 1.3).[20] In a 1911 article entitled "The Museum of the Future," AMNH president Henry Fairfield Osborn suggested the thorough-going efforts by the Museum's administrators to design an environment of uplift and edification such that merely by traveling through the imposing halls of the Museum and breathing its cultured air a visitor might be transformed:

> In the development of our halls there is a constant effort to shut out the human artificial element, to bring the visitor directly under the spell of

Nature, as under a great and infinitely gifted teacher, by making every case, every exhibit, tell some clear and simple story which appeals at once to the imagination, to the reasoning, instinct and to the heart.[21]

For Osborn, museum exhibits ought to serve as taxonomies of idealized representational types from nature.[22] Initiation into the "spell" of the natural world for the museum spectator was brought about through the narrativized exhibits and display cases that represented nature as an enclosed, emblematic miniature. Indeed, miniature life groups, which consisted of scale reconstructions of indigenous camps or homes, were very popular, especially with children, who lived "in imagination among these little 'doll people' " represented in the scenes, according to a writer in *Popular Science Monthly* in 1908.[23]

Imaginative engagement aside, as object-lessons in natural history and anthropological principles, the exhibits were meant to address the Museum spectator in a clear and unambiguous manner. Their didactic ends were achieved through the simultaneous registers of emotional affect and intellectual enlightenment via the construction of an essentialized natural world that would enchant and educate the visitor. The notion of the museum as an antidote to the harmful moral effects of emerging urban culture was not only to be found in the United States; John Maclauchlan, president of the British Museums Association, wrote in 1907 about the civilizing potential of the museum in ways typical of his American counterparts:

The crowds were better in a museum or art gallery than merely aimlessly wandering about the streets, with their not very edifying sights and dangerous temptations. . . . It is impossible for even the most stolid persons to frequently contemplate the wonders of nature, and the achievements of science and art, without, quite unconsciously to themselves, their minds being raised and refined.[24]

However, despite the best efforts of museum officials to construct the exhibit space as a closed logical syntagma, with each display case a paradigmatic unit, the spectator's encounter with the museum's public space was marked less by the intended disciplined gaze than by what Wolfgang Schivelbusch has called a panoramic perception, in many ways similar to the shopper's experience of the new urban department store.[25] Drawing an analogy between the nineteenth-century railway journey and the department store, Schivelbusch argues that just as the speed of the train "detached the traveler from the space immediately surrounding him," so the department store visitor experienced the consumer landscape "evanescently, impressionistically—panoramically."[26] If the gaze invited by the shop window interpellated the passerby into the role of consumer, the representational technologies of the life group hailed the museumgoer as a member of a civilized race who was a privileged spectator, as opposed to the passive object of a scrutinizing gaze. Indeed, with the proliferation of museum shops in the late teens and their commodification of natural history and anthropological curios, the department store window and museum life group began to assume an even greater consanguinity.[27] For present-day visitors, shopping is now perceived as an integral part of the museum experience, with satellite shops selling merchandise relating to an exhibit constituting the final room of a show, requiring all visitors to walk through the shop in order to exit the space.

It is important to remember, though, that none of the exhibits in a museum could be experienced by the museumgoer outside the framing discourses of the institution itself; merely by traversing the ethnographic exhibition halls of such grandiose public buildings,[28] museum spectators entered into an ideologically loaded space that elaborated the metanarratives of Western cultural superiority via multisensory accounts of the primitivism of other cultures. According to Bennett, the grand evolutionary narrative of scientific progress was inscribed in the very architectural design of the British Museum, where visitors enacted an evolutionary logic as they moved through the highly structured sequence of spaces and ascended the "culture-ladder from the lowest to the highest round," in the words of nineteenth-century British scientist William Henry Holmes.[29] The museum's representational technologies inscribed a preferred itinerary that each visitor was encouraged to perform; as Bennett explains: "locomotion—and sequential locomotion—is required as the visitor is faced with an itinerary in the form of an order of things which reveals itself only to those who, step by step, retrace its evolutionary development."[30] In the case of the AMNH, published guides to the Museum's exhibition halls on sale to museumgoers made explicit the inscribed geographical and evolutionary lessons by means of suggested itineraries.[31] For example, the

Museum's *General Guide* of 1911 informed visitors that the African Hall "is roughly geographical, i.e. as the visitor proceeds through the hall from south to north he meets the tribes that would be found in passing from south to north of Africa." At the end of the guide,[32] the spectator is told to "Return to Central Pavilion." In another article on the African Hall written for the *American Museum Journal* in 1911, the paradigm of an imaginary ethnographic excursion through Africa is once again evoked:

> In walking the length of the hall along the right and back along the left, one may pass in review African industry, art and tribal customs as if actually traveling north from the Cape of Good Hope to the Mediterranean, to the tribes of the Congo, and south again, west of the Congo — in other words, from the Bushmen to the tribes of the Nile and from the Sahara tribes to the Hottentots. Such a plan gives a forceful and natural arrangement for the disposition of any collection of heterogeneous materials from a region.[33]

While the pedagogic rationale for the organization of exhibits in the African Hall rested upon a somewhat paradoxical meshing of artifice and nature ("a forceful and natural arrangement"), the invitation to complete the suggested itinerary was analogous in some ways to the mobilized gaze of the early ethnographic travelogue, which, through editing and lecturer commentary, compiled touristic vignettes of native cultures in a similarly geographical logic for cinema spectators. As we shall see, similar issues of curatorial control over the experience of museumgoers would be invoked in later efforts by AMNH administrators to police the use of motion pictures themselves at the Museum.

To many observers at the time, the sheer number of objects on display in museums of natural history encouraged an undisciplined way of seeing, a distracted and distinctly modern glance associated with the nineteenth-century *flâneur*. The urban *flâneur*'s effortless transition from the boulevard into the department store, a transition channeled, in Schivelbusch's view, by "means of a carefully manipulated display of goods," was also evoked in the context of the museum and world's fair; according to an anonymous contributor to *The Outlook* in 1909, the swirling museum crowds on a bright, spring Saturday afternoon "seemed to be taking the [Agassiz Museum at Harvard] as an extension of the promenade, looking at the collections in the large as if they were scenery, and manifestly finding the scenery little to their taste."[34] The writer similarly complained of the casual and undisciplined nature of spectator attention to the informative exhibits at the 1901 Pan-American Exposition in Buffalo, New York: "The populace put itself through rigid courses of wheatsheaves and coffee berries in the Agricultural Building, and machines in the Electrical Building, stopping nowhere long enough to absorb more than one corner of an idea, and then rushed off to the boisterous Midway for dessert."[35] According to such critics, many museumgoers deemed it tiresome or unnecessary to interrupt their promenade in order to look closely at display cases and labels.

The challenge for museum designers posed by the fleeting attention span of the nineteenth-century museumgoer was discussed as early as 1869 in an article by Alfred Wallace entitled "Museums for the People." Wallace warned museum administrators that

> the eye takes in so much at once that it is continually wandering towards something more strange and beautiful, and there is nothing to concentrate the attention on the special object. Distraction is produced also by the great size of the galleries, and the multiplicity of objects that strike the eye. It is almost impossible for a casual visitor to avoid the desire of continually going on to see what comes next, or wondering what is that bright mass of colour or strange form that catches the eye at the other end of the long gallery.[36]

British museum writer Thomas Greenwood went farther in 1888, warning that the proliferation of objects and visual attractions in museums could inspire a "condition of mind as picture drunkenness or Museum drunkenness which should be guarded against."[37] Greenwood advised museum administrators to ward off such spectator intoxication through "a more extensive use of folding screens, so that anyone so disposed could shut themselves off from the crowd while they study a case or picture minutely."[38] Blocking out peripheral distractions (a feature of Schivelbusch's "panoramic perception") might give the spectator an opportunity to contemplate the object in relative seclusion, where the spectator's eye would be less likely to catch glimpse of yet another interesting-looking object located down the hall.

But curators at the AMNH also feared a different form of distraction, one that had less to do with the wandering gaze of museumgoers than with the quality of the spectator's interaction with an exhibit. The museum spectators described by Wallace and Greenwood seemed to be more entranced by the displayed objects' provocation of wonder, what theorist Stephen Greenblatt calls the "power of the displayed object to stop the viewer in his or her tracks," than in receiving the intended object-lesson of the museum display. Concerned that the spell of wonder (what Greenblatt calls "enchanted looking")[39] would leave little room for a more intellectual engagement with the object, the curatorial staff at the AMNH responded by writing long and sometimes unfathomable labels and ensuring that popular exhibits were spaced evenly throughout the exhibition space. (The contemporary recorded audio guide and interactive computer tour are modern expressions of this desire on the part of museum curators to enforce a more structured and consistent intellectual experience upon museumgoers.)

But distracted forms of looking were not the only cause for concern; some museum professionals argued that the faulty architectural design of museums was as much to blame as a distracted, wandering gaze. Francis Arthur Bather summed up the problems in gallery design in his presidential address to the British Museum's association in 1903:

The architect persists in treating a museum gallery as though it were a town hall; he overloads it with detail and decoration, which, if they do not actually jar with the subsequent contents, at least withdraw attention from them. How, finally can the museum be a place for peaceful recreation or quiet study when the architect has made every room a passage, so that the public, from the moment it enters an exhibition hall, has for its goal, not some supreme masterpiece, but the door at the other end? A tired and aimless crowd hurries through the galleries, as though it heard at its elbow the urgent voice of law repeatedly ejaculating "Move on, please!"[40]

Notwithstanding the belief of some observers that museumgoers would acquire scientific knowledge merely by passing through the Museum's exhibi-

FIG. 1.4 Hall of Northwest Coast Indians, c. 1902, showing the cedar-fabrication life group as the focal point and the separation of the hall into two longitudinal halves. (Neg. no. 384. Courtesy Dept. of Library Services, AMNH)

tion halls or being in the presence of so much educational material, AMNH officials seemed keenly aware of the need to design an ideal visitor itinerary in order to counteract the tendency toward the panoramic, fleeting, and unstable spectatorial glance. The challenge for museum administrators became how to discipline the distracted gaze of the museumgoer, to regulate an otherwise aimless ambulatory movement through the exhibitions, in which labels were disregarded and objects considered with minimal intellectual effort. Boas's 1907 description of the museum spectator conjures up the casual, wandering gaze of the modern *flâneur*: "He strolls through the halls examining something that attracts his attention here and there without much plan or purpose."[41] Indeed, Boas felt that it was the scale of the museum itself, rather than the pedagogical content of the exhibits, that appealed most to the masses: "They come to admire, to see, and to be entertained. We instruct them almost against their wish and will."[42] In Boas's view, people visited the museum in pursuit of "emotional excitement" or for "rest and recreation" and resented any attempt at systematic instruction.[43]

In accordance with the need to instruct museumgoers "against their wish and will," Boas, in a letter to Jesup in 1897, argued that the exhibits in the Museum's ethnographic halls should be laid out so as to inhibit the spectators' tendencies to meander through the exhibit in an aimless and disengaged fashion:

> When the main aisle is located in the center of the Hall, visitors will wander right to left without order, and it is impossible to compel them to see the collection in such a manner that they will have the greatest possible uplift from a short visit. By dividing the Hall into two longitudinal halves . . . visitors are compelled to see in the collection their natural sequence, and even if they pass through only one half of the Hall, will be more benefited than when seeing one alcove here, one there.[44] (See fig. 1.4.)

For Boas, the best way to accommodate the desire of museum visitors to "admire" or be "impressed by something great and wonderful" was to direct their attention to a single point that would lead systematically to a series of related points in adjacent display cases. As Boas put it: "It must be recognized that it is impossible to hold the attention of the people by the whole mass of exhibits, but that for every visitor the bulk of the material must merely give the background from which some subject that happens to strike his fancy will stand out in bold relief."[45] The underlying idea of the exhibit had to be revealed to museum spectators in subtle ways; if the object-lesson succeeded, "great truths" would be impressed upon spectators with the minimum of intellectual effort on their part.[46] Some nineteenth-century museum administrators calculated that, when not drawn to the exit sign at the end of the tunnel-shaped gallery space, the gaze of ordinary visitors would be chiefly attracted to the visually engaging spectacle of museum life groups,[47] which, as Holmes pointed out, functioned as the "key to the exhibit, the most essential idea, the feature from which the most casual observer can get a definite conception of the people and their culture."[48] But in functioning as the key to the exhibit, groups nevertheless ran the risk of overshadowing less visually spectacular displays, enticing spectators from one end of the gallery to the next (without much in between) and shaping their expectations of what natural history exhibits should look like. While the primary function of the museum group was to attract working-class visitors and elicit intellectual engagement by drawing their attention to related, and less visually intriguing, materials, this plan may have backfired in so much as many spectators paid little attention to anything other than groups; as Mark Sandberg has argued in his account of modes of spectating in the turn-of-the-century folk museum: "The disjunction between the institution's ostensible purpose and the variety of its uses by spectators highlights the fact that a museum's founding definition and its eventual social function are not necessarily identical."[49]

"A New Type of Story-Telling Picture": Debating Museum Life and Habitat Groups

> A diorama is eminently a story, a part of natural history. The story is told
> in the pages of nature, read by the naked eye. . . . [The animals] are actors in a
> morality play on the stage of nature, and the eye is the critical organ.
> — DONNA HARAWAY (1989)[50]

In an 1894 letter to Morris Ketchum Jesup, president of the AMNH from 1881 to 1908, anthropology curator Frederick Ward Putnam argued that the aim of the life group was to "at once arrest the attention of the visitor to a public Museum" and that nothing could do this as effectively as an "exhibit of man in some phase of his life." Putnam went on to describe the construction and content of the life groups:

> Characters should be illustrated first by groups made of models taken
> from life among living primitive peoples, and when relating to peoples of
> the past they should be made up from the best attainable data. Each of
> these groups should show a family or several members of a tribe, dressed
> in their native costumes and engaged in some characteristic work or art
> illustrative of their life and particular art or industry. Such a group should
> include the peculiar habitation of the people, or when this is not possible,
> a model of the habitation should be shown near by.[51]

The public appeal of the life group exhibit lay in the ways in which it captured the imagination of the museum spectator; whether or not it fulfilled the implicit aim of furthering understanding of other cultures may have been less significant for most museumgoers than the theatrical illusionism of the exhibit, with its naturalistic set, mannequins arranged in nuclear families, and strong sense of narrative.

The origins of museum life groups can be traced to numerous nineteenth-century representational forms, including large-scale circular panoramas, theatrical tableaux (where actors froze the dramatic action in poses encapsulating or heightening a narrative situation);[52] the *tableau vivant* or "living picture" parlor game (where individuals struck poses imitating dramatic scenes from painting or literature); taxidermy; and the waxwork. Life groups were also extensively used in the lavish world's fairs and expositions of mid-nineteenth-century England, which served as testing grounds for a great many innovative methods of museum display. Theatrical tableaux fulfilled several different functions on the English stage, serving both as logistical problem-solvers, as in the opening or discovery tableau, where sensational images of slaughter or mutilation could be represented as having already happened, and as climactic (or curtain) tableaux signaling the end of a scene.[53] Theatrical tableaux and the domestic *tableaux vivant*, rooted in the "genteel social entertainment on the order of charades,"[54] shared a number of semantic resemblances; their play on spectator foreknowledge of a represented scene (from history, literature, or nature), coupled with the public fascination derived from their transformational (and illusionistic) qualities, made them extremely popular Victorian pastimes.[55] In their discursive, aesthetic, and technical codes, theatrical tableaux and *tableaux vivant* anticipated the looking relations of both the life groups and early cinema.[56] But while life groups had a great deal in common with these theatrical conventions, they also represented something distinct from them, because, in spite of the illusionist setting and naturalistic detail, there were obvious differences between watching a living person imitating a still image and looking at a human facsimile modeled out of plaster. In this light, the life group shared a great deal more with the visual rhetoric of taxidermy and the waxwork than it did with overtly theatricalized displays such as the *tableaux vivant* and the moving diorama,[57] since both the life group and taxidermy enmeshed paradoxical discourses of truth and artifice, science and spectacle, terms that were to become defining antipodes in the discourses of early ethnographic film.[58]

In addition to its roots in early theatrical modes of representation, the habitat group inherited the *trompe l'oeil* techniques of earlier nineteenth-century illusionistic displays such as panoramas (in the form of 360-degree installations or moving horizontal paintings) and Daguerrean dioramas, in which semi-transparent illusionistic paintings were subjected to dramatic lighting effects that would create the illusion of movement and different times of day. According to historian Dolf Sternberger, these habitat groups combined "natural and artificial elements," their goal being "not art nor even beauty, but a new and different, a man-made Nature."[59] But what unites museum groups with these earlier forms of entertainment is less their organization as visual attractions than the kinds of discourses they generated within their respective milieux. For example, diorama scholar Karen Wonders notes that Daguerre's technique of positioning three-dimensional objects in front of a painted background landscape was attacked by artists and critics who questioned the legitimacy of using real trees in art (Daguerre defended his dioramas by claiming that he was only trying to construct the "most complete illusion").[60] John Constable argued that while Daguerre's diorama technique could be favorably compared to landscape painting, it could not qualify as true art since its primary aim was deception. This dispute suggests the double-edged nature of such illusionistic displays, since their painstaking attempts at realism might only draw more attention to the artificiality of their construction. There is little doubt that Constable's objection to the illusionistic premise of dioramas was shared by many nineteenth-century critics, and his criticism was echoed in discussions of life groups at the AMNH. But before examining these debates, let us take a closer look at how such groups were actually constructed and what they were supposed to do.

Facing the challenge of reconstructing scenes from natural and cultural landscapes, museum artists attempted to depict the backgrounds and objects in ways that were both scientifically correct and aesthetically pleasing. The preparation of life groups involved an artist accompanying an anthropologist into the field, selecting "an ideal spot [after] careful consideration of the artistic merits, as well as the ethnographical and other scientific values of the vicinity," photographing the natural setting and its details, and constructing a miniature model of the scene while in the field. Native peoples selected as figure models for the group would then have plaster cast life masks taken of their faces and, occasionally, their bodies, providing they agreed to have plaster envelop their face and body (an unpleasant experience from all accounts), which artists would then use as the basis for life group models.[61] Once the diorama background had been painted, mannequins made from head and body molds of indigenous people were clothed in actual costumes worn by the tribes and placed alongside real artifacts.

The anthropologically approved mannequins thus helped efface what Sandberg calls the " 'object-ness' of both artifact and dress, giving them a context that approximates an original connection to a body."[62] While museum spectators may have been oblivious to the fact that the human effigies were modeled on living people, for the anthropologist-curators they lent an overall credibility to the exhibit, giving a context to the artifacts and the costumes which otherwise would have sat in sterile glass cases. There is, however, as Sandberg notes, a circularity to the relationship between the props and the human effigy (one shoring up the reality effect of the other), since "without the props to activate the viewer's imagination, the mannequin remains a dummy; with them, the figure simulates agency and consciousness."[63] The result was a theatrically lit tableau that represented native life as if it were a scene from a child's pop-up storybook (see, for example, fig. 1.5). Unlike cinema, which could only conjure up its subjects through two-dimensional black-and-white images (although occasionally audiences would see colorized prints), the museum life group offered three-dimensional mannequins and objects behind its magical window, blending the uncanny presence of the human double with the authority of the scientific artifact.

Artistry in the design and implementation of life groups within the glass cases was only one stage in the overall construction process; the objects and mannequins on display required contextualization beyond the exhibit itself in the form of labels and other instructional material, although exactly how these labels were meant to present information to the public divided museum curators and professionals.[64] Holmes recommended that the exhibit representing each culture area should be supplemented by "maps, pictures, and labels" in order to present a "synopsis of its culture phenomena" (which might also include related somatic material such as "casts of the face, or even of the entire

FIG. 1.5 Apache group installed at the AMNH, 1916. In line with Boas's recommendations, the models have simulated rather than real hair. (Neg. no. 310795. *Photo:* Julius Kirschner. Courtesy Dept. of Library Services, AMNH)

figure; the skeleton or parts of it, and especially the skull . . . examples of artificial deformations and mutilations" etc.).[65] Disagreeing with Holmes, other observers, including Alfred Goldsborough Mayer, felt that most of the instructive labels in museums were either "too long to be readable or couched in too scientific terms."[66] Nevertheless, this auxiliary material played a crucial role in demonstrating evolutionary theory, since it provided additional proof of the relationship between the inherited and cultural features of a race; as Holmes put it: "The man himself as he appears in his everyday life, is the best illustration of his own place in history, for his physical aspect, the expression of his face, the care of his person, his clothes, his occupation . . . tell the story with much [greater] clearness."[67] In considering these disputes over the role of the instructive museum label, it is worth noting that for many museumgoers (non-English-speaking immigrants, illiterates, and those without the time or inclination to pause and read), the length and complexity of the labels were irrelevant; they simply weren't read.[68]

While offering specific recommendations for how museum groups should be designed for maximum legibility and impact upon spectators (including advice on labeling), Boas remained wary of attempts to attain a too-convincing reality effect in the life group, a view not shared by all curators of anthropology. Holmes, for example, argued in 1902 that "physical characters should be portrayed with all possible accuracy, and a correct impression of the disposition and social attitude of the members of the [nuclear] family group should be given. . . . [We show] how the people look, and, as far as possible, what they think and do and have."[69] However, in Boas's opinion, previous undertakings at creating life-size reproductions of native peoples had failed, because, he argued, the "surroundings of a Museum are not favorable to an impression of this sort." For Boas, "the cases, the walls, the contents of other cases, the columns, the airways, all remind us that we are *not* viewing an actual village, and the contrast between the attempted realism of the group and the inappropriate surroundings spoils the whole effect."[70] Recognizing the pedagogical limitations of the life group as an educational display ("a group does not convey any more information than a picture in an ordinary picture-book might be made to convey"), Boas recommended that life groups be judiciously used rather than have a series "illustrate different aspects of the same idea," since the "impressiveness of each is decreased by the excessive application of the same device."[71] For Boas, illusionistic verisimilitude and scientific rigor were uneasy bedfellows in the case of museum groups, a point illustrated in criticisms of contextualized group displays by Boas and others.

One of Boas's greatest concerns was that museum spectators would ignore the explanatory labels and supplementary artifacts situated some distance away from the display case in favor of a lingering, erotically charged gaze at the frequently semiclad human models cast from living indigenous peoples (fig. 1.6). Boas opposed the too-perfect illusionism of the life group, fearing that heightened realistic effects would distract spectator attention from the intended anthropological object-lesson of the exhibit in favor of a fascination with the technical means of the human facsimile. Writing in *Science* in 1907, Boas argued that

FIG. 1.6 Group in African Hall, 1911, showing two men operating a native forge for working bronze. (Neg. no. 32932. *Photo:* Julius Kirschner. Courtesy Dept. of Library Services, AMNH)

every incidental point that is added to the essentials of the exhibit will distract attention from the fundamental idea. I fear that in some cases an interest in the artificial likeness to nature may be engendered like that felt by the couriers of the Emperor of China in Anderson's fairly tale "The Nightingale," when they all exclaim on discovering that the nightingale is not a mechanical toy: "How interesting. It is a real bird!"[72]

Indeed, the 1908 description of an Inuit (Eskimo) exhibit at the AMNH in which a woman is shown cooking over a seal-oil lamp in an igloo suggests precisely the kind of fascination with the minutiae of the facsimile at the expense of a deeper intellectual engagement that troubled Boas: "The flame jets are so cleverly simulated with colored glass and concealed electric lights that they seem actually to flicker. . . . In another place a fur-muffled figure sits patiently above a hole in the ice, waiting for another fish to bite and be added to the pile already caught."[73]

To minimize the undesired effects of the life group's illusionism and theatricality, Boas advocated the use of antirealist conventions that would impart more of a general pedagogic impression than a totalizing verisimilitude. Rather than attempt to replicate nature, Boas felt it was better to underline the synthetic nature of displays. He argued that figures should be shown at rest rather than at the height of action, and that skin color and texture should be approximate only; hair should be painted, not real:

> When the figure is absolutely lifelike the lack of motion causes a ghastly impression such as we notice in wax-figures. For this reason the artistic effect will be better when we bear in mind this fact and do not attempt too close an approach to nature; that is to say, since there is a line of demarcation between nature and plastic art, it is better to draw a line consciously than try to hide it.[74]

Boas's greatest fear was that the "elements of impressiveness that life groups possessed might overshadow the scientific aim which they serve."[75] The primary purpose of the life exhibits, according to Boas, should be to catch the visitor's attention and direct it to glass cases at the perimeter of the room containing cultural artifacts, maps, and written descriptions.[76] For many visitors, however, fascination with the facsimile overwhelmed the desire to look at supplementary materials; in a discussion of the instructional work carried out at the AMNH, an anonymous author noted the look of wonder on one child's face as he stared at a life group representing Native American tanning: "One boy, who was in fact nearly a grown youth, looking at a model . . . said: 'How can they stand still?' thinking that the plaster figures were actual people inside the glass case."[77] Boas's reservations about life groups can thus offer us a potential clue about anthropological perceptions of motion pictures. In the minds of many museum curators, the immersive and uncanny qualities of both the life group and, later, moving picture, threatened to subsume a more intellectual engagement with the exhibit, privileging pure spectacle over a more rationalist discourse. In other words, the psychic links of both media to popular showmanship and phantasmagoria frustrated museum curators' efforts to enforce the primary pedagogical mission of exhibits, a factor that had serious consequences for cinema's role within anthropology.

As a popular nineteenth-century attraction, the museum life group pro-voked sharp divisions within the anthropological and scientific community, debates that were played out in other national contexts as well.[78] While the anonymous author of "Art in a Natural History Museum" argued that the museum habitat group produced "what in some cases may well be termed works of art, a new type of story-telling 'picture,' " the author was more skep-tical of life groups that involved human figures. The author suggested that "in large part the province of telling the cultures and lives of the people repre-sented in any hall [should] be relegated to mural decorations on the large wall spaces."[79] For this critic, what life groups gained in vivifying culture, they lost in scientific and aesthetic value. The AMNH itself revealed similar reserva-

FIG. 1.7 African Hall decorative panel showing a family gathered around a dwindling watering hole, AMNH, 1910. (Neg. no. 32902. *Photo:* Julius Kirschner. Courtesy Dept. of Library Services, AMNH)

tions in its 1911 *Annual Report*, when it recommended that only professional artists be recruited to undertake ethnographic murals and panel decorations (fig. 1.7): "Only an artist can represent the spirit and sentiment of the life of the various existing and extinct tribes of men, subjects that require extremely careful and exceptional caution, lest the Museum acquire mural decorations which in time will prove to be artistically poor and hence a detriment to the exhibition halls."[80]

The "exceptional caution" advised in the completion of wall murals repre-senting native life, coupled with a belief that ethnographic installations should be "relegated" to wall murals, suggests an anxiety over the suitability of high-ly illusionist exhibits such as life groups and murals. While officials and cura-tors such as Henry Fairfield Osborn, Frederic A. Lucas, and Franz Boas paid

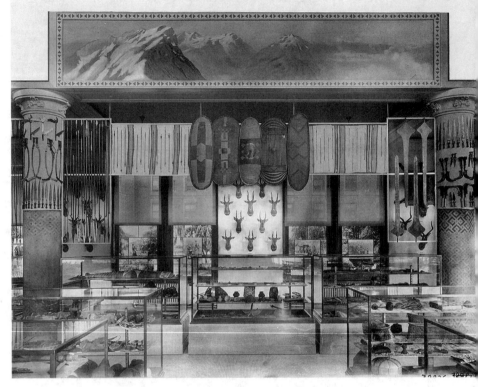

FIG. 1.8 Symmetrical integration of different methods of presenting ethnographic knowledge in the AMNH African Hall, 1909, including decorative panels, taxidermy animal heads, window transparencies, and glass cases. (Neg. no. 32926. *Photo:* Julius Kirschner. Courtesy Dept. of Library Services, AMNH)

a great deal of attention to the overall aesthetic effect of the displays and suggested ways in which art and science could be harmonized throughout the Museum's architectural spaces (fig. 1.8), Boas remained uneasy about representing indigenous life in the form of three-dimensional exhibits, since he feared that any scientific merit the life group possessed was undermined by its close affiliation with the waxwork.[81] A fear that the life group's illusionistic spell would numb the minds of museum spectators to pedagogy was replayed in later debates over the possibilities of ethnographic motion pictures, as anthropologists feared that motion pictures would similarly privilege spectacle over rational engagement.

FIG. 1.9 ARAB COURIER ATTACKED BY LIONS, completed by Jules Verreaux and first displayed at the AMNH in 1869. (Courtesy Carnegie Museum of Natural History)

A particularly compelling illustration of the life group's role as a sideshow attraction can be seen in the first group installed in the AMNH, ARAB COURI-ER ATTACKED BY LIONS, prepared in France under the supervision of Jules Verreaux, the French ornithologist and traveler (fig. 1.9). The group was initially displayed in the "Maison Verreaux" at the 1869 Paris Exposition, where it won a gold medal, and was purchased by the AMNH for display at the Museum's original Arsenal Building in the same year. The ARAB COURIER installation is particularly striking in its midscene depiction of a violent attack by two lions; one of the lions has mounted the camel with one paw on the rider's leg and the other on the camel's back. The action of attack is frozen, as if the downward movement of the camel's body would instantly resume if the group were reanimated. The life group also makes overt appeal to popular orientalist iconography, propagated at the time in international expositions; indeed, the danger, excitement, and exoticism of the image was typical of such reified views of the orientalized Other during the late nineteenth century. Writing in 1914, Lucas forgave the life group's overt theatricality and violent subject matter in the light of what he saw as its important contribution to standards of taxidermy, arguing that the work represented

> the most ambitious attempt of its day. Moreover, it was an attempt to show life and action and an effort to arrest the attention and arouse the interest of the spectator, a most important point in museum exhibits. If you cannot interest the visitor you cannot instruct him; if he does not care to know what an animal is, or what an object is used for, he will not read the label, be it ever so carefully written.[82]

The Museum's tactic of luring the spectators' attention via a spectacularized life group in the service of loftier pedagogical goals evokes the figure of the barker announcing the day's performances in traveling circuses or outside storefront movie theaters; this life group thus served a similar hailing function in attempting to attract the wandering gaze of the museum visitor.[83] But we would be foolish to ignore the implicit class connotations of this analogy between circus-goers and museum spectators; just as circus entrepreneurs sought a nondiscriminating mass consumer, so it would seem that museums lowered their expectations of the class composition of their average visitor and deliberately set out to attract lower-middle and working-class audiences.

Despite their obvious and continued popularity among museumgoers (these groups frequently ranked among the most popular museum exhibits), the efficacy of habitat and life groups was widely debated in professional discourse well into the cinematic era. In a series of articles that appeared in the April, May, and June 1907 issues of *Science*, Dr. George A. Dorsey criticized the AMNH's move away from traditional typological displays in favor of popularized groups. Dorsey decried what he saw as the marginalization of scientific knowledge in habitat groups and singled out for criticism the inaccuracies of recent life group installations featuring plaster cast models of Peruvian Indians and Inuit peoples. While Dorsey drew attention to a significant number of inconsistencies in the design of the installation (trivializing labels, a misleading portrayal of typicality, and the lack of attention to the interaction of different cultures), his primary complaint concerned the aestheticization of nature and elision of anthropological fact: "Everywhere manifest [is] the result of the conscious effort to make the cases look pretty, to have the object on one's right balance in size with that on one's left, quite regardless of whether it illustrates anything or not."[84]

Defending the habitat group against Dorsey's criticisms in *Science* the following month, Henry L. Ward, curator at the Public Museum in Milwaukee, pointed out that the great museum exhibition halls, with their high maintenance costs, could be kept open only if they appealed to the tastes of the public.[85] This difficulty of reconciling scientific aims with popular appeal in museum display was by no means unique to American institutions. In the 1890s, English amateur anthropologist and collector A.H.F.L. Pitt-Rivers was forced to modify his rigorous scientific system of exhibition design in order to satisfy the public's desire for easily accessible exhibits. Despite Pitt-Rivers's hopes that the typologically arranged specimens in his small Farnham Museum in the English countryside might serve to close working-class minds to "scatter-brained revolutionary ideas," historian William Ryan Chapman contends that the approximately three hundred local agricultural workers who visited every Sunday were more interested in the stuffed exotic animals in habitat groups than in the rows of arrowheads.[86] According to Chapman, spectator interest impelled both critics and advocates of typology toward making more realistic habitat groups.

While Dorsey argued that the divergent interests of scientists, college students, and the general public should all be met by modern museum exhibition methods, Ward believed that displays for the public should not attempt to accomplish too much:

> In other words, effectiveness is dependent on concentration in aim and in limiting the number of objects shown. It is unavoidable that such an exhibit should partake somewhat of the character of a text-book illustrated by specimens, though it is probably advisable to disguise as far as possible the mechanism of this, for people like better to think that they are discovering facts and principles than that these are forced upon them.[87]

Columbia University professor Maurice A. Bigelow advocated a middle course, arguing that while museum exhibitry should move away from the traditional "systematic system" of the taxonomic representation of zoology or native culture, organizational principles should still apply. According to Bigelow, some idea of a system was necessary, though it must be a "view of science in relation to modern life in its combined intellectual, practical and aesthetic outlook."[88] Other commentators, like the anonymous author of "Art in a Natural History Museum," published in the *American Museum Journal*, defended the group exhibit's capacity to convey scientific accuracy while at the same time to be aesthetically pleasing:[89]

> A display of specimens, in cases, unrelated, is not only uninviting, it is also uninstructive in that it tells only a small part of the truth. It can convey no idea of the life, in the instance either of animals or primitive man. Thus the "group," which shows animals in relation to each other and to their native haunt, stands for manifolded [*sic*] power to convey knowledge.[90]

The author's appreciation of the museum group constructs popular spectacle as an instrument of scientific edification: in order that a habitat or life group be instructive and impart even a limited number of scientific precepts, it had to be inviting to the museum visitor. But debates over the scientific merits of group exhibits were nothing new within the museological world and can be traced to some of the earliest attempts at illusionistic representation in taxidermic form.

Alchemy of the Flesh: Habitat and Life Groups as Trompe l'Oeil

As a showcase for the work of the artist-taxidermist, the habitat group depended upon the visualization of natural history in order to convey meaning, typifying and narrativizing nature's quarry in displays of organic perfection.[91] Early taxidermy attempts at lifelike representation with large mammals often resulted in hideous distortions of the skin and produced, in the words of pioneer English taxidermist Charles Waterton, nothing more than mere "*simulacra*":

Now I should call upon any one of these, who have given to the public a mode of preserving specimens for museums to step forward and show me how to restore majesty to the face of a lion's skin, ferocity to the tiger's countenance, innocence to that of the lamb, or sulkiness to that of the bull, he would not know which way to set to work: he would have no resources at hand to help him in that operation. . . . He could produce nothing beyond a mere dried specimen shrunk too much in this part, or too bloated in that; a mummy, a distortion, a hideous spectacle, a failure in every sense of the word.[92]

Waterton's belief that in order to revivify a specimen, the "real" must undergo a transformation and become conventionalized illustrates the narrativizing and anthropomorphizing premises behind his restorative efforts; configured this way, the animal is viewed less as an anatomical specimen than as an artist's creation, whose connotative meaning is anchored via the artificial imposition of a stereotyped (metaphorical) countenance (here, articulated through the majestic demeanor of the lion and sulky disposition of the bull). For Waterton, merely preserving the outer shell of the specimen against the ravages of time results in little more than a "hideous spectacle," a "distortion" of the animal's original splendor and a "failure in every sense of the word."[93]

Waterton's attack on amateurish attempts at taxidermy suggests not so much a professional elitism as a sense of unease about the status of taxidermy as a scientific endeavor; Waterton's fear that scientific specimens might end up as "hideous spectacles" also betrays a deeper anxiety about the prurient and morbid appeal of taxidermy, which threatened to undermine the scientific object-lesson. Waterton's rhetoric reminds us that taxidermy, as Haraway argues, had always "threatened to lapse from art into deception, from life to upholstered death."[94] If the ultimate goal of taxidermy was to convince the spectator that the animals on display had cheated or transcended mortality, then the vision could only be complete if the specimen showed no evidence of decomposition, but instead narrated a fictionalized and pristine encounter between viewer and beast that was rehearsed each time the spectator's gaze penetrated the glass.[95]

Waterton discussed the crucial role played by artistry in the taxidermy process when he described the techniques he used to preserve a toucan acquired during an expedition to South America in 1808. Writing in 1824 of how all previous efforts to preserve the brilliant blue color of the toucan's bill had failed, Waterton advised his readers to first pare away the lower mandible of the bill in order to make it transparent, and then paint it blue. This technique, he proclaimed, would make the toucan appear "perfectly natural." Waterton's acknowledgment of artifice as a prerequisite of the "real"—in order to perpetuate the impression of life, a scientist has to accept the fact of death—anticipates the crucial role played by artistry in the design and execution of museum groups (in historian Stephen Bann's words, he manipulated "reality" in order to elevate the exhibit to a greater *vraisemblance*).[96] As Lucas argued in 1914, "an important factor in the evolution of groups and their introduction into museums was the development of the art, for art it is, of making accessories, for without the ability to reproduce flowers and foliage in materials . . . half the charm and value of groups would be lost."[97] One of the habitat groups that best exemplifies the copresence of art and scientific precepts in group design and execution is the ORIZABA GROUP, an ornithological group constructed by William Peters in 1913 for the AMNH. The perspective and outlook of the display bears a striking resemblance to Frederick Church's painting *In the Heart of the Andes*, reminding us of the role of intertextuality in adding another interpretive layer to the semantic richness of habitat groups.

It is important to point out, though, that Waterton's attention to detail in his approach to taxidermy did not extend beyond the preserved specimen itself; Waterton invested more time and energy in reproducing the physical characteristics of the bird than in worrying about the location and surrounding details. In fact, the mounting of taxidermy specimens in contextualized displays did not become the norm in museums until the mid-nineteenth century; up until that point, a typological system (grouping objects according to type) was considered the most scientifically rigorous. Birds would thus be mounted and exhibited on uniform T perches constructed in front of wood panels according to predetermined taxonomies. But ornithological exhibits were not the only museum exhibits to be displayed within a typological system; the synoptic histories of indigenous material culture such as arrowheads, shields, and weaving techniques were also comparatively displayed, the governing principle being typology (what the object looked like) rather than culture area (to which cultural group and geographical region the object belonged). According to Pitt-Rivers, such displays had the aim of "showing how certain forms must have preceded or followed others in the order of their development, or in a sequence of their adoption [since the work of typology was to] unravel the true thread of events, and place the objects in their proper sequence . . . [as in] a tree of progress."[98]

One of the earliest proponents of modern habitat groups was English collector E. T. Booth, who began mounting bird groups in 1858.[99] Unlike Waterton, Booth was less interested in eliminating imperfections in the preserved specimen than in reproducing the context in which the specimen had been found, which he achieved through creating a simulacrum of the precise spot where the creature was entrapped. Booth's method attributed far greater significance to reproducing the exact conditions of the specimen's original habitat and anticipated a type of group that A. E. Parr calls the "intimate" habitat group (presenting the natural habitat of a given species). In contrast, "composite faunistic groups" (also referred to as cyclorama groups) integrated a wide variety of species into one space; through the differential use of foreground and background, these groups consisted of the "numerous intimate habitat groups of a large variety of species and environments, synthetically assembled to form a continuous display."[100] Lucas used the synthetic premise of this group to draw an analogy to cinema: "[Just] as the moving picture condenses into five minutes' time the events of days or weeks, so these groups depict in a few square feet of space the life and happenings of a much larger area."[101] Spectators' viewing habits were thus shaped by a range of related entertainments, so much so that they carried with them "expectations about viewing from experiences at competing visual attractions."[102]

Based on their experiences of looking at waxworks and native peoples performing in living exhibits at world's fairs and expositions, what spectators may have sought when standing before the hypermimetic life group was the voyeuristic thrill of gazing at a human facsimile, contextualized within an anecdotal setting or, occasionally, as an isolated figure in a glass case (fig. 1.10).[103] Casting one's eyes upon the waxy pallor of the mannequin provoked both fascination and discomfort though, as Marina Warner has argued in an essay on Madame Tussaud's eighteenth- and nineteenth-century waxworks: "[The] preserving properties and inner luminosity [of wax] symbolically challenge the corruption of the flesh and seem to overcome death. The affinity of its surface appearance with skin, wax's especially fair, glistening, slightly moist condition, lent it to the simulation of flesh."[104]

But if wax carried with it an inbuilt bias toward representing the flesh of people of Caucasian descent (or so it would seem from Warner's description of wax's "fair, glistening, slightly moist condition"), it nevertheless proved exceptionally useful in simulating human anatomy and played a crucial role in medical training; flesh, bones, muscles, nerves, and diseases could all be realistically represented, and human hair was often incorporated into the model in order to heighten the verisimilitude.[105] The coexistence of waxworks in both scientific and popular cultures cannot, however, account entirely for the phantasmatic pleasures elicited by wax simulation, a corporeal fascination that, Giuliana Bruno argues, was quickly taken up by film.[106]

An early account of the disquieting confrontation between observer and wax model was offered by the Reverent Manasseh Cutler in his description of an encounter with a wax model of Charles Willson Peale at Peale's Philadelphia Museum in 1787:[107]

I beheld two men, so perfectly alike that I could not discern the minutest difference. One of them, indeed, had no motion; but he appeared to me to be absolutely alive as the other, and I could hardly help wondering that he did not smile or take part in the conversation. This was a piece of waxwork which Mr. Peale had just finished, in which he had taken himself. . . . To what perfection is this art capable of being carried! By this method, our particular friends and ancestors might be preserved in perfect likeness to the latest generation. We seem to be able in some degree to disappoint the ravages of time, and prevent mortality itself.[108]

Cutler's description, which suggests that the human wax figure's lack of motion was offset by its otherwise convincing attributes of three-dimensionality and realistic scale, not only relates to the perfect illusionism of French film theorist André Bazin's myth of total cinema but also to the "mummy complex" which, Bazin argued, underscores film and photography's psychic roots in cheating mortality.[109] There is also the subtext of the waxwork as an act of self-preservation and focal point in Peale's Museum, implied in Peale's narcissistic decision to sculpt a wax effigy of himself. But whereas Cutler's

FIG. 1.10 Huichol Indian Arrow maker group from the Mexican Hall, AMNH, constructed c. 1901. Note the hyperrealism of the physiognomic detail. (Neg. no. 39687. *Photo:* Julius Kirschner, 1922. Courtesy Dept. of Library Services, AMNH)

reaction seems to suggest a certain affinity between the wax figure and the art of motion pictures, each representational medium possesses its own quite specific set of signifying practices. For example, gazing as long as a spectator may have wished upon life-size three-dimensional human models wearing authentic native clothing and surrounded by indigenous artifacts is quite different from viewing fleeting, mechanically reproduced, black-and-white two-dimensional images. And there were other differences, including cinema's collective audience versus the individual's or small group's viewing of life groups; the darkened versus dramatically lit viewing space; the constrained versus comparatively mobile situation of spectators; and the viewing relations imposed by the three-dimensional life group versus cinema's flat screen. A final distinction centers around the likelihood that the museum spectator's experience of the human replicant evoked the aura of the unique handcrafted object, in terms proposed by Walter Benjamin, more often than the experience of the mass-produced industrial artifact of film.[110]

However, despite these differences, some of the pleasures inherent in experiencing the ethnographic subject via the illusionistic facsimile of the human wax figure were clearly available to spectators of early ethnographic cinema: both representational media constructed safe, consumable versions of the indigene which satisfied a desire to "see" cultural difference in a narratively coherent, nonthreatening, and potentially thrilling way.[111] Like cinema spectators, viewers of life groups were invited to contemplate a group's lifelikeness *and* wonder at its artfulness; as Haraway argues in her description of the visceral and ocular appeal of the museum group:

> Each diorama presents itself as a side altar, a stage, an unspoiled garden in nature, a hearth for home and family. As an altar, each diorama tells a part of the story of salvation history; each has its special emblems indicating particular virtues. Above all, inviting the visitor to share in its revelation, each tells the truth. Each offers a vision. Each is a window onto knowledge.[112]

Haraway's description of the diorama points to its roots in a theatrical illusionism that relied upon the spectator's ability to mine certain emblems for their ideological meanings. Justified scientifically as didactic "object-lessons"

FIG. 1.11 "Pygmy group" from the African Hall, AMNH, constructed c. 1909. (Neg. no. 37529. *Photo:* Julius Kirschner, 1919. Courtesy Dept. of Library Services, AMNH)

in cultural practices and yet occupying a more liminal space in the spectator's imagination, life groups can be read simultaneously as empirical records of indigenous lives (for there's no escaping this primary function) and as meta-commentaries on the very nature of cinematic spectatorship. Our lingering gaze upon the human mannequins frozen in a storybook narrative creates meaning through piecing the bits of evidence together; in other words, a pristine image of a dramatized world is presented to the museum spectator as an offering, a site of wonder and magic (fig. 1.11).

The popularity of the life group and moving picture also suggests a spectatorial fascination with their status as different sorts of absent presences, evoking an uncanny perceptual play on the spectator's knowledge that what is shown, lifelike as it may seem, is simply an illusion;[113] like the fleeting images of native people projected onto the movie screen, the "framed and inaccessible" mannequins in the ethnographic tableaux oscillate between being lifelike and deathlike in similar ways to the ghostly figures occupying the frames of early ethnographic films.[114] As Sandberg puts it: "Mannequin tableaux, although they did not literally constitute a 'recorded' medium, approximated that status in both freezing the action and in the bodies of the wax figures themselves, which like the filmed body had a lifelike presence and yet were strangely absent as well."[115] The disquieting effect of gazing at a mannequin, as Tom Gunning argues, arose more from a conflict of messages than the notion of the naive spectator mistaking the image for reality: "Far from credulity, it is the incredible nature of the illusion itself that renders the viewer speechless . . . ; astonishment derives from a magical metamorphosis, rather than a seamless reproduction of reality."[116] Like cinema spectators, viewers of life groups were "complicit in the illusion-making and found pleasure in both the attempt and the failure of the representation";[117] they also identified imaginatively with the effigies on display, perhaps indulging in psychosexual fantasies or simply longing for a vision of life so distant from that of the modern city. It was precisely this threat of an imaginative relationship with the displayed scene that troubled Boas, who argued that phantasmatic identification with the figures was not the primary goal of the life group.

Standing in front of a glass case and gazing onto a scene was in some ways analogous to watching spatially and temporally disparate scenes of native peoples in early ethnographic films. Without wanting to push the analogy too far, I would argue that the experience of viewing life groups, especially diorama groups, which could only be seen from one side and had models of indigenous people dramatically inserted in front of painted backdrops, was not dissimilar to the experience of watching images of native peoples in early ethnographic films, especially films with no camera movement. In a great many ethnographic films concerned with native industries, for example, workers were often framed against highly connotative architectural backdrops or metonymic landscapes similar to the painted diorama backgrounds of life groups. Moving from one diorama group to another, the museum visitor experienced a series of dramatic tableaux in ways similar to the spectator of early ethnographic film, although for the cinema spectator, the movement is virtual and not lit-

eral (obviously, filmgoers are denied the sense of agency afforded museumgoers, who can choose which groups to examine, from what angle, and for how
long).

But just as a great many early ethnographic films typically consisted of temporally and spatially distinct scenes of native peoples engaged in theatricalized
rituals or industries, so the life group constructed a series of discrete immersive and syncretic representations of native peoples. A description of an Inuit
exhibit at the AMNH in *The World's Work* evokes both the immersive and disjunctive qualities of the museum life group: "Here all at once we are in the very
atmosphere of an Indian encampment or an Eskimo village. Skillfully made
figures (often actual life casts) are dressed in specimen costumes, and are seen
busy at their characteristic tasks — the women making bread, or curing hides,
and the men smoking, hunting or making weapons."[118] The "here all at once"
quality of the spectator's encounter with "the very atmosphere of an Indian
encampment" resembles the spatial and temporal dislocations of some early
ethnographic films, which, often without warning, transported the spectator
into a new geocultural location across an instantaneous cut. Moreover, reference to the museumgoer's sudden immersion in the very "atmosphere" of an
Indian encampment echoes critical and promotional commentary around
countless early ethnographic film subjects.

The spectator's momentary halt and viewing experience before each life
group corresponds on some level, then, to the film spectator's immobility and
ways of seeing cultural difference. In addition, the museumgoer's movement
between life group tableaux shares a certain resemblance with the transitions
between the sequence shots typical of early ethnographic films. If the camera's
static and frontal medium shot echoed the preferred viewing relations of the
museum life group, panoramic shots of landscape or the journey to a native
village which frequently separated tableaux of human activity in early ethnographic cinema can be compared to the panoramic perception of the museumgoer as his or her roving eye sought out yet another eye-catching life
group; walking from group to group had the same transitional quality as shots
of indigenous landscape, architecture, or transportation which often separated or even led up to scenes of native life. And yet, the act of seeing suggested
in the physical movement of the spectator as she traveled from life group to
life group in the gallery space harks back to a much earlier period of cinemat-

ic spectatorship when visitors to kinetoscope parlors would move from apparatus to apparatus to watch kinetographs of Sioux dancers or vaudeville performers. However, the link between the ambulatory qualities of kinetoscope viewing and life groups is less compelling than the connection between life groups and projected film; indeed kinetoscopes seem to foreshadow the use of video monitors in galleries, where spectators can view short films on indigenous customs before moving on to the next exhibit.

On one level, then, the museum life group seems to evoke what Anne Friedberg has called "a mobilized 'virtual' gaze," virtual because it is "mediated through representation," and mobilized because it is "rooted in other cultural activities that involve walking and travel."[119] Using the historical figure of the urban *flâneur* as a starting point, Friedberg examines a number of nineteenth-century social and cultural sites that foregrounded certain modes of looking that were to become integral to cinematic and televisual apparatuses. As we have seen, the gaze invited by museum life and habitat groups seems isomorphic with new ways of seeing enacted in a range of related late nineteenth-century architectural spaces, including shopping arcades, exhibition halls, art galleries, and winter gardens. The *flâneur*'s momentarily arrested encounter with protocinematic attractions such as museum life groups and department store display windows depended on the temporary immobility of the spectator, an immobility that, Friedberg argues, was "rewarded by the imaginary mobilities that such fixity provided."[120]

However, we should not lose sight of the fact that the mobility afforded the spectator of cinema in virtual form is, in the case of the life group, an *actual* mobility, since in order to appreciate the vistas of the museum hallways, the spectator had to physically move from exhibit to exhibit. Likewise, unlike the cinematic image, the life group object that museumgoers see is not virtual but quite tangible; it can be touched, one's face can be pressed up to the cold glass, and the object doesn't suddenly vanish before one's eyes with the passage from shot to shot as in cinema. The life group is only virtual, then, in the sense that it is a simulacrum of a distant native scene that was photographed by a museum artist before being painstakingly reconstructed in three-dimensional form within the museum. Thus, in the same way that cinema spectators are "virtually" transported to an "imaginary elsewhere and an imaginary elsewhen"[121] as they watch a film, the life group invites museumgoers to imagine they are standing in front of an actual scene of indigenous life. The spectator's movement through the museum halls thus replicates that of the anthropologist-explorer who traverses the physical and cultural landscape, encountering assorted scenes of indigenous life. In light of the primacy of physical movement required in looking at life groups, their modes of spectating seem to correspond to what I would call "promenade ethnographic cinema," a term derived from the staging techniques of medieval mystery plays.[122] In "promenade theater" (the modern term for this form of staging), the action takes place in discrete sets located around the periphery of a performance space; standing before each scene, spectators watch the action unfold, and then, cued (usually) by lighting changes, "promenade" on to the next scene which begins once the audience has reassembled. The physical configuration of museum life groups also seems to anticipate some aspects of cinema spectatorship. Boas's 1896 recommendations for the installation of life groups at the AMNH is highly evocative of the conditions of film spectatorship:

In order to set off such a group to advantage it must be seen from one side only, the view must be through a kind of frame which shuts out the line where the scene ends, the visitor must be in a comparatively dark place while there must be light on the objects and on the background. The only place where such an effect can be had is in a Panorama building where plastic art and painting are made to blend into each other and where everything not germane to the subject is removed from view.[123]

The framing and frontality evoked in Boas's discussion of diorama groups (unlike figures represented in glass cases that can be viewed from more than one perspective and that are not placed in front of painted backdrops) underscore a phenomenological similarity between the life group and the moving picture screen; not only is the proscenium framing of the diorama group similar to the shape of the cinema screen, but Boas's prescription for ideal spectatorship foreshadows the conditions for collective viewing in later moving picture exhibition (fig. 1.12). In fact, as early as 1869, Alfred Wallace recommended that seats be placed conveniently near life groups so that spectators would be encouraged to study the exhibits in greater depth. By 1908 the AMNH installed public seating in the Eskimo Hall, consisting of two skin-

FIG. 1.12 Hopi Indian Diorama life group at the AMNH, c. 1915. (Neg. no. 34627. Courtesy Dept. of Library Services AMNH)

covered sleds from Comdr. Robert E. Peary's 1893–94 North Greenland Expedition.[124] Support for the provision of seating came from some museum professionals who argued that the galleries should be places conducive to rest and recreation, since, as president of the British Museums Association Francis Arthur Bather opined, the only things permitted to rest in most museums were umbrellas. (Bather even went so far as to recommend the placement of chairs and occasional tables with flowers and books on them in entrances and galleries in order to counter the effects of museum fatigue.)[125]

In addition, museum commentator S. A. Barrett argued that the best results in museological display would be achieved only when lighting was completely controlled; he recommended using heavy shades on the windows opposite life groups, "thus giving us complete control, by means of artificial light, of the illumination without, as well as within, the group case."[126] For AMNH naturalist and taxidermist Carl Akeley, the desired effect of habitat group displays would be analogous to that of looking "out through open windows into an Africa out of doors."[127] The museum group and cinema thus present the spectator with a window on the world, what Akeley described as "a peep hole into the jungle."[128] Both are suited to what Haraway calls "the epistemological and aesthetic stance of realism,"[129] and finally, both depend upon a complex division of labor in their manufacture and execution.

Museum life groups therefore evoked some of the spectatorial coordinates of early ethnographic film-viewing in rich and provocative ways, allowing museum visitors to insert their bodies into visual fields that shared a great deal in common with the display techniques of the department store and world's fair. John Rodman Wanamaker, Philadelphia millionaire and department store magnate, was one of the earliest professionals to forge the connection between commerce and museums, arguing that the museum needed "the use of the merchant instinct to show it off to best advantage."[130] Wanamaker had long been interested in archaeology, ethnography, art, and history and in 1900 had funded curator and museum pioneer Stewart Culin's trip out West to collect Native American artifacts, which were exhibited in both his Philadelphia department store and in the University of Pennsylvania Museum, the archaeological section of which Wanamaker had helped found.[131] According to Simon J. Bronner, "Wanamaker's department store was organized like Culin's archaeological museum with Egyptian, Greek, Byzantine, and Oriental halls; the store paraded the world's ancient civilizations behind an emergent American commercial culture."[132]

Despite the enduring public fascination with life groups, institutional ambivalence toward representational modes that attempted to imitate nature too slavishly, such as the waxwork, or that petrified nature through taxidermy, suggests that the transition from the old-style "cabinet of curiosities" model of museological display to more eye-catching, sensational exhibits was by no means unproblematic. The efforts of museum administrators to control the spectator's construction of meaning through carefully designed museum itineraries can be read as an attempt to exert some control over the spectator's encounter with life groups and related display cases, although regardless of how much attention spectators gave to the individual cases and life groups, museum curators could nevertheless find some solace in the fact that scientific precepts were inscribed into the architectural design of the building, so that irrespective of how inattentive a visitor was, some vestiges of the scientific ethos might imprint themselves upon the distracted museumgoer's mind. Indeed, visitors at the AMNH frequently found themselves quite literally surrounded by ethnographic representation in the Museum's halls, since the towering walls and doorways were decorated with murals of indigenous life.[133]

In spite of the unquestionable popular appeal of the museum life group, professional concern that its reputation as crass spectacle would distract the museum visitor from the task of absorbing ethnographic lessons offers us clues for understanding anthropologists' attitudes toward cinema; indeed, the relatively late arrival of moving pictures in the AMNH (the first film was not show at the Museum until January 1908) suggests that if the too-perfect illusionism of the living village and life group ran the risk of privileging spectacle and technical gimmickry over ethnographic accuracy, the institutional resistance to exhibiting commercially produced films of indigenous peoples (nearly the only films available for exhibition at the AMNH until the mid-teens) was likewise substantial. Anthropologists' fears that the museum-going public would be more interested in the uncanny illusionism of the cinematic image or the deathly chimera of the life group mannequin than in the broader scientific principles they were intended to convey were part of more general debates about how to represent ethnographic knowledge to the nonspecialist.

But the debates generated by life groups can also be read as symptomatic of more deeper-seated anxieties about popular culture, since the ways of seeing enacted in museums of natural history were shaped as much by an emergent culture of visuality as by the specific guidelines laid down by curators and exhibit designers. Visitors to the AMNH were therefore able to try out a number of spectatorial positions while walking around the Museum and may have felt just as much at home in the halls of these intimidating palatial edifices as they did in the department stores and dime museums scattered across the same city. Furthermore, one of the most influential sites for the development of exhibition practices was the nineteenth-century's world's fair, which not only served as an opportunity for the young field of anthropology to reach a broad public, but established norms of spectating that carried over into museums and cinemas. There is, however, an inverse symmetry here in terms of the relationship forged between anthropology and popular culture in the museum and the world's fair. Whereas in the natural history museum, curators looked to a burgeoning mass consumer culture for inspiration on how to attract a new kind of spectator, at the world's fair promoters of the Midway concession stands and ethnographic villages turned to anthropology as a way to legitimize their popular exhibits, to sanction their commercial appropriation of ethnography's discourses and iconography. In seeking rapprochement between education and anthropology, the attractions of the Midway and amusement zones of world's fairs found the nascent discipline of anthropology the perfect ally in selling Otherness as visual spectacle.

2

Science and Spectacle

VISUALIZING THE OTHER AT THE WORLD'S FAIR

Yes, in truth, all the world was there.
—FREDERICK WARD PUTNAM (CHIEF OF DEPARTMENT OF ETHNOLOGY,
WORLD'S COLUMBIAN EXPOSITION, 1893)[1]

The old contemptible side-show is a thing of the past. . . . We want novelty with a point to it. It
must be beautiful novelty, or scientific novelty, or ingenious novelty, or we will have none of it.
—MARY BRONSON HARTT (REFERRING TO THE PAN-AMERICAN EXPOSITION, 1901)[2]

ECHOING THE CRITICAL controversies around life groups in nineteenth-
century museums of natural history, native villages at world's fairs and expositions provoked lively debates about the efficacy of distinctive modes of
ethnographic representation and informed scientific and popular perceptions
of early ethnographic film. An analysis of the operational and experiential
logic of native villages at world's fairs—how indigenous peoples were consumed as exhibits in both official anthropological buildings and in the more
free-wheeling concessions of the midways and pikes—offers us a clearer sense
of how representational strategies shared by the world's fair and early cinema
were perceived by leading members of the American anthropological community. As part of the social horizon of early ethnographic film, native villages at world's fairs undoubtedly played a role in shaping anthropologists'
attitudes toward precinematic ethnography; indeed, anthropologists' ambivalence about the suitability of cinema as an ethnographic tool may have
stemmed from the dubious scientific status of world's fair live attractions such

46

as Fatima's *Coochee-Coochee Dance* (1896), a performance quickly recorded for an extremely popular early Edison film. The historical coincidence of the emergence of cinema with the popularity of ethnographic villages at world's fairs (the World's Columbian Exposition in Chicago in 1893—aka the Chicago World's Fair—predates the commercial launch of Edison's kinetoscope by only one year) invites consideration of their shared phenomenological and formal features.

The rampant commercialism and commodity fetishism of world's fairs—historian Robert Rydell argues that native peoples were perceived no differently to the commodities surrounding them, displayed as "natural resources to be exploited as readily as mineral deposits"[3]—makes them especially fruitful cultural sites for exploring the complex negotiations that took place between anthropology, popular culture, and commerce in attempting to strike the right balance between education, spectacle, and profit.[4] But whereas in the museum anthropologists could select what specific aspects of popular culture to incorporate into their exhibits, at the world's fair anthropologists had far less control over how their discipline would be implicated in the overall setting, especially in relation to the displays of native peoples in the commercial amusement zones. In museums of natural history, curators were solely responsible for designing suitable representational forms for their artifacts and collections, but at world's fairs the specific signifying practices of anthropology were mediated by the fairground as a whole, which shared some, but by no means all, of the discipline's larger goals. Thus, world's fairs were something of a double-edged sword for anthropologists, providing them with both an unprecedented opportunity for museum promotion (since a great many of the objects on display ended up back in museums and were a marvelous draw for future museumgoers) on the one hand, and with a potentially disastrous public relations exercise on the other.[5]

If world's fairs served to launch the public face of anthropology to a vast popular audience, they also evoked anthropology's uncomfortable doppelgänger, popularized exhibits such as "Buffalo Bill's Wild West Show" and other for-profit spectacles that, to the untrained eye, may have looked no different from the officially sanctioned displays of native peoples. If anthropology sought to foster greater understanding of world cultures and sow the seeds for a more relativist understanding of cultural difference, the context in which it attempted to carry out this mission was hardly conducive for this kind of learning, since, as Rydell points out, at the world's fair "displays of material and natural abundance became an outward sign of inward racial 'fitness' and culture."[6] Adding to the tension was the overtly commercial impulse behind a great many ethnographic displays, which were managed by businessmen rather than curators or educators, whose raison d'être couldn't have been further from anthropology's mission of acquiring and displaying disinterested scientific knowledge. Furthermore, anthropologists responsible for organizing ethnographic exhibits frequently found themselves in the uncomfortable position of seeing their own rhetorical tropes appropriated by commercial managers. Where anthropology had once gingerly turned to popular culture for inspiration in designing popular museum exhibits such as life groups, by the end of the nineteenth century popular culture entrepreneurs had few qualms about appropriating the rhetoric of anthropology for commercial advantage.

Exploring how anthropologists attempted to exert physical and intellectual control over the representation of ethnography in both the officially sanctioned exhibits and in the amusement zones of world's fairs can suggest the institutional and intellectual tensions at play in turn-of-the-century world's fairs. Likewise, a consideration of some of the elements common to both native villages and ethnographic film, particularly the ways in which models of spectatorship evoked by such villages anticipate some of the viewing positions and phantasmatic pleasures experienced by spectators of ethnographic film, can illuminate the shared semantic resemblances of these popular visual forms.

Policing the Other: Anthropology at World's Fairs

For many Americans in the nineteenth century, world's fairs and expositions offered the first public encounters not only with exotic strangers from the far ends of the earth but with the popular face of the emerging discipline of anthropology.[7] While the American public might have read about the work of this new breed of scientist in popular magazines and newspapers or visited national repositories of ethnographic objects, the world's fair gave spectators an unprecedented opportunity to learn more about anthropology's scope and ambition. World's fairs and expositions boasted the participation of some of the most senior and influential figures in anthropology and were important public relations opportunities for the fledgling discipline; as one observer noted in 1902: "World's fairs are necessary to the proper study of mankind."[8]

Anthropologists were enlisted in the publicity machines of world's fairs and exhibitions in various ways, writing articles for popular magazines such as *Harper's Weekly* and *The World's Work* as well as the introductions or forewords to official fair souvenir handbooks. At the same time, the native villages and ethnographic concessions installed within the popular amusement zones of fairs enabled fairgoers to encounter firsthand some of anthropology's most celebrated human subjects. Peabody Museum anthropologist Frederick Ward Putnam was designated director of Department M (which included anthropology) at the 1893 World's Columbian Exposition in Chicago, and his job involved overseeing exhibits housed in the Anthropology Building (including mannequin life groups, photographs, material artifacts, and anthropometric equipment) as well as the ethnological exhibits and concessions found on the Midway Plaisance. According to Putnam, the main aim of the ethnological villages on the Chicago Midway was to disseminate ethnographic knowledge about native cultures on a "dignified and decorous basis" and to consolidate some of the anthropological learning taking place in the galleries of the Anthropology Building.[9] In the "Laboratory of Physical Anthropology" located in the Anthropology Building, visitors could gauge the extent to which they conformed to an "average" Caucasian physiognomy by examining "a perfect type of American manhood" represented in the form of male and female clay models, constructed from composite photographs based on measurements taken from more than 25,000 American volunteers who were each subject to sixty individual measurements.[10] Visitors might also compare themselves to photographs of diverse physical human types which covered one entire wall of the laboratory.[11] Stepping outside the physical anthropology laboratory directly into the American Indian exhibit at the Chicago World's Fair, the spectator was immediately presented with what must have seemed corporeal evidence of evolutionary principles explicated in the laboratory. Aimed at demonstrating theories of Western progress and the benefits of acculturation, the Native American exhibit ratified wider ideological beliefs about the degeneracy of the American Indian in the absence of Western intervention.

For many Chicago World's Fair spectators, the effect of touring the Anthropology Building, national exhibits, and some of the ethnological concessions on the Midway seemed analogous to browsing through an ethnographic encyclopedia, a comparison endorsed by some contemporaneous museum officials and journalists. Assistant secretary of the Smithsonian Institution George Brown Goode argued that the Fair would become "an illustrated encyclopedia of civilization," and *World's Work* contributor Arthur Goodrich described the Columbian Exposition as a "new edition of a world encyclopedia."[12] As part of an ethnographic smorgasbord of indigenous "types" (fig. 2.1), native peoples were incorporated narratively into what modern Dutch anthropologist Raymond Corbey calls a "*mise-en-intrigue* [in which] they were assigned their roles in the stories told by museum exhibition, world fairs, and colonial postcards. . . . The radical difference of the Other was made sense of and thus warded off by a narrative (discordant concordance) between 'civilized' and 'savage.' "[13] As a widely evoked structuring principle of the world's fair (and of the social sciences where the notion of the "criminal type" was common parlance), the "type" helped fairgoers make the transition between officially sanctioned government exhibits and Midway concessions (fig. 2.2).[14] The act of fitting cultural Others into taxonomical groups and orientalist narratives was thus a way of diffusing their potentially "disturbing difference, without annihilating the difference completely."[15] Of course, European minorities were similarly classified as types, as seen in this postcard of "Irish Colleens," from the Imperial International Exhibition of 1909 (fig. 2.3).

Midway showmen and the official scientific advisers for world's fairs responded to common problems of exhibition design in remarkably similar ways. In order to garner as much interest as possible in the native exhibits and to "manage" the potential ambivalence of spectators toward the display of cultural difference, exposition organizers supplemented relatively static displays with performances and other staged spectacles (fig. 2.4). If the ethnographic exhibit failed to attract enough public interest, the unusual and the bizarre were stressed, and quotidian life was transformed into a series of rehearsed and repeatable "stunts." The presence of jugglers and magicians, as well as the staging of mock battles or cannibalistic rituals, imbued the exhibit with a carnival atmosphere, and there are accounts of exposition visitors throwing money at the performers and being invited to touch the human exhibits in

FIG. 2.1 Postcard with caption "Assuan: Type of the Bisharin Race," made by Cairo company Lehnert & Landrock, c. 1890s. (Author's personal collection)

FIG. 2.2 Postcard of "Bedouin Milk-Seller," c. 1900. (Author's personal collection)

FIG. 2.3 Postcard of "Irish Colleens," from the 1909 Imperial International Exhibition held in London. (Author's personal collection)

FIG. 2.4 German showman Carl Hagenbeck's "Ceylon Village and Indian Arena,"
Franco-British Exhibition, 1908. (Author's personal collection)

order to increase the reality effect of the encounter.[16] At the same time, the
quotidian life of native peoples was also unproblematically transformed into a
consumable Midway spectacle, in an oxymoronic performance style that Dean
MacCannell calls "staged authenticity."[17] According to Barbara Kirshenblatt-
Gimblett, the objectificatory tendencies of the ethnographic gaze in live
exhibits turn native demonstrations of indigenous practices into frozen,
canonical artifacts which assume "forms that are alien, if not antithetical, to
how they are produced and experienced in their local setting"; through repetition, cultural performances thus become "routinized and trivialized,"[18] the
trope of performance providing the perfect representational vehicle for containing and diffusing this threat of difference.[19]

   Ethnographic villages and their concomitant spectacles predated nineteenth-century world's fairs and expositions. In 1550 at Rouen, outside Paris,
a simulated Brazilian village was constructed and populated by 50 "genuine"
Tabbagerres and Toupinabouz Indians, and 250 Frenchmen masquerading as
native "extras." The villages transformed the Rouen landscape into a Brazilian
mise-en-scène, complete with a dense forest of native and artificial flora and

imported parrots, marmots, and apes. Far from affirming Brazilian culture, the simulated settings and repeated performances over the course of the two-day event paradoxically contributed to its "erasure and negation." As Steven Mullaney explains:

> The object . . . was not to understand Brazilian culture but to perform it, in a paradoxically self-consuming fashion. Knowledge of another culture in such an instance is directed toward ritual rather than ethnological ends, and the rite involved is one ultimately organized around the elimination of its own pretext: the spectacle of the Other that is thus celebrated and observed, in passing.[20]

For Mullaney, these staged ethnographic extravaganzas constituted a "rehearsal of cultures," fueled by a fascination "geared not toward the interpretation of strange cultures but towards their consummate performance."[21] The emphasis upon performance as signifier of cultural identity tends to erase the boundaries between scientific knowledge and popular display; in this way, Kirshenblatt-Gimblett argues, the "inherently performative nature of live specimens veers exhibits of them strongly in the direction of spectacle, blurring the line still further between morbid curiosity and scientific interest, chamber of horrors and medical exhibition, circus and zoological garden, theater and ethnographic display, dramatic monologue and scholarly lecture, staged recreation and cultural performance."[22] The Rouen installation is an early instance of how semiotically rich cultural practices are reduced to reified emblems, little more than hieroglyphs, when performed out of context for the uninitiated.[23]

Native peoples were regularly exhibited in small family groups or as members of performing troupes for audiences in London and other European cities in the seventeenth, eighteenth, and nineteenth centuries (fig. 2.5). (We should remember too, that Ancient Romans paraded captive peoples and exotic animals and that Caesar brought back Cleopatra and Egyptian artifacts as physical evidence of his conquests.) While visiting London in 1850, the American artist George Catlin even flirted with the idea of curating a "floating museum of mankind" aboard the ship the *Great Britain*; stopping at international ports, the vessel could gather material (both inanimate and animate)

FIG. 2.5 Billy, Jenny, and Little Toby, the sole survivors of a group of nine Queensland Australian Aborigines who toured Europe. (*Photo:* Prince Roland Bonaparte, Paris, 1885; Royal Anthropological Institute 2000. Courtesy RAI.)

for new exhibits as it traveled from country to country.[24] As an analogous "flickering museum of mankind," early ethnographic film offered spectators a similar experience to Catlin's proposed traveling attraction, conjoining the seriousness of the natural history exhibit with the showmanship of the popular dime museum. If the logistics of maintaining a floating peripatetic exhibit were too daunting for Catlin, ethnographic film overcame similar logistical hurdles in turning an encounter with the ethnographic Other into a flexible and lucrative commodity of mass consumption.

Well before the emergence of cinema, entrepreneurs had been exhibiting native peoples and so-called freaks in their traveling dime museums and circuses. As Rosemarie Garland Thomson explains, "The early itinerant monstermongers who exhibited human oddities in taverns and the slightly more respectable performances in rented halls evolved in the mid-nineteenth century into institutionalized, permanent exhibitions of freaks in dime museums and later in circus sideshows, fairs, and amusement park midways."[25] The interpretive tropes used in exhibiting people with disabilities or physiological anomalies were also applied to peoples of color, whose ethnicity was transformed into visual spectacle for paying customers. P. T. Barnum's "Congress of Nations" and "Ethnological Congress" (fig. 2.6) began displaying "genuine ethnological curiosities" to the American public in 1883, featuring "representatives . . . from every accessible people, civilized and barbarous, on the face of the globe," including "100 Uncivilized, Superstitious and Savage People," according to the *Boston Globe*. Touted as "ethnological curiosities," native peoples were just one of many attractions on offer; human deformaties, people with "extraordinary peculiarities, such as giants, dwarfs, singular disfigurements of the person, unusual feats of strength and or agility, &c," were the mainstay of Barnum's extremely popular exhibitions and dime museums.[26] Doubly Othered in some instances by their race and "extraordinary peculiarities," these "genuine specimens" existed as ethnographic demonstrations of the prevailing hierarchical, biologically determined theories of race, theories that were deftly woven into the ideological schemas of the shows. In exploiting public interest in native peoples and peoples with disabilities, Barnum's Congress traded on prevailing discourses of progress, science, religion, nationalism, and normalcy, which helped imbue his shows with a modicum of respectability.[27] The hyperbole and controversy surrounding Barnum's dis-

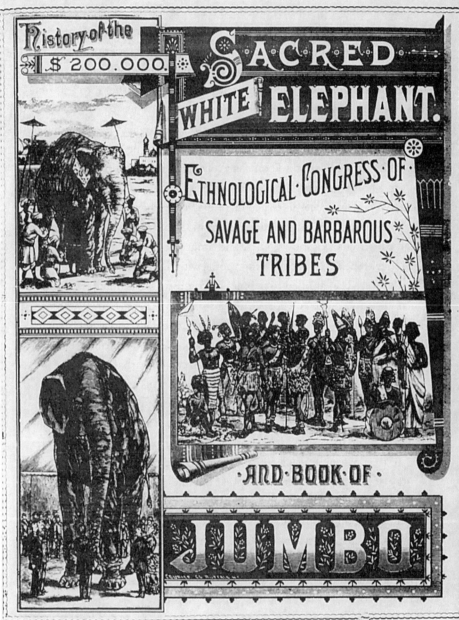

FIG. 2.6 Cover of 1884 Barnum *Courier* advertising "Ethnological Congress of Savage and Barbarous Tribes."

plays—frequent allegations that the public had been humbugged by yet another Barnum fraud (like the discovery that Zulu tribesmen were, in fact, African-Americans), together with virulently racist reviews of specific exhibits in the "Ethnological Congress" (a group of "Wild Australians" were described as the "most degraded specimens of humanity in existence" and "cannibals when they get the chance" in the *Chicago Tribune*)[28]—must have attracted the attention of at least some anthropologists who couldn't fail to notice that the reception of their own displays of native peoples at world's fairs may have at times blurred with Barnum's commercial "enfreakment" of human diversity.[29]

Barnum's "What is It?" exhibit stands as a chilling example of how the corporeal Other became a visual conundrum for nineteenth-century audiences who were invited to project their own ideas about social evolution and Darwinism onto the exhibit, since "in both its name ('What is It?') and its ingeniously evasive classificatory-type ('nondescript'), Barnum's 1860s hybrid both literally and figuratively begged the public to fill in the blanks."[30] Despite the obvious differences between the displays of purportedly "unclassifiable" native peoples—the role of "What is It?" was, in fact, played by a white actor in black face and a retarded African-American at different points in the history of the exhibit—audiences may very well have drawn upon the same kinds of interpretive viewing frames when looking at world's fair exhibits as they did at Barnum's American Museum. But Barnum was not the only North American impresario involved in the commercial display of colonized peoples; "Buffalo Bill's Wild West Show" had long featured Native Americans as part of its extensive East Coast and European tours, parading them as examples of "full-blooded" Indians and staging elaborate reconstructions of famous battles. Indeed, Buffalo Bill set up his Wild West Show just outside the main entrance to the World's Columbian fairground in 1893, reaping between $700,000 and $1,000,000 in profits.

Colonial expositions in Britain, starting with the "Great Exposition" at the Crystal Palace in 1851, were among the first to exploit a public fascination for ethnographic curiosities for explicitly propagandistic purposes. Looted objects such as ivory thrones (representing vanquished colonial royalty) were exhibited at the Crystal Palace, and an evening at the Ethnological Society of London in 1844 was devoted to the examination of "an ethnographic aboriginal," a man brought from the sailing ships docked nearby.[31] Similarly, at the Colonial and Indian Exhibition held in London in 1886, a representative sam-

FIG. 2.7 Poster for Exposition Universelle de Lyon (colonies section), 1897.

ple of subject peoples, including "Hindus, Muhammadens, Buddhists, Red Indians from British Guiana, Perak and Hong Kong" was offered as ethnographic evidence of the breadth of the British Empire's possessions.[32] Themes of race, national and cultural identity, education, progress, and imperialism were inscribed within the spatial and cultural topographies of the Colonial and Indian Exhibition that sought both to legitimize the colonial administration and educate the British public. Describing a range of rhetorical and speculatory devices, including static displays of raw materials and technologies, fictionalized dramatic interludes, and staged reenactments, Annie E. S. Coombes argues that such exhibitions mobilized "what passed in the popular consciousness as sociological investigations, historical objectivity, and anthropological knowledge" (fig. 2.7).[33]

Supported by popular scientific theories of evolution, ethnographic amusements at world's fairs buttressed white supremacy in their narratives and iconography; embodying racist attitudes toward cultural difference, imperial interests, and national progress in every aspect of their construction, ethnographic villages provided fairgoers with tangible and seemingly irrefutable evidence of the racial inferiority of non-Western peoples. These lessons were inscribed in exhibition signs (an Igorot village was labeled IGOROTTE VILLAGE: BARBARIC TRIBES at an exposition in Portland in 1905) and in the topographical relation of these signs to exhibits extolling privileged Euro-American culture. For example, the aim of the Native American village at the 1904 St. Louis World's Fair was to show that "a race which cannot of itself make the necessary strides to civilization may be helped." Such attitudes were also evoked by "scientific" rhetorical tropes which described native peoples as "specimens" and "types."[34] Evolutionary theories and racist hierarchies were thus inscribed into the architectural design of the exhibits, policy decisions over the location of ethnographic villages on the exposition site, and in the rhetoric of official promotional guides.

It should be noted, however, that the discursive and institutional contexts for such displays shifted somewhat in the late nineteenth century, when international exhibitions began to take on a more frankly nationalist and colonialist cast. The first time native peoples appeared in an "ethnographic village" (a reconstruction of a native village in which performers lived for the duration of the fair), as opposed to merely appearing at a fair or exposition, was at the

1889 Paris Exposition. This ethnological attraction so impressed one American visitor, Otis T. Mason, curator of the Smithsonian's Bureau of American Ethnology, that he enthusiastically recommended to his American colleagues that a similar display be established at the 1893 World's Columbian Exposition. Calling the Paris Exhibition the "crowning glory of anthropology," Mason described how it was possible to see "twelve types of Africans, besides Javanese, Tonkinese, Chinese, Japanese, and other oriental peoples, living in native houses, wearing native costumes, eating native food, practicing native arts and rites on the *Esplanades des Invalides* side by side with the latest inventions with the whole civilized world as spectators."[35] Beyond what was viewed as the anthropological value of ethnographic villages, the fact that they netted a profit of over $700,000 undoubtedly played no small part in persuading the Committee on Ways and Means at the World's Columbian Exposition in Chicago that similar exhibits should be featured attractions on the Midway.

World's Fairs and Popular Intertexts: Guilt Through Association

Concern that the sensationalist connotations of ethnographic villages installed in the amusement section of a world's fair might undermine the exhibit's ostensible scientific goals was voiced by scientists as early as Philadelphia's Centennial Exposition in 1876. Arrangements to establish an Indian encampment housing one hundred families were eventually shelved by exposition planners because officials feared that unless the exhibit was under strict governmental control, it could turn, in the words of Indian Commissioner J. Q. Smith, into a degraded and sensational "side-show." (The lack of government funding, together with an apathetic response to the idea by members of the Indian Affairs Committee, were other factors).[36] A reluctance to include "live Indians" in the official North American Indian Pavilion may have stemmed in part from the exhibit's uncomfortable proximity to the unofficial "Centennial City" on Elm Street. Like the Midway or Pike of subsequent American expositions, Philadelphia's "Centennial City" was a grandiose euphemism for a mile-long shantytown featuring restaurants, beer gardens, ice cream saloons, hotels, dioramas, small shows, and an extremely popular freak show "museum" where spectators paid to see such attractions as the "Wild Men of Borneo,"[37] the "Wild Children of Australia," and a collection of "Feejees" who were vouched for by the exhibitors as " 'pure and unadulterated man-eaters.' "[38] These popular attractions on Elm Street's "Centennial City," adjacent to, but legally outside, the jurisdiction of the official exposition, not only competed with the more socially sanctified exhibits but served as a negative frame of reference for spectators moving freely between the two sites. Similarly, despite the efforts of some anthropologists to maintain a serious atmosphere at the "Congress of Indians" exhibit at the 1898 Omaha Fair, most contemporary accounts suggest it more closely resembled a "Wild West show."[39]

As a response to the conflict between official and commercial sites in and around the Philadelphia fair, organizers of the 1893 World's Columbian Exposition were the first to officially sanction a specific locale within the exposition site that would include popular entertainment and ethnological concessions.[40] As its name implies, the Midway was an interstitial space that defied easy categorization;[41] sanctioned by science but designed by commerce, the Midway was the offspring of two very distinct visions of ethnography: ethnography as scientific research and ethnography as popular attraction.[42] The Midway existed as a parallel text to the official exposition, an oneiric space where ethnology, mass entertainment, and fantasy were conjoined in a heady and seductive mix; its pleasures were commonly seen as dependent upon the spectator's willingness to temporarily suspend critical faculties in favor of a multisensory experience. One journalist suggested that visitors to the Midway should be "wholly conscienceless—not like a painstaking draftsman, but like a human kodak, caring only for as many pleasing impressions as possible, not for analyzing their worth."[43] For this observer and others, while the dislocating effect of the exotic was magnified by the contiguity and variety of native cultures represented, the barrage of exotic representations also served to diminish the "singularity and difference" of the foreign exhibits from each other "as well as the particularities of their difference from Europe."[44]

As in the design of the official spaces of nineteenth-century world's fairs, theories of evolutionism were inscribed into the physical design of Chicago's Midway, with Teutonic and Celtic races located nearest the White City, West and East Asians in the center, and North American Indians at the opposite end of the Plaisance. Such topological lessons were not lost on contemporaneous observers; one critic suggested that the best way to organize a walking tour of the Midway's different races was to "behold them in the ascending scale, in the progressive movement; thus we can march forward with them starting with the lowest specimens of humanity, and reaching continually upward to the highest stage."[45] Designed to evoke utopian themes of technological progress and Western supremacism, the White City was the yardstick against which all the "barbaric peoples" on display in the Midway were measured. As Ella Shohat and Robert Stam have argued, the bombastic display of Western architecture "gave a utopian form to White supremacist ideology, legitimizing racial hierarchies abroad and muting class and gender divisions among Whites at home by stressing national agency in a global project of domination."[46] The Midway thus supported the scientific basis of evolutionary hierarchies[47] by providing an "illustration of an irrational babel of backwardness in contrast with the future-oriented rationales of progress evident in the exhibits of the industrialized white nations."[48]

One of the potential drawbacks in having a concentration of native villages, concessions stands, and refreshments in one commercial zone was that official exhibits located immediately next to the Midway were in perpetual danger of being contaminated by the heteroclite disorder of the commercial strip, as had been the case with the "Centennial City" at Philadelphia's 1876 exposition. The Chinese government, for example, which refused to be officially represented at the 1893 Chicago exposition as a way of protesting the restrictive immigration policies of the 1882 Exclusion Act, ended up sandwiched between the Ice Railway and the Captive Balloon concession, failing to win China the critical attention and prestige accorded better-located exhibits, such as that of the Japanese government.[49] Similarly, despite Putnam's pledge as Chief of Ethnology at the exposition that the "presentation of native life [should] be in every way satisfactory and creditable to the native peoples, [with] no exhibition of a degrading or derogatory manner . . . permitted," the location of the Dakota Sioux, Navajos, Apaches, and other Native American tribe exhibits near the Midway were seen to have a deleterious effect on public perceptions of the American Indian.[50]

The tensions arising between the official exhibitions of material culture in fairground buildings resembling national museums and what contemporaneous critic T. R. MacMechan described as "cheap and tawdry deception, the 'flim flam' and jingle of fakirdom" of the Midway, thus suggest the larger problems of anthropology's simultaneous quest for scientific legitimation and popular endorsement at world's fairs.[51] It also points up the fundamental differences between representing Native Americans in the form of life groups versus having actual tribal members living on the fairground. Unlike their mute, three-dimensional replicants who were viewed as anthropological specimens by fairgoers, native performers were perceived as "real" (and therefore substandard) people whose very submission to display provoked an even greater negative reaction from fairgoers. Despite being the "real thing," Native Americans were paradoxically not always deemed the most suitable conduits for ethnographic knowledge, since their tendency to provoke racist reactions in fairgoers who viewed them less as living exhibits than as despised former enemies of the U.S. government might very well have nullified the value claimed from the scientific object-lesson. Not surprisingly, native peoples had been subject to (sometimes violent) racist attacks at world's fairs since the 1870s; outbursts of racial hostility were a common occurrence at the Philadelphia Centennial where, according to one contemporary journalist, non-Western peoples were "followed by large crowds of idle boys and men, who hooted and shouted at them as if they had been animals of a strange species instead of visitors who were entitled to only the most courteous attention."[52]

Nevertheless, for some anthropologists and exposition planners, the development of a charitable countenance by "civilized" exhibition-goers was as important a justification for ethnographic exhibits as the object-lesson of native primitivism, a point driven home in anthropologist William J. McGee's contention that part of the "culture development of a civilized people [was] the growth of an altruism and a sense of justice that prescribe[d] the giving of such help."[53] Charity and evolutionary theory were by no means mutually exclusive.[54] Whether physically attacked by fairgoers or viewed as pitiable objects, Native Americans remained subject peoples whose history and current plight could be discursively molded to fit a particular ideological agenda. In the context of the exhibition, they could be appropriated into public discourses on national identity, biological determinism, and social policy and were inescapable targets for the projection of racist fears and fantasies.

Despite the hopes of the Smithsonian's Otis T. Mason that the 1893 Columbian Exposition would be "one vast anthropological revelation" with "representatives of ethnographic races in native garb and activities," the exposition ground was an infinitely more heterogeneous and contentious place than Mason could ever have imagined, a place where spectators could learn about anthropology and non-Western cultures in a multitude of ways: with the didactic "March of Aborigine to Civilization" in the Anthropology Building at one extreme, and the risqué "Street of Cairo," (modeled on the "Rue de Caire" at the 1889 Paris Exposition), at the other.[55] Despite claims for the scientific nature of *both* these modes of address, anthropologists were probably perfectly aware of the dubious pedagogical value of some of them, but could do little to censor the licentious appeal of such attractions as "Fatima — An Oriental Type of Beauty" or "The Harem Belle." While moral guardians of the infant cinema industry insisted that Edison's 1896 filmed version of Fatima's hootchy-cootchy dance be censored (a picket fence-matte masked her abdominal region), spectators on the Midway at the 1893 Chicago World's Fair could experience her eroticized dance in all its titillating glory, satiating a desire for a less mediated encounter with native peoples. In the case of Fatima's "abdominal dance" (more commonly referred to as the belly dance), Midway visitor Edward McDowell suggested that the "authorities should at least so restrict the programme that modest men and women would not be compelled to leave by a rear door ere the performance has scarcely begun," since this dance was, in his opinion, "the naughtiest of them all."[56] If Fatima's dance was uncensored on the Midway, other dances that McDowell found "startling in their audacity and suggestiveness," such as the Persian dance, were toned down for American audiences. As McDowell explained, "Out of regard for the American idea of propriety, they have for the most part omitted those movements which are considered objectionable."[57]

But concern over individual performances that threatened the norms of American propriety were minor compared to the controversies that arose around the Bontoc Igorot village featured at the 1904 St. Louis World's Fair, an exhibit that serves as a fitting reminder of the tensions existing between anthropological accuracy and prurient appeal, and one that exemplified "the fluid symbiosis between the cultural project of anthropology and the freak-making machinery of exhibitionary commerce."[58] Exhibited as one of four representative Filipino "wild tribes" (along with the Moros, Bagabo, and Negritos), the Igorots were by far the main draw on the Philippines Reservation (an average of five thousand people a day visited the Bontoc village), an exhibit of 1,200 Filipinos situated at the center of the fairground (fig.

FIG. 2.8 Igorot peoples around a fire at the St. Louis World's Fair, 1904. Notice the Euro-American fairgoers standing in the background. (Neg. no. 324132. Courtesy Dept. of Library Services AMNH)

2.8).[59] While the idealized simplicity of Bontoc village life may have been one factor contributing to its popularity, Rydell argues that the "immediate impetus to see the Igorot exhibit stemmed less from preindustrial longings than from a powerful mixture of white supremacist sexual stereotypes and voyeurism."[60] Exaggerations of cultural difference were also touted by publicity managers, such as repeated promotional references to the tribe's dog-eating habits, which not only served to differentiate the purportedly "civilized" Philippine soldiers from the "savage" Igorots but sensationalized a relatively rare cultural practice by turning it into a spectacle of savagery. But the dog-eating controversy paled in comparison to the clothing scandal in the Igorot village at the exposition.

Shortly after the Igorot exhibit opened, the Roosevelt administration grew concerned that local press reports about the scant clothing worn by the Igorot

FIG. 2.9 Cartoon mocking the breeches controversy at the Philippine Reservation, from the *St. Louis Post-Dispatch*, June 1904.

would undermine government propaganda efforts aimed at emphasizing the potential for progress on the islands, only recently acquired by the United States in the Spanish-American War. In order that the exhibit's intended tone and message be maintained, President Roosevelt felt that each Igorot should wear a "short trunk" to cover the "buttocks and front" instead of the usual G-string; in a letter written on behalf of President Roosevelt by the office of Secretary of War William Howard Taft, the former governor of the Philippines, it was reported that "the President has heard severe criticism of the Igorrotes [*sic*] and wild tribe exhibit on the ground that it verges toward the indecent. He believes either the Igorrotes and wild tribes should be sent home or that they should be more fully clad. . . . You should put more clothing on the Igorrotes and wild tribes and at the gate put signs showing how small a part of the population the Igorrotes and other wild tribes are."[61] The government eventually ordered the manager of the Igorot village to issue breeches to all the men, a mandate that "provoked much mirth, brought an outcry from anthropologists, and generated a great deal of publicity for the exposition."[62] Indeed, G. S. Johns, editor of the *St. Louis Post-Dispatch*, wrote that forcing the men to wear pants would change "a very interesting ethnological exhibit which shocks the modesty of no one into a suggestive sideshow," while University of Chicago anthropologist Frederick Starr argued that the scientific value of the exhibit would be "completely lost by dressing these people in a way unlike that to which they are accustomed."[63] Six weeks later, appeals for the need to maintain a degree of authenticity in the exhibit prevailed, and the Roosevelt administration backed down from its plan to force the Igorots and Negritos to wear bright-colored silk breeches (fig. 2.9).[64]

Not surprisingly, the controversy over Igorot attire generated a huge amount of free publicity for the exhibit, and the number of fairgoers flocking to see the Igorot in their pants-free state doubled over the course of the scandal. What the dispute revealed, however, was the explicit tension between official and popular constructions of imperial possessions; as Christopher Vaughan notes: "Courting public approval of the imperial venture through commercial ethnographic display, no matter how scientific the rubric, entailed releasing official control to the forces of the marketplace. . . . In seeking to control the image, the government had run smack against the very impulse that drew crowds to walk past two miles of exhibits showing off the latest technological and artistic achievements."[65] This exchange between government representatives, members of the anthropological community, and the popular press provides an example of how discourses of scientific accuracy, moral propriety, and public education were enlisted in battles over the value and meaning of ethnographic exhibits. In this case, the unexpected opposition between licentious appeal and disinterested scientism suggests the semantic instability of calls for authenticity in the context of ethnographic signification; veiling the male Igorot body, scientific partisans argued, made the exhibit more, rather than less, sensational and eroticized.[66]

Anthropologists were in something of a double bind, then, when forced to justify the inclusion of raunchy performers and riské exhibits; if nudity was ethnographically correct, it nevertheless ran the risk of offending Victorian sensibilities and attracting the wrong kind of publicity. French explorer-scientist Xavier Pene, organizer of the DAHOMEYAN VILLAGE at the 1893 World's Columbian Exposition and the AFRICAN VILLAGE at the 1901 Pan-American Exposition in Buffalo, attempted to ward off criticism by emphasizing the authenticity of his exhibit (REAL AFRICAN LIFE IN A REAL AFRICAN VILLAGE).[67] Pene's promotional material also boasted that while the village might be located "in the Midway," it was definitely "not of it," since "the scientific features of the exhibit of Darkest Africa differentiate it altogether from the common Midway show."[68] At the same time, one of the dangers of such insistence upon ethnological verisimilitude was the ever-present risk of violating Western taboos about the display of the human body, a risk that threatened, from the point of view of the 1901 fair's official organizers, to transform the mimetic displays into a lascivious peep show. The centrality of the body as an index of biologically determined racial identity in these installations, and in nineteenth-century anthropology more generally, was underscored by the fair organizers' emphasis on the physicality of native performers; native peoples bespoke their cultural Otherness through their bodies, reified as either "splendid specimens of humanity" or as abject sites of revulsion, as illustrated in McDowell's description of Pene's Chicago Dahomeyans as "blacker than buried midnight and as degraded as the animals which prowl the jungles of their dark land."[69]

Discourses of ethnographic accuracy, realism, and typicality therefore became the lingua franca of exposition promoters and journalists as they sought to redeem exhibits from their sometimes unsavory connotations. F. Hopkinson Smith reminded his *Scribner's* readers that the natives "eat, sleep, and dress precisely as they do at home . . . and allow no difference in their surroundings or atmosphere." Moreover, for Smith, native people existed in a timeless ethnographic present wholly discontinuous with modern life and were thus for the most part totally oblivious to the frantic pace of the bustling Midway ("there is no hurry, rush nor notice, only the indolent life of the East").[70] Smith's description of the Igorot lifestyle betrays a characteristically ambivalent attitude toward indigenous life, in which a condemnation of the purported laziness of native peoples is accompanied by a nostalgia for the less stressful life imagined to exist before modernity and a hint of envy of native people's presumed ability to transcend the modern world around them.[71] In his discussion of Midway concessions, Smith had few problems reconciling ethnographic realism with fairground artifice—what he called "the genuine and the picturesque"—as he carefully described how the buildings were facsimiles of actual locations, including a mosque described as the "prototype of the purest bit of Eastern Architecture in Stamboul."[72]

For Smith, however, the overall effect of verisimilitude was evoked most powerfully as a gendered "native element" defined through a poetics of eroticism and orientalism: "The girl instantly advances, lifts up her face and, gazing into mine with half-closed eyes, gives herself up with slow movement of her feet to that peculiar spell which seems to possess all eastern women when under the influence of the dance." Pulling back from the eroticism of his encounter with the nubile dancer in favor of a more dispassionate subject position, Smith ends his essay by vouching for the authenticity of all the native peoples on the Midway: "Nubians, the Chinese and natives of Ceylon, Dahomeny and the South Sea Island . . . are not a part of the show [but are] the people themselves."[73] The seductive dance that entrances Smith is an example of the collapse of sign and referent in a dreamlike and erotically charged ethnographic encounter; as Kirshenblatt-Gimblett sees it, Western audiences have "historically . . . long valued the inscrutable strangeness of the exotic as an end in itself" and have come to expect that mystification will be an intrinsic part of commercialized (if often scientifically endorsed) native performances.[74]

The fragmented native dance or performance imposed an entirely new use-value upon indigenous culture, turning what was essentially an expression *of* cultural identity that was embedded within a complex and intricate social web of meaning, into a three-minute *routine*, that could be watched, photographed, and quickly forgotten (the idea of colonial life as a performance is suggested in the drama ensuing in the bottom half of the image in this poster for *"Au Congo"* [fig. 2.10] appearing at the Paris Hippodrome in the 1895 Exposition Ethnographique). Paying to enter an exhibit of native people and standing on the periphery while watching everyday life go on inside the enclosure was analogous in many ways to watching ethnographic film; in contrast to actually meeting these people in their own countries, the culture under view was segmented, externalized, short-lived, and commodified to maximize legibility and difference and turn a good profit.

Because of its versatility and mechanical mode of representation, early ethnographic film was perfectly placed to take over such a project from native villages at world's fairs; not only was ethnographic film formally similar to exposition displays in terms of the kinds of looking relations established between spectator and performer, but film could take up its role in visual culture in a cheaper and more flexible manner. As Fatimah Tobing Rony has argued, "Cinema, after all, is a much less expensive way of circulating non-Western bodies 'in situ' than is circulating reconstructed 'villages.' "[75] Unlike ethnographic villages, which were tied to the spatial and temporal contin-

FIG. 2.10 Poster for "*Au Congo*," Paris Hippodrome, 1895.

gencies of the fairground (although many exhibits went on tour at the end of
an exposition), ethnographic films could offer audiences infinitely repeatable
performances or "views" that could be staged virtually anywhere there was a
projector, screen, and paying audience.

From the World's Fair to the Motion Picture Screen:
Viewing Ethnographic Villages Through a Cinematic Lens

In some respects, the display of indigenous peoples in reconstructed native villages in nineteenth- and early twentieth-century world's fairs seems diametrically opposed to their representation in early ethnographic film; whereas in the former the indigene is physically inserted into the world of the Westerner in a three-dimensional performative space, in the latter the spectator is virtually transported to the world of the distant Other. Furthermore, the amount of time spent viewing a living ethnographic exhibit would also have probably exceeded that spent watching an early ethnographic film. More significant than the divergent viewing durations, however, was the three-dimensional scale and multisensory appeal of the ethnographic exhibit, which could never be replicated on the flat, mute, and (more often than not) monochromatic movie screen. Moreover, for the fairground spectator who wished to cross boundaries between viewing subject and object, the Midway often provided opportunities for direct spectator contact with native peoples appearing in the exhibits (an experience that also relates to the reciprocal fascination of the indigenous peoples with Westerners), unlike the cinema audience's always-mediated and temporally dissociated experience of the Other. While taking a stroll along the Midway or drinking coffee at a brasserie, a fairgoer might mingle with native performers and purchase handicrafts, bric-a-brac, jewelry, spices, teas, or engage one another in other ways (Geronimo, we are told, sold his autograph for ten cents at the Omaha, Buffalo, and St. Louis world's fairs).[76] Cinema's flat, noninteractive screen couldn't begin to compete with the excitement (or threat) of an actual encounter with an exotic person of color.

The pleasure of looking was therefore experienced differently in each representational form; in the live exhibit, spectators could attempt to attract the individual attention of performers and take satisfaction in their status as privileged onlookers situated on the "right" side of the fence or roped-off enclosure. Pleasure may also have been derived from selecting precisely what to look at in an exhibit, for how long, and from discussing what one saw with an accompanying family member, friend, or bystander (fig. 2.11). While similar

FIG. 2.11 Cairo Camel Drivers, St. Louis World's Fair, 1904. (Neg. no. 338084. Courtesy Dept. of Library Services, AMNH)

discussions may have taken place during (or following) a film screening (and, also, film viewers *are* afforded some measure of freedom in selecting what to look at within the frame for the duration of the shot), cinema spectators nevertheless viewed images of native peoples from the (relative) comfort and safety of their seat, without ever having to worry about their physical proximity to the peoples displayed, direct solicitation by performers, and the risk that they themselves might become the subject of ridicule or scorn via the return gaze. For looking back was a common occurrence across the real and imaginary spaces of performance and film, with native peoples undoubtedly engaging in all kinds of resistive behavior, from an ironic, knowing, half-smile at spectators to overt acknowledgments of their status as performers. As Rony argues, "Performance at the fair was not a simply visual objectification by a flattening male gaze. Performance also invites a composing of self for spectacle, a frank gaze returned, a mocking laugh, or [even] a haughtiness."[77] Although Rony is correct in suggesting the potential for subversion in living villages (although there is little documented evidence of these exchanges), she may overstate the extent to which cinema "eliminated the potentially threatening return look of the performer present in the exposition," thus creating what she calls a more "perfect scientific voyeurism."[78] While not the equivalent of the return gaze in the live encounter between performer and audience-member, the subject's direct look at the camera in early ethnographic film can also pose a threat to the ocular certainty of scientific voyeurism, undermining, in some instances, the very ideological base upon which the cross-cultural filmic encounter is premised.

If ethnographic film offered spectators an experience of subject peoples that was quite distinct from precinematic cultural forms, it also inherited a great many of the ways of seeing associated with the world's fair exhibit. For example, both cinema and the ethnographic village incorporated tensions between ethnography as performance/spectacle and ethnography as scientific data, between popular theories of race and scientific understandings of cultural difference, and between anthropologically endorsed "authentic" representations of native culture and more commercialized versions. On a most general level, then, what unites the experience of the museumgoer, fairground visitor, and early cinema spectator is a recurring ambivalence between the spectator's desire for immersion on the one hand and for separation and distance from the threat of alterity on the other. This tension marked a diverse range of new heterotopic spaces created in the modern metropolis, spaces identified by many as emblematic of the experience of modernity itself. Spectators may thus have reconciled their desire for proximity and immersion at world's fairs with a need for separation and distance through assuming the mental disposition of the *flâneur*; like the department stores, urban arcades, and grand boulevards of the new industrialized city, the Midway was a natural habitat for the *flâneur*.[79] As Curtis Hinsley explains: "The eyes of the Midway were those of the *flâneur*, the stroller through the street arcade of human differences, whose experience is not the holistic, integrated ideal of the anthropologist but the segmented, seriatim fleetingness of the modern tourist 'just passing through.' "[80] A "kaleidoscope gifted with consciousness," a "human kodak" who cared only "for as many pleasing impressions as possible," the Midway *flâneuse* would have delighted in the riot of sounds and smells surrounding her, taking as much pleasure in observing her fellow visitors as the native performers. As one commentator noted: "the pleasantest moments are those spent in resting one's rebellious limbs upon a bench and watching the crowd. It may be less novel and instructive than some other exhibits, but it is more amusing."[81]

But the detachment associated with the *flâneur* may not precisely describe the fascination of fairgoers for ethnographic villages or their experiences of them; as Tom Gunning has argued, "[whereas] the *flâneur* flaunted a characteristic detachment which depended on the leisurely pace of the stroll and the stroller's possession of a fund of knowledge about the city and its inhabitants . . . the 'gawker' [*badaud*] . . . merges with the crowd rather than observing it from outside . . . possess[ing] no special knowledge which lifts him above those he observes."[82] Walter Benjamin's less well-known figure of the *badaud* may thus be a more accurate way of characterizing this desire to disappear into a crowd and simply stare at native peoples.[83] The figure of the *badaud* may also more closely approximate the kind of anonymity afforded spectators of early ethnographic films, who upon buying their ticket and entering the nickelodeon observed ethnographic difference from the darkness and detachment of the liminally charged auditorium. The unreflective *badaud* who identifies with the crowd in a heady rush brought on by the accelerated pace of modernity masters the art of "just looking" that was an essential component of urban streets, world's fairs, and cinema spectatorship. Indeed, the fairgoer was as much a part of the overall spectacle as the elaborately designed installations, as suggested in the following advice in "The Short Sermon for Sightseers" in the fair's *Art Handbook* for visitors at the Pan-American Exposition: "Please remember when you get inside the gates [that] you are part of the show."[84]

Despite the physical separation of native peoples and curious Euro-American onlookers in the fairground exhibits themselves, the existence of potentially transgressive spaces such as the Midway meant that boundaries between Self and Other were always subject to renegotiation,[85] as suggested in the following description of fairgoers at the 1901 Pan-American Exposition: "They plunge into the riot of nonsense with unthinking glee. They slip shrieking down the fearful dips of the Scenic Railway in company with Navajo Indians with yellow sun-rays round their eyes, and dark, sombreroed Mexicans, and low-browed, straight-haired Eskimos."[86] In entering the space of the fairground visitor, these native pleasure-seekers enjoyed a temporary respite from their public roles as "displayable" commodities; more so than the Euro-American visitors, native peoples may have sought out sanctuaries where they could forget, at least briefly, their obligations as living displays. It was perhaps this possibility to flirt with identity boundaries that Euro-American fairgoers missed most when the expositions finally closed; their visual appetites whetted from their encounters with native peoples at world's fairs, spectators may have looked to the cinema as a way of delivering similar kinds of experiences.

The spectator's status as an unofficial exhibit on the fairground, along with accounts of interaction between white visitors and people of color, underscore the heterotopic nature of Midway attractions and the world's fair generally. Michel Foucault describes such spaces as those which permit the juxtaposition within a single real place of "several spaces, several sites that are in themselves incompatible." These heterotopias, Foucault argues, are linked less to the accumulation of time (unlike museums, which "enclose in one place all times, all epochs, all forms, all tastes, the idea of constituting a place of all times that is itself outside time and inaccessible to its ravages"), than to time in its most "fleeting, transitory, precarious aspect," similar to the phantasmatic time spent on a ghost-train or fun-fair ride.[87] Indeed, one could argue that ethnographic installations at world's fairs are early versions of contemporary vacation resorts, where a tourist spends three weeks living in a simulated native environment such as a Polynesian village; in both these experiences, time is suspended, yet ironically, the experience is as much about the "rediscovery of time," a reaching back in time to access "immediate knowledge" about a culture or an indigenous people, as it is about experiencing a petrified past void of all contemporary cultural markers.[88]

In its textual practices, critical discourses, and exhibition contexts, early cinema, like the other new sites of urban spectacle, choreographed the complex juxtapositions of the urban metropole and the exoticized Other. Both ethnographic cinema and ethnographic villages constructed their spectators as virtual travelers who could be psychically transported into the world of the ethnographic Other without having to undergo actual travel; for example, visitors could experience the wholly simulated "technological voyages" such as "New York to the North Pole in Twenty Minutes," which appeared on the Pike at the St. Louis World's Fair in 1904. At the Paris Universal Exposition of 1900, fairgoers were transported around the fairground on moving sidewalks.[89] Drawing upon the techniques of precinematic dioramas and moving panoramas,[90] these voyage attractions "stressed magical transformations of landscape with their relatively short travel time as well as providing simulacra of new technological modes of travel (including ones not yet invented, introducing a utopian aspect to their travel illusions)."[91] Like film spectators, fairground riders remained immobile before an illusion of movement largely evoked by visual stimuli, although in Hale's Tours, which simulated a railway journey through the use of landscape films, the illusion was strengthened by synchronized sound effects and the mechanical rocking of the railway car theater.[92]

As precursors to such simulated travel attractions at the St. Louis World's Fair, panoramas and dioramas depicting distant and exotic lands had long been popular at nineteenth-century expositions.[93] "The Overland Route to India" at the Crystal Palace in London in 1851 was seen by 200,000 people; it was situated adjacent to "A Trip Up the Nile," "Jerusalem and the Holy Land," and the "Great Educational and Pictorial Exhibition, Geographical, Historical, and Statistical, of a Grand Tour through Europe."[94] According to historian Emmanuelle Toulet, panoramas and dioramas exhibited at the 1900 Universal Exposition in Paris featured such exotic locales as the Congo, Madagascar, the Sahara, and Fachoda, all used to rally public support for the colonial policy of the Third Republic.[95] The panorama at the Universal Exposition which most closely prefigured Hale's Tours was the Trans-Siberian; here, spectators seated on train seats watched a painted canvas unroll representing a journey from Moscow to Beijing. Machinery simulating the rolling of the train wheels and personnel dressed in Tartar and Chinese costumes enhanced the reality effect. The Mareorama, which was also a feature at the Universal Exposition, offered visitors a "Mediterranean voyage from Marseilles to Constantinople by way of Algeria, Sfax, Naples, and Venice."[96] Using actors, dancers, and musicians, the Mareorama was the most technically complex and spectacular of these animated panoramas. However, the exhibit that best evoked the viewing conditions of countless ethnographic villages on subsequent fairground midways was the "Tour du Monde," an installation integrating live indigenous performers engaged in traditional occupations before an immense oval canvas representing "Spain, Greece, Constantinople, Egypt, Ceylon, Cambodia, China and Japan."[97]

In addition to self-contained touristic rides within individual exhibitions, several fairs offered spectators the opportunity to travel between various national installations on the fairground by means of specially designed miniature fairground railways, providing visitors with tours of a vast range of global cultures in a brief journey (as well as providing a way of moving weary tourists from one part of the exhibition site to another). In this way, spectators could collapse global space into that of the fairground.[98] The ease with which exhibition-goers could travel within and between exotic locales was part of a wider culture of consumption that permeated world's fairs. However, as Annie Coombes points out, the eradication of spatial and temporal markers did not necessarily entail a similar eradication of racially inscribed Otherness. In other words, Euro-American fairgoers were repeatedly reassured of their cultural superiority through an array of discursive techniques, including the labels accompanying ethnographic installations and the racist captions on postcards and souvenir collections for sale in the exhibition halls and concession stands.

The fairground's promise to spectators of a magical access to and visual command over the world's most exotic locales and peoples was echoed in other late nineteenth-century cultural sites and technologies. If, as Coombes argues, the natural history museum offered its visitor the chance to become a global explorer who could, "through a vicarious intrepidation," gain the "experience of the seasoned traveler," the world's fair and the cinema offered their visitors a similar privilege.[99] By prescribing recommended spectator itineraries, natural history museum and world's fair guidebooks appropriated the narrative conceits of adventure fiction, the most enduring being that of the visitor suddenly discovering "himself" (and it was always a male traveler) "in the heart of" an exotic or inhospitable clime.[100]

But the natural history museum exhibit and world's fair Midway could not compete with early ethnographic cinema's limitless capacity for space and time travel. Moreover, by re-presenting a fragment of native culture ad infinitum, cinema was also able to perfect the Midway's theatrical model of regularly scheduled repeat performances for new audiences. For example, in the "Street of Cairo" exhibit at the Columbian Exposition, a bridal procession was led through the streets "every afternoon" while "several dervishes perform[ed] their rites." The caption beneath the photograph of the wedding camel in

Midway Types, a book of "illustrated lessons" from the Chicago Midway, informs the reader that while the novelty of the ceremony had worn off on its participants, "to the public the display was like a scene from a play" performed over and over again in the form of a theatrical pageant.[101]

Efforts to impose a closely regulated temporal structure upon native performances in ethnological villages are also suggested in a description of daily life in the Columbian Exposition's "Ethnographic American Indians" exhibit: "Here may be found the native Indians with canoes, fishing and hunting tackle, costumes and all the appurtenances of Indian life. They cook, make trinkets, hold their counsel and go through the ordinary routine with which their tribes have been familiar from time immemorial."[102] Quotidian life was thus transformed into a routinized performance that had to be perfectly duplicated for constantly new groups of fairground visitors. While the economic logic of performative culture on the Midway might be threatened by the weariness, resistance, and other contingencies of its live performers, cinema promised an exact and endless repeatability of the display of cultural difference, although the meanings attached to their record of indigenous life were still subject to the variations of the viewing situation.

At the same time, it is important to note that many of the native peoples encamped in ethnographic villages were no strangers to the world of performance; one of the children appearing in the St. Louis ESQUIMAUX VILLAGE had been born at the Columbian Exposition and her family had appeared at two previous world's fairs. The notion of the pristine ethnographic subject who had been brought from the "wild" to appear uncontaminated before the world hardly corresponded to the experiences of *all* native performers at world's fairs, although some people were brought from their homelands specifically to appear in an exhibit. Hyperbolic claims about authenticity were more often than not the work of advertising copywriters. Moreover, the tension between imitation and authenticity, which, as Miles Orvell argues, was a key constituent of American culture in the late nineteenth and early twentieth centuries, played an integral role in the design and execution of ethnographic villages.[103] The Inuit people who appeared at St. Louis are thus examples of what Orvell calls "iconic oxymorons," in that they embodied a central contradiction between their status as representative members of indigenous tribes and their full assimilation into Western capitalism.[104]

Not surprisingly, salvage ethnography—the mission to preserve native cultures believed threatened with extinction—became the rhetorical frame through which spectators were invited to regard the native inhabitants as relics of a forgotten age. This was especially true in the case of Native Americans. As Putnam lamented: "These people, as great nations, have about vanished into history, and now is the last opportunity for the world to see them and to realize what their condition, their life, their customs, their arts were four centuries ago. The great object lesson then will not be completed without their being present. Without them, the Exposition will have no base."[105] The daily "rehearsal" of cultural practices, some no longer practiced by Native Americans, assumed a synecdochal relationship to American Indian culture as a whole and served as an object lesson in Western ascendancy. At the same time, however, exhibits featuring Native American children from white-controlled boarding schools and Indians dressed in Western clothes were enlisted to justify the U.S. government's policy to "civilize" Indians and encourage the adoption of Western value systems. Instead of being diametrically opposed, salvage ethnography *and* a desire to see Indians abandon their cultural heritage in favor of full assimilation were both part of a dialectic that revealed a great deal about American ambivalence toward the colonial Indian subject.

The parallel regimes of spectatorship of ethnographic film and world's fairs were rehearsed in a culture of material excess, imperial expansion, and rampant commercialism, where, as Rydell points out, "woven into the dream world of goods was a hierarchical continuum of material and racial progress that signified nothing so much as the distance traveled from 'savagery' to 'civilization.' "[106] While there are obvious ontological differences between ethnographic films, photographs, postcards, and curios, each offered audiences a visual experience that was born of a new commodity culture in which a glimpse at exotic Others could be bought in similar ways to soap and washing detergent and where visitors were invited to make the museum gift shop and the fairground concession stand part of their overall itinerary. Indeed, late nineteenth-century advertisers borrowed the ethnographic iconography of the Other in devising advertising campaigns and commodity packaging. Legendary Indian characters, for example, were transformed into consumer icons that could be emblazoned on the labels of soaps, hair preparations, perfume, and coffee; severed from history, these images invited Euro-Americans to enter into a collective fantasy about Native American identity which flattered white consumers at the same time as it buttressed racial mythmaking and cultural imperialism. As a result, Jeffrey Steele argues, "Forcibly removed from any contexts that would threaten the imaginative security of consumers, American Indians . . . were . . . turned into fetishized images that satisfied the hunger for entertainment and disposable commodities."[107]

Along with a multitude of other cultural goods that exploited images of alterity for commercial gain, ethnographic villages promulgated a fascination for visualizing native cultures that was taken up by moving picture entrepreneurs. Launching a veritable craze for film's representing peoples of color following the success of the World's Columbian Exposition in 1893, world's fairs appearing in the first decade and a half of the twentieth-century provided a mutually reinforcing environment for the growth of commercially produced ethnographic films and native exhibits. But early cinema also provided filmic analogs of many of the subjects that had proven popular at world's fairs (including depictions of Native Americans, Inuit people, and Asians), sometimes creating historical documents of the villages and their performers.[108] Edison's early filmmaking company shot three films of the Inuit exhibit at the ESQUIMAUX VILLAGE at the 1901 Pan-American exhibition: *Esquimaux Village*, *Esquimaux Game of Snap-the-Whip*, and *Esquimaux Leap Frog*.[109] In the first film, a man on a sled pulled by two huskies and another man on foot race frantically back and forth between a model igloo in the background and a pond in the foreground. The frenetic movements of the performers in long shot and lack of textual information about the purpose of the action lend it a comic quality; interpretive clues can only be mined from the Arctic iconography (snowscape, pond, igloo, and huskies) and Inuit clothing and artifacts. As a result of the obvious fake background and brevity of the film, Inuit life is reduced to a pathetic mime, a charade performed for the camera and for the daily visitors who stood before the ESQUIMAUX VILLAGE. Fixing the very brief fragments of native performance in the photochemical film process, these early films of native exhibits replicate the commercial Midway's logic of the reiterated and stereotyped performance of cultural otherness, but in so doing, they fail to deliver on what must have been the most compelling aspect of the exhibit, its liveness and immediacy.[110] Rather than make a case for a direct chain of influence between native villages and ethnographic cinema, these early films of "staged authenticity" at world's fairs point up cinema's inadequacies when faced with the challenge of reconstructing an already reconstructed perform- ance (in addition, a static camera with no panning device located at the perimeter of the exhibit was bound to have produced a somewhat impover- ished view of the performers' actions).

A contrasting example made eight years later, however, is Pathé's *The Toua- regs in Their Country* (1908).[111] Despite the title, which implies that the Touaregs will be seen on location in Africa, we soon realize that they are not in fact in Africa at all, but have been transplanted to a European location either as part of a world's fair "living village" or as an attraction in their own right. The "unwitting evidence"[112] of the deciduous trees, perimeter wooden fence, and European rooftops gives away the ruse, and, if we are left in any doubt as to whether we are in Europe, the "courier attack" reenactment (a dramatic icon first popularized in the ARAB COURIER ATTACKED BY LIONS life group) which begins halfway through the film confirms our suspicions that the Touaregs are performing set-pieces in a reconstructed village

The Touaregs in Their Country functions as a *mise-en-abyme* of sorts, since the Touaregs, already encamped as a traveling troupe in a European city, are invit- ed to reenact scenes from their daily lives, including a dramatic courier ambush (fig. 2.12).[113] From the outset, the performers seem to struggle to take their roles as ethnographic subjects seriously; in the opening shot, for exam- ple — a medium shot of three relaxed-looking Touaregian women standing in front of a tent (fig. 2.13) — the woman in the center soon begins to break down and laugh (accompanied by the woman on her right), while in the second shot (also a medium shot), two young boys in the center of the frame surrounded by their eight siblings and parents jockey for a better position in front of the camera before order is restored. The relaxed demeanor of the Touaregs points to a certain familiarity with Western recording technologies, and their laugh- ter and jostling for position indicates more than a little awareness of what it means to be filmed. The camera's proximity to the subjects in these scenes also suggests a relatively informal relationship between filmmaker and those filmed, since the intimate medium shots of the "domestic scenes" showing women and children are rare for a period when most ethnographic subjects were filmed in medium long shot (fig. 2.14). Likewise, the considerable range

FIG. 2.12 Frame enlargement of courier attack from *The Touaregs in Their Country* (Pathé, 1908).

FIG. 2.13 Frame enlargement of three women from *The Touaregs in Their Country* (Pathé, 1908).

FIG. 2.14 Frame enlargement of mother and child from *The Touaregs in Their Country* (Pathé, 1908).

of camera setups suggests that the operator was afforded a great deal of freedom. These contrasting examples of films featuring performers from ethnographic villages drive home a number of points about early ethnographic film: that the installations themselves could serve as filmic subjects (but with varying degrees of success) and that their modes of address could be thinly disguised but never entirely removed from texts which may contrive to be representations shot on location but were as constructed as the native villages that inspired them.

Like museum life groups, native villages at world's fairs provoked professional and popular debates over ethnographic representation and the public mission of anthropology in ways that helped shape anthropologists' attitudes toward early cinema. Anthropologists saw two challenges in organizing exhibits at world's fairs: how to dignify their fledgling discipline amidst the garish commercialized displays of consumer culture of the Midway and how to negotiate the considerable logistical difficulties of recruiting and overseeing several hundred native peoples who set up temporary homes on the exhibition grounds. If, as Gunning has argued, the world's fair trained spectators for participation in a new commodity-based visual culture by raising the act of spectating to a "civic duty and technological art" — every Midway exhibit listed in the *Official Guide to the World's Columbian Exposition* sold merchandise of some sort or charged a fee for performances — then anthropology's efforts to circumscribe its intellectual concerns within a strictly scientific framework may have been undermined by the sensational appeal of the Midway.[114] Popular understanding of ethnography at the 1893 Chicago Exposition was thus negotiated within the spectacularized consumer culture of the Midway, becoming another commodity that fairgoers could buy.[115] Giving "visible form and legitimacy to an emerging culture of abundance," world's fairs were part of a proliferation of popular representations of native peoples, what Martin Heidegger characterized as the "age of the world picture," brought about as a result of modernity and a totalizing reconceptualization of the world as a series of capturable sights.[116]

The primacy of the visual as a conduit of scientific knowledge, the emphasis on spectator mobility, both real and virtual, and the values of didactic consumerism linked the nineteenth-century experiences of the department store shopper, the natural history museumgoer, the Midway gawker, and the early film spectator. While these sites coexisted and were part of a complex web of popular representations, what unites them is an emergent visual culture that created the conditions of possibility for ethnographic representation in popularized form. As Gunning explains:

> Decades before the cinema, urban experience and an emerging commodity culture had already carved out a visual receptivity into which the film experience crept like a hermit crab. As part of the modern emphasis on the act of consumption, this world of visual stimulus was designed to convert passersby into gawkers, and gawkers into purchasers, as the link between visual pleasure and a commodity culture was forged.[117]

But if the museum life group and the Midway attraction were both involved in rendering the world as a didactic spectacle, an object to be viewed and consumed, the lessons obtained from the museum life group revealed that "integrated ideals" were often compromised in the service of entertainment, which meant that exhibits in the Anthropology Building at the Columbian Exposition were probably viewed with the same mix of curiosity and prurient appeal as the sideshows and concessions on the Midway.

Not surprisingly, like their colleagues in museums of natural history, anthropologists had to steer a difficult path between official and commercial culture at world's fairs; conscious of their public reputation and role as harbingers of modern, "scientific" theories of race and culture, anthropologists worked to design exhibits that would bespeak their pedagogical responsibilities in clear and unambiguous ways. However, if the challenges anthropologists faced in contending with the "commercial contamination" of ethnography in the entertainment zones of world fairs proved substantial, they could at least resume their professional positions as museum curators or professors after the fair was over. But anthropologists would not escape the pervasive tensions between the scientific and popular missions of their discipline; debates over the appropriateness of popular versus scientific modes of ethnographic representation and the challenges of integrating cinema into museums' educational programs found another battleground in the museum of natural history. Before considering how cinema was taken up by anthropologists and used within the museum of natural history, we must first examine nineteenth-century anthropological photography, the final piece in our precinematic puzzle and one that played a crucial role in shaping anthropologists' attitudes toward cinema as a mechanical recording technology. Indeed, some of the most evocative evidence left behind by the world's fairs and expositions consists of photographs which bridged the divide between scientific articulations of racial theories and popular fascination with the ethnographic Other.[118] As objects which could be bought, sold, traded, hoarded, and lost, they provoked a form of gawking that was similar to and yet distinct from that associated with life groups and native villages.

3

Knowledge and Visuality
in Nineteenth-Century Anthropology

The science of anthropology owes not a little to the art of photography.
—EDWARD B. TYLOR (1876)[1]

AS PART OF a modern fascination with images of the Other at the end of the nineteenth century, photographs of native peoples circulated freely in both public and private spheres, offering many Americans their first glimpse of exotic peoples; taking the form of book illustrations, slides, postcards, *cartes-de-visites*, stereographs, cabinet cards, newspaper and magazine illustrations, ethnographic photographs were mass-produced by a range of different manufacturers and easily found their way into the homes and hands of a wide range of Americans. While photographs performed a similar discursive function as life groups and native villages, and were even integrated into some of these displays, they did not communicate to a mass audience in quite the same way; photographs—while public in the sense of their ubiquity at world's fairs, state fairs, circuses, tourist destinations, dime museums, and the print media—were better suited to more private and discrete viewings than life groups and native villages. As tangible objects of varying shapes and sizes, photographs were not constrained by the same contingencies of time and space as life groups and villages. But despite the obvious ontological differences across these representational forms, they nevertheless provoked similar debates about the legibility of anthropological knowledge when represented in visual form. For this reason, taking a closer look at ethnographic photography can also tell us a great

86

deal about how anthropologists responded to mechanical imaging techniques and possibly explain why film was never taken up by the discipline with the same enthusiasm as photography.

But before reaching any hard and fast conclusions about anthropologists' perceptions of cinema, we should examine the rhetorical construction of the medium as a scientific recording device within anthropological journals and private memoirs from the late nineteenth century and consider anthropology's relationship to a very modern form of looking associated with the *badaud* or gawker. Examining anthropology's relationship to photography can also give us a better sense of how the discipline came to define itself *in relation to* visuality and how that discourse was marshaled in the service of loftier scientific goals and ethnographic accuracy. In order to appreciate the challenges motion picture technology presented to the nascent discipline of anthropology, we should first consider the effect photography had upon what Jonathan Crary calls the "intelligibility of visuality."[2] In other words, what impact would mechanically produced images have upon anthropology's intellectual mission at the end of the last century, and was visuality perceived in broadly utopian terms or in a more prosaic, functionalist manner? In particular, we should consider the relationship of corporeal evidence collected by mechanical means with traditional modes of ethnographic inscription, such as engravings, sketches, diagrams, and written accounts. Would, for example, mechanically obtained evidence produce a very different kind of anthropological object to more traditional forms of data collection? Would photography supply anthropology with an apodictic tool or did the science require the accreditation of more established methods of inscription? What particular "truth effects" were associated with each method of representing ethnographic knowledge? If, as Christopher Pinney has argued, photography's "quantifying and reality appropriating capacities perfectly suited the realist and quantitative aspirations of anthropology," why did cinema fail to win similar support among anthropologists?[3] Were equipment costs and technological inexperience the only factors in anthropologists' reluctance to use cinema or were there other factors that should be taken into consideration?

Before the invention of cinema, photography *was*, at least for a while, the darling child of the fledgling discipline, hailed in both British and American anthropological circles as the sine qua non of advanced scientific practice.

However, its status within the discipline could never be taken for granted, and despite the eulogistic praise heaped upon photography from such notables as Edward B. Tylor, debate ensued about what kinds of photography were better suited for anthropological investigation as well as the attendant risks of photography's too close an association with popular culture. So while enduring for almost half a century, anthropology's love affair with photography was destined to end; by the time motion pictures were fully institutionalized in the mid-teens, photography was no longer viewed with the same epistemological reverence as it had been in the latter half of the nineteenth century. At a time when anthropology was striving to establish its scientific credentials, photography shifted from being an indispensable research tool to an ancillary device.

Before looking in depth at the governing principles of three distinct photographic practices (anthropometric photography; relatively candid photographs of indigenous peoples taken by anthropologists in the field (with varying degrees of staging); and commercially produced portraits of native peoples sold as *cartes-de-visites*, cabinet cards, and picture postcards), a more general discussion of the kinds of truth claims made on behalf of photography is called for. At the end of the third leg of our journey into the precinematic origins of ethnographic film, we might also consider the distinct modes of spectating engendered by ethnographic photography and film, distinctions that seem to blur in the case of the long-take, single-shot ethnographic film which suppresses movement in favor of a lingering, some would say erotically charged, look at cultural difference.

The Still Camera as a "Truth Machine"

Of all the human senses, sight assumed a position of unquestionable dominance in nineteenth-century anthropology; it was tales of what intrepid travelers, colonial officials, and missionaries had *seen* on their trips to the far corners of the earth in the form of drawings, sketches, engravings, watercolors, paintings, and cultural artifacts that thrilled the general public and scientific societies alike and that provided the much sought-after evidence of racial inferiority and so-called barbaric practices. After the invention of photography, however, such nonmechanical forms of visual evidence were judged by some to have been limited by the eyes *and* imaginations of their producers, mere *interpretations* of what had been seen rather than empirical proof. According to such critics, a sketch or watercolor of an ethnographic scene, no matter how carefully rendered, lacked the immediacy and objectivity of an anthropological photograph. As the curator of the British Museum, William Henry Flower, argued in 1882:[4] "Photographs . . . with their histories carefully registered, of any of the so-called aborigine races, now rapidly undergoing extermination or degeneration, will be hereafter of inestimable value. Drawings, descriptions and measurements are also useful, though in a far less degree."[5]

While painterly renderings of indigenous life might continue to be "useful," they could not compete with the "inestimable value" of the photograph. Needless to say, to contemporary observers ethnographic photographs produced during this period are no less tainted by the romantic imaginings of nineteenth-century scientists as their artistically rendered counterparts. Beyond our current awareness of the inherent manipulation of the photographic image, historians have pointed out that a great many of these photographs were subjected to extensive retouching and other techniques that altered the relationship of the sign to its referent.

In contrast to the later case of cinema, the medium of photography appeared to achieve rapid and widespread professional legitimation and application within anthropology soon after its invention;[6] in the late 1840s, French physician and naturalist E. R. A. Serres added daguerreotypes representing the "physical characters of diverse racial types" to his collection of anatomical specimens and other materials.[7] Similarly, Harvard naturalist Louis Agassiz commissioned photographer J. T. Zealy in 1850 to produce fifteen daguerreotypes of African-born slaves living in South Carolina as part of Agassiz's anthropometric studies in support of the extremely racist polygenetic model of human development, a theory positing the separate genetic roots of white and black races.[8]

A case for the usefulness of photography within American anthropology was made as early as 1859, when Joseph Henry, secretary of the Smithsonian, argued that because "the Indians [were] passing away so rapidly," the young medium should be enlisted as part of a mammoth project to record indigenous cultures threatened with extinction. Henry argued that unlike engravings, sketches, and other subjective artifacts, photography could guarantee "a far more authentic and trustworthy collection of likenesses of the principal tribes

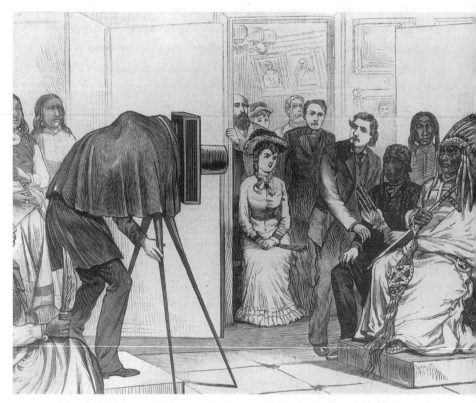

FIG. 3.1 Ponca and Sioux delegates being photographed by Charles M. Bell. From *Frank Leslie's Illustrated Weekly*, September 10, 1881. (Courtesy National Anthropological Archives, hereafter NAA)

of the U.S."[9] But as this engraving of Charles M. Bell photographing Ponca and Sioux delegates illustrates, the studio portraitist was in great demand among whites and native peoples, as can be seen from the mixed clientele and framed portraits on the wall of his Washington, D.C., studio (fig. 3.1). Within British anthropology, the privileged status of photographic evidence over evidence in the form of writings or drawings was argued in the British journal *Nature* in 1876, when Tylor suggested that most engravings of "race-types" found in books were "worthless," since they either failed to capture the special characteristics of race or caricatured them. "Now-a-days," Tylor charged, "little ethnological value is attached to any but photographic portraits."[10]

In Britain, professional and amateur anthropologists had at their disposal published handbooks containing detailed instructions for gathering ethnographic data (including the taking of photographs) in remote imperial outposts. Published jointly by the British Association for the Advancement of Science and the Royal Anthropological Institute in 1874, *Notes and Queries on Anthropology* was viewed as one of the most comprehensive of these fieldwork handbooks, with four editions published between 1874 and 1920. Designed to be used by "travelers and residents in uncivilized lands" who it was thought could produce "factual, 'unbiased' "[11] field material under the tutelage of the handbook, and as a theoretical and methodological bridge between "stay-at-home" anthropologists and field observers, *Notes and Queries* contained practical advice about how and in what order to collect data.[12] The manual aimed "to promote accurate anthropological observations on the part of travelers, and to enable those who are not anthropologists themselves to supply the information which is wanted for the scientific study of anthropology at home."[13] Aimed mostly at British travelers, scientists, and officials who may come into contact with native peoples for extended periods of time, *Notes and Queries* had very little practical application for American anthropological research, where anthropologists undertook most of their ethnological investigations themselves; indeed, *Notes and Queries* was criticized by American anthropologists at the time for its antiquarianism and evolutionary precepts.[14] But in an era when British anthropologists still got most of their research secondhand from colonial administrators, missionaries, and travelers, the handbook was viewed as a useful regulatory device that would help individuals structure their research.

One of the ways these amateur ethnographers attempted to bolster the accuracy and impartiality of what they had "observed" was by taking photographs. C. Read, author of the preface of the ethnographic section of the 1892 and 1899 editions of *Notes and Queries*, set out to explain the role of photography within field investigations; seeing the camera as an indispensable research tool, Read argued that researchers should devote as much time as possible to taking photographs, "for by these means the traveler is dealing with facts about which there can be no question, and the record thus obtained may be elucidated by subsequent inquirers on the same spot."[15] *Notes and Queries* was personally endorsed by Alfred Cort Haddon, who wrote the photography section of the 1899 edition. Haddon had been interested in photography's utility as an ethnographic recording device for some time; in an 1895 lecture to the British Folklore Society, Haddon argued that photography could render the study of folklore accessible to a lay audience since "most of the aspects of folklore were easily illustrated [by photographs], and thus the facts could be made to appeal to the eye as well as to the ear."[16]

Haddon also proposed establishing an archive of folklore photography to be managed by the British Folklore Society (amateur photographers would be invited to send their photographs of autochthonous objects and customs to the archive). By these means, Haddon argued, "not only would facts be recorded, but new workers would be pressed into the service of our science."[17] In the *Notes and Queries* entry on photography, Haddon discussed techniques and the equipment the traveler should take on an expedition. Haddon recommended that a number of portrait "types" should be procured ("full face and square side view") as well as "unarranged groups," which should be taken "instantaneously so as to get perfectly natural attitudes, for it must never be forgotten that when a native is posed for photography he unconsciously becomes set and rigid, and the delicate 'play' of the limbs is lost."[18] Haddon promoted the use of photography in the collection and dissemination of ethnographic knowledge as a bridge between professional and amateur anthropologists. Like many of his colleagues, Haddon did not question photography's truth-telling capacity.

However, Haddon's confident assurances about photography's veracity cannot, I argue, be read entirely at face value. What these endorsements seem to suggest is a desire on the part of anthropologists to validate their discipline in a time of great scientific upheaval; with medical breakthroughs occurring almost every day and daring new theories explaining the origins of mankind entering the fray, what anthropology needed most was a research tool that would silence skeptics who doubted the subject's legitimacy within the sciences. Convinced, therefore, that the photochemical processes binding image to collodium base would imbue photography with a veneer of objectivity, anthropologists took every opportunity to underscore photography's utility. This desire to bolster anthropology's reputation *through* photography's discursive stratagems makes perfect sense, then, given the subject's short life span and lack of rigorous training programs in universities; what photography could offer anthropology most was reassurance about visuality as an appropriate conveyor of scientific fact. But exactly what kinds of photographs were best suited for the transmission of ethnographic knowledge was by no means a settled affair.

The Veridical Properties of the Camera: Anthropometric Photography

Photography's ability to produce objective and verifiable data was frequently asserted by anthropologists throughout the second half of the nineteenth century, especially within the practice of physical anthropology, concerned as it was with the systematic study and classification of physical man.[19] At a time when evolutionism dominated nineteenth-century anthropological theory, systems of racial classification and measurement occupied the efforts of many anthropologists; the near-obsessive measuring, classifying, charting, and ranking of human physiognomy in physical anthropology (as well as pseudo-sciences such as phrenology and craniometry) can be read as responses to the wider challenge of how to make sense of observable physical and cultural differences among the peoples of the world. Photography's indexicality brought scientific respectability to anthropometric studies simply because the insolubility of the image offered the appearance of legitimate evidence.

The mechanical nature of photography and its power to preserve traces of anatomical difference also appealed to nineteenth-century anthropologists. According to historian David Tomas, the anthropological appeal of photography for nineteenth-century ethnographers resided in its "descriptive permanence and its ability to reproduce the kind of 'tedious minuteness' of factual detail required by the science"; the photograph's facility for iconographic detail "forestall[ed] an aesthetically impregnated subjective vision" that threatened to dilute the scientific observer's objectivity.[20] Writing on the "Ethnology of the Motu" in the *Journal of the Anthropological Institute* in 1878, W. Y. Turner noted that the objective properties of the photographic camera would prevent subjective biases from "polluting" the data, since "one difficulty in determining the question of race arises from the fact that different writers describe the same people in quite different ways." It was infinitely better, Turner argued, "not to rely on written descriptions only, but to secure if possible photographs of natives."[21] Indeed, for Turner, what separated the photographic record from the engraving or illustration was the speed at which an observer could identify racial characteristics when two images were placed next to each other: "For the purpose of comparison, my photographs are so arranged as to place that of a Motu between a Papuan and a Malayo-Polynesian, so that a *glance* will decide to which of the two great families . . . the Motu belongs."[22] Similarly, in 1886, British anthropologist Edward Horace Man endorsed the scientific utility of the photographic camera, arguing that "more correct information [could] be obtained from photography than from any verbal description, however minute and careful."[23]

As a mode of scientific inscription, anthropometric photography was premised upon the notion that a mechanically reproduced image of the human body obtained via standardized photometric methods could permit the recovery of "reliable and comparative morphometric data."[24] Two of the most influential systems were devised by the Englishmen Thomas Henry Huxley and J. H. Lamprey in the 1860s. Huxley's system required that subjects be photographed naked alongside measuring instruments placed at a fixed distance from the camera, according to a series of standardized somatic and cephalic poses (fig. 3.2).[25] Two full-length photographs would be taken of each subject, one frontal and the other in profile, supplemented with full-face and profile portraits of the subject's head (a forerunner of the contemporary mug shot).[26] Huxley argued that the lack of uniformity in anthropological photography greatly diminished its scientific value, since comparative studies of physiological types were more difficult to conduct on randomly posed photographs than on bodies inserted into regulated visual contexts; according to Huxley: "[While] great numbers of ethnological photographs already exist . . . they lose much of their value from not being taken upon a uniform and well considered plan. The result is that they are rarely measurable or comparable with one another and that they fail to give the precise information respecting the proportions and the conformation of the body, which . . . [is of paramount] worth to the ethnologist."[27]

J. H. Lamprey claimed that his system of classification, consisting of photographing native peoples in front of perpendicular lines suspended across a wooden frame (fig. 3.3), "greatly helped . . . the study of all those peculiarities of contour which are so distinctly observable in each group" and served as "good guides to their definition, which no verbal description could convey, and but few artists could delineate."[28]

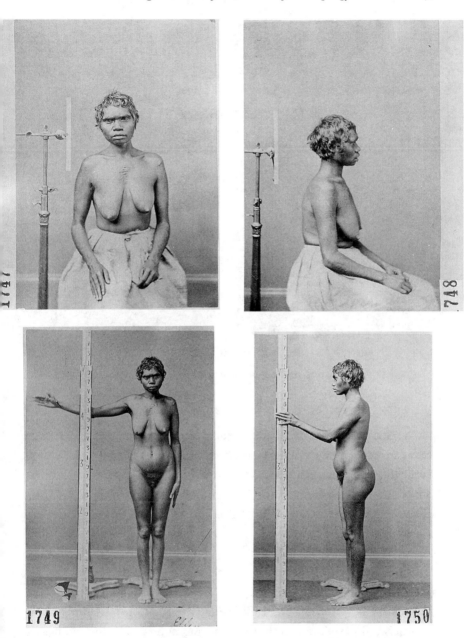

FIG. 3.2 Four views of Ellen, age 22, a South Australian Aboriginal woman photographed according to T. H. Huxley's instructions, c. 1870. (Royal Anthropological Institute 1747, 1748, 1749, 1750. Courtesy RAI)

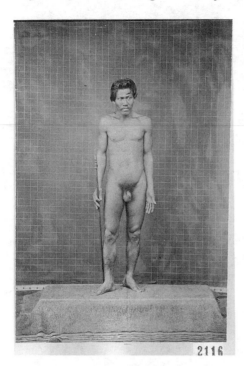

FIG. 3.3 Front and profile view of a Malayan man photographed by J. H. Lamprey, c. 1868–69. (RAI 2116, 2117. Courtesy RAI)

One goal of anthropometric photography was to make the native body legible as an ethnographic sign, since the detection and measurement of individual anatomical features were seen as offering the perfect solution to the problem of how to guarantee objectivity and "truth" in anthropological investigation. Cultural theorist David Spurr argues that within this cartographic gaze, "the eye treats the body as a landscape . . . proceed[ing] systematically from part to part, quantifying and spatializing, noting color and texture."[29] Flower, for example, argued that "physical characters are the best, in fact the only true tests of race, that is of real affinity; language, customs etc., may help or give indications, but they are often misleading."[30] In an operation of optical empiricism, Flower reads from the mute and nonreciprocating bodies of native peoples the signifiers of race, understood as indelible manifestations of an inner character, vital to the project of racial and social classification.[31]

The promise of mathematical precision in the quantity and diversity of measurements obtained in a single sitting convinced many anthropologists of anthropometry's utility in the project of racial classification and criminal identification.[32] The anonymous contributor to "Current Notes in Anthropology" in 1893, for example, offered a taxonomy of somatic information that could be obtained via anthropometry: "We learn the . . . inclination of the shoulders; the relations of the hip and chest dimensions in the two sexes; the development of the breasts in both sexes; the projection of the gluteal region; the proportion of trunk to extremities, and a number of other physical peculiarities."[33] In India, the caste system worked in anthropometry's favor and was a key factor in its successful implementation between the 1890s and the teens. Several anthropologists and colonial administrators based in India at the time argued that culturally imposed restrictions on intermarriage between ethnic and social groups had kept the "genetic muddying of the population" to a minimum.[34] The perceived lack of a "national type" in India was thus viewed by colonial administrator Herbert Hope Risley as one of anthropometry's saving graces, since "in contrast to most other parts of the world, where anthropometry ha[d] to confess itself hindered, if not baffled, by the constant intermixture of types [which] obscur[ed] the data ascertained by measurements . . . in India the process of fusion was arrested long ago."[35] The statistics gained from anthropometry were viewed as indices of political allegiance mapped onto the physical surface of the body—what Pinney calls "a sociological form of fingerprinting"—which had obvious utility for the colonial power. Furthermore, as a way of explaining the caste system (and as a way to displace the political resonance of Hindu social organization), discourses of biological determinism and ritualism were used to undergird ideological constructions of Hindu society as nonmaterial and fragmented by multiple ethnicities, constructions that served India's ruling colonial class.[36]

A close relative of anthropometric photography, the human locomotion studies of Eadweard Muybridge, which used between twelve and twenty-four cameras set up in five positions to photograph sequential stages of movement against a common background,[37] acquired the status of scientific documents as a result of the gridlike backdrop Muybridge used (which was virtually identical to Lamprey's) and his decision to photograph many of his subjects naked (although in contrast to Lamprey and Huxley, Muybridge supplied his subjects with an array of props, including chairs, buckets, and handkerchiefs). The iconography of dispassionate science in the gridlike background, the decontextualization of the undressed subjects, and the serious nature of the informing research context were meant to legitimize Muybridge's research, and to no doubt deflect attention away from the prurient content of the images.[38]

Influenced by Muybridge's human motion studies, French physiologist Étienne-Jules Marey developed his own method for analyzing the range, velocity, and sequence of various phases of human locomotion. Marey's chronophotographic camera (*fusil photographique*) had a slotted-disk shutter that opened and closed intermittently to expose twelve images per second on the perimeter of a rotating glass plate. As a technology for charting and disciplining the national and colonial body, Marey's chronophotography shared a number of discursive features with anthropometry; both practices transformed subjects into anonymous ciphers of scientific knowledge and were implicated in broader institutional structures of corporeal control. Marey, for example, produced geometric chronophotographs in which the human body was transformed into a flat graphic trace devoid of any distinguishing features. Clothing his subjects in a black body-suit and strategically marking their joints with shiny buttons connected by metal bands, Marey computed with mechanical precision the successive attitudes of the human body in motion from the lines and dots. However, the model of vision inscribed in Marey's geometric chronophotography was in many ways a radical departure from the structures of knowledge implicit in anthropometry's appropriation of photography as a "seeing technology." Marey rejected analogical detail in favor of graphic notation in his geometric chronophotography. He also eschewed the "surface verisimilitude" and textual detail of the photographic image, preferring instead a graphic inscription free of pictorial, spatial, and depth cues. In so doing, Marey stripped away the flesh of his subjects in order to access the working mechanisms of a human body that resembled an animate machine.[39] However, if Marey removed from the human body all distinguishing features, save possibly gait, one could argue that anthropometric photography enacted a similar process of cultural desublimation by insisting that native subjects be photographed undressed. Divesting the body of the indigene of such markers of culture as dress, ornamentation, and jewelry, the anthropometric photographer transformed native people into anatomical specimens.[40]

However, if the scientific patina of photographs of naked bodies in standardized poses alongside measuring instruments in front of gridlike back-drops appealed to anthropologists and scientists alike, the process of extracting anthropological data from photographs was fraught with technical difficulties. The problem of maintaining the verticality of the anthropometer, coupled with the challenge of ensuring the exact and uniform positioning of a subject's head and arms, led to disputes within anthropometry over what and how measurements should be consistently applied.[41] The laboratory settings and anthropometers were ultimately more effective, however, in evoking a gloss of scientific objectivity and rigor than in producing useful statistical information; according to Pinney, the apparati served more of an emblematic and compositional function rather than a guarantor of scientific utility, since it was extremely difficult to obtain accurate measurements from these instruments when factors such as their distance from the camera were hard to regulate.[42] Despite these drawbacks, proponents of anthropometric photography invested a great deal of faith in the visual sign (what Pinney calls "the truth of photographic scientism") as a means of bolstering prevailing social and evolutionary theories, which used photographs as evidence of the racial inferiority of native peoples.[43]

Not surprisingly, anthropometric photography came under a measure of criticism from turn-of-the-century anthropologists. British botanist-turned-colonial administrator-turned-anthropologist Everard im Thurn (1852–1932) argued that as a visual system of data collection, anthropometric photography suggested nothing of the living culture of the people under investigation,[44] since the images produced were "merely pictures of lifeless bodies." Indeed, im Thurn argued that native people "might indeed be more accurately measured and photographed for such purposes dead than alive, could they be conveniently obtained when in that state."[45] What im Thurn was invoking here was the common practice of measuring the cadavers of non-Western peoples in state hospitals in Paris (and elsewhere), a practice that Flower argued should be undertaken with native cadavers in British hospitals. At the Musée d'Histoire in Paris, Flower noted: "All the bodies of persons of outlandish nationalities dying in any of the hospitals . . . are dissected by competent and zealous observers, who carefully record every peculiarity of structure discovered, and are thus laying the foundation for an exhaustive and trustworthy collection of materials for the comparative anatomy of the races of man."[46]

Following im Thurn's suggestion, it would seem that data extracted from a cadaver could be more extensive and reliable (and more easily obtained) than information gathered from living specimens.[47] This quest by French anthropologists and others to pursue the study of physical anthropology is a vivid illustration of what Foucault calls the "microphysics of power," in which the bodies of social subjects become the sites upon which an obsessive quest to quantify, log, calculate, and control racial difference is played out, sometimes in a macabre fashion.[48]

In condemning anthropology's use of photography to obtain minute somatic detail from mute scientific objects, im Thurn not only questioned the utility of these photographs as anthropological knowledge but, in Pinney's words, "cooly suggest[ed] the abandonment of what had been a quite clearly articulated anthropological privileging of the still and the silent over the quick and the living."[49] But in criticizing the practices of physical anthropologists, im Thurn was also questioning the very utility of the concept of race as a scientific category. What im Thurn advocated was a more candid approach to fieldwork photography, a method of photographing native peoples that was opposed to the dehumanizing tendencies of physiological photographs, and that viewed "race" less as a classificatory index than as a lived experience, a complex of social and cultural influences that helped determine an individual's identity as a member of a social group.

Nineteenth-Century Fieldwork Photography

Working and traveling as a curator and colonial administrator between 1881 and 1897, im Thurn gained extensive knowledge of the Indian peoples of Guiana and viewed photography, in Donald Taylor's words, as "an intrinsic, if aesthetic and humanizing part of [anthropology]."[50] Im Thurn's classic 1893 article "Anthropological Uses of the Camera," was an attack on the scientific appropriations of photography as an anthropometric tool in favor of a more naturalistic fieldwork photography.[51] Arguing that the camera "seems to be insufficiently appreciated and utilized" by the "traveling anthropologist," im Thurn suggested ways in which the camera could be used to record native life "under the most natural conditions."[52] An analysis of im Thurn's photographic work leaves one in little doubt that he attempted to practice what he preached;

FIG. 3.4 Father and sons taken by Everard im Thurn, c. 1889–90. (RAI 610. Courtesy RAI)

his photographs appear remarkably unstaged, although there is no way of knowing definitively which photographs were posed and which were sponta-neous. Shunning anthropometric or other obviously staged compositions, im Thurn's photographs represent individuals in fairly intimate groupings who retain a degree of dignity in front of the camera (fig. 3.4).

But not all photographers working within the field were as sensitive to intersubjective relations as im Thurn, and it would be wrong to imply that field photographs, by dint of their in situ status, were necessarily less manip-ulated and staged than their anthropometric counterparts; in many instances, they were simply staged *differently*. For example, British colonial administrator Capt. F. R. Barton's photographs taken in Papua New Guinea around 1905 range in content from being highly aestheticized pictorialist compositions to dehumanizing anatomical studies. Not surprisingly, many of Barton's staged images fall less within the scientifically defined boundaries of anthropologi-cal photography than within an earlier nineteenth-century pictorialist tradi-tion (fig. 3.5). According to Marta Macintyre and Maureen MacKenzie, Barton's vision is a "parody of Classicism. . . . The girls become artists' mod-els, choreographed by Barton to emulate the postures of Hellenic sculptures."

FIG. 3.5 British colonial administrator
Capt. F. R. Barton's photograph of a
Motu girl, c. 1905. (RAI 20535.
Courtesy RAI)

The erotic content of the images—Barton was ostensibly concerned with
practices of tattooing the female torso (which for the Motuan people were
associated with female attraction, fertility, and marriageability)—also evince
a libidinously charged encounter with indigenous sexuality, a barely masked
desire for closer contact.[53]

Another pioneer of the more candid style of fieldwork photography was the
Irish-American ethnologist James Mooney, who between 1887 and 1906 made
hundreds of portraits of Native Americans, as well as recording material culture and ceremonial life.[54] Mooney's more naturalistic style of fieldwork photography and his sensitivity to native/white relations mirrored the sensibilities of im Thurn; like im Thurn, Mooney saw the benefits of establishing a
rapport with his subjects and was respectful of Native American wishes. When
photographing the Ghost Dance for the first time in 1891, Mooney avoided
using the flash so as not to "incite panic in the entranced dancers," and he
offered subjects payment for the privilege of taking photographs and/or making copies of prints.[55] According to Ira Jacknis, Mooney's focus was "not the
particular slice of life privileged by the camera, but the ongoing flow of native
experience . . . an interest in the actual conditions of native life, seen as part

of a dynamic and continuous history."[56] Consequently, Mooney documented indigenous culture in its entirety and supplemented his photographs with a range of alternative media, including phonographic recordings, verbal notes, and song transcriptions.[57] In spite of the uneven technical qualities of Mooney's photographs (some are over- or underexposed and the composition is often careless),[58] they are, as Jacknis points out, ethnographically sophisticated in their relatively spontaneous and candid quality.

Despite their technical shortcomings, it is possible to see a germ of later ethnographic filmmaking praxis in Mooney's approach to fieldwork photography, especially his attentiveness to issues of intersubjectivity and the ethics of cross-cultural image-making. Mooney's photography anticipates modes of ethnographic enunciation that had not yet found expression in cinematic form, including the attempt to encompass several aspects of a culture, in place of the more typical concern with a single cultural feature, such as ceremonial life, food preparation, or artisanal work. Had Mooney taken a moving picture camera with him into the field (and, given his multimedia approach to ethnographic recording, it is somewhat surprising he didn't), the films he produced might have been significantly different from those of his contemporaries.

Gaining the confidence of the local people was for anthropologists like James Mooney and Everard im Thurn, "one of quite the most essential matters" if one was to avoid producing "ordinary photographs of uncharacteristically miserable natives," which, in im Thurn's opinion, resembled photographs of "badly stuffed and distorted birds and animals."[59] Taking photographs of native peoples required a measure of cooperation on the part of subjects, since the long exposure times of the wet-collodium plate system and the unfamiliar properties of the camera provoked resistance in some communities, although as this photograph of a Zulu village taken by a Trappist monk in 1896 attests, the rigid pose of the subjects was by no means an iron-clad indicator of their attitudes toward the camera, as the children gathered around the camera and the Zulu warrior who has taken up the role of photographer seem to suggest a fairly relaxed demeanor around recording technology (fig. 3.6).

While Frederick Archer Scott's wet-collodium system (which produced a glass negative from which prints could be made and which dominated photography from the 1850s through the 1880s) opened up photography to new users, few dynamic aspects of indigenous culture could be represented pho-

FIG. 3.6 Trappist monk staging a photograph of Zulu warriors, Natal, South Africa, 1896. (Courtesy Pitt Rivers Museum)

tographically since, as Rudolph Arnheim explains, "the equipment was too bulky to catch anybody unawares, and the exposure time was long enough to wipe the accidents of the moment from the face and gesture. . . . A sort of otherworldly wisdom was symbolized by the fact that any momentary motion vanished automatically from those metallic plates."[60] The tedious length of time required to pose for the wet-plate photograph (forcing the subject to "suffer as much as a surgical operation" in Barthes's words) thus gave many of the native peoples photographed a strained, frozen expression reminiscent of the mannequins in museum life groups.[61] Given the length of time they had to stand still and the intimidating-looking apparatus, it is hardly surprising that Louis Agassiz's photographic subjects developed suspicious attitudes toward the camera (furthermore, they had no idea what Agassiz intended doing with their images), as evidenced in the description by Agassiz's wife, Elizabeth, of native reactions to being photographed: "There is a prevalent superstition among the Indians and Negroes that a portrait absorbs into itself something of the vitality of the sitter, and that any one is liable to die shortly after his picture is taken. This notion is so deeply rooted that it has been no easy matter to overcome it."[62] However, we must also consider the fact that such imputations of native superstition may have served as a convenient scapegoat for scientists and anthropologists who failed to win the trust of native peoples (or compensate them sufficiently for the intrusion, physical discomfort, and generosity of time).[63]

The negotiations involved in procuring individual portraits became that much more fraught in the case of multiple sitters, as Man discovered when he tried to organize a group photograph of Shom Pen villagers in 1886: "I exposed two or three dry plates, but owing to the dense over-hanging foliage, and the difficulty of making the Shom Pen understand the necessity of all keeping still together for two or three seconds consecutively, the exposure proved insufficient."[64] Similarly, when Tosco Peppe's photographs of the Juangs from Bengal were published in the *Descriptive Ethnology of Bengal* in 1872, one caption noted that "Mr Peppe had immense difficulty in inducing these wild timid creatures to pose before him, and it was not without many a treat, that they resigned themselves to the ordeal."[65] Repeated reminders of the challenges or risks involved in taking photographs of native peoples should be read with a certain degree of skepticism, though, since inflated egos and exaggerated accounts of personal challenges were very often the result of self-aggrandizement rather than documents of fact.

Notwithstanding the possibility for exaggerated claims, feelings of resentment and discomfort at being photographed register immediately with the spectator of this photograph of young Mexican women taken by Norwegian anthropologist Carl Lumholtz in 1898; the sterile white backdrop and averted gazes of all but one of the women tell us a great deal about their perceptions of the photographic encounter (fig. 3.7). While many native peoples apparently could be persuaded to pose for the camera and have anthropometric measurements taken, some tribes adamantly refused. Such testimony from anthropologists suggests the complex social interactions around visual technologies when they are used in anthropological fieldwork, and the fact that the camera was by no means perceived uniformly by different tribes. In the case of Lumholtz's 1914–17 expedition to Borneo, attitudes toward the camera varied

FIG. 3.7 Four Mexican Huichol women against a white backdrop. *Photo:* Carl Lumholtz, c. 1890s. (Neg. no. 43195. Courtesy Dept. of Library Services, AMNH)

widely, from tribe members visibly shaking with fear or having tears in their eyes while being photographed or measured, to men and women seeming to relish the prospect of being able to dress up in their finest clothes and jewelry for the camera.[66]

Two photographs of Mohave Indians (Jack and Smokestack) taken in front of a woodland backdrop replete with naturalistic props at the American Museum of Natural History in 1895 are vivid illustrations of how the construction of ethnographic meaning in photographs depended a great deal on the setting as well as the instructions given to subjects regarding pose, direction of gaze, and demeanor. In the first image (fig. 3.8), the hands held by the side of the body, the hair dressings brought forward over the shoulder, along with the symmetrical positioning of the feet, contribute to the feeling of submission hanging over this image. Jack and Smokestack are constructed as representatives of their environment in similar ways to the token props on the ground; their faces seem strangely distanced from their passive bodies, grim-

FIG. 3.8 Mohave Indians Jack and Smokestack photographed at the American Museum of Natural History, 1895. (Neg. no. 3767. Courtesy Dept. of Library Services, AMNH)

ly acquiescing to the photographer's instructions for the duration of the shot. In the second, slightly closer photograph (fig. 3.9), however, Jack and Smokestack have taken up entirely different poses, pushing their hair over their shoulders, raising or folding their arms, and looking at the camera with a degree of indignity. Now while it is entirely possible that the unidentified pho-

FIG. 3.9 Jack and Smokestack appearing more relaxed in front of the camera, 1895. (Neg. no. 3768. Courtesy Dept. of Library Services, AMNH)

tographer played as much of a role in staging this second photograph as the first image—explicit directions may have been given regarding *all* aspects of the pose—one can't help but interpret the second image as an act of defiance on the part of Jack and Smokestack, in which Native American agency and self-determination chip away at the power relations of the previous image.

A dislike of the intrusive nature of still photographers and culturally bound (metaphysical) fears about the meaning of photography were only half the story. Anthropologists also had to contend with the considerable technical and logistical difficulties involved in taking photographs. As a result of both the unwieldiness of photographic equipment (fieldwork researchers had to carry two hundred pounds of equipment, chemicals, glass plates, a darkroom tent, a huge camera and attendant black cloth in order to take photographs), the often inhospitable climates, and the complexity of mid-nineteenth-century photography, anthropologists were glad to enlist the services of professional photographers on expeditions. In addition, one of the most frequently filmed aspects of indigenous life, native dances, could be photographed only if artificially posed, and nighttime ceremonies had to be reconstructed for the camera during daylight. However, some of the drawbacks of the wet-collodium plate process were alleviated with the dry plate process, which allowed photographers to use preprepared plates in their cameras. However, it was not until the Kodak roll-film camera (with the marketing slogan, "You Press the Button, We Do the Rest") was invented in 1888 that photography found its way into the hands of a far more diverse group of individuals.[67]

Commercial Uses of Anthropological Photography

While some anthropologists took up the camera themselves as an instrument of field research, a significant number of the photographs employed in comparative ethnological studies were originally produced for commercial distribution. Anthropologists seemed to have few qualms using photographs obtained via commercial distributors as ethnological evidence in the same manner as photographs they had taken themselves. However, a concern with iconographic verisimilitude led British anthropologist M. V. Portman to reject the prevailing soft-focus pictorialism of artistic photography in favor of the visual rigor of sharp focus: "a good *focusing glass* . . . should always be used as our object is to get great and accurate detail, not to make pictures. 'Fuzzygraphs' are quite out of place in anthropological work."[68] A print with maximum sharpness of detail and without the aestheticizing techniques associated with some commercial photographs was thus of greatest documentary value to most anthropologists. Despite Portman's attack on the pictorial style

FIG. 3.10 Australian Aborigine Clarence River photographed in the studio of J. W. Lindt in the early 1870s. (RAI 670. Courtesy RAI)

of many photographs produced for mass consumption, some anthropologists paid scant attention to the provenance of photographs and had few qualms combining photographs made by travelers, missionaries, colonial administrators, expatriates, and commercial studios with their own images when illustrating monographs.

The indigenous peoples represented in these commercial stereographs, *cartes-de-visites*, and postcards were frequently represented by studio portraitists as essentialized specimens of objectified and racially monolithic categories with little attention paid to the subtleties of tribal or ethnic identity or the subjectivities of those represented.[69] The cultural purity of the anthropological object was evoked in theatricalized, diorama-type studio backdrops which transported native subjects into imaginary quasi-narrative tableaux (fig. 3.10). Walter Benjamin criticized what he called the "painterliness" of this style, which elided the social identities of subjects by placing them in front of scenic backdrops and retouching the image.[70] Roslyn Poignant has offered a metaphorical reading of the act of transplanting colonized people from their native habitats into the fictive mise-en-scène of the photographic studio: "Their removal from the bush to the constructed studio set, which is dressed with authentic local plants, parallels their actual displacement as the land's owners. With their weapons laid aside and their wildness neutralized by the studio ambiance, they have been transformed into specimens—like the plants around them" (fig. 3.11).[71] This is a vivid illustration of what Shohat and Stam call the colonialist zeugma yoking "native" with nature, an enduring conceptualization in nineteenth-century constructions of native peoples.[72] George Catlin, for example, exemplifies this trope in his discussion of the "inevitable" extinction of "man" and "beast" in their plight against civilization. Collapsing discourses of the Noble Savage with those of Manifest Destiny, Catlin argued that

Nature has nowhere presented more beautiful and lovely scenes than those of the vast prairies of the West and of *man* and *beast* no nobler specimen than those who inhabit them—the *Indian* and the *buffalo* —joint and original tenants of the soil, and fugitives together from the approach of civilized man; they have fled to the great plains of the West, and there under an equal doom, they have taken up their last abode, where their race will expire and their bones will bleach together.[73]

FIG. 3.11 An unidentified Dakota Indian man posing against one of photographer David F. Barry's numerous backdrops, c. 1880s. (Courtesy NAA)

ADEN — Somaly woman

FIG. 3.12 Somaly woman illustrative of "type" convention, c. 1890s. (Author's personal collection)

As we saw in the context of world's fairs and expositions, commercial ethnographic subjects were predominantly photographed as exotic or eroticized types, the neutral background in such portraits serving to eliminate all defining markers, de-territorializing the image and elevating the human body to the position of primary signifier of racial difference and eroticized beauty (fig. 3.12). Other ethnographic photographs inserted depictions of human activities such as fire-making into a priori taxonomical classifications, such as physical type, clothing and body decoration, rituals, technology, and material culture.

The production of lavish ethnographic photographic albums pioneered by the organizers of the 1893 World's Columbian Exposition exploited the semantic authority of the scientific "type" and included such titles as *Midway Types: A Book of Illustrated Lessons About the People of the Midway Plaisance* and *Portrait Types of the Midway Plaisance*. As a conceptual category, the "type" photograph drew upon the scientific connotations of the specimen as a way of classifying cultural or ethnic groups,[74] borrowing the visual iconography of the scientific

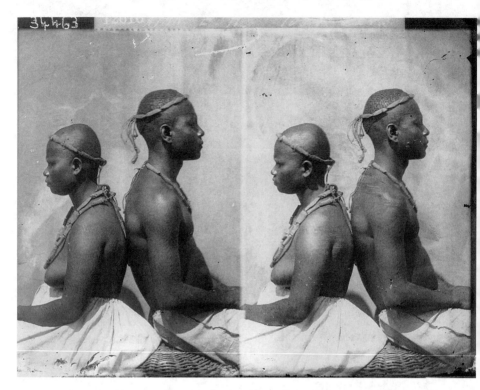

FIG. 3.13 Stereograph of Andamanese man and woman photographed by E. H. Man, c. 1900. (RAI 34463. Courtesy RAI)

specimen through physically and synechdocally isolating the subject, as seen here in this stereograph of an Andamanese man and woman (fig. 3.13). Transformed into what visual anthropologist Elizabeth Edwards calls an "abstract essence of human variation," the type traded on the connotative authority of the anthropometric photograph through its use of standardized frontal and profile poses, often in front of a white sheet or similar neutral background (see fig. 3.7).[75]

The iconography of the "type" also found a home in early ethnographic film (see *Indian and Ceylonese Types* [Eclair, 1913], which features nothing but typological images of South Asians, and *On the Edge of the Desert* [France, 1920] for especially vivid examples), functioning as a coded moment when film and photographic signification appear to collapse. The extent to which this trope had become conventionalized in early ethnographic film is suggested in a 1905 Pathé release in which a French vaudeville performer impersonates different character types using Grand Guignol-inspired masks. The film, *French Types*, consists of nothing but exaggerated front and profile shots of French stereotypes. That the visual coordinates of the anthropometric view could be parodied so easily here is testimony to the currency of the "type" as a rhetorical (and ideological) construction in turn-of-the-century popular culture, notwithstanding the celebrity status of the impersonator for French audiences.

Connotative props were frequently used as markers of alterity in these conventionalized representations, and it was not uncommon for commercial photographers to exchange props and costumes across diverse subjects. In some cases, negatives or prints were retouched to accentuate body painting obscured in the photographic process; in other cases photographers would create the impression of body painting where none had been present.[76] Photographic prints from the same negative often appeared in different formats with new captions, printers, and attribution.[77] As in other fields of photography, plagiarism was routine; photographers put their names on other photographers' work or retouched the image to distinguish it from the original negative. As commodities that were traded across international borders, photographs were governed by market forces that stressed availability to meet popular demand at the expense of ethnographic accuracy. The production of tourist postcards in Samoa, for example, illustrates the circuitous nature of systems of production and exchange: photographs of Samoans were sent to England for printing, shipped back to Samoa for sale, and then returned to England in the hands of English travelers.[78]

Like their counterparts at world's fairs, commercial publishers of photographs exploited ethnography's legitimating discourse when promoting collections. Aimed at readers with no direct experience of the native peoples represented, these images appeared in popular publications and in the form of lithographed postcards, photo-based woodcuts, and half-tone engravings.[79] The camera's introduction into the consumer market coincided with the founding of the National Geographic Society in the United States by Gardiner Greene Hubbard in 1888, although *National Geographic* magazine did not start using photographs until eight years later. Early illustrations in the magazine were produced by steel engraving which, despite their high quality, incurred prohibitively high production costs. *National Geographic* therefore entered the magazine market at a propitious moment in terms of photography's institutionalization within the quality magazine industry; but it also bespoke a great deal more than simply the ubiquity of photography as a popular medium and hobbyist pastime. As Catherine Lutz and Jane Collins argue, "The magazine relied on sharply focused, easily readable photographs to bolster its claim that it was presenting an unbiased, unmediated view of the world, a claim that went hand in hand with the assertion that all written material was accurate, balanced, and fair."[80]

Two of the most frequent devices for enhancing the anthropological significance of photographs were cropping and retouching. While the latter technique was considered a routine procedure to correct environmental conditions such as poor lighting, historian Iskander Mydin argues that retouching and other techniques must be regarded "not merely as manipulation but instead as an incidental photographic closure of time and space so that an 'ethnographic present' could exist."[81] Franz Boas, for example, retouched some of John H. Grabill's photographs of Kwakwaka'wakw dancers taken at the Columbian Exposition in 1893 when he published them in his 1897 book *Social Organization and Secret Societies of the Kwakuitl Indians.* In one photograph, a naturalistic background connoting a contemporary Northwest landscape replaced the original location, and all details, excluding the central figure, were removed from the image. As Jacknis points out in his analysis of Boas's photography, such retouching, as well as the photograph's provenance, were rarely acknowledged in Boas's accompanying text,[82] an omission which suggests that issues of authenticity in visual data were not subject to the same standards of scientific rigor as written accounts. In another photograph from the Northwest (fig. 3.14), Boas used a blanket held up by himself and George Hunt to serve as a neutral backdrop for a photograph of an informant demonstrating cedar-spinning. Erasing contemporary signs of modernity and transforming the process into an isolated activity void of geographical markers, the photograph was taken as part of a study for a life group representing the uses of cedar installed in the AMNH's Hall of Northwest Coast Indians in 1902.

Pinney notes that anthropologist Charles G. Seligman differentiated photographs that he had not retouched (what he called "real" photographs) from those images that had been manipulated (what he called "more or less faked"

FIG. 3.14 Franz Boas (*left*) and George Hunt hold up a blanket to serve as a neutral backdrop for a photograph demonstrating cedar-spinning taken in 1894. (Neg. no. 11608. Courtesy Dept. of Library Services, AMNH)

images). By identifying photographs that he considered "false," Seligman made a preemptive strike against his photographs being mistaken for commercial prints. This strategy depended upon the supposition that if only a few of Seligman's photographs were "false," the vast majority must, by implication, be "true."[83] Such disclaimers were necessary, as Pinney explains, because "the anthropological genre is marked off from the commercial genre only by particularistic captions marked by a specificity of group and location."[84] Here, again, we see evidence of anthropologists attempting to elevate their discipline above the contaminating influences of popular culture. Anthropology's relationship to visuality is an important point of self-definition for scientists such as Seligman who seem keenly aware of how the subject's reputation may be tainted by charges of manipulation or deception. Because of the permeability of boundaries between anthropological photographs and commercial prints, the visual was something of a double-edged sword for anthropologists, providing them with the much-needed empirical evidence of cultural difference they were after, but always at the risk of discreditation, either on the grounds of manipulation or dishonesty (claiming, for example, that they had taken a photograph when it had, in fact, been commercially bought).

But for most anthropologists, the provenance of an ethnographic photograph mattered less than the kinds of illustrative or pedagogic uses to which it could be put. When accompanied by a detailed caption in a scholarly text, a commercially produced photograph would undergo a process of decontamination and become acceptable as ethnographic evidence (in similar ways, commercially shot ethnographic film footage exhibited within a scientific lecture might acquire the status of scientific evidence by force of the scholarly prestige of the lecturer or the elite connotations of the venue). Given the extensive interpenetration of scientific and popular ethnographic photographs in the nineteenth century, and the fact that no single textual feature distinguished nonanthropometric photographs from other photographic genres, it's hardly surprising that countless photographs created within the contexts of missionary work and anthropological expeditions found their way into commercial markets.

However, the highly prescriptive interpretive meanings imposed upon the photograph via captioning or discursive uses (popular press illustration, stereograph, *carte-de-visite*, or scientific plate) is also reminiscent of the contextual determinants of the reception of early ethnographic film, since the ethnographic status of filmic actualities was to a large extent shaped by the film lecturer and the exhibition context, and in the case of both photographs and films, the intended meanings of visual texts were rarely trusted to "speak for themselves," but were insistently circumscribed by the exhibition context, be it a caption accompanying a photograph, a didactic intertitle, or a comment uttered by a lecturer.[85]

Despite the complex and interconnected relationships surrounding film and photographs, these technologies differed in their perceived ability to represent indigenous lives; they placed very different demands, both practical and ideological, upon anthropologists, and for these reasons must be understood on their own terms. In the same way that mass-produced ethnographic portraiture was often formally indistinguishable from photographs made by anthropologists, ethnographic films shot within the context of ethnographic research were often impossible to differentiate from their popular counterparts. Under these circumstances, it is not surprising that the ethnographic status of nineteenth-century photographs seems less a matter of textuality than a product of the specific reception communities in which they circulated.

The semantic instability of visual modes of ethnographic enunciation that straddled both scientific and popular genres may very well then have been the kiss of death for ethnographic filmmaking. In terms of the risks it posed to science, cinema shared more in common with the life group and the ethnographic village than the photograph; perceived by most anthropologists as a means of display rather than a genuine research tool, the "dangers" cinema posed to science were closer in substance to those of staged mass entertainments than the limited objectivity of the photograph. But having said this, there are a number of correspondences between early ethnographic films (and actualities in general) and photography, that force us to reevaluate how ethnographic meaning is negotiated in each medium. The first way in which distinctions between early ethnographic film and photography tend to blur relates to the textuality of much early nonfiction film; marked by long takes and occasional medium long shots rarely linked in cause-and-effect logic, films of native peoples offer few cues for spectator anticipation and recollection fundamental to the operation of narrative cinema. In this regard, early ethnographic films challenge Pinney's distinction between photography's surplus of meaning and cinema's constraint of meaning through "narrative chains of signification."[86] This opposition also ignores the fact that photographs, like films, can contain emphatic narrative cues. While spectator interpretation of these early cinema tableaux was inflected by the film's subject, genre, and reception context, the long-take, static long-shot film typical of the pre-1903 period gives spectators considerably more time to peruse the contents of the frame, often a landscape and its (frequently motionless) inhabitants for the duration of the shot.[87] It should be pointed out, though, that editing-in-the-camera was far more frequent during the early cinema period than previous accounts have allowed; for example, early Edison films show signs of editing within a single camera placement, and as André Gaudreault has demonstrated, about 20 percent of Lumière's films contain frequent camera stoppages and even splices.[88] Notwithstanding this degree of editing within early cinema, the decision to film a scene of ethnographic interest may have been determined not by the kinesthetic qualities of the profilmic, but by the fact that it contained people who were interesting to look at irrespective of whether they moved or not. In this way, the long take, which allowed a more contemplative reading, coupled with the relative lack of on-screen movement in many early ethnographic films, makes the very act of viewing more similar to that of looking at a still image; the long take with no camera movement invites the spectator to scrutinize the frame with a concentration and intensity that may even exceed that given up to a photograph.

This relatively unconstrained exploration of the filmic image by the spectator is reminiscent of Roland Barthes's idea of the photographic *punctum*, an uncoded detail that attracts the attention of the viewer such as a fold in a dress, the position of a hand, or an object in the frame.[89] According to Barthes, *punctum* was not present in motion pictures in the same way as it was in photography, since the kinetic quality of the filmic image worked against the evocation of *punctum*; as Barthes explained: "In front of the screen, I am not free to shut my eyes; otherwise, opening them again, I would not discover the same image; I am constrained to a continuous veracity" (55). But Barthes's description pertains less to the single-shot, long-take films of the early cinema period than to classical Hollywood films whose systems of editing depend less on the long take as a paradigmatic unit. Indeed, the decentered visual compositions of many early ethnographic films seem to contain a surplus of *punctum*, often in the form of tiny details or incidents occurring at the margins of the frame. For early film audiences with few opportunities to view images of native peoples from exotic regions, such a frame must have contained a plethora of ethnographic detail warranting inspection (and repeat viewing).

According to Barthes, a photograph's inimitable feature, its *noeme*, deteriorates when it is projected as a moving picture because, when a still image is animated, the "pose is swept away and denied by the continuous series of images" (78). Barthes also argues that unlike photography, which cannot invoke the sense of a future, cinema is protensive, less melancholic than photography and therefore too " 'normal' " and "life-like."[90] But I would argue that a great many early ethnographic films (especially Alfred Cort Haddon's films of Mer Islander dancers and Walter Baldwin Spencer's of Australian Aboriginal ceremonial dances) evoke far more pathos than do their still photographs of the same performances. The films' pathos arises from the immense dignity of the indigenous performers, our respect for their native ceremonies and plight as colonial subjects, and, most importantly, a nostalgia associated with viewing moving images of people who are no longer living, yet who seem so alive for the duration of the film. Spectator affect here may be a product both of the highly expressive nature of the ceremonies performed for the camera and of the visible deterioration of the aging film stock. The ontological form of early cinema may, then, have created a different set of "looking relations" between film subject and film viewer, inviting the more contemplative gaze frequently associated with photography in place of that of motion pictures.

Meanings evoked by such images were also governed by metanarratives external to the specific viewing context, such as the master narrative of "Progress" and "Civilization" that permeated turn-of-the-century world's fairs. As Raymond Corbey points out, "narrative plots [were] as pervasive in the civilizatory, imperialist, missionary and scientific discourses of the period as in the three-dimensional spectacles that, to a considerable degree, were governed by these discursive activities."[91] In addition to the vocal or textual positioning of the image by the visible or invisible narrator, the ethnographic meaning of the visual artifact was subject to the vagaries of audience response. The challenges to historians in accounting for the role of such powerful but implicit metanarratives and the vicissitudes of reception suggest some of the difficulties in determining how the meanings of ethnographic films and photographs were negotiated in the early part of this century.

The trafficking of nineteenth-century ethnographic photographs across scientific and popular markets thus established a precedent for commercially produced ethnographic films, although unlike photographs made within scientific contexts, which frequently found their way into commercial markets, only a small number of ethnographic films shot by anthropologists actually made it onto popular screens for the simple reason that so few of them were made. Why, then, did cinema never become the "instrument" of the physical anthropologist in the same way that the photographic camera formed the basis for anthropometric photography? The answer to this question can be found in part in the discursive construction of cinema (or chronophotography) by two figures who are credited with experimenting with technology that would eventually usher in cinema: Étienne-Jules Marey and Félix-Louis Regnault. A brief look at what they had to say about the scientific uses of cinema should give us better purchase on the kinds of paths ethnographic film *did not follow* at the end of the nineteenth century.

When working with new technologies for animating the human subject, Marey and Regnault operated from separate epistemological assumptions; while both saw chronophotography as the solution to the problem of how to represent movement that escaped detection by the human eye, their views on cinema's utility as a scientific instrument were quite distinct. Regnault shared with Marey an interest in cinema's capacity to expand vision in time, and had used Marey's chronophotographic camera to record the movements of native West Africans at the Exposition Ethnographique in Paris in 1895.[92] Regnault argued that an analysis of movement, particularly unconscious movement, was an indispensable part of physiognomical and anthropological research. If photographs offered insufficient evidence of how the human body moved through space, the chronophotographic camera could revivify the subject, and in so doing permit a detailed "reading" of the human body through the synthesis of individual photographs of native subjects as a series of projected images. As Fatimah Tobing Rony has argued in her groundbreaking research on Regnault, chronophotography for Regnault could transform ethnography and sociology into "precise sciences," facilitating in the process the close analysis of what he called *le langage par gestes*, a language idiomatic to the pre-literate body of the native. Unlike Regnault, though, Marey could not have cared less for lifelike projection since it could only show what the human eye itself could see; what interested Marey was cinema's ability to *transcend* rather than to replicate vision. As Marey explained:[93] "Cinema produces only what the eye can see. . . . It adds nothing to the power of our sight, nor does it remove its illusions, and the real character of a scientific method is to supplant the insufficiency of our senses and correct their errors. To get to this point, chronophotography should renounce the representation of phenomena as they are seen by the eye."[94] Marey's belief in "scientistic functionalism" (Noël Burch's phrase) led him to see "the synthesis of movement as a gross redundancy from his cognitive point of view"; for Marey, the illusion of movement in projected film would do little to advance scientific understanding of the mechanics of movement.[95]

Chronophotography was therefore of far greater use to Marey in its analytic form than in its synthetic state as projected illusionistic movement, however "satisfying and astonishing that resurrection of movement may be."[96] An apparatus that merely reproduced movement as perceived by the human eye was thus of little use to Marey, since the image "would be attended by all the uncertainties that embarrass the observation of the actual movement."[97] Marey was unimpressed with the commercial and merely depictive applications of cinematographic technology, arguing that "the absolutely perfect projections that naturally arouse the enthusiasm of the public are not those, speaking personally, that captivate me the most," and despite being heavily influenced by Muybridge's locomotion studies, he was ultimately leery of the showmanship quality of Muybridge's lecture-demonstrations.[98]

What Marey's and Regnault's contributions to the prehistory of ethnographic cinema represent, then, are dead ends in terms of the direction ethnographic film would finally follow. As a physicist interested in the anthropological potential of imaging technology, Regnault was clearly on the same page as anthropologists such as Haddon and Spencer, who, within five or so years, would use motion pictures as part of ethnographic fieldwork. But Regnault's interest in movement studies, recorded in a similar fashion to anthropometric studies, was not where the impetus currently lay in ethnographic film at the start of the twentieth century. To be sure, there are isolated incidents of anthropologists replicating Regnault's study by having native peoples demonstrate walking, squatting, and jumping for the camera, but for those *few* anthropologists who did consider using cinema (and the emphasis here is definitely on the few), motion studies were not especially important, particularly when the limited amounts of costly film could be put to better use in the service of recording ceremonial activities or aspects of material culture such as basket-weaving or pot-making. Ironically, then, anthropologists interested in using film during its infant years shared a great deal more with commercial manufacturers such as Edison and Biograph than Regnault and Marey, singling out something to film not because it would stand as empirical proof of racial difference, but because it captured a cultural activity or process threatened with extinction and because it would make an interesting film.

The exceptional use of the motion picture camera by a few turn-of-the-century anthropologists thus occurred in the absence of a clearly defined intellectual project for film within anthropology; one might even go as far as to say that cinema's emergence in the mid-1890s was a case of unfortunate bad timing given anthropology's shift away from visuality toward textuality. The only guiding principles that two of early ethnographic films' pioneers—Alfred Cort Haddon and Walter Baldwin Spencer—could follow when they took motion picture cameras with them into the field were their prior experiences of using photography. If the larger intellectual shifts and philosophical ruminations on the utility of the visual within anthropology suggest some of the reasons why cinema was not embraced by most members of an international community of anthropologists between 1895 and 1915—although I should stress here that this is not to imply that anthropologists suddenly stopped taking photographs or abandoned all attempts at using film—they also underscore the singularity and importance of the efforts of Haddon and Spencer to incorporate film into ethnographic fieldwork. With this in mind, let us now turn to the early ethnographic filmmaking of these men and consider what happens to the ethnographic image when it is vivified by the motion picture camera.

PART II

EARLY ETHNOGRAPHIC
FILM IN SCIENCE &
POPULAR CULTURE

4

The Ethnographic Cinema of Alfred Cort Haddon
and Walter Baldwin Spencer

The Cinematograph has become not—as some people imagine it to be—a showman's plaything, but a vital necessity for every . . . institute, laboratory, academy and museum; for every traveler, explorer and missionary.

—CHARLES URBAN (1907)[1]

In medical, surgical and natural science, anthropology, botany, entomology, and natural history generally, the motion picture presents wonders and facts scarcely possible of realization.

—THOMAS CLEGG (1910)[2]

THE CONFIDENCE OF these early motion picture industry professionals concerning the scientific and pedagogical value of cinema as a research tool seems to suggest an early rationale for cinema within anthropology and the sciences. However, Urban's claims for cinema as a "vital necessity" for missionaries, scientists, tourists, and state administrators and Clegg's yoking of scientific objectivity with scopic thrill ("wonders and facts") mask a more complicated history of the fate of motion pictures within anthropology. These two optimistic and triumphant judgments from members of the fledgling motion picture industry, opinions designed as much to legitimize filmgoing for a middle-class audience as to make a case for cinema's relevance for science, also belie the more complex and contested fortunes of cinema within anthropology. If the motion picture trade press was keen to cover film experiments taking place within medicine and the natural sciences, it had a harder time reporting the use of motion pictures within anthropological fieldwork, for the simple fact that around the time Urban and Clegg trumpeted cinema's role within education, no more than a handful of anthropologists around the world had ever used a motion picture camera to film native peoples. Among the first group of experimenters were Alfred Cort Haddon and Walter Baldwin Spencer.

When Haddon took the unprecedented step of taking a Newman and Guardia moving picture camera he had bought in London for £25 with him on his second expedition to the Torres Strait (i.e., the group of islands between the northeast coast of Australia and Papua New Guinea) in April 1898 (he had first visited the Strait ten years earlier in 1888), he had no prior experience of working in the new cinematic medium. Along with the camera, Haddon brought thirty 75-foot rolls of film, two wax-cylinder phonographs, and assorted photographic equipment, including the experimental Ives and Joly apparatus for taking color photographs.[3] Overcoming considerable technical and logistical hurdles, Haddon shot approximately four and a half minutes of footage of Mer Islanders and Australian Aborigines performing ceremonial dances and demonstrating fire-making. Three years later, in 1901, Haddon's English colleague Walter Baldwin Spencer followed his friend's advice to take a "kinematograph" with him on his expedition through Central Australia; equipped with a Warwick Bioscope, Spencer filmed a remarkable range of Arrernte ceremonies and went on to exhibit his films on extended lecture-tours in Australia and Britain.

Despite this brief flurry of interest in ethnographic cinema between 1898 and 1901 and *some* discussion of the positivist uses of the moving picture camera within physiology in continental Europe, anthropology's growing professionalization in the 1900s and teens ultimately coincided with a diminution of interest in the visual in the first two decades of the twentieth century.[4] Whereas the photographic image of the native body had once served as a classificatory index for mid-nineteenth-century evolutionist theories of human development, visual imaging techniques were now considered sadly lacking in representing the more subtle and complex questions of cultural patterning and belief systems that interested anthropologists at the time. No longer providing answers to the questions anthropologists were frequently asking, textual verisimilitude was relegated a backseat as anthropologists increasingly concerned themselves with collecting data expressive of the deeper cultural structures they were now eager to explore. What this move away from the visual points toward, then, is an enduring paradox in the history of visual anthropology, a tension between the apparent sufficiency of the ethnographic image—its excess of visual detail on the one hand versus its discursive insufficiency on the other, the fact that while it may appear to tell us a great deal about a particular social or cultural practice, it nevertheless remains "annoyingly mute" (in ethnographic filmmaker and theorist David Mac-Dougall's words) about what these cultural forms and symbols might actually mean in broader anthropological terms.[5]

But these paradigmatic shifts within anthropology do not fully explain why Haddon and Spencer were among a handful of anthropologists to see the utility of cinema within ethnographic fieldwork; we must also consider the very real logistical difficulties of using film in the field as well as ideological resistances to cinema as cheap amusement (in 1898 cinema was still something of a novelty, akin to any new invention that garners lots of interest before entering the mainstream). It is only by appreciating the daunting prospects of using film in inhospitable climes with no technical support (save the manufacturer's leaflet) that we can begin to grasp what the stakes might have been for anthropologists, who were only too pleased to get themselves and their vital supplies into the field in one piece without having to worry about the fate of their very expensive, state-of-the-art technology.

The Ethnographic Filmmaking of Alfred Cort Haddon

British by birth, both Walter Baldwin Spencer and Alfred Cort Haddon began their careers as zoologists. In 1881, Haddon was appointed to the chair in zoology at the Royal College of Science in Dublin, where, according to George W. Stocking Jr., he lived "in a kind of cultural exile among a quasi-colonial population." Upon losing the chairship in zoology at Melbourne University to Spencer in 1886, Haddon began making plans for a first major research trip to the Torres Strait, an "archetypically Darwinian" project "to study the fauna, the structure, and the mode of formation of coral reefs" (fig. 4.1).[6] Arriving in the Torres Strait in 1888, Haddon devoted a great deal of his time to the study of native culture, sketching (fig. 4.2) and photographing the Mer Islanders and collecting artifacts which he planned to sell on his return to England in order to recoup some of the expedition's expenses. Haddon rendered a great deal of

FIG. 4.1 Alfred Cort Haddon photographed during his first expedition to the Torres Strait in 1888. (Courtesy Cambridge Museum of Archaeology and Anthropology, hereafter CMAA)

what he saw in the Torres Strait in visual terms—even illustrating letters sent home to his son Ernest with colored sketches of indigenous dance, musical instruments, canoes, and his living quarters as seen in this 1888 letter (fig. 4.3), an important clue perhaps in our understanding of his eventual decision to use film and sound recording in the field. Given his bias toward the culture rather than the marine biology of the Torres Strait Islands, Haddon's professional interests shifted in the direction of anthropology during the expedition, compelling him to return ten years later to collect more data for a monograph he planned to write.[7]

After much protracted organization, Haddon and his six-member expedition team left England for the Torres Strait in April 1898. Traveling with him were experimental psychologist W. H. R. Rivers and his two students, Charles Myers and William MacDougall; Sydney Ray, a specialist in Melanesian languages; Charles Seligman, a doctor interested in native medicine; and Anthony Wilkin, a King's College (London) undergraduate and trainee field anthropologist, who was recruited to take charge of photography and assist with physical anthropology measurements (fig. 4.4).[8] The expedition was

FIG. 4.2 Sketch of sword mask from 1888 expedition. (Courtesy CMAA)

sponsored by Cambridge University, various scientific societies, the British and Queensland governments, and the private funds of expedition members.[9]

One of the many legacies of Haddon's 1898 Torres Strait Expedition—and one of the least discussed within the history of visual anthropology—was his unprecedented use of cinematography and wax-cylinder sound recording.[10]

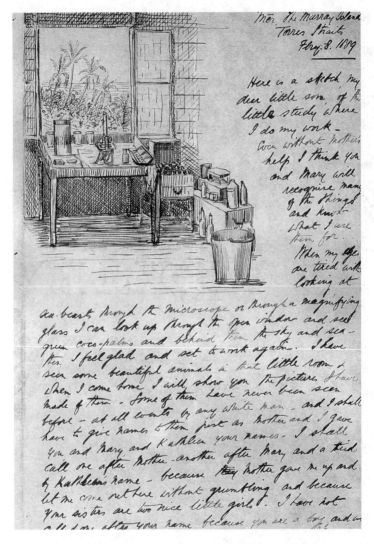

FIG. 4.3 Illustrated letter sent from Haddon to his son Ernest in 1888. (Courtesy CMAA)

W. H. R. Rivers's "genealogical method," a theoretical framework he developed during the expedition for producing information about members of a
local clan from which general social laws could be formulated, had a far greater
impact on anthropological theory than did Haddon's film or phonographic
recordings.[11] While Haddon's enthusiastic endorsement of photography with-

FIG. 4.4 Haddon and the expedition team, 1898. Haddon (*seated*) with (*left to right*) Rivers, Seligman, Ray, and Wilkin. (Courtesy CMAA)

in anthropology might account in part for his decision to use film and sound recording in the field, there is nowhere in Haddon's extant writings any clear rationale for what role cinema might have played in capturing what Jay Ruby calls "visible symbols embedded in gestures, ceremonies, rituals, and artifacts situated in constructed and natural environments."[12] The fact that Haddon put Wilkin in charge of much of the expedition's photography suggests a real commitment to photography as a research tool (why else would Haddon tie up one of the expedition members with such a task?); it may also have freed Haddon to work on other aspects of the research and to devote his energies to the more complex of the two media at the time, the cinematograph.[13]

As a result of delays in shipment of the motion picture film, Haddon didn't start using the cinematograph until September 5, 1898, six months into the seven-month expedition, and his films were shot over a few days on Mer

(Murray) Island in the Eastern Strait. Unfortunately, Haddon's camera sustained damage during transit, which meant that the film often jammed; to make matters worse, the nitrate film deteriorated quickly in the tropical heat of the Islands.[14] Writing to his wife Fanny, Haddon noted somewhat despondently that "I have tried to use [the cinematograph] once or twice and have got some results I hope—but the camera usually jams and I lose a great deal."[15] Reflecting upon his experience of filming a Malu-Bomai ceremony performed by Mer Islanders wearing specially made masks, Haddon had little confidence in either the equipment or his abilities as a filmmaker: "As often happened the machine jams and the film is spoiled. I am afraid that this part of the outfit will prove a failure."[16] But Haddon's fears may have been largely unfounded; Haddon's film processor, J. Guardia, sent Haddon a frame enlargement in June 1899 accompanied by the encouraging news that "there is nothing much to complain of with a machine that produces work of this quality practically on the first trial and under admittedly unfavourable circumstances. We tested all the films, and developed those that promise good results."[17]

Like all anthropologists in the field, Haddon had to negotiate with the Islanders and missionaries to gain access to cultural practices, and he admitted that "even with good intentions and a friendly disposition on the part of the native there were many real difficulties in the way of getting information." In Haddon's case, however, the language barrier was mitigated by the extensive history of missionary activities on the islands, as Haddon explained: "We communicated by means of jargon English, which, owing to the school instruction most of the natives had undergone, was not of so crude a character as is generally the case."[18] The recording of native songs and language was an important part of the expedition; Myers, for example, used the phonograph to record songs (fig. 4.5), ceremonies, and even the sound of Islanders grieving.[19]

The first of the five single-shot films that Haddon made depicts a Malu-Bomai ceremony at Kiam;[20] the second and third films show Mer Islanders performing dances on a beach; the fourth features Mer Islanders demonstrating fire-making; and a fifth film portrays five visiting Australian Aborigines performing what Australian film historians Pat Laughren and Chris Long call the "Shake-A-Leg" dance in the same beach location as the second and third films.[21] The brief single-take Malu-Bomai ceremony film features three

FIG. 4.5 Myers seated with the phonograph, Ulai singing sacred songs, and Gisu beating the sacred drum "Wasikor" during the 1898 expedition. (Courtesy CMAA)

dancers who shift their weight from one leg to the other as they move in a tight circle in front of the camera. As the film begins, the three men stand behind one another (the third slightly off-frame right), slowly shifting their weight from foot to foot in a rocking motion with their arms at their sides and their hands extended at right angles from their bodies. The rhythmic movements intensify as the men lift their legs and shake their entire bodies, and the dancer in the foreground, followed by the other two, turns his body away from the camera in a counterclockwise direction and moves slowly round in a circle until he has resumed his starting position (fig. 4.6). This circular pattern is repeated twice in the 50-second shot.

The second of Haddon's films (seventy seconds long) shows three Mer Islanders, wearing Dari headdresses and *labalabas*, performing a processional dance on a beach. The camera frames the beach and ocean beyond, with palm

FIG. 4.6 Frame enlargement from Haddon's film of Malu-Bomai ceremony at Kiam, 1898. (Courtesy CMAA)

trees frame right and a small canoe behind a wooden fence at the center of the image. The medium long shot begins as the three men slowly enter from frame right and dance in a circular pattern from right to left, rotating their bodies and periodically crouching down on the ground and rhythmically moving their hands (fig. 4.7). The men perform these twirling and crouching movements three times before exiting frame right. According to Laughren and Long, Haddon's camera jammed at this point; when the shot recommences, the dancers are in the same location, although they move in a straight line with different leg movements in the remaining seven seconds of the shot. A slightly different camera setup is used in the third beach film (twenty-one seconds), with the camera positioned to the right and closer to the dancers. Three Mer Islanders enact a similar dance to the first film, although this time they perform in a straight line with knees raised higher than the first dance as they wave their hands from side to side next to their heads.

FIG. 4.7 Frame enlargement from Haddon's film of three Mer Islanders with Dari headdresses and *labalabas*, performing a processional dance on a beach, 1898. (Courtesy CMAA)

FIG. 4.8 Frame enlargement from Haddon's film of Pasi, Sergeant, and Mana demonstrating drill method of fire-making, 1898. (Courtesy CMAA)

Haddon's fourth film was shot in a forest opening with shadows of trees spilling into the righthand side of the frame. Three Mer Islanders, Pasi, Sergeant, and Mana, are shown in medium long shot sitting cross-legged on the grass demonstrating the drill method of fire-making, which involves twirling a stick between their palms on top of a wooden block (fig. 4.8). The 30-second film of the fire-making is the only one in which a performer reacts to the presence of the camera, when the man seated frame left looks repeatedly in its direction. The three men are centered in the frame, and while most of the action is performed by the man on the right, who takes charge of rubbing the fire stick, our attention is also directed toward the aesthetic qualities of the composition, especially the texture of the grassy clearing, mottled effect of the shadows, and the symmetrical arrangement of the Islanders in a triangular formation.[22]

The beach location from Haddon's second and third films is the setting for his fifth film (seventy seconds), which features a dance by five visiting Australian Aborigines; one of the five men beats out a rhythm by hitting a long pole with a stick while the other four dancers shift their weight from leg to leg and clap their hands. Following a jump cut, the same four men perform the "Shake-A-Leg" dance, standing with their legs apart and wobbling their knees and thighs. After a second jump cut the dancers clap their hands in a similar fashion to that seen in the opening.

Of the five films that Haddon shot, the one we know the most about in terms of what may have motivated Haddon to film is the Malu-Bomai ceremony, which had fascinated Haddon since his first trip to the Strait in 1888 and which he had photographed extensively. While Haddon had learned about Meriam initiation rites during the 1888 expedition, he had to wait until the second trip to collect more data on the Mer cult and persuade two Mer Islanders, Wano and Enocha, to reconstruct the Malu-Bomai ceremony for the motion picture camera. Making models of the elaborate masks[23] worn during the ceremony out of cardboard used for packing supplies was a symbolically charged act for the Islanders, since these reenactments rekindled ritual beliefs and practices that had been suppressed through missionary activities and the Islanders' conversion to Christianity some thirty years before Haddon's arrival (fig. 4.9). The intercultural negotiations involved in preparing for the ceremony, which would include sound as well as film recording, were complex to say the least;

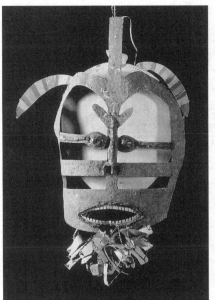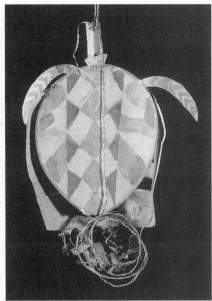

FIG. 4.9 Front and back of Malu-Bomai mask worn by dancer in Haddon's film (1898), now in the collection of the Cambridge Museum of Archaeology and Anthropology, Cambridge, England. (Courtesy CMAA)

Myers noted in his journal six weeks before the dance was filmed that Haddon had been trying to persuade the older Islanders to arrange a performance of the "now obsolete ceremonies and dances of Malu" and that one of the men admitted to Myers that he was afraid to perform the ceremony for fear that he might lose his position in the church. "With great difficulty" Myers was able to record a few Malu songs on his phonograph.[24] Wano and Enocha wanted to donate the ten shillings Haddon had paid them for their mask-making labor to the annual missionary meeting, although, somewhat ironically, they ended up concealing the masks from church officials when they brought them to show Haddon at the weekly prayer meeting.[25] Traditional Islander beliefs, Christian faith, and salvage ethnography all collided around the Malu-Bomai ceremony, a fact not lost on Haddon who, according to anthropologist-curator Anita Herle, was "acutely aware of the contrast between traditional Island Custom and the realities of Islander life, which was strongly influenced by traders, colonialists, and missionaries."[26]

Haddon's decision to film the Malu ceremony also raises important questions about how visually rendered ethnographic information was discursively constructed at the time. Did the film of the ceremony invite a very different way of "seeing" cultural difference that had more in common with popularized representations of native peoples? Did it, in fact, influence Haddon's construction of the event for the general readership of his 1901 book *Head-Hunters: Black, White and Brown*? Elizabeth Edwards, for example, sees a tension playing out in the contrast between Haddon's suppression of the lyricism and exoticism of the Malu-Bomai film in his description of the ceremony in his expedition reports intended for a professional readership[27] (the six-volume *Reports of the Cambridge Anthropological Expedition to the Torres Straits*, published between 1901 and 1935)[28] and the evocative description of the same dance in *Head-Hunters*:

> The grotesque masks worn by ruddled men, girt with leafy kilts, had a strange effect as they emerged from the jungle and very weird was the dance in the mottled shade of the tropical foliage, a fantasy in red and green, lit up by spots of sunshine. . . . [The mask was] covered with a ruddled turtle-shell . . . representing a human face, which had a beard of human jaw-bones; above the face were leaves and feathers, and hanging from it behind was a painted carapace of a turtle, the latter was supported by a long string by the second Zogole. The third Zogole bore a turtle-shell mask representing a hammer-headed shark, on which was a human face; it was provided with human arms and hands, and decorated with leaves, feathers, and turtle-shell figures of birds, frogs, and centipedes.[29]

Knowledge is thus evoked quite differently in the *Reports* version of the dance than in *Head-Hunters* (one cannot imagine for a minute that Haddon would have referred to the dance as "a fantasy in red and green" for scientific readers of the *Reports*); this contrast, Herle argues, "reveals a different way of looking and understanding [and] highlights the difficulty in translating revelatory experience into academic text as well as Haddon's attempt to engage different audiences at a time when field-based anthropology was attempting to position itself."[30]

Haddon's staged fragments of Islander dances and industries exist as much as aestheticized versions of the salvage ethnography paradigm, with its "vanishing race" ideology and melancholic "structure of feeling," as they do scientific articulations of ethnographic information about native communities.[31] As staged reenactments, the dances and ceremonies transport the intended viewer back into the mythic past of Islander ceremonies, or rather, as Edwards puts it, "transports the mythic past to the present through performance."[32] It is tempting to see, then, in Haddon's cinematically inspired re-creation of the Malu ceremony for the *Head-Hunters* reader an alignment of visuality itself with the senses and the emotions rather than the rationalist rhetoric of the expedition's *Reports*. So where Haddon's *Head-Hunters* description of the Malu-Bomai ceremony attempts to evoke the phantasmatic excesses of the original ceremony, and capture something of the visceral and tactile quality of the dance, which could only be hinted at in the photographs, his dispassionate *Reports* entry more closely parallels the discursive tenor of his still photographs of the same event. Moreover, Haddon's cinematic study of the Malu-Bomai ceremony provides a compelling sense of "being there" among the Islanders, a feeling of copresence at an event which is absent in photographs of the same scene (see fig. 4.6 of Malu-Bomai). One is also struck by the way the film negotiates several different and potentially contradictory modalities: the theatricality of the performance, intimations of the subjectivities of the Islanders, and the putative certitude of scientific knowledge. Edwards argues that the tension between the conditions of possibility for *scientific* knowledge and the conditions of possibility for the *subjective* experience of a native community is "enhanced by the nature of [film] and photography, the realism of which heightens and makes theatrical, yet paradoxically allows the impression of authenticity of experience through mimetic scientific devices."[33] But where Edwards does not differentiate between photography and film's mimetic potency as tools of ethnographic reconstruction, cinema, with its heightened verisimilitude and kineticism, raises prescient questions about the readability of cinematic and photographic sign-systems as anthropological knowledge.

As the disparity between the description of the Malu-Bomai ceremonies in *Head-Hunters* versus that in the *Reports* reveals, at the same time cinema offered a solution to the problem of ethnographic representation, its mimeticism created a new set of issues that had less to do with methodology and scientific accuracy than with how the visceral qualities of the film image could be reconciled with principles of ethnography. It was cinema's ability to render the ethnographic body with such fidelity, ocular pleasure, and tactility that perhaps presented one of the greatest challenges to anthropologists; film, with its inalienable lifelike qualities, may have posed troubling questions to the privileging of sight as the paroxysm of anthropological knowledge. But what was it exactly about film that touched a nerve?

Looking at Haddon's film of the Malu-Bomai ceremony, one is struck by the tactile quality of the cinematic image, the way in which the flat spatial composition and surface textures of the image seem to drift out toward the spectator not just visually but through a simulated sense of touch. This sense of tactile closeness to the cinematic image has been identified with so-called haptic or haptical cinema, defined as "relating to or based on the sense of touch."[34] While Noël Burch is credited as among the first to theorize the idea of haptic space in relation to early cinema, his conceptualization of haptic space as a phenomenon that "grows from the increased use of varied shadow and the idea of an invitation into believable room, into boundless space" is somewhat confused, as Antonia Lant has shown.[35] Notwithstanding the blind spots in Burch's argument, his contribution to an *idea* of haptic cinema has opened up possibilities for critical engagement with what is undoubtedly a slippery and controversial concept. In different terms, and long before Burch wrote about haptical cinema, Frances Hubbard Flaherty—wife, photographer, and cinematic collaborator of documentary filmmaker Robert Flaherty—characterized the viewing encounter between ethnographic subject and film spectator in a manner evocative of haptic cinema. Flaherty describes an ethnographic film of a potter as a quasi-spiritual conjoining of the cinematic spectator with the on-screen performer, a coming together of the virtual body of the performer with the real body of the viewer: "The motion picture camera can follow . . . movements closely, intimately, so intimately, that as with our eyes we follow, we come to feel those movements as a sensation in ourselves. Momentarily we touch and know the very heart and mind of the [performer]; we partake, as it were, of his life, we are one with him."[36] Laura U. Marks has also argued that there is a more "dynamic subjectivity between looker and image" in haptic visuality than in optical visuality because, in the former, the spectator's eyes are akin to organs of touch and seem to reach out and "feel" the image through a form of "embodied perception."[37]

The axial movements of the Malu-Bomai dancers in the lush forest setting and the jerky rhythm of the circular dance has a somewhat mesmerizing effect as the dancers are seemingly brought to life by the twitching of their lower bodies at the start of the film; while the three dancers stand one behind the other, for a split second our eyes seem to trick us into thinking that the lead dancer has magically replicated himself as the two other dancers step out from behind his body. The chiaroscuro effect of the forest light gently caressing the masked bodies of the dancers in their circular movements seems to render them at once two-dimensional *and* three-dimensional; indeed, the dancers seem to oscillate between their ontological status as two-dimensional figures merging with the background (their costuming adds to this effect) and bodies that penetrate space in front of the spectator, thus creating a tension between foreground and background. Could it be that early cinema's predilection for offering the spectator a sensorially rich ethnographic experience (richer, one could argue, than even the still photograph) threatened to turn ethnographic knowledge into something that defied scientific logic, since it was more closely affiliated with the senses than the intellect? In any event, early cinema, with its kineticism and tactility may have threatened the certainty of ethnographic knowledge at a time when theories of kinship and language — theories that were inherently resistant to visual representation — were displacing the pursuit of the visual correlates of racial hierarchies in turn-of-the-century anthropology.

In this regard, Haddon's films display little of the obsessive care with which French physician Félix-Louis Regnault arranged the profilmic and filmic elements of his 1895 comparative physiological studies of the native body, including background, blocking, and shot scale.[38] Distinct from Regnault's goal of the rigorous scientific recording of a taxonomy of human movement, Haddon's filmmaking seemed motivated more by a romantic longing to preserve Islander culture than a need to categorize people on the basis of human typology. Haddon's staged fragments of native ceremonies and industries thus exist as much as contextualized anthropological "views," by dint of their location shooting and what Tom Gunning calls a "cinema-of-attractions" mode of address in which the act of display is explicitly foregrounded, than as physiological studies of Torres Strait Islanders and Australian Aborigines.[39] However, if Regnault's and Haddon's respective interests in motion photography and cinematography were driven by their own specific research agendas (we mustn't forget that Regnault's background was as a physician), they both nevertheless saw in motion picture technology a *demonstrative* function which, Edwards argues, was akin to the visual thinking and planning taking place in the natural sciences. Like Regnault's chronophotographs, Haddon's films and photographs were undertaken primarily to verify the scientific evidence gathered firsthand on the Torres Strait Islands. As Edwards explains: "The development of central photographic strategies was not intended as mere illustration, but as an integral part of the presentation, proof and transmission of evidence."[40] But anthropological images are never produced in a social vacuum; in considering how a corpus of photographs or films materializes in ethnographic expeditions, we must also disentangle the intricate web of social relations which always enmesh image-making. This is often easier said than done, although in cases where fieldwork diaries and other records are extant, it *is* possible to identify the kinds of social meanings attached to photography.

Surviving fieldwork diaries and other contemporaneous evidence suggest that photography was already familiar to Torres Strait Islanders and formed the basis for complex interpersonal relations between Islanders and European scientists; as Edwards points out, "the display, projection through magic lantern shows, exchange and gift of photographic images played a central role in the Expedition's social relations with the Torres Strait Islanders."[41] Furthermore, as Edwards notes, Haddon anticipated photography's potential as a vehicle for social interaction by bringing along two magic lantern projectors and a collection of lantern slides of both general-interest subjects and of Islanders from the 1888 expedition on his follow-up expedition.[42] Haddon would routinely give prints to Islanders he had worked with, and once word got out that free photos could be obtained, Islanders crowded Haddon's verandah asking for "pikkis." In one journal entry, Myers recalled how he would pretend to take photographs of entire families dressed up in their Sunday best "after posing them with much care and amusement. Flash calico is always worn on these occasions and is frequently lent from one man to another."[43] There is even some evidence of native reaction to the publication of photographic illustrations in *Head-Hunters*, a rare glimpse of native subjectivity considering the period in which Haddon was working. Writing to Haddon some four years after the expedition, Mer Island teacher and expedition informant J. S. Bruce reported that

The Murray people were very pleased with the illustrations. Debe Uale and Jimmy Rice looked long and earnestly at their photos. . . . But you should see Ulai and Uano wading carefully through it. Uamo rose 100% in my estimation. He is never tired of having a look and telling me that "he made that" i.e. the Bomai [mask]. . . . Pasi was the man that I expected of all men to take an interest in it, but I cannot say he did nor old Harry.[44]

Other issues are more difficult to resolve by recourse to surviving evidence of exchanges between Europeans and Islanders, including the question of Haddon's own attitudes toward and use of his Torres Strait films. As a result of the technical problems Haddon encountered with the motion picture camera, he did not attempt to shoot any film for the remainder of the expedition and wrote his wife Fanny informing her that unless Newman and Guardia had already sent films to Borneo (the next leg of the expedition), then they need not bother.[45] Haddon's exasperation at trying to get the camera to work on Mer Island no doubt changed his mind about shooting film on Borneo. Additionally, Haddon never wrote about the ethnographic significance of his films and, as far as we can ascertain, exhibited them on no more than a handful of occasions, which may say something about their marginal status as ethnographic evidence within the corpus of materials brought back from the Torres Strait. Whatever Haddon's reasons for not promoting, exhibiting, or discussing his films upon his return — it is difficult to say with certainty why he was never given more credit for his films or why he didn't trumpet their groundbreaking status upon returning to England — there's no doubt that his first impressions of filmmaking were distinctly negative. But Haddon's inability to feel fully in control of the cinematic apparatus may have been only partly to blame for his subsequent disinclination to use film; lacking intertitles and entirely dependent on expert contextualization in order to be made legible to both scientific and lay audiences, Haddon was left with the question of what exactly *could* be done with his films in the absence of an intellectual framework for ethnographic film. Given that the films were less amenable to scientific explication than the photographs Haddon had taken — he used photographs for note-taking as well as illustrative purposes and stylistically altered them to underscore their ethnographic detail — all Haddon could really do was exhibit them on special occasions when he could be present to talk about them.

In this context it is useful to consider the role played by movement in determining the quality, utility, and legitimacy of the ethnographic knowledge obtained by the motion picture camera as opposed to those features captured by the photograph. In other words, how do Haddon's films encode ethnographic knowledge differently from his photographs? As stated earlier, Haddon had photographed the Malu-Bomai dance during his first expedition to the Torres Strait and had even depicted the climax of the Malu ceremony in a watercolor showing the three performers wearing masks and performing before a large seated audience (fig. 4.10). Notwithstanding their enormous significance as emblems of cultural life no longer practiced by the Islanders, Haddon also probably selected the Malu-Bomai dance, beach dances, and fire-making on the basis of how well these scenes had previously photographed or been rendered in visual terms, a standard practice for aspiring motion picture camera operators. One of the key factors governing the mode of representation employed by early filmmakers was current practice in photography; as Burch has pointed out, the innumerable street scenes shot by the Lumières emulated professional norms popularized by the picture postcard.[46] Haddon's choice of subject matter may, therefore, have been guided by three factors: his judgment of their ethnographic significance; their prior representation as photographs; and how well they embodied the medium's capacity for representing motion. Some of the photographic images published in Haddon's six-volume account of the expedition (which range from seemingly unstaged dances framed in low-angle setups to tightly controlled anthropometric images in which an Islander is photographed in frontal and profile close-ups against a white background) suggest some of the possible ways in which film may have been deployed to gather data. Indeed, Haddon's talent as an artist and his background in biology (with its own visual biases and emphasis on illustration) may help account for his general interest in photography and cinema.[47] Haddon was also a decided fan of diorama life groups, recalling once that he had gained "more pleasure and instruction" from seeing life groups at the 1851 Crystal Palace Exposition than from anything else. In a discussion of the pros and cons of life groups in 1908, Haddon felt that he owed a "very great debt of gratitude to the Crystal Palace authorities for having these lifelike imitations of people in their surroundings."[48]

While Haddon may have been thinking about the ethnographic potential of cinema, about how film could be used as a research document or how images

FIG. 4.10 Watercolor of the Malu-Bomai ceremony drawn by Haddon, 1898. (Courtesy CMAA)

of native peoples moving through space could generate usable ethnographic data, these intellectual concerns were subordinated to the more urgent challenge of simply getting the camera to work. There is no doubt that Haddon saw the value of compiling as much empirical data as possible on Torres Strait Islander life; during his first trip to the Torres Strait he had talked about the "importance to science of the recording of all customs and beliefs of the natives." It is probably with this in mind that he undertook his filmmaking. While Haddon did not discuss his reasons for using cinema as part of his fieldwork or ruminate on the medium's potential as an ethnographic tool, he did refer to the motion picture camera as "an indispensable piece of anthropological apparatus" in a letter to Baldwin Spencer and suggested that Spencer try to sell his own films to a commercial motion picture company: "I have no doubt your films will pay for the whole apparatus if you care to let them be copied by the trade," he wrote.[49] While we have no evidence that Haddon ever made his films available to a nonscientific audience, the fact that he urged the possibility upon Spencer suggests a pragmatic approach to ethnographic filmmaking as well as an awareness of public demand for images of the Other.

The only records I have come across of Haddon ever publicly exhibiting his films are from 1900 and 1905: in 1900 he showed them during a talk given before the Royal Geographical Society, and in 1905 he screened them as part of a lecture series at Cambridge University's Pathological Laboratory and at the Anthropological Institute in London (Haddon had been appointed Lecturer in Ethnology at Cambridge University in 1900).[50] The Cambridge lecture was mentioned in Leonard Donaldson's *The Cinematograph and the Natural Sciences* (1912), one of the first books to explore the relationship between cinema and science. Describing the event as a "very successful and vivid representation of a certain type of savagery," Donaldson made a case for the inclusion of the cinematograph in all anthropological expeditions, as it could provide "concrete proof of an explorer's achievements."[51] Putting together lantern slides, films, and sound recordings into an evening's lecture on the expedition (even attempting sync-sound with the films and phonograph recordings of the Malu-Bomai ceremonies), Haddon anticipated what would become technically possible through digital technologies a century later. A report on the Anthropological Institute lecture from the *Daily Telegraph* (London) declared that "this [was] the first occasion on which the cinematograph [had] been employed for the purpose of anthropological research," although it is noteworthy that Haddon apparently waited five years before exhibiting his films before the scientific community again.[52] In this regard, Haddon may have followed the example of Spencer, who began making plans to tour with his films and slides before leaving the field in 1901. What is clear is that Haddon played a pivotal role in Spencer's decision to film the Arrernte, and that Spencer sought advice from Haddon on a range of issues including which camera to use and how much film to take.

The Kinematograph in the Field:
The Ethnographic Filmmaking of Walter Baldwin Spencer

Like Haddon, Spencer's ethnography evolved from his zoological research. Following two years of medical training at Owens College in Manchester, Spencer entered Exeter College Oxford to study natural science on a four-year scholarship. In 1886, at the age of twenty-seven, he was appointed to the newly established professorship in biology at the University of Melbourne, where he found himself too preoccupied teaching natural sciences and campaigning for better academic facilities to be able to conduct substantial scientific research. Spencer's introduction to ethnographic fieldwork came with his participation in the 1894 Horn Expedition to Central Australia, although his research was largely limited to zoology, as E. C. Stirling, director of the South Australian Museum and lecturer in physiology at the University of Adelaide, took responsibility for the expedition's anthropological work.[53]

It was during this expedition that Spencer met Frank Gillen, who was to become his friend and longtime collaborator. As stationmaster of the transcontinental telegraph station at Alice Springs and "sub-protector" of the local Australian Aborigines, Gillen had a good working relationship with members of the Arrernte tribe and over the years had been an avid collector of ethnographic miscellany (twenty-five pages of Gillen's research on the manners and customs of the Arrernte were published in the report of the Horn expedition).[54] In November 1896, Gillen arranged for the Engwura ceremony to be held in Alice Springs during Spencer's summer vacation; the infrequently held ceremony attracted Australian Aborigines from great distances, and Spencer was introduced to the tribe as Gillen's *wetecja*, or younger brother.[55]

According to Stocking, Spencer and Gillen's three-month stay at or near the Arrernte camp represented an unprecedented ethnographic opportunity to witness and photograph Australian Aboriginal customs; using pidgin English, they were able to question the Arrernte who visited their shelter to chat in-between dances (fig. 4.11). However, Spencer's biographers D. J. Mulvaney and J. H. Calaby argue that Spencer's and Gillen's ability to interpret the belief systems of the Engwura cycle of ceremonies was limited owing to a number of factors, including the compromises and adaptations introduced as a result of the participation of so many Aboriginal groups in the Engwura; the anthropologists' overreliance on young tribal men as interpreters; and the linguistic barriers which meant that they "never knew what was coming next, and were obliged to be constantly on the watch."[56] In spite of—or perhaps in response to—these cross-cultural barriers, Spencer and Gillen devoted a great deal of time to photographing the Engwura ceremonies.[57] Gillen had been a keen amateur photographer before he met Spencer and took advantage of the expe-

FIG. 4.11 Spencer seated with a group of old Arrernte men who acted as leaders during the Engwura ceremony, Alice Springs, 1896. (Courtesy Museum Victoria, Australia [hereafter, MVA])

rience gained during the Horn expedition to improve his technical skills and concentrate on ethnographic subjects.[58] It was not until 1901, however, when Spencer and Gillen managed to fund an expedition across Australia from south to north, that a moving picture camera was enlisted to record ethnographic data.[59]

Spencer and Gillen's yearlong expedition to Central Australia covered a distance of 1,600 miles, mainly through desert terrain on camel-back.[60] Mounted Trooper Harry Chance was employed as driver, cook, and handyman for the fee of ten shillings a day, and two Charlotte Waters Aborigines, Purunda and Erlikiliaka, expert at handling the twenty horses used during the expedition, were also recruited (fig. 4.12).[61] Spencer and Gillen took along an Edison concert phonograph using 5-inch diameter wax cylinders to make sound recordings, and a Warwick Bioscope camera bought from Charles Urban's Warwick Trading Co. in London to shoot moving pictures.[62] Spencer's decision to

FIG. 4.12 The 1901 expedition gathered outside Frank Gillen's house, Alice Springs. *From left to right:* Purunda, Gillen, Chance, Spencer, Erlikiliaka. (Courtesy MVA)

include film and sound recording in his expedition seems to have been inspired, at least in part, by Haddon's enthusiastic endorsement of the cinematic equipment. Writing Spencer from Dublin, Haddon declared:

> You really *must* take a Kinematograph or a biograph or whatever they call it in your part of the world. Get an ordinary commercial one. If you order from London . . . I would place myself in the hands of the Warwick Trading Company. . . . I have asked them to send you a catalogue. I have stated what you want it for.[63]

Haddon also suggested that Spencer take a phonograph with him, and he offered Spencer a number of practical tips on the use of wax cylinders of maximum diameter to optimize tone, the effects of humidity, and the problem of "getting your natives to sing loud enough."[64] Spencer was skeptical about obtaining usable phonograph recordings, fearful that the Arrernte would be "awfully frightened of it and imagine that we are carrying their voices away with us."[65] Gillen was less optimistic about using the film camera than the phonograph, expressing concerns about the effects of the heat on the apparatus: "I am not happy about the Cinematograf [*sic*], will they stand the heat you think?"[66] Gillen also worried about Spencer's lack of technical expertise, asking Spencer in a letter: "Have you had any experience working the machine and if not, where are you going to gain it?"[67] The first phonograph recordings were made at Stevenson Creek, six hundred miles north of Adelaide, on March 22, when Gillen, after persuading a number of Arrernte tribe members to sing Corroboree songs and recite indigenous place names into the phonograph, played the recordings back for the performers. Arthur Cantrill notes that Spencer deviated from the usual practice of having selected singers perform close to the recording horn and instead decided to have the horn cover the entire group, a choice that resulted in a more authentic effect even if the sound quality was inferior.[68]

Spencer first used the moving picture camera to film a sacred Rain Ceremony known as *Kurnara* in the tribal settlement Charlotte Waters. In fact, Charlotte Waters and Alice Springs were the only film locations used, as Spencer feared the heat and rigors of transportation would damage the camera and film stock.[69] Spencer's inexperience as a camera operator and the unpredictable nature of the Rain Ceremony performance led to a considerable amount of guesswork and improvisation on Spencer's part, as he recalled in his 1912 account of the expedition: "It is not a very easy matter to use [the cinematograph] amongst savages. As they move about, you never know exactly where they will be, and you are liable to go on grinding away at the handle, turning the film through at the rate of perhaps fifty feet per minute, and securing nothing."[70] Spencer elaborated on these early filmmaking challenges in his 1928 book *Wanderings in Wild Australia*:

> We had no idea what the rain ceremony was going to be like, so that all
> I could do was to stand the machine on one side of the ceremonial ground,
> which was simply an open space in the scrub, focus for about the centre of

it and hope for the best. The lens allowed for a fair depth of focus, but the field of action covered by the natives was large and I had *not*, as in more recent machines, a handle to turn [in order to pan the camera], making it possible to follow up the actors as they moved about very much from side to side of the ceremonial ground. . . . The chief difficulty was that the performers every now and then ran off the ground into the surrounding scrub, returning at uncertain intervals of time, so that now and again, in the expectation of their sudden reappearing, and fearful of missing anything of importance, I ground on and on, securing a record of a good deal of monotonous scenery but very little ceremony.[71]

As Spencer recalled, in spite of his considerable photographic experience, he was a complete novice at operating a moving picture camera and had only the manufacturer's cursory instructions to guide him in the field:

A diagram showed how to fix the film in the machine, so as to make it run round, but no instructions had been sent as to what rate to turn the handle, so I had to make a guess at this. The focusing glass was, of necessity, small and you could only get a sideways and not distinct view of it, but after a little practice with a blank spool, I felt equal to a first attempt in real life.[72]

After Spencer familiarized himself with the workings of the camera, he still had to contend with the intense desert heat and aridity which shrunk the wooden camera casing and allowed dust to settle on the mechanism and unexposed film. Spencer complained that the dust "seem[ed] to be able to penetrate everything, even the specially made shutters and slides of the cameras" and frustrated his frequent lubrication of the camera's mechanism with Vaseline. The heat and dust also affected the photographic plates, resulting in fogged images; Spencer, in an effort to light-proof his camera, stuffed the instrument's cracks with "black worsted and porcupine-grass resins."[73] Despite these environmental handicaps, Spencer proudly declared the films as "the first attempt ever to obtain moving representations of the ceremonies and dances of Australian aborigines."[74]

Spencer shot thirteen brief films of various Arrernte ceremonies during the

FIG. 4.13 Preparation for Tjitjingalla ceremony photographed by Spencer, 1901. (Courtesy MVA)

expedition, recalling later that "some of the negatives were quite good [while] others indifferent."[75] He devoted the greatest attention to his third subject, the Tjitjingalla ceremony, an event he had first witnessed in 1896. Spencer represented the ceremony in eight shots: two of its preparations, five of the ceremony, and one of the Arrernte men discussing the event.[76] Striking in these preparation shots is the relaxed demeanor of the men, who seem oblivious to the presence of Spencer or the camera; some have their backs to the camera and at no point turn around to see what Spencer is doing (fig. 4.13). The men's disposition may indicate their familiarity with the anthropologist's recording devices, as they had already been extensively photographed by Spencer and had even heard their recorded voices played back on the phonograph.

The Tjitjingalla ceremony depicted in Spencer's films involves a small group of men seated to the right of a wurley (a small bush structure) while a group of six men carrying wooden staves and wearing elaborate cone-shaped head-dresses and white body paint dances in the space to the seated group's left (fig.

FIG. 4.14 Tjitjingalla Corroboree showing wurley structure photographed by Spencer, 1901. (Courtesy MVA)

4.14). During the dance the performers intermittently enter the center of the frame from the left and move around in a clockwise direction in alternating small and large circular sweeps before exiting frame left. In Spencer's words, "the dancing itself was of a very simple nature," since the men moved in a line, wheeling backwards and forwards toward the seated internal audience, always with a "very characteristic prancing and high knee-action."[77] Spencer's reference to the performers retiring into the darkness away from the light of campfires suggests that the ceremony, which usually took place at night, was staged during daylight for the benefit of the motion picture camera.

As Arthur Cantrill notes, the camera setups in Spencer's five shots of the Tjitjingalla ceremony are relatively diverse, ranging from an opening long shot of the group, to a medium shot in which the camera is moved to the right by approximately 45 degrees, and to a reverse angle of the ceremony. For the fourth shot, the camera was returned to the same position used in the second shot and moved slightly to the left in the final shot, which at 2 minutes and 22 seconds is the longest in the series.[78] According to Cantrill, Spencer's decision to provide multiple viewpoints of the ceremony through the changing camera setups is an early example of editing in the camera and may have been a logical extension of his photographic work and scientific drawings where an event was often recorded from more than one perspective.[79] Indeed, Spencer's deviation from the single-camera setup characteristic of most early actuality films may have been his response to the challenge of producing an accurate visualization of the ceremony.

The difficulty of gaining access to the full cultural significance of rituals like the Tjitjingalla ceremony was discussed by Spencer in *Across Australia*, his popular account of the expedition:

The only thing which we could find out about the Tjitjingalla was that the last scene was supposed to represent the actions of a party of men who were anxious to persuade one special man celebrated for his wisdom and strength, to join them [fig. 4.15]. The bush wurley was supposed to belong to him, and the idea was that they had got between the old man and his camp while he was away out in the bush and that when he came back again they tried to prevent him from going into his wurley, and finally succeeded in persuading him to join them and to place himself at their head. This, however, may be nothing more than a meaning now attached by the Arrernte to a performance which was originally intended to represent something quite different.[80]

Spencer's admitted difficulties in deciphering the historical and cultural significance of indigenous ceremonies has implications for considerations of the kinds of knowledge privileged by visual, as opposed to lexical, forms of ethnographic inscription. One possible danger was that the visual record of an event would come to stand alone as evidence of native ceremonial life in the absence of accurate and detailed contextual information on the genealogy of a ceremony and its cultural meaning(s) for tribal members. The implicit problem was that a few photographed and filmed images of a cultural group,

FIG. 4.15 Final dance in Tjitjingalla Corroboree photographed by Spencer, 1901. (Courtesy MVA)

through their repetition and lack of context, would assume a metonymical relationship to the culture as a whole, analogous to the logic at work in typological photographs of native peoples. Certain cultural events become conventionalized as essentialized icons so that representations that fall outside the parameters of the already known are seldom made publicly available. Haddon encountered the same problem as Spencer during his first trip to the Torres Strait in 1888; describing his findings in the *Journal of the Anthropological Institute*, Haddon noted that anthropologists studying familiar as well as exotic cultures came up against similar interpretive stumbling blocks: "Even among ourselves there are comparatively few educated people who can give a trustworthy account of sights they have seen long ago, or who can repeat fairy stories correctly, or give an intelligible and logical account of their religious beliefs and of their sacred legends."[81]

Spencer filmed several other Arrernte ceremonies during his 1901 expedition, including the Unnirringita (grub) Ceremony, the Snake Ceremony, the Eagle-Hawk Ceremony, the Sun Ceremony, and a Women's Dance. The recording of the last ritual consists of a long shot of thirteen women standing in a straight line facing the camera in ceremonial costume and white body paint. Three Arrernte men are seated in profile in the left foreground. The women hold wooden staves throughout the dance which they tap against their upper thighs while shifting their weight from leg to leg as they gradually advance toward the camera. The film ends as two women standing at the left end of the line break away from the others and move offscreen. From his own account, Spencer was less than overwhelmed by this dance, describing it as "a very tame affair, in which the women stood in a row and swayed themselves about."[82] However, this is one of the few dances Spencer filmed that involved women, and he must have been cognizant of the secretive nature of many women's ceremonies from which Arrernte men (other than musicians) were barred. The midground presence of internal male spectators who occasionally glance in the camera's direction, along with the camera's distance from the women, creates a tension within the profilmic space, suggesting that Spencer and Gillen had to physically and metaphorically keep their distance from women's ceremonies, even when under the watchful eye of three Arrernte elders.

The challenges of filming such often-spontaneous performances included Spencer's inability to follow moving subjects with a fixed camera that had no panning or tilting facilities, although, as Cantrill argues, Spencer's cinematography, particularly his grasp of composition in deep space, improved dramatically between April 3 and May 11, when he completed his filming at Charlotte Waters.[83] It is impossible to gauge the extent to which Spencer was able to direct the staging of the dances and ceremonies he filmed (recommending a suitable time of day or location, for example), although as he became more experienced as a camera operator, he seems to have made a number of calculations about the suitability of certain ceremonies and rituals for sound recording and filming. It was not unusual for Gillen and Spencer to receive last-minute notice of an impending performance to which they had to rush, laden down with the cinematograph and photographic apparatuses. Moreover, on at least one occasion, there is a suggestion that the Arrernte performers did not follow directions they had been given for keeping the action of the ceremony within the frame; as Gillen recalled:

In the afternoon we went up to the Creek to witness a sacred ceremony of the Echunpa or big lizard totem but the confounded performers, two in number, instead of performing within the field covered by the Bioscope made a wide semicircular sweep which took them out of the field and practically wasted a film. I used language, Spencer smiled grimly, and in provokingly calm tones said philosophically "it's no use getting excited."[84]

Besides reflecting the logistical difficulties of using the phonograph and cinematograph in areas north of Charlotte Waters and Alice Springs, Spencer and Gillen's decision to restrict their filming and sound recording to these locations may have been due to their familiarity with the Arrernte living in the vicinity of these telegraph stations. As Spencer pointed out, the phonograph and cinematograph were only used "amongst natives to whom we were well known."[85] The comment suggests that Spencer felt comfortable using the camera and phonograph only with members of the Arrernte with whom he had a previous relationship (and with whom he could communicate through a translator). Spencer's remarks also allude to the delicate power relations operating in anthropological fieldwork and the kinds of pressures placed upon anthropologists using conspicuous and technically-demanding contrivances such as the cinematograph and phonograph. The ceremonies and rituals anthropologists filmed were very often one-off events, which meant that Spencer had no means of rerecording a ceremony or ritual unless it was restaged for the benefit of the camera. Spencer therefore relied a great deal on Arrernte elders for detailed exegeses of the structure, sequence, and meaning of cultural rituals (fig. 4.16).

In locations where Spencer and Gillen were completely unknown to members of Australian Aboriginal communities, the challenge of interpreting the ethnographic data—what Spencer described as getting at "the 'why' of things," the "essential" or "fundamental idea" behind a performance—seemed to outweigh the allure of recording unfamiliar events. The moving picture camera could communicate cultural knowledge only to an initiate capable of decoding the significance of an event, although even on these occasions anthropologists still struggled to get at "the idea which [was] present in the native mind," because, as Spencer pointed out, on certain occasions the native himself or herself could "offer no explanation."[86]

FIG. 4.16 Spencer, Gillen, and Arrernte informants at Alice Springs, 1896. (Courtesy MVA)

Constrained by the 3-minute rolls of film[87] and lack of a panning device,
Spencer attempted to edit in the camera when filming complex ceremonies, a
skill he finessed once he became familiar with the general outline of a ritual
and could confidently omit sequences he felt were either repetitious or
insignificant. In so doing, Spencer made aesthetic as well as anthropologically informed decisions about which parts of a ceremony to film and which to
omit because, in his words, they were "monotonous" (a term he frequently
used to describe Arrernte corroborees). To avoid the "blur on the screen"
which Spencer believed would occur each time he stopped and restarted the
camera (Cantrill notes there is in fact no blur, merely one or two overexposed
frames), in his later films Spencer made a continuous recording of only the last
three minutes of a ceremony, a practice that suggests he explicitly anticipated
which parts of the ceremony to exclude and which to record.[88]

After Spencer and Gillen had completed their sound and moving picture recordings on May 20, they concentrated on glass-plate photography using a Goerz-Anschutz quarter-plate hand camera and a half-plate camera fitted with the same manufacturer's lens and focal plane shutter, modified to resist heat and hard use. According to Mulvaney and Calaby, Spencer was a skilled still photographer and set up improvised darkrooms in telegraph station houses at each major stopover where he developed, enlarged, and printed his photographs under extremely taxing conditions. Before leaving Alice Springs, Spencer and Gillen had taken 243 photographs, a number that increased to 500 photographs by the end of the expedition. In addition to the ceremonies, Spencer photographed examples of material culture such as fire-making, "typological studies," and more informal shots of the Arrernte (fig. 4.17).

Despite Spencer's claim that all his photographs were "first hand—nothing prepared, and no posing. Most . . . were snapshots with a hand camera, for it was a matter of 'press the button' when the chance occurs," the numerous anthropometric photographs Spencer took have more in common with the highly interventionist techniques prescribed in *Notes and Queries* for conducting comparative physiological analyses than candid fieldwork images.[89] The less appealing aspects of such anthropometric procedures (for both measured and measurer) were suggested by Gillen's diary entry for September 10: "Spencer measuring blacks all morning. A disagreeable task but it must be done." Native responses to such invasive sessions were also recorded by Gillen; on July 11 he wrote: "Atwaintika was measured yesterday by Spencer and it was most amusing to watch the look of half wonder on his face when the Anthropometric instruments were being applied to his head."[90]

During the expedition itself, Spencer sent photographic prints to friends as well as to newspaper publisher David Syme, who used the images in articles written by Spencer for Syme's illustrated Melbourne weekly *The Age*. Spencer had accepted a thousand-pound sponsorship fee for the 1901 expedition from Syme in exchange for regular articles and photographs sent from the field.[91] Gillen made frequent references to Spencer's preoccupation with writing these pieces during the expedition, noting in one journal entry that Spencer was "embodying in highly popular form much of [our] material."[92] This commercial sponsorship no doubt influenced Spencer's judgments about which aspects of his ethnographic research were suitable for a scientific versus a gen-

FIG. 4.17 Relatively candid photograph of Arrernte women with baby, 1901. (Courtesy MVA)

eral audience. On the one hand, Spencer's typological photographs showing frontal and profile shots of native peoples were made under the governing principles of what we'd now call physical anthropology that demanded standardized, quantitative data about Australian Aboriginal physiognomy, data that was likely to have bolstered racist claims about the purported inferiority of so-called savage peoples. On the other hand, Spencer's more spontaneous fieldwork photographs reached the general public via Syme's newspaper, and were exhibited along with phonograph recordings and cinematography in Spencer's public lecture-screenings. However, recognizing that the outcomes of his professional research should not be limited to the scientific community, Spencer had few qualms exploiting popular fascination with Australian Aborigines; building upon public interest in the expedition that had been garnered though the publication of updated illustrated reports on the expedition in the Melbourne *Age*, Spencer organized a lecture tour in which he would exhibit films as well as photographs he had shot during the expedition. According to Cantrill, a theater entrepreneur was hired to organize the lecture, and advertisements were placed in the entertainment pages of local newspapers.[93]

Spencer began his public lectures series in 1902 when he resumed his duties at Melbourne University, an institution facing financial difficulties and fierce attacks from *The Age* for its purported "educational sterility, administrative inefficiency, and its professorial indolence."[94] In order to boost the university's public reputation and to raise funds for its science laboratories, Spencer arranged to deliver ten public lectures throughout Victoria on "Aboriginal Life in Central Australia" (fig. 4.18). In addition, lantern slides were made available for public sale at two pence each. At Spencer's first public lecture on July 7, 1902, an audience of two thousand, including the governor, paid two shillings each, filling Melbourne's Town Hall.[95]

Advance publicity promised audiences that "a brief account will be given of scenes and ceremonies which have been selected as typical of savage life. The various ceremonies will be illustrated by lantern slides, cinematograph views, and phonograph records."[96] Spencer's confidence in the public's interest in the lecture-screenings was supported by less formal means of publicity; as he put it, "the facts were discreetly mentioned and spread abroad, that some difficulty was experienced as to whether it was quite fit and proper to exhibit in public cinematograph pictures of natives who do not wear all the clothing that they ought to."[97] In forewarning his audience, Spencer may have been following the advice of his friend Lorimer Fison who suggested that the "only way to deal with the [undress views] . . . is to say in plain terms beforehand in the paper and ads what they are, and to tell the women not to come unless they are prepared in the interests of science to witness painful sights. I think that this will fill the Hall. If you give your lecture, I think the undiscriminating slides ought to appear, and I don't see what anybody can complain of if they are told plainly beforehand what to expect."[98] That Spencer may have been somewhat conflicted over how moral propriety could be reconciled with ethnographic accuracy can be seen in the following remark:

I can select a series of slides to which even the most strict Presbyterian elders could take exception but then this would mean elimination of the best things. What I would like to show would be the real native and though anyone who is interested, genuinely, in savages, would look at the pictures from a purely ethnological point of view, it is rather doubtful as to whether an average audience would not be shocked.[99]

FIG. 4.18 Cover of Savage Club "Smoke Night" program in which Spencer lectured and showed "limejuice" (lantern) views and phonograph records, Melbourne, 1902. The handwritten caption on the projected image reads, "A belly dancer from Central Australia."

Spencer's concerns that photographs of the Arrernte might offend the sensibilities of his Victorian audience recall the worries voiced by museum curators and world's fairs organizers over the prurient appeal of hypermimetic exhibits, including the controversy over the Native American exhibit at the

1876 Centennial Exposition. At the same time, the showman in Spencer may have steered a calculated path through the censorship issue, courting controversy in order to maximize publicity. That Spencer had always intended his images to be seen by lay audiences is apparent from his arrangement with Syme and the decision to tour with the material upon his return from the field. Spencer seemed to have few qualms turning aspects of his fieldwork into sensationalized entertainment, and even thought he compensated members of the Arrernte tribe for their paricipation in his image-making with hatchets, knives, tobacco pipes, tobacco, flour, and tea, some Arrernte were deeply unhappy about sacred ceremonial secrets being revealed to outsiders.[100] In addition, Cantrill notes, "Spencer deceptively told the elders that he would be revealing the secrets only to two colleagues who were 'men of immense weight among the tribes of the south-east,' " rather than to large audiences in Australia and Britain.[101]

Spencer's use of a range of visual and aural technologies to collect ethnographic data thus suggests a sophisticated understanding of the utility of photographs and sound recordings as ethnographic data *and* commodities that could be bought and sold and commercially exploited. Moreover, Spencer's decision to sell his photographs provides further evidence of a nascent visual anthropology forging ties with the general public and the discipline itself being yoked to a potentially transgressive visuality. This seemingly minor point has great resonance for some of the issues explored in this book, however, since it shows a certain symbiosis between anthropology and mass culture at a very early stage; it also hints at how anthropology's self-identity was bound up with its relationship to popular culture. The extent to which anthropology could comfortably represent itself through visual means was an issue Spencer may have grappled with while planning his expedition, although as we have seen, other than his reservations about the graphic nudity shown in some images of the Arrernte, Spencer was reconciled to portions of the audience misconstruing the images.

Whether Spencer had any real misgivings about his ethical behavior throughout the buildup to the lectures is somewhat beside the point though; whatever Spencer thought, the enormous success of his Australian and British lecture tours suggest that turn-of-the-century audiences were quite willing to forgo Victorian standards of taste and decency for the duration of Spencer's lecture-performance, providing they got a closer look at Australian Aborigines living in the wild (as the lessons from the world's fairs clearly show). Moreover, where they may never have dared enter a debased site of popular amusement such as a dime museum or traveling circus, they could justify their attendance at Spencer's lecture as a result of the dignified venue and scholarly credentials of the lecturer. Spencer's decision to go ahead with this original plan to show uncensored images of the Arrernte undoubtedly paid off, as suggested in this review of the multimedia lecture from *The Age*:

> The sacred ceremonies and dances connected with rainfall were depicted by the cinematograph, and other weird songs, which accompany the dances, were given by the phonograph. The whole of these records, of which there was a great number, were remarkably clear, and gave a better conception of the customs of the aborigines than would the perusal of all the literature on the subject.[102]

Another Melbourne newspaper, *The Argus*, called the event "diversified entertainment," no doubt a reference to Spencer's skill in combining scientific edification and visual spectacle through the slides, films, and phonograph recordings.[103] Striking here, too, is Spencer's replication of Haddon's early attempt at a mixed-media presentation, evidence perhaps of Spencer taking yet more advice from Haddon vis à vis motion pictures, or of both men having similar ideas about how sound and image could be combined to produce more integrated, contextualized knowledge about native customs.

Part of the appeal of Spencer's presentations of Australian Aboriginal culture to general audiences in Australia and Britain no doubt lay in their ideological affinity with the general prevailing discourses of social evolutionism;[104] framed by widely circulating and mutually reinforcing discourses of science, race, and colonialism, this naturalized ideological system offered Spencer's nonspecialist audiences a "conceptual universe" within which his ideas about and images of Australian Aborigines would circulate.[105] Spencer was quick to build upon his successful Melbourne engagements with a tour to other cities in Australia and Britain, giving a total of sixty-three public lectures to packed houses between 1902 and 1904.[106] In addition, Gillen, following a script prepared by Spencer, also lectured on the expedition, using slides and phonograph recordings in a similar fashion to Spencer.[107]

Optimism Followed by Antipathy

Each new imaging technology has presented anthropologists with historically contingent logistical, epistemological, and ideological challenges. Unlike their earlier experience with photography, anthropologists attempting to use the new medium of moving pictures faced unprecedented financial and practical hurdles.[108] Late into the teens (some twenty years after Haddon and Spencer shot their films), anthropologists, scientists, and explorers were all quick to mention the arduous task of shooting film in the field; writing about his experience of filming wildlife as part of a two-man crew in Northwest Quebec in 1919, Albert Britt pointed out that the weight of the filmmaking equipment was a daunting prospect for explorers venturing into the wilds: "Lift a movie camera sometime" the author dared the reader. "Then lift a tripod . . . [and] a couple of thousand feet of film in the magazines. Then imagine this weight added to an outfit that is already too heavy for the portages."[109] But even the promise of cheaper and more portable cameras in the teens failed to have much impact on prevailing attitudes toward cinema, since the hardships of intemperate climates, remote topographies, degradable film stock, and technical inexperience continued to put off all but the most intrepid of travelers.

Despite Haddon's and Spencer's interest in ethnographic film, cinema remained a decidedly ancillary method of ethnographic data collection within turn-of-the-century anthropology. One of the obstacles Haddon and Spencer faced was how to create an appropriate representational genre for film, since, as Ira Jacknis, has argued, new ethnographic modes do not evolve in a vacuum, but "in tandem with changing theoretical and institutional conditions."[110] The greatest hurdle anthropologists faced using a moving picture camera to record ethnographic data was making the films legible as scientific documents; in other words, what kind of useful knowledge (other than pictorial records of dances or native industries) could ethnographic films leave behind for subsequent anthropologists?

Unlike written ethnography, ethnographic film could convey none of the certainty that came with a logocentric view of fieldwork that dominated anthropology; indeed, some of the questions raised by the filmmaking of Haddon and Spencer still animate theoretical discussions of ethnographic cinema, including cinema's potential to create forms of ethnographic knowledge different from those produced within written ethnography and film's potential to uncover "structures of experience" that evade the written text, allowing access to an emic (insider's view) in place of an etic (outsider's perspective).[111] In contrast to written forms of inscription, ethnographic films were often considered little more than visual field notes, illustrations that were interesting to look at but did little to advance ethnographic theory, an attitude that remained largely unchallenged until pioneers like Margaret Mead and Jean Rouch made a case for the importance of ethnographic cinema in the 1950s.

One of anthropologists' most serious reservations about motion pictures, and a concern that goes back to life groups and native villages, was that the spectacularized, moving ethnographic image, with its surfeit of illusionistic detail and lack of context, would paradoxically show too much and reveal too little. Spencer's own frustration at his lack of access to the cultural significance of some of the Arrernte ceremonies he filmed suggests his own recognition of the limitations of visual notation in the field and betrays a wider anxiety about the control the anthropologist could exert over moving images in the period before editing and camera movement were standardized. An example may illustrate my point; as a result of Spencer's improvised and imperfect efforts to frame the Arrernte's movements in some of the ceremonies, the ethnographer's mechanized gaze is rendered less perfect and seems more fragile and contingent in the moving pictures than it does in still photographs, with the implied risk that the dancers will move out of the camera's range and frustrate our visual sovereignty over the spectacle. At the same time, because the film camera can powerfully evoke both the profilmic landscape and human figure, the performers featured on film come across as individuals with subjectivities and cultural identities rather than objects reified by the dehumanizing gaze of the ethnographic sideshow.

Ironically, cinema's ability to represent reality with such compelling verisimilitude may have contributed to anthropologists' ambivalence about the medium, since the sense of agency afforded native peoples for the duration of a performance also threatened to undermine the specular authority of an idealized scientific observer. As Rosalind Morris argues, ethnographic film always contains a " 'surplus' of meaning, a beyond of expression that exceeds the film's translatability to different subject positions."[112] At the same time,

Spencer's films demonstrate the extent to which ethnographic filmmaking can wrest native ritual and performance from their "systems of meaning," in Morris's words, creating the sense not only "that the image is distanced from its supposed referent but also that what it signifies has been loosened from its moorings in the historical world."[113] Thus the indeterminacy surrounding the ethnographic image demanded constant policing by anthropologists, since spectators of visual anthropology seldom possessed the kind of extrafilmic information required to decode an image's intended meaning. Faced with the challenge of reigning in the connotative power of the filmic image, anthropologists had few ways of enforcing preferred meanings beyond their physical presence at each screening (until, that is, intertitling became the industry norm). For most professional contemporaries of Haddon and Spencer, the cinematographic apparatus was too unwieldy, too troublesome, and too conspicuous to afford the kind of detailed documentation that was increasingly expected of twentieth-century anthropologists.

Early ethnographic film thus grappled with similar epistemological and ethical issues to nineteen-century photography. Take the issue of access, for example; a great deal of important ethnographic material could never be represented in visual form for various reasons, including the sacred or private nature of the activity (such as circumcision rites or childbirth practices), native people's refusal to be subjected to the physical coercion and loss of privacy that often accompanied filmmaking, and, most importantly, the limited use-value of images that could not explain deeper cultural structures. Within British anthropology, for example, the study of kinship and social organization represented significant intellectual areas of cultural study not amenable to visual representation. Anthropologists were thus limited to photographing or filming views or events that could be made to stand in for more complex and implicit structures. Because a great deal of the tribal infrastructure and cultural practices could not be rendered visible in this manner, anthropologists had to rely upon events that could serve as cultural metonyms and be legible as anthropological evidence.

Another reason for the antipathy toward cinema among some anthropologists may have stemmed from its roots in popular culture. For early twentieth-century anthropologists whose only encounter with cinema were the kinds of attractions one might expect to see at Coney Island in New York or the

Egyptian Hall in London, moving pictures seemed to be at odds with the mission of anthropology. Unlike photographs of native peoples, which could be purchased, retouched, recaptioned and made to enunciate ethnographic knowledge, the meanings of motion pictures representing distant cultures were far harder to circumscribe, unless an anthropologist lectured with the films—which anthropologists like Haddon and Spencer did—or used intertitles to inscribe meaning through internal contextualization. If most anthropologists weren't interested in becoming producers of motion pictures, they may also have been reluctant exhibitors, consumers, and occasional critics of early commercial cinema.

That anthropologists such as Haddon and Spencer made their filmmaking accessible to wider communities thus takes on greater significance when we consider the odds stacked against them. Surrounded perhaps by colleagues hostile to motion pictures and embarrassed at the lowbrow hype accompanying public screenings of their films, Haddon and Spencer seemed not in the least bit interested in nurturing ethnographic filmmaking; spawning no protégés, Haddon never touched a motion picture camera again and Spencer waited some ten years before venturing into the field with a camera. But the fact that Haddon, and Spencer in particular, were aware of (and perhaps willing to capitalize on) the popular curiosity surrounding native peoples cannot be ignored and speaks to the enormous public fascination with images of alterity that seem to permeate turn-of-the-century popular culture. It is to the parallel world of commercial filmmaking that we now turn to prise open this curiosity for cross-cultural imaging.

5

"The World Within Your Reach"

POPULAR CINEMA & ETHNOGRAPHIC REPRESENTATION

To the World, the World we show
We make the World to laugh
And teach each Hemisphere to know
How lives the Other Half.
—LYMAN H. HOWE (1909)[1]

~~~ ~~~

IN 1885, English impresario John Robinson Whitely described a procession of Buffalo Bill's American Indians marching outside his Washington, D.C., hotel as a "a show that presented living and moving pictures of a fast-vanishing phase of national existence, on the ever-receding frontier line between the territory of the white man and the happy hunting grounds or 'reservations,' of the redskins."[2] When Whitely subsequently booked Buffalo Bill's troupe for an appearance at the 1888 Four National Exhibitions Show in London, he described the powerful dislocating effects of the spectacle upon the audience: "Those visitors positively seemed to lose their sense of local habitation, and to feel themselves altogether transported in body beyond the Atlantic when they passed across the bridge leading from the Main Building into the vast arena."[3] But Whitely was not the only entrepreneur to appreciate the popular appeal of ethnographic spectacles; six years later, in the fall of 1894, Thomas Alva Edison invited members of "Buffalo Bill's Wild West Show," then appearing in Ambrose Park, Brooklyn, to perform before his latest technological wonder, the kinetoscope, in his Black Maria film studio.[4] The enlistment of

Native American performers by Whitely and Edison are but two instances of a pervasive fascination with images of the exotic Other in turn-of-the-century popular culture, a public demand catered to across the gamut of entertainment forms, from legitimate theater to dime museums, and, eventually, to motion pictures.

Despite a resurgence of scholarly interest in the range of early photographic practices involving non-Western peoples,[5] early ethnographic filmmaking has received much less attention among historians. While scholars have acknowledged the filmmaking endeavors of a handful of anthropologists before 1920, most early nonfiction films featuring native peoples were made *not* by professional anthropologists for gatherings of scientific peers, but by commercial producers for popular consumption in nickelodeons. If Lyman H. Howe's 1909 publicity doggerel promising audiences enlightenment about "how the other half lives" through laughter and education may seem a far cry from professional ethnography, early commercial promoters of ethnographic filmmaking nevertheless sought legitimacy from the discursive authority of anthropology. Like the operators of natural history museums and world's fair attractions, early commercial filmmakers invited audience members to take up the role of virtual ethnographers. The countless fragmentary and ephemeral cinematic glimpses of non-Western peoples screened by nickelodeon operators and by itinerant lecturers who depended on the lure of the exotic for their livelihood are reminders of the common ground between a modern culture of curiosity and the emerging science of ethnography. Indeed, these practices embodied the fears of many anthropologists that such commercial ethnographic filmmaking might not only contaminate serious anthropological research but threaten to become indistinguishable from it. Analyzing the near-obsession of early commercial filmmakers with native peoples as cinematic subjects and considering the ways in which their films can be read as ethnographic texts,[6] this chapter surveys a range of popular ethnographic filmmaking between 1894 and 1915, including the travelogues of such celebrities as Burton Holmes, Lyman Howe, and Frederick Monsen. Fundamental to any consideration of such noncanonical ethnographic filmmaking is the question of how it is possible to think about films produced by commercial film companies such as Edison, Biograph, and Pathé and exhibited by lecturer-showmen such as Holmes and Howe as "filmed ethnography"; in other words, how such early commercial films might be read as early examples of ethnographic filmmaking at a time when the term *ethnographic film* had not yet been coined.[7] How, for example, did these films codify ethnographic knowledge for popular audiences, and to what extent did they appropriate the rhetorical tropes of the travel novel, the souvenir postcard, and the lantern-slide lecture? To what extent did lecturer-exhibitors, writers of film intertitles, and early film journalists draw upon the interpretive schema of anthropology when framing the reception of these films for mass audiences? What effect did this discursive poaching have upon anthropology's own reputation and self-perception as a discipline with strong ties to visual culture? Did it matter to film promoters that anthropologists themselves weren't particularly interested in ethnographic film? And finally, how were these films discursively enmeshed in wider debates about cinema's potential as a civilizing apparatus and as a tool of colonial propaganda?[8]

This chapter begins with an analysis of some of the earliest motion picture records of native peoples, films of Native Americans shot at Thomas Edison's New Jersey studio in 1894 — testimony not only to the enduring popularity of American Indians as filmic subjects in early American cinema but to a broader fascination with the exotic in late nineteenth-century popular culture. Following this we explore the status of the reconstruction as ethnographic evidence, the fascination of early filmmakers with indigenous dance as an icon of alterity, and the complicating effects of the return gaze in a wide range of early ethnographic films. Next, the chapter examines the commercial travelogue's debt both to discourses of ethnographic objectivity and to the commercial imperatives of a burgeoning film industry and considers the travelogue in relation to cinema's potential as a civic educator and tool of colonial propaganda. The chapter concludes with a comparison of one of the most famous ethnographic films of the pre-*Nanook* period, Edward Sheriff Curtis's *In the Land of the Head-Hunters*, with the filmmaking of a lesser-known figure working at the same time, Joseph K. Dixon. Curtis and Dixon typify a new breed of ethnographic filmmaker whose fascination with Native American culture inspired them to reconstruct and record aspects of Indian life before it vanished forever. The filmmaking efforts of Dixon and Curtis recapitulate some of the theoretical motifs of this chapter, including debates over authenticity and appeals to the ideology of the Noble Savage. They also present us with an opportunity to consider how at least some Native Americans responded to their portrayal in early ethnographic cinema.

Edison the Ethnographer: Filming Native American Dance

Filmed by Thomas Edison's cameraman W. K. L. Dickson at Edison's New Jersey studio in 1894, *Sioux Ghost Dance* and *Indian War Council* are among the earliest surviving filmed records of Native Americans.[9] The synthetic form of the Wild West Show, which combined elements of the circus, the parade, the carnival, the stage spectacular, and the melodrama into a single event, made it particularly amenable to cinematic translation, and Edison invited such celebrities as Annie Oakley, Eugene Sandow, and Anabelle Whitford to perform before his new kinetoscope.[10] In addition to *Sioux Ghost Dance* and *Indian War Council*, Dickson filmed *Buffalo Bill* and *Buffalo Dance*, the latter film featuring seventeen Native Americans. Antonia Dickson, early cinema critic (and sister of Edison's cameraman), captured the mood of Edison's studio in her 1895 article, "The Wonders of the Kinetoscope":

> Buffalo Bill marshals his heterogeneous suite — lustrous-eyed Moors and Arabs, turbaned and bejeweled; dashing Texan cowboys in shadowy sombreros and cavernous boots; sleepy-eyed Celestials and agile Japanese; fierce Cossacks and picturesque Albanians; impassive Indians in pomp of war paint and plumes. These resolve themselves into strange combinations — into the Omaha war dance, the Sioux ghost dance and Indian war council; into wonderful feats of swordsmanship, lasooing and shouting.[11]

Dickson's extravagant and stereotypical adjectives evoke a menagerie of exotic performers, suggesting a human carnival under the supervision of the white adventurer–field marshal.[12] A review of the event in the New Jersey *East Orange Gazette* offers a more sober, though no less dramatic account of the proceedings:

> The affair in the theatre started with an exhibition of rapid firing in a circle by Col. Cody, which was followed by a war dance by the Indians. The latter was given in full war paint and feathers, to the music of native drums

and was accompanied by the usual brandishing of tomahawks and scalping knives. Next came a war council between Buffalo Bill and the chiefs in
which the participants passed the wampum belt and smashed the pipe of
peace. A group of pictures of the entire party was then taken and the performance closed with a buffalo dance to native drum music by the three
great chiefs present, Last Horse, Parts of His Hair, and Hair Coat.[13]

The debt of the new medium of cinema to earlier cultural representations
of Native Americans can be seen in the already-jaded critic's description of
"the usual brandishing of tomahawks and scalping knives." In all likelihood,
though, the films of the Indian dancers elicited a far more complex spectatorial response than that suggested in these two contemporary accounts.
Displacing the Native American figures from their lived social context to the
limbo background of the Black Maria studio serves to isolate the dancers and
underscores the unsettling effect of their provocative visual address to the
spectator. The performers' proximity to the camera, allowing the revelation
of costume and facial detail, together with the possibility for repeat viewings
of the kinetoscope loop, creates a viewing experience that one imagines would
have been quite different from that at the live Wild West Show performance.
At the same time, despite its name, the Ghost Dance depicted in the Edison
film was not the solemn circle dance associated with the contemporaneous
Native American "Ghost Dance" movement started by Indian spiritualist
leader Jack Wilson but another circle dance featuring three performers.[14] In a
case of historical accuracy taking a backseat to advertising hyperbole, by titling
the film "Sioux Ghost Dance," Buffalo Bill (or possibly Edison or even the
Indians themselves) no doubt hoped to capitalize on public interest at that
time in the Native American movement. Helping to frame the reception of
both the cinematic and live versions of the *Sioux Ghost Dance* is the tradition of
the Noble Savage, which had long presented the American Indian in an inno-
cent, pristine, and Edenic existence before the corrupting influences of
Western civilization.[15] Drawing upon a language of racialized iconography,
the Noble Savage was a long-standing and fluid ideological construction,
capable of incorporating ambivalent and often contradictory Western attitudes toward native life.[16] Though some spectators may have viewed Buffalo
Bill's Native American dancers as a poignant reminder of a people "doomed"

to extinction and not made a connection to the Ghost Dance movement, Jack Wilson's "Ghost Dance" nevertheless provided an ominous backdrop to the film's reception, a more defiant sensibility possibly evoked in the feisty gesture of one of the Sioux dancers in Edison's film.[17] While the context of the Wild West Show reassured audiences that these dances were to be consumed primarily as entertainment rather than as documentary records of Indian-white relations, the performers in Edison's films, unlike in the Buffalo Bill show, had fewer contextualizing markers and were thus more ideologically fluid. Moreover, the semicelebrity status of the Indian performers as members of "Buffalo Bill's Wild West Show" and the *mise-en-abyme* quality of the *Sioux Ghost Dance* (a filmic reconstruction of a Wild West Show's reenactment of a Native American "Ghost Dance") point up the difficulty of prising open the meanings of early cinema's actualities for contemporaneous audiences.

For the majority of photographers, cinematographers, and tourists who traveled to Native American communities in the American Southwest before 1915, visual spectacle was decidedly the main draw; the exotic costumes, live snakes, and unfamiliar dancing offered a thrilling mix of the abject and the spiritual. It mattered little to most filmmakers that the films made of the Snake Dance were poor substitutes for what Peggy Phelan calls the "undocumentable event of performance . . . performance's independence from mass reproduction."[18] Despite the static camera's distance from the dancers and the short duration of these on-location dance films, they were extremely popular with urban cinema audiences. The Snake Dance was also an attractive subject for itinerant "high-class" lecturers such as Burton Holmes (who in 1898 and 1899 sent his cinematographer Oscar Bennet Depue to Oraibi, Arizona, to film the "most famous Moki rite") and for wealthy independent adventurers like Theodore Roosevelt, who commissioned a film of a Hopi Snake Dance as late as 1913.[19] Illustrations of the Snake Dance appeared regularly in advertisements for railway companies bringing tourists to the American Southwest, including this one (fig. 5.1), from a 1902 brochure for lecturer Burton Holmes.[20] Holmes described the Snake Dance as "a spectacle unique in its impressive savagery," although he reassured viewers uneasy about the disquieting nature of the dance that the "horror of the exhibition is dispelled by the dash and spirit with which the celebrants perform the dangerous and thrilling rite."[21]

ONLY
ROUTE
TO ·
THE

GRAND

CAÑON

OF

ARIZONA

AND THE

MOKI SNAKE DANCE

DIRECT ROUTE TO HAWAII

Santa Fe Route

THE ATCHISON, TOPEKA & SANTA FE RAILWAY

FIG. 5.1 The touristic appeal of the Moki Snake Dance was exploited in this advertisement which appeared in Burton Holmes's publicity materials for 1902.

Because of its kineticism and visual appeal, dance offered a "raw," almost tactile representation of "Indianness" for many turn-of-the-century spectators. Rubbing shoulders with anthropologists and amateur and professional photographers, cinematographers flocked to the Southwest to record native ceremonies from the mid-1890s through the mid-teens, as seen in this Ben Wittick photograph (fig. 5.2). In 1897, more than two hundred white spectators

FIG. 5.2 Hopi priests performing the Antelope Snake Dance near the Dance Rock at Walpi Pueblo, Arizona. Note the camera tripod in the lower left corner of the frame. (Photograph taken by Ben Wittick on August 21, 1897. Courtesy National Anthropological Archives)

attended the Walpi Snake dance in Arizona, twice as many as previous years. The enormous drawing power of the Snake Dance was explained by professional photographer George Wharton James in 1900 ("Here the Snake Dance is given in more dramatic form than in any other of the four villages where it is performed"), although for government officials the drama's popular appeal was cause for some concern.[22]

Given the critical and commercial value associated with claims for ethnographic authenticity, some image-makers and anthropologists worried publicly about the impact of crowds of photographers and filmmakers upon native performances; James, for example, in the premier issue of the photographic monthly *Camera Craft* in 1902, complained of the deleterious effects of the presence of cameras upon the "authenticity" of the Snake Dance, criticizing what he saw as the misrepresentation of Snake Dance performances by tourist photographers and journalists and claiming that the performances were not dances of spectacle but prayers for rain and a blessing of the harvest. James decried the surfeit of white spectators with still (and, in some instances, moving picture) cameras, which resulted in parts of the performance either being cut or altered by performers intimidated by the encroachment of the observers: "It cannot be said that the changes are to the advantage of the photographer. They render his work less *certain* and *effective*, and it will not be long before one can write a learned and accurate paper from the standpoint of scientific ethnology on 'the change in religious ceremonies owing to the camera.' "[23]

James's concern in 1902 with both what he saw as the negative impact of white observers on indigenous rituals and the camera's inability to differentiate between an "authentic" performance and a fake or imperfect rendition is an early instance of these perennial disputes within ethnographic filmmaking. At the same time, James's dismay over the contamination of "pure" ethnographic rituals by the cameras of Western observers implicitly exempts his own photographic practice from the same charge; it is the cameras of less enlightened or socially credentialed witnesses, not his own, which threaten to corrupt the ethnographic integrity of the event. Strikingly absent in James's hypocritical attitude toward Indian dances is any discussion of the complex social and economic transactions inevitably involved in gaining photographic and filmic access to other cultures; also characteristically absent in James's complaint is any consideration of the subjectivities of the native peoples, about what *they* thought about the incursion of white tourists into their communities and how their lives commensurably changed.

Public safety was also deemed a factor in efforts to police the native dances. Writing in the *Annual Report* of the Bureau of American Ethnology in 1900, Jesse Walter Fewkes worried that the "germs of the degradation of the religious character of the Walpi Snake dance" were already detectable, that the crowding of Western spectators posed a serious safety issue (the walls and roof of the pueblo would crumble under the weight of hundreds of onlookers, he feared), and most seriously, that a time would come when the Snake Dance would "cease to be a religious ceremony, the secret rites would disappear, and nothing [would] remain but a spectacular show."[24] Moreover, according to Fewkes, the younger performers in the ceremonies were more profoundly affected by the presence of white spectators than their elders:

> When gazed upon by so many strangers, some of the Snake men appeared to be more nervous, and did not handle the reptiles in the fearless manner which marked earlier performances. The older members of the fraternity maintained the same earnestness, but the more youthful glanced so often at the spectators that their thoughts seemed to be on other subjects than the solemn duty before them, and they dodged the fallen reptiles in a way not seen before at Walpi.[25]

Like the dancer's defiant glance at the camera in Edison's *Sioux Ghost Dance*, the performers' acknowledgment of the spectators threatens not only the integrity of the ceremony (and the personal safety of the performers) but also signals the impossibility of conceptualizing Indian identity outside the context of contemporaneous Native American–white relations. Fewkes's rhetoric of germs, contamination, and degradation to describe the contact between native peoples and nonnative image-makers remains an enduring feature of ethnographic discourse throughout the twentieth century, where Western contact is seen to threaten the imputed pristine and timeless world of the Noble Savage.

Anxiety about the impact of Euro-American spectators was also voiced by the native peoples themselves, who complained of the deleterious effect of outsiders on the ceremonies and tried to ensure that public exhibitions were kept separate from secret, private ceremonies, although Fewkes claimed that because of the influx of visitors, some Indian men joined Snake societies for a chance to be in the limelight, rather than for religious reasons.[26] But in many respects the voices of native peoples were doubly silenced in the process of accumulating photographic evidence of their ceremonial lives; not only were members of the pueblos put under enormous pressure to perform regularly for a seemingly endless stream of tourists, but their subjectivities were all but erased in the essentializing tendencies of the filmed and photographed Snake Dances. Responding to the suppression of Native American subjectivity from these photographs, Native American curator Jaune Quick-To-See Smith argued in 1984 that native peoples could find little to identify with in the corpus of images produced by the photographers and camera operators who flocked to the Southwest (despite the importance of the ceremonies as expressions of pueblo spirituality): "Government surveyors, priests, tourists, and white photographers were all yearning for the 'noble savage' dressed in full regalia, looking stoic and posing like a Cybis statue. . . . We cannot identify with those images."[27]

With these aspects of the cultural position of Native American dance performances in mind, let us return to a consideration of Edison's Native American films. Four years after the Black Maria kinetoscopes were made, Edison revisited the subject of American Indian dance, commissioning a series of films shot on location in Arizona in 1898 and 1901.[28] With the exception of *Panoramic View of Moki-Land*, the five films in the 1901 Native American series were all shot on location in Walpi, Arizona, and consist of views of the Snake Dance shot at different points in the ceremony. The most visually striking of the series, *Moki Snake Dance by Wolpi Indians*, frames a group of snake dancers in a high-angle medium long shot (the camera probably located on an adobe rooftop) which includes internal spectators (most of whom are white) at the right-hand corner of the frame. The film begins with the dance already in progress and shows the dancers holding snakes in their mouths. The single-take film records the dance without changing position, with the exception of some camera reframing at the beginning of the shot.[29]

What differentiates the mechanics of sight in *Moki Snake Dance by Wolpi Indians* from the series of 1894 and 1898 films is that James White's camera explicitly adopts the point of view of the Euro-American spectators who sit on lower levels of the adobe wall on the right side of the frame. As with *Line Up and Teasing the Snakes* (1901) and *Parade of Snake Dancers Before the Dance* (1901), the film validates the cameraman as ethnographer through its use of internal spectators (who mirror the theater spectators watching the film); and even though three white men can be seen in *Buck Dance* (1898), the fact that they are stationed in the extreme background looking at the camera suggests that they are part of the spectacle as opposed to detached observers implicitly identified with the camera operator and film spectator. The presence of nonnative spectators also signals the status of the film as a reconstruction, almost certainly staged for the tourist market, rather than performed as part of a cycle of ceremonies.

More specifically, the closing glimpse in *Moki Snake Dance* of a white woman leaning forward from her standing position against an adobe wall in order to secure a better view of the performers suggests the gendered appeal of early actualities, and how nakedness as a complex sign system resurfaced in the context of the early Indian western. According to Fred J. Balshofer and Arthur C. Miller, part of the allure of early "Indian films" for female viewers, in addition to their evocation of a sublime landscape, was the spectacle of male nudity.[30] Unlike spectators witnessing the Snake Dance firsthand, film audiences were free to view the ethnographic spectacle from the safety of cinema's displaced representation, a safety doubly bracketed in this film by the implicit point of view of the on-screen white onlookers. The mixture of repulsion, fear, fascination, and reassurance conjured up by *Moki Snake Dance* speaks to both the voyeuristic appeal of the ceremony and the comforting distance provided spectators by the moving picture apparatus.

These issues beg the question of the relationship between Edison's Black Maria films of 1894 and those made on location in 1898 and 1901: what is the effect of location shooting upon the construction of ethnographic meaning? While less exhibitionist in style than Edison's 1894 films of Indian dancers, the 1898 films nevertheless fall squarely within the category of a cinema of attractions. In the absence of extrafilmic information in the form of a printed synopsis or film lecturer who might elucidate the significance of what was filmed, spectators view the films from the position of curious, yet removed, onlookers.[31] If the effect of the 1898 dances is less visceral than their 1894 counterparts, the location setting nevertheless contributes to their significance as archival records for Native American historians. The 1898 and 1901 films, with their glimpses of Indian ceremonies performed *in situ* by ordinary tribe-members, offer ethnographic insights unavailable to viewers of Edison's 1894 professional performers. While the location settings and internal audiences may evoke a greater degree of ethnographic authority in the 1898 and 1901 films than in the earlier studio films, this is not to suggest that the later films provide a transparent record of indigenous culture. What they do provide is a record of the way in which culture was *performed* for outsiders visiting the region during this period.

The ethnographic value of these early Edison films derives in part from the camera's status as a historical witness to these dances, although, as Philip Rosen explains, indexicality in the absence of explication leaves a great many questions unanswered. In the context of ethnographic film, these questions include the meaning and informing context of a performance, the degree of staging, the intended uses of a film, and native attitudes toward the film shoot. While there is very little information available on this last issue, there is evidence that Navajos performing dances for Edward S. Curtis deliberately subverted the dance's meaning by performing it backwards for the camera.[32] In so doing, Christopher Lyman argues, the performers could preserve the sacred status of the ceremony.[33] The camera's presence as a historical witness to these events is by no means a guarantor of ethnographic "truth"; indeed, the indexical power of the moving picture can paradoxically render a situation less readable than an account obtained by nonvisual means, as Rosen explains:

When [a] representation is explicitly said to be valuable because of the presence of the apparatus, the indexicality of the image—the image emerges as insufficient in itself. It must be explained, sense must be made, the very shape of the image requires verbal explication and pinpointing. . . . The closer the image comes to being reduced to pure presence, the more it threatens to become unreadable and requires explication.[34]

Ethnographic knowledge is therefore frustrated by the presence of the performing native body as an ethnographic sign; in the absence of narrative organization or decoupage, the fact of filmic enunciation—the sheer exuberance of the performing body in space—overshadows such issues as the nature of the ceremony, why it is being performed, and under what circumstances.

Performing Bodies

Edison's two-part *Kanakas Diving for Money* (nos. 1 and 2), shot in Honolulu in 1898, offers early filmic evidence of the centrality of the ethnographic subject as a body-to-be-performed for nonnative audiences. But it also offers a glimpse of native subjectivity inasmuch as the Kanakas expect to be rewarded for their diving stunts or, rather, will dive *only* in search of the coins that are tossed at them. The scopic appeal of black bodies frolicking in and around water can be seen in this poster for the 1896 Joly *cinematographe* system which in the top right corner shows a black woman bathing her baby in a river and children diving into a river or lake (fig. 5.3). Visually organized as discrete attractions, the seven filmic images radiating out from the projector show a range of bodies moving in space, whether as dancers, boxers, or gardener-comedians, as seen in the 1895 Lumière film *L'Arosseur Arrosé* inscribed in the lower central arc of the image. That the ethnographic Other is included in this early catalogue of filmic subjects should come as no surprise, given the popularity of exhibits of native peoples at world's fairs, "Buffalo Bill's Wild West Show," and Barnum's "Ethnographic Congress."

In *Kanakas Diving for Money* (no. 1) six young boys swimming next to a massive ocean liner in the harbor dive underwater for coins tossed to them from offscreen (reminiscent of the money tossed at native peoples at world's fairs); the slightly elevated medium long shot captures the boys' legs thrusting out of the water and their pleading with the onlookers for more coins. A similar setup is used in Edison's *Native Women Coaling a Ship and Scrambling for Money*, part of a series of films shot in the West Indies in 1903, although after the money-diving sequence, the camera pans to the left to reveal a long, antlike line of women with coal carried in baskets on their heads entering the bowels of a ship docked in the harbor.[35] In this case, however, the coin retrievers are male and the coalers female, a gendered division of labor in which women assume the typically male role of manual labor while the men's bodies are constructed as performances. Performance thus functions within a transactional economy that is laid bare in these two films; the large ships, from which the coins are tossed, evoke the colonial power upon which the people of the

FIG. 5.3 Joly *cinematographe* system from 1896.

islands are dependent for survival. The offscreen coin-throwers who instigate the spectacle before the camera implicate the viewer in the economic exchange; in a sense it is the nickelodeon audience's own money that is being thrown at the divers, money advanced by the filmmaker from the theatrical box office to the poorly paid extras.

While historians might wish to speculate on the ways in which indigenous peoples are rendered as "spectacles-to-be-watched" in commercially produced films, in most cases there is little if any reliable information on the arrangements made between camera operator and native peoples (such as compensation for appearing in a film). In almost all cases, the only surviving evidence we have of this encounter is the film itself. The nature of a subject's performance for the camera is determined by a multiplicity of factors, including his or her relationship to the filmmaker and the context of the profilmic event, whether a ritual or ceremony, craft-making, hunting, or a view of a public or private space. The specific context in which images of native peoples were obtained is an important consideration when the trope of performance is evoked in discussions of early cinema, since where and under what circumstances a film was made will surely have some bearing upon its status as filmed ethnography. For example, filming native peoples who traveled with world's fair native villages and who performed daily under the scrutiny of the Western eye (such as *The Touaregs in Their Country*) is considerably different from shooting film on location where native peoples have little experience of Western contact. Likewise, paying a subject to demonstrate basket-making or perform a native dance is different from setting up a camera in a public place and letting it record until the film runs out. Two films that capture the visual logic of what I shall refer to as the presentational versus the observational approach (the former being a more explicitly staged performance than the latter) are *Egyptian Fakir with Monkey* (from Edison's 1903 Egyptian series, which exemplifies the presentational mode) and an unidentified film illustrative of the observational approach shot in Liberia in 1910 from the Abbé Joseph Joye Collection at the National Film and Television Archive in London.[36]

As the title implies, *Egyptian Fakir with Monkey* consists of a circuslike routine involving a fakir, a performing monkey, and a goat. The actual locale, including palm trees, a large white tent, and an ornate wooden chair, distinguishes this film from studio productions in which a vaudeville act is staged for the camera, as in Edison's early kinetescopes. As the monkey goes through its repertoire of tricks (while the goat remains motionless on a three-legged stool), including twirling a stick with its tail, dancing to the beat of the fakir's drum, and performing a mock swordfight, we are conscious of people going about their business in the background. As a result, the dense naturalistic mise-en-scène inflects how we mine the film for meaning beyond the familiar figure of the performing monkey. The film evokes a certain tension between the authentic Egyptian location which identifies the fakir as a member of a living culture and the monkey routine which connotes popular urban amusements and the emblematic construction of the Other as someone who exists solely to entertain Westerners. The conflict between the two registers is partially resolved shortly before the end of the film when, after a jump cut, an Egyptian man is shown standing in the midground staring fixedly at the camera. The presence of a second person imbues the performance space with social significance, as we now have two actors in front of the camera. Through its reflexive organization, *Egyptian Fakir with Monkey* paradoxically undermines the trope of the ethnographic subject as a body to be performed at the same time it validates it; the popular iconographic sign of the Egyptian fakir, replete with fez and long gown, reinforces stereotypical constructions of non-Westerners while the film disrupts the trope of the ethnographic Other as performer by having an Egyptian man reclaim the performance space from (or at least share it with) the fakir.

In contrast to *Egyptian Fakir with Monkey*, certain scenes from the 1910 Liberian film from the Joye Collection suggest a degree of trust between filmmaker and native peoples; the camera, at eye level for most of the film, frames the action in medium close-ups, as opposed to the typical medium long shots of this period. The Joye film has a relatively sophisticated structure, opening with an establishing long shot of a crowd of men gathered for a religious procession before offering a series of medium long shots of men and women preparing their hair (fig. 5.4) and dancing. A medium long shot of a group of seated women and children at campsite (fig. 5.5) follows medium shots of the religious procession (fig. 5.6); camera angle, shot scale, and duration all suggest that the Liberian women and children felt relaxed around the filmmaker since some people have their backs to the camera and others are in profile. No one looks in the direction of the camera.

FIG. 5.4 Frame enlargement of women braiding hair from 1910 Joye Collection film.

FIG. 5.5 Frame enlargement of campsite from 1910 Joye Collection film.

FIG. 5.6 Frame enlargement of religious procession from 1910 Joye Collection film.

FIG. 5.7 Group of seated women and children from Lowell Thomas's *Lawrence of Arabia*, 1917. (Imperial War Museum [IWM 42]. Courtesy IWM)

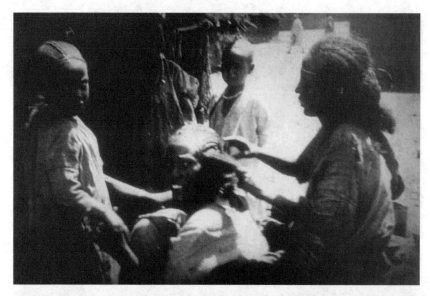

FIG. 5.8 Return gaze seen in frame enlargement of woman turning toward camera at end of hair-braiding sequence in 1910 Joye Collection film.

FIG. 5.9 Frame enlargement of male head-shaving scene from 1910 Joye Collection film.

A very similar camera setup can be seen in Lowell Thomas's 1917 *Lawrence of Arabia* (reassembled by the Imperial War Museum, London), in which a group of women and children are filmed at fairly close proximity (fig. 5.7). Here, the camera operator does not appear to be an intruder within the social space of the film, or at least fails to elicit an easily discerned reaction from the people as evident in the film. In the Joye film, however, the camera becomes more conspicuous when it moves closer to the action, as in the hair-braiding scene outside a hut.[37] Seemingly oblivious to the camera at the start of the shot as she sits in profile, the woman whose hair is being braided suddenly turns and smiles at the camera at the end of the shot, as do two children who enter the frame in the middle of the action (fig. 5.8). The low-angle medium close-up gives the impression that we, too, have been invited to attend the hair-braiding process, our presence explicitly acknowledged through the salutation at the end. In contrast, the succeeding shot of male head-shaving is less intimate in scale; the camera is frontal, in full medium shot, with the action strictly centered and with less casual wandering about by others in the frame (fig. 5.9). In the Joye film's final two shots, depicting a man drumming before a crowd of about twenty men and young boys (fig. 5.10) and two women dancing before a large crowd (fig. 5.11), we see evidence of what David MacDougall calls an "unprivileged camera style," close to the performers and inside the circle of onlookers. Relinquishing the position of a detached observer who sets up his camera on the top of a roof or on the front of a moving vehicle, the style of the unprivileged camera is "based in the assumption that the appearance of a film should be an artifact of the social and physical encounter between the filmmakers and the subject."[38]

Egyptian Fakir with Monkey and the 1910 Joye Collection film illustrate some of the difficulties involved in classifying films of this period as ethnographic based on textual evidence alone, since in the case of the Joye film there is no extant evidence of who shot the film, where it was exhibited, and how it was received (the film is identified only by the collector and a number). While the Joye film seems far more sophisticated narrationally, spatially, and ethnographically in terms of what it reveals about a West African Muslim society, we have no way of knowing how contemporaneous audiences extracted ethnographic meaning from it. One clue may lie in considering the kinds of images filmmakers assumed audiences would be interested in looking at during this

FIG. 5.10 Frame enlargement of man drumming from 1910 Joye Collection film.

FIG. 5. 11 Frame enlargement of two women dancing surrounded by crowd at the end of 1910 Joye Collection film.

FIG. 5.12 Opening shot of *Picturesque Colorado* (Rex Motion Picture Co., 1911).

period. Examining what the camera operator chose to frame and scrutinizing the demeanor of native people in front of the camera, we can speculate on how certain ethnographic images assume ascendency in Western imaginings of what native peoples living in exotic places should look like; what the moving picture camera itself signified to native people (although, for obvious reasons, this can never be fully known); and what larger knowledge structures were being evoked in the film. We might also consider the formal and aesthetic choices made by a camera operator in relation to how native peoples from different parts of the world have been traditionally imaged—for example, the way in which certain native groups quickly become identified with a narrow range of stereotypical types. An analysis of *Picturesque Colorado* (Rex Motion Picture Co., 1911) may be illuminating in this regard.

Picturesque Colorado opens with a medium long shot of two Native American men in full feather headdresses performing a war dance in front of four women and a small child at Manitou, Colorado (fig. 5.12).[39] Like the woman from the opening of *The Touaregs in Their Country*, who could not contain her embarrassment at being in front of the camera, an Indian woman standing on the left-hand side of the frame struggles to maintain her composure and ends up stifling her noticeable giggles with her hand. Perhaps as a result of the subversive effect of this laughter on the tone of the scene, the camera operator somewhat unexpectedly begins to slowly pan away from the dancers to take in a view of the extensive cliff dwellings as the Indian woman is given a chance to regain her composure. Why did the filmmaker choose to pan away from the group at this point, as opposed to editing in the camera or leaving the camera position unchanged? The operator may have felt that the laughter undermined the nostalgic tone evoked by the dance and, rather than have the serious mood of the shot sabotaged by this act, decided to frame something else. Alternatively, we can read his decision to pan as a direct symptom of the overexposure of Indian dances, which by this date no longer captivated the public's imagination as they had done ten years earlier. In other words, perhaps the cameraman himself was simply bored by the dance and, anticipating the audience's shared response, decided to move on. Alternatively, given the film's title and explicit remit to represent a *range* of Colorado sights, the brevity of the Indian dance sequence may have been quite intentional. Whatever the cameraman's motivation to pan away from the dancers, the camera movement nevertheless has an impact on our perception of the native performers, who are "left behind" in favor of the cliff dwellings; the shot is followed by views of the mountainous landscape taken from a moving vehicle. Indeed, the second explanation gains credence in subsequent scenes of the film which show Euro-American tourists vacationing on top of Steamboat Rock and Glenwood Springs. The Indian dancers are presented as merely one attraction among many others for tourists in "picturesque" Colorado; in the process, they are transformed into touristic icons which, like other aspects of modern life, can be consumed quickly, without the need for lengthy contemplation.

Native peoples are represented here, then, not as possessors of a land but as mere figures in a landscape, not dissimilar to the mannequins seen in museum life groups. *Picturesque Colorado* also reverses the common ethnographic film-editing trajectory from wide shots of a landscape to physiognomical close-ups of its inhabitants. The typical movement from the landscape to the body of the Other is exemplified in the 1913 Eclair film *The Oasis of El-Kantara*, which opens with long shots of the oasis and ends on a medium close-up of two young Arabian boys grinning for the camera. As Lucy Lippard argues, "Around the turn of the century, Indians were the photogenic counterparts of today's 'lookouts'—roadside scenic vistas, ready-made 'views,' 'nature' viewed from a static culture."[40] But ethnographic representation is touched by tourism in another way; the tourist, as Catherine Russell has noted, is also an ethnographer, because he or she imagines him or herself capable of producing certain kinds of knowledge about cultural difference, such as information gleaned from a tourist guidebook and from firsthand encounters with native culture, without need for the rigors of scientific investigation.[41] This conflict between the ethnographic body as a spectacle to be looked at and as the repository of vibrant information about how cultural difference is experienced is doubly dramatized in the case of such commercially produced films; while both early cinema and anthropology were fascinated with the body as an overdetermined sign, the tension between these different levels of representation becomes acute in films that have the surface "look" of ethnography but are motivated by an entirely commercial agenda.

The textual features of these early ethnographic films thus offer us a palpable sense of how native peoples were transformed into public views. This is particularly striking in shots of individuals going about their life in a social space that is suddenly altered by the camera operator's presence, as in *Egyptian Market Scene* and *Market Scene in Old Cairo, Egypt* (both produced by Edison in 1903). These films are early examples of the camera's disruptive effect on the ebb and flow of a marketplace; the Western camera operator, perhaps merely part of the crowd until the moment he sets up his camera, undergoes a metamorphosis as he fixes on an appropriate spot and begins to crank the handle; as Belgian theorist Livio Belloï explains: "Renouncing motion, focusing on a fixed point in space, the operator *leaves the crowd*, singularizing himself. From strolling to immobilization, from fusion to distancing, the stroller transforms himself, at this precise moment, into an *observer*."[42] In his analysis of the role of the cameraman in early Lumière films, Belloï argues that the process of filming is the result of an interaction between observer and onlooker, neither a spontaneous encounter nor one in which the camerman exerts total creative control over the profilmic. At the moment the cameraman sets up his equipment, he and his machine become what Belloï calls "poles of attraction and centers of visual attention," as opposed to invisible recording devices.[43] With its metallic glass eye fixed on a crowd or group of individuals, the camera undergoes another metamorphosis as it is transformed into an attraction that pulls people's wandering gaze over to its boxy head and three-legged frame.

The Return Gaze

Itself a technological novelty at the turn of the century, the motion picture camera frequently became the center of attention in films made in both public and private spheres.[44] In *Egyptian Market Scene* (mentioned above), which is photographed in a slightly high-angle medium long shot, our gaze onto the bustling market is returned by a boy in the foreground who never takes his eye off the camera; as the camera's pan continues, he is joined by a man wearing a white turban in the extreme foreground who also stares fixedly at the camera. The camera's slow, surveillance-like pan from left to right brings into view other market traders who glance in the camera's direction, until the shot ends framing yet another man standing screen right looking directly at the audience. In many ways, by foregrounding the status of the cinematic apparatus as both a "seeing technology" and a "technology to be seen," this film becomes an exercise in the art of reciprocal "looking" as much as a micro-ethnography of Egyptian markets. The boy's refusal of the camera's invisibility may have elicited any number of unexpected outcomes in terms of the effect of the return gaze on traditional constructions of exotic or oriental scenes.

As something of an emblematic moment in early ethnographic films and travelogues (see, for example, the two young boys timidly holding out their hands in the frame enlargement from Lowell Thomas's *Lawrence of Arabia* [fig. 5.13]), the return gaze can have diverse implications for the ideological meanings of a film and its effect on an audience; in what manner and context a filmed subject chooses to look at the camera will affect how we make sense of the return gaze. In a number of ethnographic process films, for example, an indigenous artisan will often look up at the camera while continuing with the work activity, be it constructing a clay pot or a bamboo mat. It should be noted, though, that artisans occasionally chose not to look at the camera for the *duration of a film* as seen in this frame enlargement from *Die Mauerische Topfer* (*The Moroccan Potter*, c. 1910) (fig. 5.14). Framed in a medium long shot at the start of the film, the Moroccan man is completely preoccupied with making his pot and makes no eye contact with the camera. After a jump cut, the cam-

FIG. 5.13 Frame enlargement of two young boys with women begging in front of the camera from Lowell Thomas's *Lawrence of Arabia*, 1917. (IWM 42. Courtesy IWM)

FIG. 5.14 Frame enlargement from *Die Mauerische Topfer* [*The Moroccan Potter*] (c. 1910).

FIG. 5.15 Group of Arabian boys staring at the camera from Lowell Thomas's *Lawrence of Arabia*, 1917. (IWM 42. Courtesy IWM)

era moves in slightly closer to the subject to get a better view of the hands at work on the potter's wheel, but this has no impact on his demeanor. When workers do acknowledge the presence of the camera, this cursory glance, I would argue, can either be read as a gesture of inclusion, in which the worker looks up from his or her labor to the camera operator as if to say "see, this is how it's done," or, as a nervous reaction to the presence of the camera and operator, more of a "oh you're still here" kind of response. A second type of return gaze takes the form of the "camera-as-celebrity," in which native peoples (often children) run to keep up with a camera stationed on a moving vehicle. This is the case in the opening of the 1923 British film *Street Images* shot in China, or in the frame enlargement of Arabian boys staring at the camera from Thomas's *Lawrence of Arabia* (fig. 5.15).[45]

William Alfred Gibson and Millard Johnson's 1906 film *In Living Hawthorne* is a stunning instance of how the viewer is directly addressed from a number of different stances; as David MacDougall has argued, this film exemplifies the itinerant film-unit model from the early cinema period in which filmmakers would visit rural areas and shoot footage that would be shown the following day in a rented space. The camera in this film seems to be the equivalent of the royal visitor garnering enormous public interest (from adults but especially children), eliciting, as MacDougall points out, an almost knee-jerk reaction to the self-exposure that comes with being looked at:

> The glance into the camera evokes one of the primal experiences of daily life — of look returned by look — through which we signal mutual recognition and affirm the shared experience of the moment. It is the look of exchange that says, "At this moment, we see ourselves through one another." The encounter produces a phatic reversal of roles, in which the reviewer seems to be regarding himself or herself with the eyes of the other.[46]

A third form of return gaze is the sustained stare at the camera, which is by far the most provocative and potentially disruptive to the discursive organization of a film. The question evoked by the variety of modes of the return gaze is the extent to which these moments when the spectator's gaze meets that of the subjects might be read as acts of defiance or as gestures of subversion.[47]

Fatimah Tobing Rony argues that unlike the situation at world's fairs, where the return gaze represented a threat to the security of the white onlookers, in cinema the return gaze is unthreatening to spectators, due to cinema's "more perfect voyeurism."[48] However, I would point out that, in certain instances, the cinematic return gaze breaks the circuit of power between the spectator's gaze and the "to-be-looked-at-ness" of the Other by making the spectator acutely aware of the intrusive nature of the filming and by triggering a nearly automatic reaction to the discomfort of being stared at. In this regard, while not threatening in the same literal sense as being conscious of someone staring at you standing six feet away at a world's fair native village, there is nonetheless something unsettling about being reminded of our status as onlookers, intruders, and outsiders. In the case of cinema, something compels us to stare back at the person looking directly at the camera (the darkness of the cinema auditorium mitigates against prolonged looking away from the screen); we may even identify with their curiosity and/or discomfort (how many of us recoil at the prospect of being filmed on the street as we go about our business, or, even worse, at being stopped and filmed without our permission). In contrast to Rony, then, I would say there is a paradoxical quality to the return gaze that is unique to film; while it signals the filmmaker's agency as a gatherer of images—*we* collect images of *them* and not vice versa—at the same time it carries with it a subversive or defiant element, a look that *could* be transcribed as "I see you looking at me and don't like it." While this acknowledgment of our looking subverts our status as voyeurs (although there is, in my opinion, something pleasurable, as well as disconcerting, about being stared at), it also threatens the certitude of our visual sovereignty over the people represented in the film. It may be more accurate to read the return gaze as an example of the kinds of social interactions between colonizer and colonized taking place in the "contact zone," Mary Louise Pratt's term for the interstitial social spaces of the colony, a place where native cultures are never simply overcome by the presence of the colonizers, but remain in productive tension with them.[49] As a space in which "geographically and historically separated [peoples] come into contact with each other and establish ongoing relations," the contact zone incorporates the "interactive, improvisational dimension of colonial encounters so easily ignored or suppressed by diffusionist accounts of conquest and domination."[50] In this regard, the return gaze suggests the dissonance between the illusion of complete control exerted by colonial authorities and a recognition of its fragility and discursive complexity. In the absence of textual or paratextual clues as to the nature of the interaction between filmmaker and filmed—whether the process was coercive or consensual—we must tread with care when it comes to making sweeping assertions about the "colonial gaze" of early ethnographic film.

Given that the return gaze can take on many different forms, from an accidental glance at the camera to a sustained form of direct address, and even a form of reverse ethnography in contemporary ethnographic cinema, where indigenous filmmakers have made Westerners the object of the gaze,[51] it is irreducible, therefore, to any singular interpretation and long predates cinematic representation. Take, for example, Albert Eckhout's painting of Tarairiu Indians (on the cover of the present volume), which speaks to a very cinematic way of seeing cultural difference (fig. 5.16); the widescreen composition and

FIG. 5.16 Tarairiu Indians painted by the Danish artist Albert Eckhout in the 1640s. (*Photo:* John Lee. Courtesy the National Museum of Denmark, Department of Ethnography)

kineticism of the dancers even seem to foreshadow Thomas Edison's *Sioux Ghost Dance* and *Indian War Council*. The third dancer from the right returns our gaze in a way similar to one of the dancer's in *Sioux Ghost Dance*, who solicits the spectator each time he completes the circular pattern of the dance. Unlike the Edison film, Eckhout's painting features internal spectators (whose gaze seems directed as much to the viewer of the painting as to the dancers) and two women who whisper secretly with hands over their mouths. Like the return gaze itself, their presence in the painting complicates the intersubjective relations of the ethnographic encounter, forcing us, I would argue, to think about the representation as precisely that—a representation.

While the look at the camera in such films as Pathé's *The Touaregs in Their Country* seems to say, "I see you watching me," in films such as *Egyptian Boys in Swimming Race*, which are organized more explicitly around a staged performance, the look is more of a summons, along the lines of "Look at Me!" The unintentional effects of the return gaze can also be seen in another film from the 1903 Edison Egyptian series—*Market Scene in Old Cairo*—which is formally structured by a long, sweeping pan.[52] A high stone wall enclosing the marketplace at screen-left serves as a logical starting point for the pan in this film; the shot opens onto a rich topography of baskets, boxes, and other bric-a-brac, although a man seated with his back to the wall quickly draws our attention away from the merchandise and onto his gaze, which, while he remains visible in the frame, is fixed on the camera. However, the camera's presence is acknowledged with greater consequence two-thirds of the way through the pan, when a man wearing a uniform and a fez scatters the people standing in the foreground of the shot and stands looking at the camera for the remainder of the film. His intervention disrupts both the tempo of the film's action and our reading of the scene; suddenly confronted by an official who has the power to empty the frame, we are reminded of the exigencies of filming in public spaces in non-Western cultures and how easily our ability to see can be thwarted. At the same time, it is unclear what might have motivated the official to clear the space: he may, for example, have disapproved of the attention the curious onlookers paid to the Western camera operator or to the presence of the filmmaker in the bazaar. Alternatively, he may have been trying to help the filmmaker get a better shot of the market and its environs and took it upon himself to direct the scene.

Another example of a local authority figure exerting control over profilmic events can be seen in Edison's *Egyptian Boys in Swimming Race*, filmed on the banks of the Nile River in March 1903. As the organizing principle of the film, the swimming contest creates a measure of narrative suspense as each boy scurries out of the water and solicits the camera operator for a reward for his efforts. The camera is on land about 100 feet from the swimmers who, at the start of the film, are barely visible in extreme long shot. The movement of the actors within the profilmic space is determined both by the cameraman, who planned the film around the swimming race (which moves toward the camera), and an on-screen stage director who ducks in and out of the medium shot to yank the boys into a neat line and to ensure that they all raise their right arms at the end of the race.[53] Despite its comic conclusion, this film invokes issues of corporeality central to our understanding of the textual forms of early ethnographic film. The boys' movement in the film from extreme long shot to medium shot encapsulates the gradual shift in early cinema from the tableau toward closer shots of the body, a shift in which the moving picture camera substituted the full figure with "multiple fragments . . . assembled under a new law," to quote Walter Benjamin.[54] One could also argue that the commercial filmmaker-ethnographer's fascination with the naked body of the Other provided the scopic motivation for cinema's disembodied gaze.

The reactions of native peoples to being filmed were occasionally remarked upon by early cinema writers, as in a 1907 description of Pathé's *Picturesque Java* in which the reviewer noted that the "several hundred" Javanese children were "conscious . . . before the camera, dancing and cutting capers before the lens." Equally remarkable to many critics was the apparent obliviousness of the filmed subjects to the presence of the camera, as in the review of Warwick's *A Primitive Man's Career to Civilization* (1911) from *The Bioscope*, where the critic noted that "savages, unconscious of the camera's proximity, [were] busy making weapons in the most primitive fashion."[55] However, if film reviewers occasionally remarked upon native peoples' behavior in front of the camera, they did so without considering what effect (if any) the return gaze or refused gaze (when an individual deliberately turns his or her head away from the camera) might have upon a film's claims to ethnographic veracity. Nevertheless, the underlying assumption seemed to be that films representing people going on with their daily life as if they weren't being filmed were more authentic than films which drew attention to their constructedness through acknowledgment of the camera. As we shall see, commercial filmmakers were keen to draw upon notions of authenticity and ethnographic verisimilitude which circulated in the legitimating worlds of professional anthropology and museology at the turn of the century.

The Travel Film as Filmed Ethnography

It is as if Mr. Howe had literally lifted out great moving incidents, living scenes as it were, from the most interesting parts of the world and set them down before one.
— *Philadelphia Enquirer* (1908)[56]

Of all the ethnographic genres in circulation during the early cinema period, it was the travel film (or travelogue) that most consistently co-opted the idea of ethnographic accuracy, fusing anthropological discourse with the rhetoric of the infant travel industry. The promotional conceit of "being there without being there" was the linchpin of most advertising campaigns and film reviews.

F I G. 5.17 Burton Holmes (*right*) and his cameraman Merl Levoy, setting up a shot in the middle of a Paris street, c. 1910. (Courtesy Museum of Modern Art [hereafter, MOMA])

It is worth exploring exactly how such films were constructed as ethnographic texts and what kind of experience they promised spectators in exchange for their money. Popularized by professional lecturer E. Burton Holmes (1870–1958) (fig. 5.17), the term *travelogue*,[57] or travel picture, as it was also called, functioned within what Charles Musser calls "an already extensive practice of nonfiction screen presentations."[58] Such films were shown as part of the illustrated lecture in major U.S. and British cities between 1897 and the early 1920s (fig. 5.17). Scenes from everyday life shot in urban, rural, and exotic locations lent the vaudeville lineup a cosmopolitan gloss as audiences were transported from continent to continent with every change of reel or scene.[59]

The illustrated travel lecture combined elements of touring educational exhibits and demonstrations of scientific and technological inventions with more sensational forms of entertainment, such as the dime museum, Wild West Show, and P. T. Barnum's troupe of human and natural exhibits.[60] In the travelogue, spectators were invited to become vicarious travelers through a discourse of armchair tourism that became the lingua franca of film reviewers between 1908, when brief film reviews began to appear in the *Moving Picture World*, and 1915. Film titles such as *A Trip Through the Holy Land* (Urban Eclipse, 1907), *In and Around Havana, Cuba* (Edison, 1911), and *From Durban to Zululand* (Edison, 1913) constructed the film spectator's experience as virtual travel, with the geographic itinerary of the journey literally inscribed into the film's title. The traveling lecturer-exhibitor commodified alterity by means of a consumable package of voyeuristic pleasure and rationalist rhetoric of uplift, comfort, and affordability. In this manner, the travelogue echoed the appeal of contemporary cultural venues such as the Hale's Tours cinema installations in several U.S. cities and the 1904 St. Louis World's Fair thrill-ride attractions which promised to transport visitors "New York to the North Pole in Twenty Minutes" or the fair's miniature railroad which ferried passengers through reconstructed villages of exotic peoples.[61] However, if amusements that offered spectators enthralling glimpses of faraway continents represented a democratization of tourism, they nevertheless perpetuated, according to Lauren Rabinovitz, "ethnocentric notions . . . by making faraway cultures into commodities that could be enjoyed for the price of admission."[62] Cinema thus "not only supported American intervention and domination over other peoples but also legitimated American imperialism and consumption of other national spaces."[63] If the average audience member could not afford (or felt disinclined) to globe-trot around the world, he or she might nevertheless experience distant lands by embarking on "little journeys" (as one critic called travel films) each time they attended a film screening. For the "stay-at-home" who lacked either the "time or money to see the great wonders of the world," travel pictures offered "the advantages and pleasures of travel without any of its defects, discomforts or inconveniences"[64] (fig. 5.18).

One of the most successful and prodigious turn-of-the-century travel lecturers was Lyman H. Howe (1856–1923), who prospered for many years after many of his competitors had gone out of business.[65] Travel lecturers such as Howe began using moving pictures in lectures around 1896–97, producing what Musser calls a "cinema of reassurance" in which middle-class sensibilities and elitist cultural values were ideologically inscribed into the lecture-performance.[66] Howe and other showmen drew their audiences from both church-based organizations and middle-class cultural, educational, and fra-

FIG. 5.18 Advertisement for travelogues on London bus, c. 1900.

ternal groups that sponsored illustrated travel lectures as part of a broader mission of uplift through education and exposure to the arts.[67] Howe's promotional materials spoke directly to the pedagogical and cultural preoccupations of these groups; his "22nd Semi-Annual Tour" in 1906 (fig. 5.19) was promoted as "an entertainment of merit, refinement, amusement, and educational value," while an advertisement for Howe's "Lifeorama: The Epitome of Moving Pictures" in 1909 described the exhibition as "the epitome of the truest realism that can be anchored in sight and sound."[68] According to the *Moving Picture World*, the mind was "ever kept in motion, ever stimulated, ever refreshed, ever excited."[69]

Travel film lecturers such as Howe and Holmes exerted a great deal of authorial control over their film exhibitions and were responsible for designing the program, ensuring the smooth transition between stereopticon slides, moving pictures, and phonograph recordings, and for setting the tone of the evening through the juxtaposition of films and spoken commentary.[70] As an interpretive agent, the lecturer provided a metacommentary on the slides and films featured in the program, perhaps using audience reaction to specific

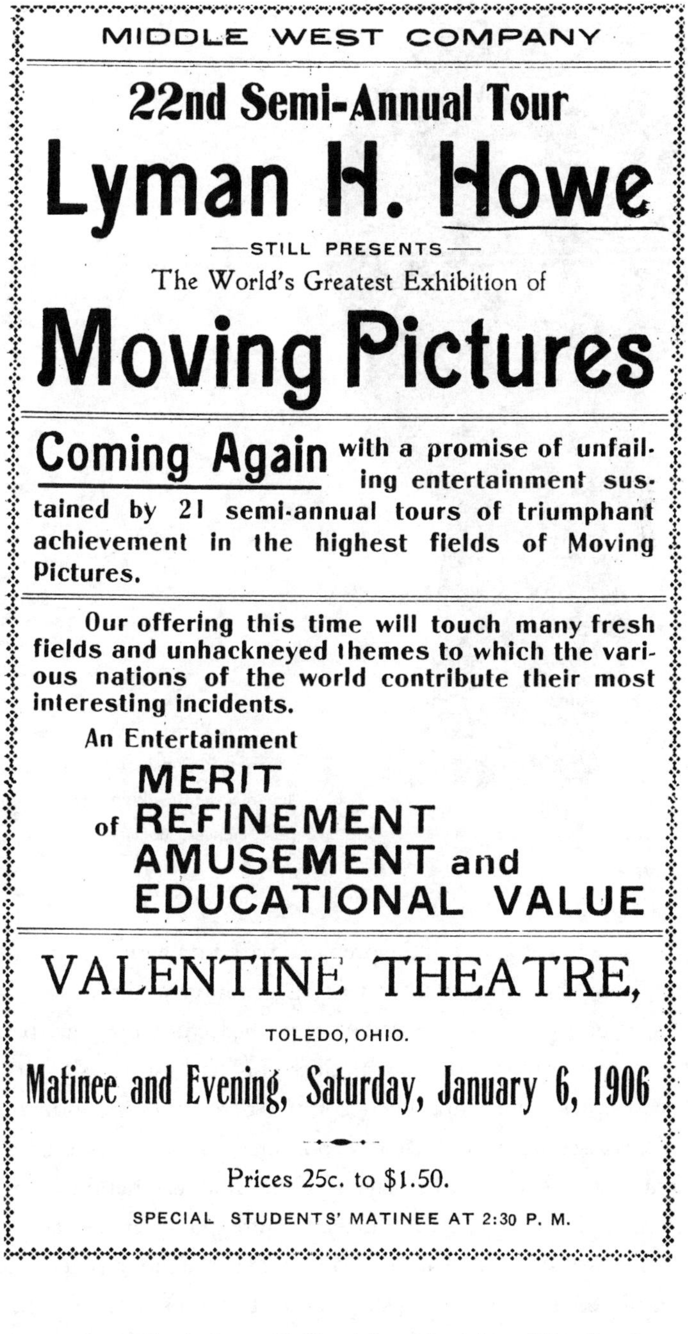
MIDDLE WEST COMPANY

22nd Semi-Annual Tour

Lyman H. Howe

—STILL PRESENTS—

The World's Greatest Exhibition of

Moving Pictures

Coming Again with a promise of unfailing entertainment sustained by 21 semi-annual tours of triumphant achievement in the highest fields of Moving Pictures.

Our offering this time will touch many fresh fields and unhackneyed themes to which the various nations of the world contribute their most interesting incidents.

An Entertainment

MERIT
of REFINEMENT
AMUSEMENT and
EDUCATIONAL VALUE

VALENTINE THEATRE,

TOLEDO, OHIO.

Matinee and Evening, Saturday, January 6, 1906

Prices 25c. to $1.50.

SPECIAL STUDENTS' MATINEE AT 2:30 P. M.

FIG. 5.19 Flier for Lyman H. Howe's "22nd Semi-Annual Tour," 1906.

FIG. 5.20 Burton Holmes dressed in
Japanese kimono for lecture series on
Japan at the Brooklyn Institute of Arts
and Sciences, 1909.

images as a cue to depart from the prepared narration with extemporaneous
comments about his experiences of visiting a country.[71] In addition to high-
lighting specific aspects of the mise-en-scène, the lecturer may have peppered
his talk with racist quips about the inferiority or "backwardness" of so-called
primitive peoples, especially when compared to modern, industrialized
America (this discourse would also have bolstered notions of national and cultural identity, reinforced by the playing of the American national anthem at
the beginning or end of a performance). Lecture tours were not confined to
large cities, which suggests that the geographic and demographic makeup of
audiences played no small role in shaping the lecturer's commentary. Given
the aleatory quality of much early exhibition practices, audiences could have

made any number of thematic and associative connections between individual scenes in films and between films that may or may not have been made explicit by the film lecturer. The exhibitor was also capable of exerting some degree of control over the film itself, either by removing, shifting, or disregarding intertitles or subjecting it to tinting or toning.[72] The ethnographic status of films representing indigenous peoples was largely determined by the film lecturer and exhibition context; indeed, for some early traveling film exhibitors, audience fascination with the exotic became part of the lecture-presentation itself, as showmen donned national costumes to add a soupçon of "authentic" culture and visual color to the film-lecture performance (fig. 5.20).[73] The films' textual cues were thus mediated by contextual and intertextual determinants, so much so that ethnographic meaning was always subject to the myriad possibilities of presentation and viewer negotiation.

The relationship between the travel lecture and the travelogue film (which was often used to illustrate the lecture) is quite complex; the travelogue footage screened during an event was probably not shot by the lecturer himself, since it was fairly routine for lecturers to recruit camera operators to shoot film. This was the case with Burton Holmes's relationship with Oscar Depue, his projectionist, who was also responsible for shooting Howe's films. Moreover, where and when films were shown during the program (which may have changed from venue to venue or even from lecture to lecture) would clearly have had some bearing on the overall effect of the performance. For example, the program for Holmes's 1909 "Around the World Series" (fig. 5.21) contains lecture titles (which often varied slightly) that give us no indication of what moving pictures were likely to be shown during the course of the lecture. However, the lecture synopses that always accompanied the program announcements in the *Brooklyn Institute of Arts and Sciences Bulletin* did identify motion pictures through the use of block capitals (nonfilm sequences are listed in lower case). Thus regarding Part I of "The New Japan To-Day," which may or may not have been the same lecture as "The Cities of Japan To-day" and "The Country of Japan To-day" from the spring 1909 lecture announcement mentioned above, all we know is that travelogue footage of Japan was shown fourteen times during the first part of the lecture, including such titles as "Life at Busy Corner Along Tokyo's Broadway" and "Wedding Procession of the Mikado's Daughter." While we have no idea how long each film seg-

The Burton Holmes Lectures

A SPECIAL COURSE OF
Five Beautifully Illustrated Lectures
IN THE MUSIC HALL, ENTITLED

'AN AROUND THE WORLD SERIES"
BY

MR. BURTON HOLMES
WITH
NEW COLORED VIEWS, NEW MOTION PICTURES
And NEW PANORAMIC SCENES,
ON WEDNESDAYS

MATINEES AT 4   EVENINGS AT 8.15

FEBRUARY 17—Hawaii To-day
FEBRUARY 24—The Cities of Japan To-day
MARCH 3 —The Country of Japan To-day
MARCH 10—Java and Ceylon
MARCH 17—Round About Paris (Also New)

Mr. HOLMES encircled the globe during the Spring and Summer of 1908, and returns with new material for his lectures.

The Opening Sale of Course Tickets
WILL BE ON
TUESDAY, FEBRUARY 2d, at 8.30 A. M.

THE MATINEE { To Members (with Coupons), for the Course - $1.50, $2.00, $3.00
LECTURES   { To Persons not Members, for the Course - $3.00, $4.00, $5.00
THE EVENING { To Members (with Coupons), for the Course - $2.00, $3.00, $4.00
LECTURES   { To Persons not Members, for the Course - $4.00, $5.50, $7.00

THE INSTITUTE TICKET OFFICES

ACADEMY OF MUSIC, BOX OFFICE . . . . . .   8.30 A. M. until 9.00 P. M.
FREDERICK LOESER & CO. (Piano Rooms, Fourth Floor) . . . . 8.30 A. M. until 6.00 P. M.
ABRAHAM & STRAUS (Near Hoyt Street Entrance) . . . . 8.30 A. M. until 6.00 P. M.

FIG. 5.21 Program for Burton Holmes's "Around the World" lecture series at the Brooklyn Institute of Arts and Sciences, spring 1909.

FIG. 5.22 Photograph of an unidentified camera operator shooting the celebrated Torii Arch at Miyajima, Japan, 1908. The arch is the subject of the concluding film in Burton Holmes's lecture "The Old Japan Today." (Courtesy MOMA)

ment lasted or what the contextualizing remarks may have been, we do have a detailed road map of the evening's entertainment, helpful in establishing what lecturers such as Holmes and Howe may have thought their middle-class audiences were most interested in looking at.[74] Moreover, unlike the titles of the lectures, which were short and to the point, the descriptions of the travel films left little to the imagination. For example, the film "Curious Serving Customs in the Japanese 'Yadoya' or Hotels" appeared in the lecture "The Old Japan Today" (fig. 5.22) while "How the Javanese Population Bathes and Launders Itself in the River Jjiliwong" was shown as part of the lecture "Java: The Eden of Netherlands India."[75]

Ideology in the travel film operated both through a proliferation of meanings as well as a containment of meaning, as it had in travel writing, including the suppression of significant aspects of the encounter between the traveling party and native peoples in favor of a romantic mystification of the traveler's experience.[76] "Manners and customs" descriptions of the indigenous people were usually contained in separate sections of the novel, rather than integrat-

FIG. 5.23 Flier for Lyman Howe's "29th Semi-Annual Tour," 1909. The shows boasted "The Wonders of Abroad, World's Masterpieces in Animated Photography," or what Howe described as the "Supreme triumph of realism."

ed into the narrative, to be "pulled out of time . . . preserved, contained, studied, admired, detested, pitied and mourned," in Pratt's words.[77] The conventional suppression of native subjectivity also extended to the laborers accompanying the traveling party; if mentioned at all, they appeared as abstractions, "exotic, comic, or pathetic spectacle for the eyes of the European . . . [while the European is] a self-effaced seer whose intervention seems to define the parameters of what is seen."[78]

This opposition between the possessor of the gaze and its recipients is illustrated in a flier for Lyman Howe's "29th Semi-Annual [Lifeorama] Tour" from 1909, in which the framing of Howe's Victorian countenance in the photograph positions him as the omniscient seer, looking directly at us as well as perhaps at himself, since the ornate frame suggests that Howe might be gazing at his own reflection in a mirror (fig. 5.23). The recurrent notion of a world inhabited by rapidly disappearing native "types" is evoked in Howe's maxim

"See Them Now or Never," a reference both to the limited engagement of the films (when the exhibitor returned the following year it would be with new titles) and to a discourse of salvage ethnography, the idea that audiences must act quickly and see the cultures represented in these films before they vanished forever.[79] This idea of time travel back to a more "primitive" past is visually inscribed at the top of the flier where the transportation motif infers a forward movement away from a "savage past" (as depicted on the right-hand side of the image) and toward a civilization as symbolized by Howe. The illustration also borrows the iconography of parades on the midways of world's fairs and in "Buffalo Bill's Wild West Show," and the less organized line of people in national costume at the bottom of the page resembles an encyclopedia entry on indigenous costume. As this advertisement vividly shows, homogenizing native peoples into a collective "they" in travelogues acts as a normalizing discourse which codifies difference and fixes the Other in a timeless ethnographic present.[80] Within this constellation, according to anthropologist Johannes Fabian, anything "he" does, or is, is not a particular historical event but an instance of a pregiven custom or trait.[81] In this manner, Pratt argues, "encounters with the Other can be textualized or processed as enumerations of such traits."[82]

But the ethnographic travelogue also shared something with another close relative of the travel novel, the picture postcard, a form that reified the identities of indigenous peoples in ways similar to the travel film and travel novel (figs. 5.24 and 5.25). As an illustrated form of colonial discourse, the postcard produces what Algerian cultural theorist Malek Alleloula calls a "pseudo-knowledge" about the colony, a knowledge deprived of most of the markers of the material conditions of colonial life.[83] In his penetrating study of postcards originating in Algeria from the turn of the century through the 1920s, Alleloula argues that erotic photographs of Algerian prostitutes masquerading as *Algeriennes* are the products of a "ventriloquial art" which revives the phantasm of the harem in a cheap, mass-produced art form that straddles two spaces: "the one it represents and the one it will reach."[84]

A similar process of reification and cultural stereotyping is at work in a 1907 *Moving Picture World* promotional description of *From Cairo to Khartoum*, which constructs the exotic Other as simultaneously alluring and threatening:[85]

FIG. 5.24 Postcard with caption "Jeune femme bédouin," c. 1890s. (Author's personal collection)

FIG. 5.25 Two Tunisian women embracing in a pose characteristic of Algerian postcards analyzed by Malek Alleloula, c. 1890. (Author's personal collection)

Wild, fantastic parades . . . a fierce charge of Arabs . . . afford wonderful glimpses of the manners and customs of these barbarous tribes. . . . Arab market scenes at Cairo [that] are deliciously novel to Western eyes— men, women and children of all shades of black and brown chatter and gesticulate, squat, walk or stand as they buy or sell wares and produce . . . veiled and unveiled women, rough and unkempt men, burmoused [*sic*] and turbaned—all make up a sum of wonderful Oriental variety and animation that will live for years in the memory.[86]

The string of oppositions in this description—wild parades versus market scenes, squatting versus standing, buying versus selling, veiled versus unveiled women, unkempt versus turbaned men—construct the Orient as a world of vivid contrasts and constant motion that will "live for years in the memory." But these binaries also serve another purpose. In employing some of the conventionalizing tropes of the travel novel, adjectives such as "wild," "barbarous," "curious," "picturesque," "quaint," "strange," "weird," and "queer" become the hallmarks of Otherness in published descriptions of these films, functioning essentially as an ideological shorthand for deeply embedded views about racial difference and the place of the Orient in the Western imaginary.[87] Another example may illustrate my point: a review of Holmes's lecture, "Japan: Land of Flowers," frames the cross-cultural encounter in terms of its excess of "picturesqueness" and "quaintness":

> Then in motion pictures they went through many of their dances for the express edification of the motion picture machine and the audiences which it was to reach. Always they were graceful, always picturesque and quaint, always there was about them an atmosphere of unreality as if they were characters out of a fairy story and not real performers . . . dancing before a *real camera*. Other motion pictures showed a funeral procession which, while solemn as was befitting the event, had the same air of unreality, the same picturesqueness and quaintness.[88]

The slippage between the rhetoric of realism and the picturesque in this review suggests the difficulty of discussing these films within the context of ethnography, a scientific endeavor that has traditionally avoided overtly subjective or lyrical accounts of native peoples. Where the only evidence of a film having been made is an extant promotional description or review, the writer's frequent emphasis upon the "quaintness" and "picturesqueness" of the event frustrates certainty about both the precise content of the scene and the broader cultural context and meaning of the performance. While the review's repeated references to the atmosphere of unreality created by the filmed dances and funeral procession may be read as an attempt to evoke the oneiric effect of these ceremonies, we may wonder why the author makes a point of contrasting the "unreal" effects of the dancing with the "realness" of the camera. Perhaps fearful of the audience mistaking the "unreal" dances and funeral procession for a fabrication of reality, the reviewer is at pains to point out that if the performers seem as though they are characters lifted from a fairy story, the means by which they have been mechanically reproduced is unmistakably "real."

The films shown in Holmes's lecture "Japan: Land of Flowers" also point up the ambiguous status of the "real" in early cinema, an intermingling of the registers of artifice and reality that is not uncharacteristic of critical reaction to early actualities, and that is signaled in the reenactment as a way of representing events that could not otherwise be filmed. Rather than deny any knowledge of the reenacted status of the Japanese dances, the writer points out that the dances have been performed for the "express edification of the motion picture machine and the audiences which it was to reach." However, if the public had an interest in viewing a representation of a noteworthy or picturesque event, this representation was under no obligation to render reality with complete exactitude, although there are clearly *degrees* of artifice and constructedness across films produced during the early cinema period. Oppositions between real and faked, authentic and fabricated, and genuine and imitation were nevertheless subject to flexible interpretation in the early cinema period.[89] In addition, the problem of differentiating "authentic" travel films from reconstructions and reenactments (a strategy of countless popular films portraying ethnographic subjects as well as coronations, executions, military campaigns, boxing matches, and safaris in the pre-1905 period) blurs the boundaries between fact and fiction.[90]

For turn-of-the-century audiences, the "reality effect" of early actualities may have depended on the mobile subject positions they were invited to take up while watching films; for example, in the case of the early boxing film, identification may have shifted from that of patriotic citizen to silent witness and ringside fan with each change of reel. According to film historian Dan Streible, fake fight films elicited such a range of spectatorial reactions because "they derived from two conflicting practices: accepted forms of re-presentations, and dishonest misrepresentations contrived to deceive."[91] Similarly, in the case of early ethnographic travelogues, audiences may have assumed very different relationships to the images of filmed native peoples, depending on the exhibition context and textual cues. In the case of early ethnographic cinema, the extent to which audiences were able or inclined to separate the faked from the "real" was perhaps in part determined by their previous exposure to native cultures. Thus, audiences judged the cinematic depictions to be more or less real based on exhibition practices associated with precinematic forms

FIG. 5.26 Photograph captioned "Singular City of Seoul." Holmes shot films in Korea circa 1908 and probably included these ethnographic images in a lecture on Korea given at the Brooklyn Institute of Arts and Sciences in 1909. (Courtesy MOMA)

of ethnographic representation and the framing discourses of verisimilitude. For example, we have no way of knowing how Holmes might have framed the image of Korean children shot circa 1908, his comments perhaps directed toward the children, the style of the housing, or the water channel running diagonally across the frame (fig. 5.26).

But if early cinema audiences often seemed disinclined to enforce rigid distinctions between reconstructed and authentic performances (or simply acknowledged the artifice without being overly bothered by it), filmmakers themselves adopted a very different public stance on issues of accuracy and authenticity. In this regard, itinerant showmen frequently made extravagant claims about their films that were parroted in descriptions, reviews, and features published in the professional and popular press. On the subject of Howe's *The Grand Canyon*, one anonymous critic noted that the film contained "real Hopi and Navajo Indians in their native haunts around the canyon . . . [instead] of the type of Indian or near-Indians that are usually exploited by show-men. . . . [This] real type is unmatted and unsullied by any influences but those of their native haunts and environment."[92] In cases where very little information survives on how audiences may have responded to the realist claims made by film promoters and reviewers (or even what a film consisted of, in the frequent case where there is little, if any, description of individual scenes from a lost film), all that remains of a film is ephemeral material from trade journals, newspapers, and popular magazines.[93] By examining how these materials intersected with existing signifying practices, we can better understand how ethnographic travelogues constructed meaning and appealed to audiences. Notwithstanding the presentist biases that inevitably color contemporary readings of this material (the fact that we can never step outside our subject positions as modern viewers of these films and their supporting materials), we can still find clues as to how discourses of ethnography were evoked and refracted in surviving documentation.

Given the impossibility of knowing precisely how audiences framed their understanding of ethnographic realism, it may be more useful to consider how audience expectations were met or challenged in these early ethnographic travelogues. For example, a description of the 1905 Pathé film, *In India: Marriage of the Nephew of the Maharajah of Tagore*, suggests that what audiences expected to see in films representing non-Western cultures played no small role in influencing what was singled out for discussion in the trade press (and flagged in publicity materials):

> We see the natives, with stolid, serious expressions on their dark faces marching along to the strains of their own weird music. . . . Some Indian maidens then execute a peculiar Indian dance, making motions with their hands as if in imitation of snakes springing forward and retreating. The whole scene is one of splendid color, *just what one would expect to see in India.*[94]

Ethnographic verisimilitude is measured by this reviewer on the basis of how an image of India lives up to one's preconceptions of the country and its people ("just what one would expect to see"). The experience of watching actuality footage of South Asian dancing for the average spectator may, then, have differed little from gazing at a fictional rendition (or even looking at a film poster), as both involve the sensation of "having already witnessed" a phenomenon that novelist and literary critic Walker Percy calls the "symbolic machinery" that helps spectators form an image of a place, event, or practice before they submit their gaze to the actual thing. According to Percy, a spectator's imagined version of an object or phenomenon can never fully escape the internalized culturally constructed way of seeing it, which may end up appearing more "real" than the firsthand account.[95] Pathé's images of Indian dancers may thus have shared a number of semantic resemblances with other established representational forms and been experienced by spectators in much the same way as fictional renditions, as audience expectations of what an Indian dance should look like would have been shaped by a limited repertoire of images drawn from popular illustrations, the circus, the theater, and painting, or what Jonathan Culler calls the sight as a sign of itself.[96] German film historian Martin Loiperdinger argues that this trafficking between the significatory codes of actuality and fiction goes both ways, since audiences familiar with topical problems within Western culture during the period, such as infant mortality, may have experienced fictional films like Biograph's *The Country Doctor* (1909) as documentary.[97]

For many early film spectators, there was undoubtedly something unique about submitting one's gaze to a moving image of an indigenous dance, as opposed to staring at a frozen still; cinema's "mobile, virtual gaze"[98] afforded the spectator the opportunity for virtual travel and vicarious identification with both the filmmaker and the subjects represented on the screen, what one critic in 1907 argued was "just the tonic that thousands of tired women and dissatisfied men need[ed], and which could not be paid for anywhere else than in the nickel theatre."[99] The movie critic of the Rochester *Times* went so far as to argue that the travel film not only "gratif[ied] the universal longing to travel much more satisfactorily" than did travel literature (Jules Verne's *Around the World in Eighty Days* served as a standard comparative text in several reviews) but gave audiences an opportunity to "girdl[e] the globe" with all the "atmosphere and fascination of actual travel": "People comprising the large audience in the Pabst Theater last night could scarcely believe they were sitting comfortably in stationary theater chairs, for there is enough of that convincing atmosphere about Lyman Howe's Lifeorama pictures to transport the spectator to the scene depicted."[100]

Promising virtual travel to distant and often inhospitable lands, early travelogues obviated the need for physical travel in the minds of several writers and were deemed a worthy substitute for the cumbersome, visually impoverished, and more expensive encyclopedia. Addressing would-be exhibitors as well as companies with motion picture interests, the *Motion Picture World* promoted cinema as a form of accelerated learning that could compress knowledge about the world and its peoples into easily assimilable vignettes. As a living encyclopedia that could sate the audience's presumed thirst for knowledge about the ancient and modern world and that would "leave the mind impressed precisely as would the actual visit," the travel film was rhetorically constructed as the next best thing to real travel to exotic locales, which, for most nickelodeon audiences, was beyond their economic means.[101] The same idea recurs three years later in a 1913 review of Howe's films: "[The travel film] is fulfilling a mission that is as far reaching in its scope as the halls of learning and culture. . . . When you leave the theater after a two and half hours world tour with Howe, you have derived more real satisfaction, wholesome entertainment, and beneficial knowledge than can be gleaned from a score of dramatic or musical offerings."[102] Not only did cinema offer unique pedagogic advantages over the traditional arts, but it was perceived as a more cost-efficient and intellectually worthy means of vicariously experiencing distant lands and peoples:

The moving picture machine, for less than $5 worth of admission tickets
. . . will take you on a journey into every quarter, nook and corner of the
globe that has been discovered and show you scenes that even the most
inveterate of explorers and globe trotters, who may have spent $500,000 in
their travels, have never seen. . . . One man doing nothing but traveling
for ten years could not visit all the places and witness all the scenes that the
moving picture machine will show you this month.[103]

Filmgoers who attended Howe's lecture in Milwaukee in 1909 were assured
that they did not "need to visit [a] country in order to acquire knowledge of
the customs and habits of [a] people," a point echoed in a *Moving Picture World*
editorial from the following year: "So clearly and graphically are the scenes
presented that one may acquire a reasonably accurate knowledge of distant
lands and their inhabitants for the expenditure of a few cents per week; and
there is no heavy expense or hardship for actual travel."[104] Clear from the
hyperbole surrounding these accounts of the travelogue as virtual travel is the
degree to which they echo, and perhaps parody, the serious accounts of ethnographers, another possible reason why anthropologists felt uneasy about
commercially produced ethnographic films. While no one would have confused the serious work of anthropologists with such showmanship claims of
film promoters, there is no doubt that their allusion to discourses of visuality—the idea of cultural difference as something to be "witnessed" or "seen"—
dramatizes some of the persistent commonalities and tensions between popular culture and anthropology.

In trade and popular press accounts of travel films, writers often argued that
the promise of vicarious travel offered audiences by such showmen could be
greatly enhanced through the use of mechanical sound effects and the human
voice: "Accompanying spoken dialogue and sound adds immensely to the realism and makes the audience forget for the moment that they are really looking at views, but are spectators at actual events," wrote one reviewer.[105]
Exhibitors often went to great lengths to reproduce illusionistic sound effects,
placing recruitment ads for sound-effects personnel in the trade press (fig.
5.27); for example, audiences watching Howe's "Lifeorama" films of the battle of Port Arthur heard "the clanging of sabers, the rattle of musketry, the
fanfare of trumpets, the roll of the drum, the booming of the cannon . . . in

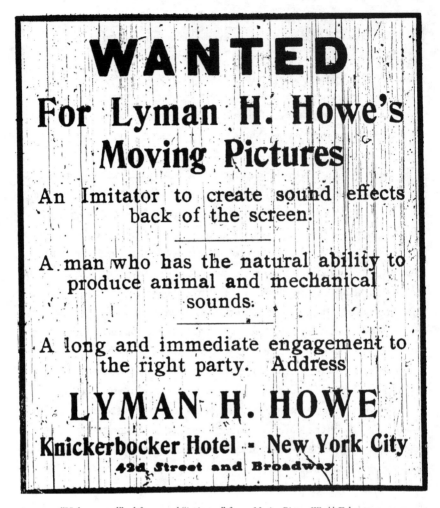

FIG. 5.27 "Help wanted" ad for sound "imitator" from *Moving Picture World*, February 13, 1909.

short [everything] that brings the scene close to home until the spectator fairly lives in the atmosphere and is transported in imagination to the spot where history is being made."[106] If the sound effects of warfare that helped evoke the Port Arthur battle scene were designed to be largely mimetic and naturalistic, the reproduction of indigenous speech was subject to far greater artistic license and often served to reinforce racist notions of native languages as little more than childlike and incomprehensible "chatter." For example, the

Pittsburgh Leader's reviewer of "Lifeorama" noted that while the sound of railroad tracks being laid was created simply "by clashing pieces of iron together," Mr O. J. Tasker, the technician responsible for the voices, "nearly talked himself blue in the face speaking the language of coolies."[107] Another reviewer referred to "an outburst of joyful appreciation [when] . . . the natives seen in the pictures were heard chattering in their jargon."[108]

As this discussion of the role of sound suggests, recovering the experience of turn-of-the-century audiences of these films and understanding how their ethnographic content was interpreted must accommodate evidence beyond the filmic image, since live sound accompaniment (as well as the noise generated by audience members responding to the films) transformed the film exhibition into a unique performative event.[109] As Rick Altman has argued, "Not only are the performances themselves forever lost, but even their traces have systematically fallen prey to the low esteem accorded ephemeral and tributary phenomena like silent film sound."[110] Given the brevity of most films in the pre-1900 period, lecturers like Howe alternated moving pictures with phonograph recordings (as well as using the phonograph to create sound effects for the moving images), which meant that moving pictures were either used to highlight certain aspects of the lecture or appeared as special attractions at the end of the show.[111]

But the inclusion of live sound in film-lectures is just one of several factors complicating our understanding of the early ethnographic travelogue; the uncertain provenance of films exhibited during an exhibition program also complicates accounts of how ethnographic meaning was constructed in these lecture screenings, since films shot by camera operators employed by lecturers (or on occasion, lecturers themselves) were undifferentiated from those purchased from commercial production companies.[112] Given that both sorts of films were typically programmed as part of a single evening's refined entertainment, it is difficult to know with certainty which films had been shot by the lecturer and which were commercial releases produced by manufacturing companies. In his lecture "More About Paris" (1909), for example, Holmes exhibited films produced by Charles Urban, Pathé Frères, Léon Gaumont, Raleigh and Robert, as well as material shot by his own assistant, Oscar Depue. Questions of authorship are further obscured by the fact that the film negative was subject to manipulation by film colorists who hand-painted individual frames; Holmes employed Japanese artists, along with his regular colorist Helen E. Stevenson,[113] to hand-color the negative of films shown in the lecture "The New Japan Today."[114]

Relying upon extant prints of early travelogues for ethnographic meanings is thus fraught with difficulties, since factors relating to the overall design and tone of programs undermine the sovereignty of the print as the self-sufficient sign-event. As Dutch archivist Nico de Klerk notes, rather than being the sole arbiter of meaning, the print was "an arena where the claims of all these forces were negotiated."[115] For example, it was common practice in America to screen comic and trick films—what one Baltimore film critic referred to as "tension relievers"—between travel films, in order to vary the program or to signal an upcoming intermission.[116] Comic films and magic shows were also staples of the illustrated lecture program, as evidenced by a 1903 Holmes lecture in which "interesting scenes from all over the world . . . were interspersed with a diverting lot of comedy pictures and marvelous magic productions that baffle all attempts at explanation."[117] In 1914, Howe showed a film from the "Rastus" series which "kept the audience in laughter" as well as "trick pictures of sambo annexing a chicken only to make the horrifying discovery that he has bagged a skeleton."[118] The overt racist content of these comic films cannot have been lost on exhibitors, who may have used them to draw explicit comparisons between the indigenous peoples represented in the travelogues and the African-Americans portrayed condescendingly in the comic shorts. Ethnographic meaning would therefore have circulated within and between the texts that comprised the lecture and been derived from a wider cultural matrix of Eurocentric ideas on racial hierarchies and white supremacy.

Moreover, prints used by early exhibitors were also often composed of compilation footage and retitled for commercial release; some of the footage from Pathé's *The Touaregs in Their Country* (1908), for example, shows up under the title *An African Village* (Kleine, 1908). In contrast to the intertitles used in the Pathé version, which offer a literal description of upcoming scenes (including "The Turban as Head-Dress," "Departure of a Caravan," and "Assaulting a Courier"), the titles in the Kleine print are more informal and colorful in style (a scene of a little boy and his mother is introduced by the title "His Mother's Pride"; another intertitle describes the Touaregs as "fierce warriors and fighters").

FIG. 5.28 Cartoon of English lanternist and inveterate traveler Frank E. Butcher of the well-known firm W. Butcher and Sons, Ltd. (Supplement to *The Bioscope*, February 16, 1911)

Likewise, footage from American millionaire-adventurer Paul J. Rainey's *African Hunt* (1914) was reedited and given the title *Scenes of African Animals*.[119] Lecturers would often recycle their own films with new titles years after they had initially been shown; Frederick Monsen, in his 1913 program "The Other Side of the World," exhibited the same films under new titles that he had shown in his 1906 program, "The Garden of Allah: The Sahara Desert" at Carnegie Hall. Idiosyncratic retitling and creative repurposing of film footage thus makes it difficult to identify films and to say with certainty when they were shot, by whom, and for what particular purpose. Notwithstanding this uncertainty, it is probably safe to say that the majority of ethnographic travelogues made during this period were shot by commercial cinema operators or itinerant showmen who lacked expert knowledge of the indigenous cultures they filmed. Instead, the figure of the filmmaker was probably closer to that pictured in a 1911 cartoon of English lanternist Frank E. Butcher marching from the Middle East to Africa and Japan in search of stereotypical displays of marketable alterity (fig. 5.28). Producing a synoptic and impressionistic view of native peoples, the choices these camera operators made about what to shoot and what to ignore were no doubt driven by commercial imperatives and a desire to satisfy audience expectations; a film series shot in Japan, for example, would not signify "Japaneseness" to an American audience unless it featured geisha girls dressed in kimonos.

But satisfying audience expectations wasn't always so straightforward. The desire to get a closer glimpse of native cultures was always tinged with ambivalence, as the lessons learned from world's fairs had shown. Rather than participate in the proscribed moral and intellectual underpinnings of the ethnographic object-lesson, spectators might be repulsed or fascinated by what they saw. Described by Homi K. Bhaba as a paradoxical response to non-Western cultures in which "otherness" is "at once an object of desire and derision," ambivalence was central to spectators' reaction to representations of cultural difference in the ethnographic travelogue.[120] But ambivalence was textually inscribed in the ethnographic travelogue in other ways; audiences were presented with images of a world undergoing rapid change, and while some spectators may have enjoyed or taken pride in seeing the iconography of Western mastery and imperial might, others may have lamented the loss of an "ethnographically pristine" way of life. Indeed, Jennifer Peterson argues that travelogues lulled spectators into a state of poetic reverie, a mode of spectatorship quite distinct from the experience of viewing fiction.[121] But despite the travelogue's capacity for provoking nostalgia, scenes representing the impact of modern technology such as cars, telegraph poles, and modern advertising on indigenous culture were routinely juxtaposed with images of autochthonous life, such as market trading, child-rearing, or agricultural techniques (see, for example, Holmes's lectures "The Old Japan Today" and "The New Japan Today"). Audience attitudes toward the native peoples depicted were complicated by their ambivalence toward the encroachment of the modern world on communities that were typically depicted as existing in near-total ignorance of the onslaught of modernity. Ambivalence was thus central to the experience of viewing the travelogue, functioning, in Peterson's words, "not only as a descriptive attitude but a constitutive mechanism."[122] The experience of the archaic or allochronic Other for turn-of-the-century motion picture audiences was inextricably bound up with the audience's own complex relationship with the forces of modernity that were transforming work and everyday life in Western metropoles. This tension is strikingly visualized in this advertisement for a British motion picture camera which associates the cinematic apparatus with the iconography of the timeless sphinx. Egypt's place within the social imaginary of early cinema was figuratively played out in countless films and ads from the period (fig. 5.29).[123]

Another informing context for the reception of commercial films of ethnographic content were the discourses of national identity, civic participation, and cultural uplift which dominated many turn-of-the-century discussions of urban leisure activities. A number of questions are relevant in this regard: In what ways were the travelogue and ethnographic film in general enlisted by government officials, educators, and metropolitan spokesmen as part of a broader mission of instilling civic responsibility and national identity? How did film reviewers and publicists respond to public policy statements about the governability of colonial peoples and domestic subjects through their pronouncements on travelogues? And finally, how did anthropologists react to films that encroached on their own territory, not just through their subject matter but also through the rhetorical construction of ethnography?

FIG. 5.29 Ad for Powers' Cameragraph from *The Biograph*, March 30, 1911.

Early Travelogues as Colonial Propaganda

The five cent audience is always interested in desirable subjects that will describe
the occupations, subjects, customs . . . and chief racial characteristics of the nations.
— *Moving Picture World* (1908)[124]

While most anthropologists felt disinclined to incorporate moving pictures
into their arsenal of fieldwork techniques, commercial production companies
continued to produce massive numbers of ethnographic travelogues between
1907 and 1913. An explanation for the continued demand for travel films was
offered by *Moving Picture World* columnist Louis Reeves Harrison in 1912: "We
hunger to see other parts of the earth, possibly from keen curiosity, probably
for the purpose of making discoveries in general as to what is going on in lives
and conditions remote from our own."[125] But travelogues could also furnish
information about new ethnic groups that were immigrating to the urban centers of the United States, as Harrison noted in the same article:

We can not gain too much knowledge of the many interesting varieties
of peoples who are gradually merging with our own population. Their history, their industries, their arts, their monuments, their customs, their
sports, their comedies and their tragedies give charm and variety to screen
presentations and offer a live stimulus to thought.[126]

Films depicting the cultural practices of peoples rapidly converging in cities
in the industrial Northeast of the United States not only entertained nickelodeon audiences but functioned as a popular memory of distant homelands
for new immigrant audiences in America. The prominent debates over the
effects of immigration upon the American "generic stock" provided a vivid
backdrop to discussions of the utility of travelogues; as anthropologist George
W. Stocking Jr. notes, "with mounting concern over the problem posed by the
'new immigration' and the outbreak of race riots in the years after 1900, the status of the immigrant and the [African-American] were issues agitating many
liberals."[127] In 1904 secretary of the Smithsonian Samuel Pierpoint Langley
announced that the Bureau of American Ethnology (BAE), formed in 1879,

would complete a "Biological Sketch of the People of the United States," an ambitious research project surpassing anthropology's previous involvement in issues of governmentality and social control. For Langley, the opportunity to conduct this research came at a propitious moment, since

> the ethnic elements of all nations and races are assembling in America, and are rapidly coalescing. It is the first occurrence of its kind known in history, and is the beginning of an era fraught with the deepest possible interest, historic, scientific, and national. It affords a great, and probably a last, opportunity to witness and record the intermingling of the racial elements of the world and the resultant physical, mental, moral, and pathological interactions in all stages and in every phase.[128]

Langley's suggestion that this era will be "fraught" with national, historic, and scientific interest evokes the nativist subtext of his research proposal, namely, fears that the amalgamation of different races and ethnic groups not only threatened white hegemony but might eliminate whiteness altogether. Despite the assurances of scientific neutrality in Langley's choice of objective verbs ("witness" and "record"), the research "opportunity" presented by the infusion of racial and ethnic groups into American society was accompanied by a deeper sense of unease over the long-term impact of "physical, mental, moral, and pathological interactions" between Euro-Americans and racial minorities.[129]

In this context, the ethnographic travelogue and its portrayals of both distant civilizations and cultural groups emigrating to the United States served to inspire and rationalize constructions of national identity. Recognizing that actualities could play a crucial role in education, ethnic assimilation, and social policy in the industrial metropole, film industry leader Charles Urban made a case for cinema's social remit:

> The entertainer has hitherto monopolized the cinematograph for exhibition purposes, but movement in more serious directions has become imperative, and our object is to prove that the cinematograph must be recognized as a national instrument by the Boards of Agriculture, Education, and Trade, by the War Council, Admirality, Medical Associations, and every institution of training, teaching, demonstration and research.[130]

The BAE had in fact undertaken such a project in 1901, accepting a proposal from University of Southern California professor of biology, O. P. Phillips, to make moving pictures "representing the industries, amusements, and ceremonies of the Pueblo Indians and other tribes in New Mexico and Arizona."[131] The purpose of the project was to make

> absolutely trustworthy records of aboriginal activities for the use of future students, as well as for the verification of current notes on fiducial dances and other ceremonies. . . . The camera was kindly furnished in the interests of science by the Armat Moving-Picture Company. . . . Despite accidents that happened to the apparatus the work was fairly successful, yielding about a dozen kinetoscope ribbons, in connection with which about a hundred excellent photographs were made.[132]

The tone of the BAE's report on moving pictures, including the insistence that the films will be "absolutely trustworthy records" produced "in the interests of science," suggests an undercurrent of unease within scientific circles about commercial cinema's role as an ad hoc ethnographer. In fact, in response to Phillips's letter of introduction, Professor William J. McGee of the BAE expressed skepticism about Phillips's chances of success in procuring useful footage, given the challenges of filming native ceremonies on location. While not dismissing these difficulties, Phillips reassured McGee that with "a little maneuvering . . . [and] a little silver on the side," he was always able to get what he wanted.[133] The BAE's annual report reassured its members that, despite the fact that the Armat Moving-Picture Company was a commercial enterprise, it was simply supplying equipment to Phillips, who could presumably be entrusted with the task of producing ethnographically accurate records. Several years after its 1901 decision to hire O. P Phillips to produce actuality films of Indian cultural life, and perhaps in response to the criticism of the depictions of Native Americans in the Indian one-reelers released between 1908 and 1911,[134] the BAE approached the Selig Polyscope Company in 1911 about making films of "the more important Indian ceremonies before it is too late."[135] While there is little extant material on the outcome of this collaborative venture, by 1917 the BAE had had a change of heart about working with commercial companies and noted in its annual report that requests to use

Indian actors in "made-up exhibitions of their old time customs and dances" would be routinely rejected unless Indians were featured in "present day scenes."[136]

Farther afield, early motion pictures could be used to promote the colonies as sites for economic exploitation and emigration and to reinforce the work of missionaries;[137] as British commentator Thomas Clegg argued in the *Motion Picture World*, "Colonial governments have long recognized [cinema's] usefulness in bringing to the very doors of the people at home, the importance, value and beauty of . . . dependencies, not only as a means of inducing emigration, but of securing the introduction of fresh capital for further development."[138] While Clegg is referring here to colonial uses of cinema within the British Empire, cinema's potential as a civilizing apparatus was exploited by almost all Western governments with imperial interests across the globe. French publicist F. Laurent, for example, outlined the benefits of French colonial cinema in the journal *Le Cinéma*: "One indisputable advantage of the geographical film is that it helps link the colonies to the mother country. It shows us all the outlets offered to French enterprise by our vast overseas possessions. . . . The cinema will be the best emigration agency of the future."[139] As well as appealing to the roving eye of the modern spectator, the travel film also presented a unique opportunity for disseminating what Noël Burch calls "the banalization of the scandal of colonization."[140] Suggestive of the implicit alliance between the early commercial ethnographic filmmaker and imperial power, the book jacket for Elmer Tracey Barnes's *The Motion-Picture Comrades in African Jungles* (1917) depicts the colonial-garbed cinematographer turning the handle of his camera in the presence of two armed white escorts (fig. 5.30).[141] The discretely organized scenes on the cover of Barnes's book evoke cinema's temporal and spatial fragmentation and, with the exception of the graphically dominant white male and colonial encampment, are built around a nature-versus-civilization opposition. One has only to examine catalogs of commercial film producers alongside the titles of popular adventure writing from the period to see how early cinema followed the geographical itineraries and ideological rationales of colonial expansion; for example, Edison's films were marketed under the label "Conquest Pictures," and Tom Gunning notes that early film catalogs presented a "nearly encyclopedic survey of a new hyper-visible topology, from landscape panoramas to microphotography."[142] The acquisition of new territories, coupled with the explosion of tourism,

FIG. 5.30 Book jacket for Elmer Tracey Barnes's *The Motion-Picture Comrades in African Jungles* (1917), showing the adventurer-explorer having penetrated the far reaches of Africa with his motion picture camera.

meant that itinerant cameramen and production companies could set up base in colonial expatriate communities and shoot films of native societies under the protection of the governing authority.

But the travel film served a more complex function in the imperial metropole. As well as justifying colonial and imperial expansion, it suggested the potential of cinema as a civilizing apparatus in the transformation of native peoples from ungovernable "savages" into modern colonial subjects; as one trade press critic put it, cinema was none other than an "agent for civilization" and could be productively used "as a tool for social transformation" in the hands of the right people.[143] In 1912, U.S. Secretary of the Interior Dean C. Worcester devised a program to use cinema as part of a propaganda effort to educate members of the Bontoc Igorot, Ifuago, and Kalinga tribes in the U.S.-occupied Philippines. The main aim of these government-produced educational films was to inculcate Western standards of hygiene among the indigenous subjects, although as a way of sustaining audience interest colonial administrators decided to exhibit nonpropaganda subjects (featuring both Western and native cultures, according to anthropologist Emilie de Brigard) between the propaganda films.[144] But the decision to show films representing white Americans was probably motivated by another subtext, the idea that exposure to "civilized" culture would reinforce the object-lesson by representing white metropolitan culture as the ideal to which colonial subjects should aspire.[145]

The frequent and consistently favorable references in the motion picture trade press to cinema's applications within colonial propaganda, anthropology, and scientific education were part of the emerging industry's larger ideological and commercial effort to elevate film exhibition through the trumpeting of its civilizing and pedagogical missions. The author of an article entitled "Making the Devil Useful" in the *English Journal* set out to defend cinema from vituperative attacks by arguing that film was neither "an invention of the devil"[146] nor "excessively satanic," but in fact had a "great deal in it at the present stage of its development."[147] Not surprisingly, the kinds of films the anonymous author had in mind were educational subjects. For many film reviewers, actualities were considered a welcome respite from the flood of fictional subjects, with their last-minute rescues and tales of crime and corruption. In particular, the travel lecture was singled out by some critics as offering a more sedate form of entertainment, what one critic called "positive brain rest." However, while a reviewer in 1912 noted that Pathé's *Tunisian Industries* came "as a relief to the more dramatic themes which form the staple of the moving picture theater entertainments,"[148] not all ethnographic travelogues might have qualified as "brain rest," since many actualities contained scenes of graphic violence which would have been censored from fictional films, including the brutal slaying of a buffalo in Pathé's *Madagaskar: Manners and Customs of the Saklavas* (1910). If these films evoked Peterson's sense of poetic reverie, they also offered spectators action and excitement through exotic locations, editing, and the live comments of the lecturer, as suggested in this 1909 review of Howe's lecture at the New York Hippodrome: "The mind was kept ever in motion; ever stimulated; ever refreshed; ever excited. I cannot conceive of a more delightful and rational way of passing an evening."[149]

Motion picture trade press promotion of cinema's anthropological mission can be interpreted as evidence of the perceived general popular appetite for ethnographic material and of the industry's attempt to both create a market for educational films *and* to elevate the general cultural position of the medium. In 1907, for example, the *Moving Picture World* reported that scientists who were conducting research for the Berlin Academy of Science had

> secured excellent photographic and cinematographic records illustrating the life and customs of the aboriginal Veddahs of Eastern Ceylon. The Veddahs are the descendants of the primitive race which inhabited Ceylon prior to the Hindoo conquest. Their number is steadily decreasing and today there are probably not more than two thousand throughout the island.[150]

In the process of viewing commercially produced ethnographic films, audience members could vicariously experience what the putative ethnographer had witnessed firsthand; and if they had the economic means to purchase a camera and a ticket to an exotic locale, they too could join the ranks of amateur ethnographers. An industry representative writing in the *Moving Picture World* in 1909 went so far as to chide explorers who embarked upon expeditions equipped only with a still camera: "The world has been pretty well covered by the stationary photograph," the author opined; "people are demanding motion as is evidenced by the excitement created by aviation photographs." The author offered the following recommendation:

Whenever a scientific or geographical expedition is to be undertaken we would put in a claim for the presence of the moving picture camera in the equipment. . . . The various film manufacturing concerns are always to the fore with the moving picture camera in their enterprises. It now remains for the private individual, the traveling photographer, explorer, geographer and the like never to undertake his journeys without a moving picture camera, as he is always sure to find a market for his pictures and interest a large section of the public.[151]

Thinking perhaps along the same lines as Baldwin Spencer, who had made his photographs and films accessible to a lay audience in 1901, the writer underscored the public desire for thrilling actuality footage, a fascination that would lead to the production of such adventure "classics" as Martin and Osa Johnson's *Simba: King of the Wild Beasts* (1928) and *Congarilla* (1932), and Merian C. Cooper and Ernest B. Schoedsack's *Chang* (1927) and *King Kong* (1933).[152] However, the writer's plea to professionals engaged in exploratory work may also have been motivated by interests more proprietary than altruistic, including the lucrative deals that could be negotiated for distribution rights to popular hits.

Two individuals who heeded the call of the *Moving Picture World*'s editorialist were Joseph K. Dixon and Edward Sheriff Curtis, filmmakers who operated within distinct commercial and institutional contexts, but whose ethnographic films were motivated by a shared interest in resurrecting the "real" Indian from the stereotyped depictions of the commercial film market and in constructing a more pristine (and therefore more "authentic") image of the American Indian.

The Ethnographic Filmmaking of Joseph K. Dixon and Edward S. Curtis

An American reverend who had gained experience as a photographer working for Kodak in 1904, Joseph K. Dixon was hired by the department store magnate John Rodman Wanamaker in 1906 to "carry out educational work in the Philadelphia department store and to lecture on educational subjects such as poetry, presidents, nature and music."[153] In 1908, Dixon was commissioned by Wanamaker to lead an expedition to the Crow Reservation in Montana to obtain photographs and moving pictures, and to shoot a film adaptation of Henry Wadsworth Longfellow's epic poem *Hiawatha*, all to be shown in Wanamaker's department stores as part of Dixon's series of educational lectures.[154] Dixon also shot footage of the first Crow mission school, an annual Crow encampment known as the "Tepee Capital of the World," and a reenactment of the Battle of the Little Big Horn, which employed U.S. Cavalry and Crow Indians in place of Sioux.[155] A review of the 1908 film series in the trade journal *The Nickelodeon* reported that Wanamaker's decision to sponsor the films was motivated by a desire to "preserve, via film, the primitive red man in all his ancient regalia and glory—with bows and arrows, tomahawks, tom-toms, bonnets, war clubs etc."[156]

Dixon's goal to "perpetuate the life story" of the Indian was, however, riddled with contradictions. On the one hand, his attempt to document Native American culture was firmly entrenched in a discourse of salvage ethnography; Dixon declared that in photographs and films of Native American culture, "every effort was exhausted to eliminate any hint of the white man's foot" in order that the "spirit of the native environment" would dominate. On the other hand, Dixon was interested in explicitly inserting Native Americans into white history, as evidenced in the battle reenactment.[157] Likewise, Dixon's footage of the Crow camp and Crow Fair in Montana represents Crow life as coterminous with that of white Americans, contrary to Dixon's pledge to "eliminate any hint of the white man's foot." The presence of Western clothes and supplies in the Crow camp's shop, and scenes showing Crow girls (flanked by nuns) attending the first Crow mission school, along with other shots of white tourists on their way to the annual Crow Fair all document the presence of white institutions in Crow culture. Because of this textual evidence of white copresence in Native American life, the film resists whole-hearted endorsement of the ideology of salvage ethnography. Instead, Dixon's film offers a polysemic representation of Indian life depicting white cultural and economic infrastructures existing alongside thriving native practices such as the Crow Fair. Dixon's films of Native Americans were thus animated by a central tension between the idea of the Indian as historically copresent with white society and that of the Indian living in the timeless "ethnographic present" of the Noble Savage.

The conventional suppression of the historical copresence of Euro- and Native Americans in favor of a mythical and allochronic (timeless) construction is also vividly illustrated in the work of photographer and filmmaker Edward S. Curtis. Although Curtis condemned conventional studio portraits of Indians as inaccurate, he did not always practice what he preached; for example, when he took his studio-tent with him on expeditions to reservations, he painstakingly concealed every trace of a subject's contact with Euro-American culture. Like his commercial rivals, Curtis furnished his Indian sitters with props such as feather bonnets, masks, and costumes, which often circulated indiscriminately across his photographs of different tribes. In some photographs Curtis dressed his subjects in wigs to conceal their contemporary hairstyles, and he cropped and retouched prints to remove all signs of white contact, thereby perpetuating homogenized and petrified notions of "Indianness."[158] Curtis's pictorialist photographic style, modeled on nineteenth-century painting traditions—where the image was subjected to the aestheticizing techniques of soft-focus, carefully staged mise-en-scène, lighting effects, and sepia toning—won him accolades from both reviewers and high government officials. Writing to curator E. H. Harriman in 1905, President Theodore Roosevelt congratulated Harriman for exhibiting Curtis's photographs in New York, calling Curtis's representations of Indians "genuine works of art . . . [that] deal with some of the most picturesque phases of the old time American life that is now passing away."[159] By convincing his Native American photographic subjects to "abandon themselves to the old life and forget the present and their environment," Curtis believed that future generations would have access to this repository of an idealized American past.[160]

Dixon himself made similar claims on behalf of his work; in the introduction to his 1913 book *The Purpose and Achievements of the Rodman Wanamaker Expedition of Citizenship to the North American Indian* (produced in conjunction with the expedition film), Dixon claimed that "historic values have been preserved. . . . These records are systematic, extensive and constructive. . . . They not alone furnish exact data, but they are in addition a record of the environment, homes and types of the tribes so that a hitherto unavailable source of information is afforded by yielding data for comparative study."[161] Dixon's rhetoric suggests the use of film as a tool of surveillance and discipline for the classification of Native Americans; indeed the "data" gathered by Dixon's moving pictures were consistent with a tradition of fabricated and idealized versions of Native American cooperation and assimilation, as in *Club Swinging, Carlisle Indian School* (Biograph, 1902).

Like that of Dixon, Curtis's work as a photographer and filmmaker is rife with paradoxes. In an effort to produce a more authentic motion picture of Native Americans than his commercial competitors, a film that would "illustrate the period before the white man came," Curtis decided to shoot "documentary material" for *In the Land of the Head Hunters* which would then be used to illustrate a dramatic story based on a Kwakwaka'wakw (Kwakuitl) myth.[162] These scenes include visually striking shots of the figures of the Thunderbird, Wasp, and the Grizzly Bear paddling in canoes, as well as footage of clam diggers and ceremonial dancers in animal and bird masks and costumes. Rejecting what he saw as the artifice of commercially produced films featuring Native Americans, Curtis set out to make "genuine Indian pictures," that would be "far more valuable than regular dramatic subjects."[163] But in his attempt to represent the "real life" of the Indian, Curtis paradoxically suppressed all visual evidence of the actual contemporary lives of the Kwakwaka'wakw, preferring instead to represent Kwakwaka'wakw culture in a remote nineteenth-century past that had to be extensively re-created by members of the tribe who participated in the film. But there are other ironies at play here; by giving more attention to topics such as war, romance, and ceremony at the expense of everyday images of Northwest Coast Indians, Curtis's film did breathe life into the iconography of Kwakwaka'wakw culture as a result of his decision to commission members of the tribe to construct ornate building facades, totem poles, masks, and costumes (he even paid many of the Indian men who appeared in *Head Hunters* to shave their beards and wear wigs in order to conform to mythologized constructions of "Indianess").[164]

To be sure, Curtis had more success re-creating Kwakwaka'wakw culture than Dixon had reconstructing the Battle of the Little Big Horn. After a slow start, Dixon's restaged battle quickly degenerated into farce as many of the Indian actors (and white cavalrymen) failed to take their performances seriously, spoiling the desired dramatic effect — for example, by refusing to play dead properly. As Susan Applegate Krouse explains:

The Custer battle re-enactment is not the most successful of Dixon's photographic attempts. . . . Shots are fired wildly into the air, Indians club soldiers with their guns, and the dead rearrange themselves more comfortably. One Indian pulls the tail of his feathered headdress out from under him, and then resumes his dead act. Rather than a serious historical re-enactment, the battle quickly disintegrates into a farce.[165]

The realism of the battle was also marred by incoherent staging and direction; Custer's cavalrymen and Indians enter the frame from all directions and the camera breaks the 180-degree rule by representing the battle from both sides, in both long and medium long shots. As the cameraman struggles to keep the highly kinetic action within the camera's range of vision, he pans to reframe the action (or, in some cases, in *search* of the action, as the frame empties of all combatants). Without warning, the battle comes to an abrupt end, signaled only by the dispersal of the Indians, who exit frame right. Notwithstanding the unconvincing performances and inexperienced cinematography, the smoke and realistic costuming convey at least a sense of the real-life drama of the Custer battle, and the closing pan showing the battlefield littered with bodies and riderless horses is quite effective.

It is unclear how wide a commercial release (excluding Wanamaker's department stores) Dixon's 1908 film enjoyed. According to Krouse, Dixon was so disappointed with the Custer reenactment that he only used photographs of the battle when lecturing, although if a review of the film from the *Nickelodeon* can be trusted, a version that included the Custer battle as well as footage of Indian agriculture and native industries did get released. Given Dixon's own reservations about the success of the reenactment, it is odd that this reviewer should have singled it out for praise, noting that the scene had been "so realistic that women and children who witnessed it fainted when some of the Indians fought as though their lives depended on it."[166] For this reviewer, the credibility of the Crow performances was contradictorily associated with their own duplicity, as "in many cases," the reviewer explained, "the Indians had to be searched for lead cartridges which they tried to conceal." Angry at a stray blank bullet from a cavalryman's gun which had lodged in the leg of one of the Crow, "it was thought for a time that the Indians were about to engage in battle in reality, in which case the soldiers would have been in a bad plight, as they had nothing with which to fight except 10,000 rounds of blank ammunition."[167]

Fears that Native Americans were dangerously untrustworthy as performers in films based on Indian life led motion picture author Ernest Alfred Dench to offer three reasons why "real" Indians should not be employed as actors: first, that receiving a salary would merely keep Indian actors furnished with "tobacco and their worshipped 'firewater' "; second, because "they put their heart and soul into work, especially battles with the whites, and it is necessary to have armed guards watch over their movements for the least sign of treachery";[168] and third, because whites are "past masters" at playing Indian roles and, with clever makeup, are indistinguishable from real Indians.[169] Dench's warnings of the danger of using real Indian actors suggest some of the submerged structures of racial stereotyping, or what Sander Gilman describes as the need to perpetuate a "sense of difference between the 'self' and the 'object' which becomes the 'Other.' " For Gilman, "the mental representation of difference is but the projection of the tension between control and its loss"—a tension that takes on a physical form as the Other.[170] Dench's strategies for dealing with repressed mental representations of racialized Others, according to Gilman's psychoanalytic model, reflect the internalized fears of the dominant culture that insurrection is always a potential threat, especially when large numbers of Native Americans congregate.

But despite these claims for the mutability of whiteness and the ability of white actors to masquerade as Indians, some film studios, (including Kalem), cultivating a reputation for ethnographic accuracy in the silent film era, went out of their way to stress the authenticity of their performers. The realistic mise-en-scène of *Fighting the Iriquois in Canada* (Kalem, 1910) was noted by one reviewer who claimed that spectators knew little "of the time and trouble taken by the Kalem producers and scenic artists to delve into the libraries and art museums to get the correct data for these pictures and the accurate dress of the period."[171] In preparation for their 1913 film *The Cliff Dwellers*, Kalem's art directors visited the American Museum of Natural History for visual tips on Indian clubs, cooking vessels, and other artifacts.[172] Anthropology was thus used as a legitimizing discourse by the Kalem Company and other commercial studios, which could boast of having consulted with one of the nation's premier institutions for the anthropological study of Native Americans in preparation for their latest production.

Like the Kalem Company, Edward S. Curtis also turned to established scientific institutions to lend credibility to his commercial efforts. Curtis told philanthropist J. Pierpont Morgan (from whom Curtis sought sponsorship for his twenty-volume book project on the North American Indian) that he planned to turn over his completed fieldwork to scientific authorities for editing and scholarly commentary, a move he felt would imbue his work with "unquestionable authenticity."[173] In acknowledging his limited skills as an ethnographer, Curtis nevertheless hoped to exploit the legitimizing authority of anthropology and, in the process, enlist the backing of wealthy donors. At every opportunity, Curtis sought to distinguish *In the Land of the Head Hunters* from what he saw as fake film of Native Americans produced by commercial companies. In a 1912 letter to Charles D. Walcott, secretary of the Smithsonian Institution, Curtis claimed his aim was to record as carefully as possible the domestic and ceremonial life of Native Americans, so that each picture would be an "unquestioned document" instead of "caught fragments of a superficial, indifferent matter."[174] At the same time, Curtis acknowledged that the film was "a compromise between what I would like to make if I was in a position to say—the public be damned—and what I think the public will support."[175] This tension was echoed in a review of *Head Hunters* from the *Independent* which justified Curtis's decision to embed his ethnographic reconstruction within a fictive narrative: "In accordance with the taste of the times," the reviewer noted, Curtis "has adopted a dramatic framework."[176]

However, Curtis's hopes that *Head Hunters* would find wide commercial success by meeting "the tastes of the masses or those who are looking for amusement only" were not borne out.[177] W. Stephen Bush, in his laudatory review of the film in *Moving Picture World* in 1914, suggested that it was not "a feature for the nickelodeon or the cheap houses, but it ought to be welcomed by the better class of houses that are looking for an occasional departure from the regular attractions and that want to give their patrons a special treat."[178] Emphasizing the class-based appeal of such educational films, Bush compared *Head Hunters* to Wagner's *Ring of the Nibelungs* and *Parsifal*:

Mr. Curtis has extracted from his vast materials nothing but the choicest and nothing but that which will please the eyes and stir the thoughts of an intelligent white audience. All the actors are full-blooded Indians. The Indian mind is, I believe, constitutionally incapable of acting; it cannot even grasp the meaning of acting as we understand it. Probably nobody understands this better than Mr. Curtis. The picture speaks volumes of the producer's intimacy with the Indians and his great power over them. They are natural in every move; the grace, the weirdness and the humor of their dances has never been brought home to us like this before.[179]

Beyond flattering his "intellectually superior" readership's ability to distinguish "real" Indians from whites in makeup, Bush's reference to the "naturalness" of Curtis's "full-blooded Indians" also pays tribute to the familiar image of the American Indian as Noble Savage. Likewise, Bush's ease in essentializing Native Americans and his praise for Curtis's privileged access to and power over his subjects suggests the heroicized figure of the white showman-explorer.

The pictorial qualities of Curtis's film were also celebrated by poet and early film theorist Vachel Lindsay in 1915, who discussed the film in the context of recounting his visits to the Chicago Art Institute and New York's Metropolitan Museum of Art in search of "sculpture, painting, and architecture that might be the basis for the photoplays of the future."[180] Based on this research, Lindsay argued that "the photoplay of the American Indian should in most instances be planned as a bronze in action [although] the tribes should not move so rapidly that the panther-like elasticity is lost in the riding, running and scalping."[181] For Lindsay, the "action moving picture" called for the qualities of bronze figurative sculpture, owing to the metal's supposed elasticity and its ability to highlight "tendon, ligament, and bone" rather than muscle. Praising Curtis's film as a "work of a life-time . . . [and] supreme art achievement," Lindsay contended that *In the Land of the Head Hunters* abounded with such "noble bronzes."[182] In his aesthetic analogy to bronze as the classical medium for the representation of movement, Lindsay's racial coding speaks as much about white cultural assumptions about the exotic and aestheticized Other as about classical iconography (later in the same chapter he describes the representation of Africans in a comedy about cannibalism as

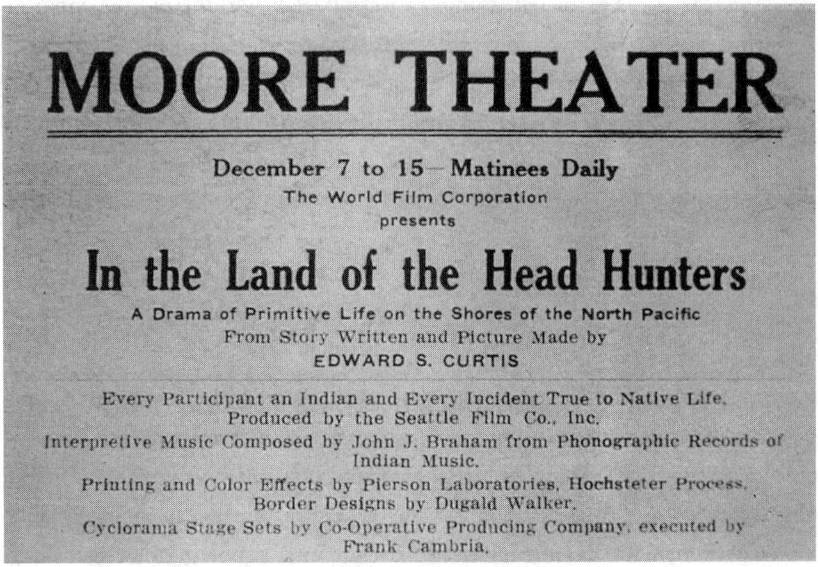

MOORE THEATER

December 7 to 15—Matinees Daily
The World Film Corporation
presents

In the Land of the Head Hunters
A Drama of Primitive Life on the Shores of the North Pacific
From Story Written and Picture Made by
EDWARD S. CURTIS

Every Participant an Indian and Every Incident True to Native Life.
Produced by the Seattle Film Co., Inc.
Interpretive Music Composed by John J. Braham from Phonographic Records of
Indian Music.
Printing and Color Effects by Pierson Laboratories, Hochsteter Process.
Border Designs by Dugald Walker.
Cyclorama Stage Sets by Co-Operative Producing Company, executed by
Frank Cambria.

FIG. 5.31 Advertisement for Edward S. Curtis's *In the Land of the Head Hunters*, 1914.

being "like living ebony and silver").[183] Despite such elevated praise for Curtis's film, it was not a box-office success, and after a brief run at the Casino Theater on Broadway and 89th Street in New York and at the Moore Theater in Seattle (fig. 5.31), it vanished into obscurity.

In a similar manner, Dixon's films were also quickly forgotten, although not before being shown as part of a special lecture cohosted by the American Museum of Natural History and the American Scenic and Historical Society in New York in 1912 and at the Panama-Pacific International Exposition held in San Francisco in 1915.[184] Dixon's lecture at the AMNH, "The Last Great Indian Council: The Farewell of the Chiefs," drew upon films and photographs he had shot during the 1909 expedition, which, like the 1908 trip, was to the Valley of the Little Big Horn in Montana.[185] Guests at the lecture were left in little doubt as to the significance of Dixon's films as historical documents; the aim of the expedition, they were told, was "to make a permanent record of the manners and customs, the home life, the sports, games and wars, of the North American Indians," a record that would be obtained "with the consent and cooperation of the United States Government of Washington."[186]

The portentous language used throughout the program suggests a defensive strategy aimed in part to disassociate Dixon's films from less valorized images of Native Americans then appearing on New York City movie screens. But in exploiting a discourse of scientific impartiality to authenticate his film and photographic work, Dixon also acknowledged the place of art by calling his films "pictorial" records based on "faithful and comprehensive transcripts of Indian customs and costumes." Dixon's screening at the AMNH is a striking example of how institutions and discourses of both science and commerce collaborated in constructing notions of "truth," accuracy, and realism in early ethnographic film. Dixon's collapse of art and science in his "faithful pictorial" oxymoron indicates just how imbricated both discourses were in the ethnographic filmmaking of figures such as Joseph K. Dixon and Edward S. Curtis. For a representation to be considered authentic, it had to be aesthetically pleasing in the pictorialist style predominant among turn-of-the-century photography that aspired to the status of an art form.

In addition to considering the discursive and intellectual contexts of commercially inflected ethnographic filmmaking, it is also important for historians to address the question of Native American responses to their representation in both nonfiction film and in the countless westerns produced between 1909 and 1914. Native American reaction to their portrayals in this ubiquitous early film genre was occasionally reported in the motion pictures trade press and in letters to the editors of newspapers, although there is no way of verifying the native identity of these contributors, since they may have been written by editors to bolster specific views. In 1911 the *Moving Picture World* reported the visit to Washington, D.C., of a group of Native Americans organized in order to complain about their filmic treatment. The delegation charged that "moving picture promoters in order to get thrilling pictures of the Indians have used white men costumed as Indians in depicting scenes that are not true pictures of the Indian and are in fact grossly libelous" and urged congressional action to regulate moving pictures.[187] In an implicit defense of the representation of Native Americans in the early film western, the editor of the following issue of *Moving Picture World* published a letter purportedly from a Native American reader in Rochester, New York, which, while attacking filmed westerns for their exaggeration of the fighting prowess of white protagonists (such as five pioneers chasing away twelve Indians), praised the majority of films for their accurate portrayal of Indian life.[188] Given the fragmentary nature of the extant public record, it is difficult to evaluate Native American responses to their depictions in early motion pictures based on the slim evidence in the film trade press.

In any event, there seems to have been an increased emphasis placed upon verisimilitude in the western after 1910, a move that had implications for producers of ethnographic film.[189] A 1911 *Moving Picture World* editorial entitled "The Make-Believe 'Indian' " denounced the hypocrisy of critical demands for realism at a time when the roles of Native American characters continued to be played by white actors. Linking the representation of the American Indian as Noble Savage to the ideology of salvage ethnography, the reviewer asked why, "while we still have the real Indians with us . . . cannot thoroughly representative films be produced, making them at once illustrative and historic recorders of this noble race of people, with their splendid physique and physical prowess?"[190] Indeed, reviewers were often scornful of the liberties taken by commercial studios in their use of the Native American experience: "It is too often the case," wrote the *Moving Picture World*, that "nowadays in Western pictures and also in historical pictures, inaccuracies and anachronisms occur."[191]

Around the same time, film critic Stephen Bush enumerated a taxonomy of stereotypes of Native Americans used by filmmakers of the western, noting acerbically that "we have Licensed Indians and Independent Indians — the only kind we lack are real Indians."[192] Similar protests were raised from anthropological quarters; writing to the *New York Times* in 1914, Alanson Skinner, assistant curator of the department of anthropology at the AMNH, complained that "from the standpoint of a student, most of the picture plays shown are ethnologically grotesque farces. Delawares are dressed as Sioux, and the Indians of Manhattan Island are shown dwelling in skin tipis of the type used only by the tribes beyond the Mississippi."[193] Criticism was voiced even in the *Moving Picture World*, the industry stalwart, when contributor C. H. Claudy condemned the histrionic acting of whites playing Indians in releases by Kalem, Pathé, and Lubin; according to Claudy, "Many a picture is spoiled . . . by the overdoing of a part. . . . No other kind of Indians that the popular mind conceives, ever gesticulated so violently, so rapidly, so much. They lose all dignity, all realism, when they spend most of the time with their arms in the air!"[194] (See fig. 5.32.)

FIG. 5.32 White actor Owen Moore playing Little Bear in still from *The Mended Lute* (Biograph, 1909). (Courtesy MOMA)

In the context of demands from inside and outside the motion picture industry for greater ethnographic accuracy and to distinguish their work from that of the commercial film studios, both Dixon and Curtis boasted of their painstaking efforts to achieve verisimilitude. In an attempt to avoid the kind of inaccuracies typical of most films about Native American life, Curtis employed the Anglo-Native American George Hunt to collaborate on *In the Land of the Head Hunters*; Hunt would be responsible for recruiting most of Curtis's cast and serving as a cultural adviser. Hunt had gained experience as a native informant working for Franz Boas as a photographer and guide for the Jesup North Pacific Expedition organized by the AMNH between 1897 and 1902.[195] While Curtis employed George Hunt as an adviser, cast Hunt's son in the male lead, and used a number of Hunt's other children and grandchildren as extras, Hunt was nevertheless critical of Curtis's overall approach. In Hunt's opinion, Curtis failed to present the most important cultural elements from a Kwakwa̱ka̱'wakw viewpoint, and elevated visual spectacle above cultural contextualization.[196] At the same time, perhaps seeing a potential rival in Joseph K. Dixon, Curtis disparaged Dixon's Wanamaker expedition films, complained of Dixon's plagiarism (without specifying the nature of the infringement), and called Dixon's photographs from the expedition "fakey illustrations."[197] Franz Boas, too, was critical of Curtis's "ethnography" among the Kwakwa̱ka̱'wakw, arguing that Curtis's search for sensation led him to grossly manipulate the "truth" about Northwestern culture. The intricate professional lineages between Franz Boas, George Hunt, Edward Curtis, and Joseph Dixon during this period attest to the ambivalent and contested ethnographic status of Dixon's and Curtis's filmmaking. Apart from actualities produced by commercial manufacturers, there was very little ethnographic filmmaking with which to compare to Dixon's and Curtis's films. Thus, for elite audiences who weren't interested in fictional "Indian" films playing at the local movie theater, Dixon's and Curtis's creations afforded a rare opportunity to view films of Native Americans within the socially sanctified space of the museum of natural history. Moreover, beyond the accounts of critics and the comments of George Hunt, historians lack a clear idea of what the Kwakwa̱ka̱'wakw themselves actually thought of *In the Land of the Head Hunters*, although following the discovery, restoration, and renaming of the film by anthropologists Bill Holm and George Quimby in 1972 (it's now called *In the Land of the War Canoes*),[198] contemporary Kwakwa̱ka̱'wakw have had the opportunity to not only serve once again as collaborators on the restoration project but to recuperate the film as part of their cultural history.[199]

Finally, it is important to note that the films of Dixon and Curtis exemplify a proto-auteur mode of ethnographic filmmaking that was to reach a paroxysm in Robert Flaherty's *Nanook of the North* (1922). When considered in the context of Edison's early ethnographic films and the ubiquitous commercial travel films of the turn of the century, the work of Dixon and Curtis suggests some of the changes within commercial ethnographic filmmaking in the first fifteen years of the century and signal some of the characteristics of the adventurer genre of the late teens and twenties associated with husband-and-wife teams Martin and Osa Johnson and Carl and Mary Jobe Akeley. By the midteens, ethnographic film had reached a crossroads of sorts, with brief actualities shot in exotic locations no longer having the same hold on the popular imaginary in the face of increasingly sophisticated feature-length fiction films such as D. W. Griffith's *Birth of a Nation* (1915); at the same time, the general filmic appeal of the ethnographic Other was still potent, confirmed by the huge box-office success of Flaherty's *Nanook of the North*.

In the most general terms, cinema, as an icon of modernity, in part took over the project of naturalizing racial hierarchies inherited from other nineteenth-century visual technologies, such as living exhibits at world's fairs, *cartes-de-visites*, and Barnum's "Ethnological Congress." The experience of viewing early ethnographic film may have been determined as much by the recognition of familiar representational tropes as it was by a sense of wonder at their mechanical means of reproduction. Presented in the motion picture trade press and elsewhere as the pinnacle of Western technological progress, the cinematic apparatus was itself a potent symbol of the ideological power of Western technology and colonial might. It comes as no surprise, then, that as an "epistemological mediator"[200] between the world of the spectator and that of the subaltern, cinema functioned as a powerful vehicle for the dissemination of racist and colonialist ideology. This is suggested in a 1914 review of *Beasts of the Jungle*, which compared a Congo African ("the lowest type of mankind") with a chimpanzee ("the highest type of Simian"). A "picture such as this," the reviewer continued, "brings to our minds the theory presented by Darwin and we are forced to wonder if he was not right, as the animal exhibits an intelligence seemingly much greater than that of man."[201] In more hysterical, negrophobic terms, the reviewer of *From Durban to Zululand* free-associates through a panoply of Western literary classics and contemporary popular culture. After describing the Zulus as "satyr-like," the author declared that "this remarkable spectacle would take the pen of a Dante to describe fully. It is like a dream of the Inferno, or one of Little Nemo's adventures. A great line of black, ferocious-looking Zulus with feathered headplumes, rising and falling to uncanny heathenish music in honor of their English masters!"[202] Despite the fact that the film reviewer could not hear the "heathenish music" to which the Zulus were dancing, he felt confident enough of its revulsive qualities to describe it for the reader.

Presented with images of the racialized Other to which they had a strong visceral response, reviewers frequently drew upon familiar stereotypes or literary metaphors for interpretive frames of reference. In the absence of contextual ethnographic information on the meaning of what was happening in the frame (a problem facing professional film critics and, on occasion, even anthropologists), reviewers resorted either to bald-faced racism, "Noble Savage" stereotypes, ironic quips (as in the reference to the Zulu's dancing being in "honor of their English masters") or the occasional open admission that they didn't have the faintest idea as to what was actually going on in the film. The latter position is implied in the 1910 *Moving Picture World* review of *In Africa*. After introducing Africa as a "little known and marvelous land," the reviewer declared that "a detailed description of the various scenes would be tiresome, and after all would mean nothing"; instead, the author merely recommended that audiences go and see the picture themselves with its "wealth of life and movement and its glimpses of a distant part of the world."[203]

As part of the social and cultural horizon of turn-of-the-century popular culture, ethnographic films drew upon the visual lexicon of well-established precinematic forms at the same time as they redefined some of the classic emblems of native representation through stylistic and ideological reworkings. While filmic images of native peoples shared a number of textual features with their visual antecedents, these images increasingly came to be defined through a uniquely cinematic lens that created new possibilities for cultural expression and the dissemination of ideology. Early ethnographic film practice was thus accompanied by a discourse of ethnography that was shaped as much by the intertextual frames of racialized entertainment as it was by the scientific ethos of anthropology. Turn-of-the-century anthropologists may therefore have been discomforted by the fact that a rhetoric of salvage ethnography circulating in professional anthropology was indistinguishable from trade press claims about cinema's unmatched potential to produce unimpeachable visual records. Recalling Lyman Howe's advice to "See Them Now or Never," a 1907 *Moving Picture World* editorial cautioned that "the march of civilization is so rapidly defacing native customs that it is of the greatest importance that cinematographic means be adopted to place them on record. For this purpose the Cinematograph is an ideal agent, for by its aid we obtain a truthful and permanent record of native customs, ceremonies, etc."[204] In place of the sharply focused ethnographic monograph (which was quickly becoming the standard anthropological research artifact), ethnographic travelogues instead offered a kaleidoscopic and fragmentary view of native cultures. At the same time that anthropology was adopting the techniques of the long-term participant-observer, the ethnographic travelogue's promise of a "thousand and one pictures" of exotic peoples across the globe may have reminded anthropologists too much of the concession stands of world's fair midways.

By trading on notions of ethnographic accuracy, filmic realism, and scientific legitimacy, films with ethnographic content made by commercial manufactures, itinerant lecturers, and photographer-filmmakers such as Edward S. Curtis and Joseph K. Dixon negotiated the conflicting demands of science and popular culture in complex and creative ways. Moreover, it should be noted that the relationship between science and popular culture was dialectical rather than oppositional, with both sides evolving simultaneously within a modern culture of curiosity: just as science and anthropology looked to popular culture as a way of publicly presenting their findings, so too did popular culture turn to the rhetoric of science and anthropology to market its products to a middle-class audience. A discourse of ethnography was variously used as a legitimizing strategy by these filmmakers; in the case of Dixon and Curtis, it was used to disparage commercially produced "caught fragments" of native life in favor of their own more "authentic" films; in the case of the hundreds of travel films produced by manufacturers such as Pathé, Kalem, and Biograph, it was bound up with discourses of uplift, education, and tourism.

As the examples discussed above make clear, where there is no extant information on a film's production or exhibition history, textual evidence becomes our only point of entry. For better or for worse, we base our arguments largely on what we see in the surviving cinematic fragments, rather than on the contextual material that might produce a more nuanced reading of a film. In spite of these limitations, an analysis of recurring textual features, including the presentational quality of early ethnographic film, the trope of performance, and the effect of the return gaze *can* suggest some of the ways in which stylistic tropes became conventionalized in the early cinema period. But if formal analysis alone cannot excavate the sedimented layers of ethnographic meaning nor illuminate how these films were embedded in broader institutional and ideological systems, scrutiny of the exhibition site of early ethnographic film can open up avenues of investigation that have so far been neglected by early cinema scholars. It is to the American Museum of Natural History that we now return in order to see how ethnographic film found a home among its sister technologies, the magic lantern, and the diorama life group, for it is only by examining film's prospects within the natural history museum that we can best appreciate how the tensions between popular culture and anthropology played out around the controversial subject of film.

PART III

FIRST STEPS:

THE MUSEUM &

EARLY FILMMAKERS

6

Early Ethnographic Film at

the American Museum of Natural History

One man in a million may see the actual thing . . . but every man may go to Seventy-seventh
Street, Central Park West, and see as accurate a representation of it as art and science may show.
— SHERMAN LANGDON (1906)[1]

Here is a museum that is fun, a museum that is a feast to the eye, and at the
same time a museum which proposes to teach you something in spite of yourself.
— "THE SPECTATOR," IN REFERENCE TO
THE AMERICAN MUSEUM OF NATURAL HISTORY (1909)[2]

LOCATED IN New York City, the center of the early U.S. motion picture
industry, the American Museum of Natural History (AMNH) might be expected to have played a pioneering role in the early exhibition of motion pictures within American museums (fig. 6.1). With many motion picture distributors located in Manhattan and a commercial structure of film exchange in
place by 1906–1907, the AMNH's use of early scientific and ethnographic film
might have sparked similar activities among rival institutions. That the
AMNH failed to capitalize on public interest in motion pictures until 1908,
well into the nickelodeon period, is somewhat surprising, considering the
widespread appeal of early film travelogues and educational subjects. The marginal status of early film at the AMNH is even more anomalous given the Museum's interest in popular museum formats such as life groups and the illustrated lecture, although the earlier disputes provoked by life groups at the
AMNH might have made the Museum's administration cautious about exploiting motion pictures there.

FIG. 6.1 Exterior of the American Museum of Natural History, 1907. (Neg. no. 45674. Courtesy Dept. of Library Services, AMNH)

By exploring the conditions of possibility for early ethnographic film at the American Museum of Natural History between 1908 and 1919, from the slow initial acceptance of the medium to a wider acceptance of film's pedagogical role within public lectures at the Museum, this chapter constructs what Foucault calls an "effective history" of moving pictures at the AMNH, a history sensitive to the ruptures, displacements, and contingencies of knowledge occasioned by cinema's entry into the Museum.[3] A careful analysis of how motion pictures were gradually incorporated into the institution's programs for members and children can shed light on the wider discursive construction of cinema as a vehicle for scientific knowledge. The sometimes testy exchanges between Museum officials and guest speakers who employed film in their invited lectures, along with the challenges Museum officials faced in integrating AMNH-sponsored anthropological expedition footage into public programs, illuminate wider professional attitudes toward moving pictures during the period while evoking earlier arguments about the pedagogical role of life groups within the Museum. As motion pictures became a regular feature of the AMNH's educational programs and public lectures, a number of senior Museum officials variously described how film might best be adapted to the institution's scientific and civic mission, anticipating contemporary debates over the efficacy and utility of film as an instrument of scientific knowledge.

Even after 1908, when motion pictures began to be integrated into the AMNH's public lectures and children's events, there continued to be discussions over the precise role of motion pictures in Museum-organized anthropological expeditions and in the institution's public programs. Not surprisingly, the status of film became enmeshed within long-standing professional debates about other popular forms of museum display, such as the illustrated lecture and the life group, and while there are no explicit comparisons made between the two representational forms in the discourse, it is possible to see how motion pictures engendered similar kinds of anxieties for the Museum's curators. The complex interactions among Museum staff, visiting lecturers, AMNH-sponsored anthropologists in the field, and professional commentators provide compelling testimony not only of the unstable and contentious nature of film as a transmitter of anthropological knowledge but also of the interdependency of anthropology and popular culture in turn-of-the-century New York, the center of the burgeoning film industry.

The experience of viewing motion pictures in a space of socially sanctioned edification and uplift such as the American Museum of Natural History was by no means identical to the experience of watching the latest one-reeler in a cramped and noisy Lower East Side storefront theater. Films representing native peoples were thus part of a discursive practice that cannot be reduced to a singular site or textual meaning, and there is no easy way of determining precisely what kinds of ethnographic meanings such films engendered for historical spectators, since there are few remaining traces of their exhibition contexts. Nevertheless, taking a closer look at the museum as a reception site will flesh out our understanding of the emergence of ethnographic film and offer us vital clues in pinning down scientific perceptions of cinema at the beginning of the twentieth century.

Visual Antecedents: The Illustrated Lecture at the AMNH

The earliest record of lantern slides being used at the AMNH goes back to 1880, when Albert S. Bickmore, the Museum's founder and first superintendent, secured approval from the trustees to begin offering a formal educational program. Similar developments were under way in other major natural history museums, including the Smithsonian and the Peabody. The inaugural AMNH event, a lecture entitled "Corals and Coral Islands," used hand-colored slides and coral specimens from the Museum's exhibit cases. The illustrations were projected on a screen through a doorway from an adjoining room and, according to John R. Saunders, were presented in an informal and conversational style.[4] It is important to note how the spoken lecture, the magic lantern slide, and the artifact on display created different orders of scientific knowledge in lectures such as "Corals and Coral Islands." The impracticality of using actual objects in large lectures, where people sitting at the back of an auditorium had obstructed views of the lecture podium, meant that a projected image of an animal or specimen (what Barbara Kirshenblatt-Gimblett calls "second order" materials) was essential if audiences were to grasp the significance of what was being explained. "First order" materials (the actual artifacts) would therefore have served two purposes: they authenticated what was being shown on the screen and inspired audience members to examine specimens at closer range after the lecture.[5]

Instruction of children at the AMNH started in 1893 when assistant curators began offering talks and informal lectures in the library on Saturday mornings. Formal cooperation with the New York City Board of Education began in 1895, organized by the AMNH's education supervisor Henry M. Leipziger, who delivered most of the early natural science and fine arts lectures, which were given on Tuesday nights. Between 1886 and 1903, Museum Superintendent Bickmore devoted considerable time to purchasing negatives from photographers and building up the Museum's collection.[6] By 1898 the Museum's annual report boasted that "photography has become of increased importance both in connection with exhibition and publication. We have now developed an almost perfect system of photography."[7] Illustrated lectures at the Museum proved extremely popular, addressing subjects across the fields of natural history, art appreciation, modern industrial life, anthropology, and geography. A review of an illustrated lecture series on Paris from the *American Museum Journal* in 1900 offered an explanation for the special appeal of slides: "In this latest series of lectures there are thrown on the great 25 foot screens over 300 views of stereoscopic clearness and depth, illustrative of the most glorious city in the world. Compared with these views, ordinary photographic reproductions can only faintly suggest the charm of the reality."[8] The role of the illustrated lecture within the Museum's mission of education and uplift was argued in 1900, when Leipziger made a case for its importance in appealing to working-class Museum visitors. According to Leipziger:

> To the thousands of toilers in this city what an opportunity is afforded by the lectures to the people to get a glimpse of the great world. How, by means of the picture thrown on the screen, are the words of the lecturer clarified and intensified. The eye and the ear are both appealed to, and the knowledge thus gotten remains. So if we can make the pleasure of our people consist in the delights of art, in the beauties of literature, and in the pursuit of science, and gradually turn them away from so much that is lowering, are we not doing a real public service . . . and if we can turn our youth away from the street corner to the temple of nature, are we not helping them to that end?[9]

For Leipziger, the illustrated lecture served a double function; not only did it appeal to less cultured Museum audiences, who might otherwise find recreation in unwholesome pursuits, but it also ensured that the scientific aims of the object-lesson impressed themselves deeply upon the consciousness of all Museum visitors, since "the knowledge thus gotten remains."

In addition to the enormous popularity of stereoscopic slides as visual aides in the museum lecture, several prominent advocates of illustration used museum-owned slides in public lectures given in New York City (the same men later pioneered the introduction of moving pictures at the AMNH). When delivering a lecture as part of the New York City Board of Education's lecture series, the AMNH's Roy Chapman Andrews used colored lantern slides from a whaling expedition to help his audience "feel and hear the rush of the sea, the roar of the gun and the thrill of the hunt."[10] Andrews also used lantern slides in New York society fund-raising dinners, thrilling his audience with tales of adventure and scientific exploration. Operating the magic lantern projector was no small feat, however, as AMNH scientist Raymond Ditmars discovered when he gave an illustrated lecture before one of New York City's largest screens at the Sixty-Ninth Regiment Armory. According to Ditmars, "Two theatrical electricians fed the fifty-ampere arcs of special stage stereopticons, and after their labors, they looked as if they had crawled from a coal hole." Their efforts, however, did not go unnoticed; as Ditmars recalled, the "immense and brilliantly illuminated pictures were received with prolonged applause."[11]

By 1911 the AMNH possessed more than 35,000 catalogued lantern slides, 12,000 of them colored, illustrating "plant life, animal life, industries, customs of people, and physical geography."[12] At this point in the development of educational services, the slides were not loaned to agencies outside the Museum, although in 1915 the Museum's department of education decided to bear the cost of distributing slides and opened a branch of the AMNH primarily for teaching in Washington Irving High School. As part of the new lending service, slides could be borrowed separately, in groups, or in lecture sets, accompanied by full descriptions to aid teachers in preparing their presentations. However, the Museum's annual reports for 1915 noted that few schools had access to the lantern or blackout facilities necessary to exhibit slides: "The use of slides has been limited by the fact that many schools are not equipped with class rooms which can be darkened, or do not possess stereopticon lanterns. There are, however, 35 schools in the city which are making frequent and regular use of these slides."[13]

While the establishment of the Museum's magic lantern lending library signaled institutional recognition of the role of visual aides in the science lecture, opposition to the practice persisted. One of the main criticisms voiced was that lecturers tended to use too many slides at the expense of detailed verbal explication of the subject at hand.[14] Blame for this trend was often placed squarely on the audience itself, who, curators argued, had come to expect that lectures would be copiously illustrated. Writing in *Science* in 1908, AMNH director Frederic Lucas complained that "formerly lectures were given because the speaker had something to impart, but . . . unnaturally, the pictures [magic lantern slides] have come to be regarded as more important than the words, or at least more desired by the public."[15] The AMNH's curator of public education, George Sherwood, seconded Lucas's criticism of the overuse of slides: "The most common mistake made by the lecturers that we have is the tendency to show more slides than is desirable."[16] Meanwhile, on the other side of the Atlantic, British curator Frank Woolnaugh complained about the quality of some manufacturers' slides, noting that "those of some makers still leave much to be desired," although the increased demand of the past few years had, Woolnaugh argued, "brought about considerable improvement" since almost all natural history subjects were now taken from "real life."[17] Not surprisingly, fears that magic lantern slides might prove to be too powerfully diverting and distract audiences from the attention required for the scholarly explication of scientific ideas were echoed in subsequent internal Museum debates about the use of motion pictures. In the case of cinema, moreover, curators had additional issues to worry about.

Film Enters the Museum

Unlike life groups, which were permanently (and on occasion temporarily) installed in the Museum galleries and over which curators had complete sovereignty, motion pictures entered the Museum through the side door, so to speak, initially under the control of the visiting lecturer, especially before the Museum began its own film collection (consisting of films shot by AMNH curators as well as purchased titles) in the mid-teens. Booking a lecturer and his films (and they were almost always male to begin with) involved a certain amount of risk to Museum administrators; vouching for the credentials of the lecturer was one thing, but ensuring that the films screened lived up to the scholarly reputation of the institution was another. An analysis of the Museum's interaction with lecturers suggests that disputes arising over the use of motion pictures were often less about film's intrinsic worth as a conveyor of scientific knowledge than about how films would be integrated into the spoken part of the lecture. While it is unclear whether the Museum vetted every film shown at the time, there is evidence that curators had seen at least some of the films before their public exhibition. The use of film at the AMNH therefore involved a basic contradiction; motion pictures were desirable in their mass appeal, but this appeal was exactly what was most suspect and subject to censorship. While I have come across no extant material on the reception of the first film exhibited at the AMNH—it was used to illustrate a lecture given by O. P. Austin entitled "Queer Methods of Transportation" on April 8, 1908—the March 1908 edition of the *American Museum Journal* advertised the upcoming lecture as

> a view, by moving pictures and stereopticon slides, of the curious methods of travel and transportation encountered in a trip around the world; the crude methods of the Tropics and the Orient are contrasted with the modern systems of Europe and America, and some suggestions are presented regarding the possibility of development of the Tropics and the Orient through the introduction of modern methods.[18]

It is perhaps no coincidence that the first film to appear at the Museum should foreground issues of modernity and Western industrialization; implicated in discourses of colonialism and imperialism, the cinematic apparatus had itself become a metaphor for progress and technological advance, a point that might not have been lost on some members of the audience who were reacquainting themselves with cinema, or perhaps viewing a film for the first time.

As is the case with the vast majority of travelogues of the period, there is no way of ascertaining the provenance of the films used in Austin's lecture, including whether Austin had shot them himself or had rented them from a commercial agent for the occasion. We do know that once film began appearing regularly in the public program, staff in the AMNH's department of education cooperated with visiting lecturers and, in at least one case, took on the responsibility for film rental. In 1909, Dr. Hugh Smith of the U.S. Bureau of Fisheries requested that the Museum rent four titles from Miles Brothers Film Exchange of New York City, since Smith felt that these films would "illustrate my remarks nicely."[19] It is unclear who paid for the rental of the films, although in the case of Claude N. Bennett, who delivered a lecture entitled "The Panama Canal: The Eighth Wonder of the World" in the spring of 1911, the speaker insisted that if the Museum wanted moving pictures, they would have to pay for their rental from the General Film Company. Records indicate that the Museum refused to pay for Bennett's films, even though they were exhibited as part of the lecture. The Museum's initial refusal to pay for the rental of films (it is unclear from the extant documentation whether the Museum eventually acquiesced and made funds available) suggests the Museum's expectation that lecturers would supply film material that they either shot themselves or acquired from commercial sources. In any event, the day before his lecture at the Museum, Bennett had written the curator of public education, George Sherwood, informing him that "except to gratify your wishes, I do not care whether the moving picture films are used or not."[20] Bennett's correspondence with the Museum is an example of the sometimes testy exchanges between invited lecturers and Museum officials; Bennett reminded Sherwood that his $25 lecture fee was half what he normally charged institutions and that he had only agreed to appear at the Museum because it was a public institution with a "fixed schedule of fees from which you cannot vary."[21]

Decisions on funding, suitability of material, and editorial control over the early use of film by guest lecturers at the AMNH were made on a case-by-case basis. For example, in arranging a subsequent lecture by Dr. Smith in December 1913, Museum director Lucas gave Smith strict instructions on which portions of the rented footage shot by Roy Chapman Andrews in the Pribilof Islands could be used:

We understand that these motion pictures give an excellent idea of some of the life of the Pribilof Islands, including seals, sea lions, reindeer and natives. We would wish to use probably no more than 2,600 feet of the film; for instance, we would not care for the skinning of the seals, portions of the film that duplicate over other sections, or parts that are not especially good.[22]

In this instance, Lucas had clearly taken it upon himself to prescreen the films in order to make a decision on how their use would best conform to the institution's pedagogical philosophy. Lucas was not shy about offering specific directives on the amount of film that could be used in the lecture or censoring sequences deemed unsuitable for the Museum's audiences, such as the skinning of the seals. Lucas's casual listing of "natives" along with the regional wildlife also suggests that few, if any, distinctions were made between films with explicit ethnographic content and those related to natural history or the natural sciences. For example, there is no discussion of the specific kinds of challenges ethnographic films might present to the illustrated-lecture format in either lecturer correspondence or in internal Museum documents, despite the fact that from the lecture titles alone, it would seem that a significant number of films with ethnographic content were exhibited at the AMNH between 1908 and 1915.[23]

If the use of motion pictures within the Museum's public lectures was not addressed in internal memoranda before 1908, subsequent AMNH-lecturer correspondence refers repeatedly to disputes over the suitability of specific film sequences for the Museum's audiences. In 1912, for example, Museum president Henry Fairfield Osborn advised lecturer Capt. Frank E. Kleinschmidt that in future talks involving Kleinschmidt's motion picture, *Hunting Big Game with a Cinematograph in Alaska and Siberia*, the lecturer should "omit the [seal] killing and not extend the series [of the polar bear] too long."[24] While Osborn did not explain the reason for his injunction in any detail, the graphic nature of the violent imagery was surely the source of his complaint (a poster for Kleinschmidt's second film, *Arctic Hunt* [1914], described it as containing "exciting, dangerous, sensational situations pictured while hunting animal life").[25] However, a review of Kleinschmidt's first film in the *Philadelphia Telegraph* in 1912 cited the same polar bear hunt scene as the one the commercial audience was "most impressed with." The reviewer continued: "Here the pictures are so nearly perfect that the illusion is quite compelling and one imagines oneself aboard the schooner pursuing the polar bear mother and the cub as they swim along the ice flows, the little fellow with his teeth fixed on the mother's stumpy tail."[26] What are we to make, then, of President Osborn's admonishment of Kleinschmidt to censor the same scene that a journalist had singled out as the source of greatest audience approval? On one level, it suggests the culturally contingent nature of meaning across the film's distinct exhibition sites, since the responses from Osborn and those reported by the anonymous Philadelphia reviewer may have been determined in part by the imputed class tastes of their respective audiences. The critic's references to the film's nearly perfect illusionism might also be read as a displacement of the audience's sadistic pleasures in viewing the hunting scenes. Fearing the effect such graphic footage might have on the sensibilities of the Museum's members, Osborn felt duty-bound to register his displeasure with Kleinschmidt and to prohibit such footage from finding its way into future screenings at the AMNH.

But this was not the only time the Museum-as-film-exhibitor asserted its authority on visiting lecturers; James Barnes's 1914 film *From Coast to Coast Through Central Africa*, compiled from footage shot during the AMNH-sponsored expedition Barnes had undertaken with British naturalist-filmmaker Cherry Kearton, was also subject to editorializing by the AMNH.[27] Sherwood demanded that Barnes change a revised intertitle that used the word "playground" in describing an animal watering hole back to the original intertitle "African Animals in their Home," because, as Sherwood declared, "the Museum stands for science and must therefore adhere strictly to facts."[28] That this seemingly insignificant semantic shift across alternate intertitles elicited such a principled response from Sherwood is symptomatic of the Museum's sensitivity toward the use of figurative language in ostensibly scientific presentations. It also betrays a more general and long-standing fear about the trivializing effects of popular modes of address upon scientific standards. As historian Nancy Leys Stepan argues in her work on race and gender analogies in nineteenth-century science, "one reason for the controversy over metaphor, analogy, and models in science is the intellectually privileged status that science has traditionally enjoyed as the repository of nonmetaphorical, empirical, politically neutral, universal knowledge."[29] J. Hillis Miller's explication of the function of the label or the caption in placing a picture "back within the context of some diachronic narrative" may be relevant here, as is Roland Barthes's theoretical work on photography, captioning, and connotation.[30] While not completely opposed to the use of illustration in public lectures, Osborn seems to exemplify Miller's argument that illustration "to some degree interferes with [a] text," and, in this case, with science's own master narrative of truth and objectivity.[31] Thus, every editorial change Osborn was able to impose upon visiting lecturers represented a small victory of science over pseudoscience, separating the Museum from some of the undesirable associations of popular culture. Osborn's behavior suggests that illustration for him threatened to interfere with science's master narrative of objectivity. Furthermore, in a congratulatory letter sent to Barnes following a successful AMNH screening, Osborn suggested that Barnes "add a map clearly showing the tribal divisions and territories" in future screenings.[32] For Osborn, the map's objectifying classification of tribal groups and geographical areas ensured the priority of rational knowledge over visual spectacle.

The Museum's efforts to censor specific film segments and police the language of motion picture intertitles are merely two examples of the measures Sherwood and Osborn took to regulate the use of motion pictures at the Museum in the teens. In another context, Sherwood wrote to Lee Keedick, self-described "Manager of the World's Most Celebrated Lecturers," suggesting that in children's presentations at the Museum, lecturers should show lantern slides of each exhibit before screening moving pictures. As late as 1919, Osborn wrote Sherwood insisting that either a taxidermy specimen, a slide of a Museum habitat group, or a photograph of the group should be displayed in order to "connect moving pictures with the serious side of zoology."[33] In 1920, Osborn felt compelled to admonish Sherwood that "the educational must not be swallowed up by the popular aspect of our lectures."[34] The fearful prospect that the seductive illusionism of the moving image would undermine more scholarly aims underscored the precarious equilibrium between science and spectacle which Osborn strove to maintain for Museum audiences. That the Museum wanted *some* measure of popular spectacle is evident from the institution's ongoing efforts to popularize its exhibits, and the large number of diorama life groups and taxidermy specimens installed during this period are testimony to this shift. However, unlike permanent exhibits, which could be designed according to scientific principles and contextualized via labels, moving pictures rented from commercial exchanges or brought to the Museum by visiting lecturers were something of an unknown quantity to curators, due in large part to cinema's relative newness as a medium and to motion pictures' associations with cheap amusements.

It is perhaps worth emphasizing the fact that the viewing public at the Museum would have been exposed to a wide array of popular ethnographic imagery at that time, some of it represented in vulgarized form in freak shows, circuses, and vaudeville programs, as well as in more salubrious form in commercial motion picture travelogues. Fearful of the touristic and unscientific profile of many itinerant lecturers who sought to exhibit their latest trave-logues at the Museum, Osborn carefully vetted those lecturers invited to appear at the Museum, and also kept a watchful eye on exactly how moving pictures were to be incorporated into the illustrated lecture. Osborn's insis-tence that spectators not be permitted to get caught up in the illusionistic lure of the moving image is thus part of a defensive strategy adopted to minimize the risk that Museum-goers might misconstrue the lecture's ostensible scien-tific aims. In attempting to contain the illusionistic appeal that vivified filmed zoological and biological studies, Osborn sought to mitigate cinema's dis-tracting kinetic and spectacular qualities by ensuring that the content of the film's images and intertitles, the subject of the lecture, the relationship of the film to magic lantern slides, and the controlling vocal sanctioning of the speaker would all preserve the scientific seriousness of the talk.

Osborn's insistence that either physical artifacts be displayed or slides be shown *before* motion pictures in public lectures also suggests an opposition between the presumed nonscientific nature of mimetic movement and the reflective qualities of stasis, even in the form of a magic lantern slide. Osborn's concern that scientific principles would be undermined or trivialized in the case of unaccompanied moving pictures invokes a hierarchy of visual repre-sentation in which stasis is afforded greater scientific exactitude than move-ment and spoken or written texts imbued with more authority than visual images. Thus the lecturer's task became, in the words of theorist Roger Cardinal, to orient the gaze of the spectator by "marshaling perceptions of detail within a cohesive and dogmatic order and . . . narrativizing the image by changing simultaneity into sequence, haptic mosaic into story."[35]

Osborn's injunction that Museum lecturers use still images or taxidermy specimens before screening moving pictures also reflected concerns of Museum officials about the unsuitable nature of much of the commercial footage used by lecturers. In the spring of 1917, as Museum department heads met to reassess their policy on public programs, Sherwood outlined the difficulties of reconciling scientific legitimacy and audience appeal:

> The policy that we have followed fairly closely in the past is to consider that the lectures to the members are primarily for the purpose of keeping them in touch with the specific work the institution is doing, and conse-

quently with the progress that is made in lines of science that is germane to the work of the museum. Every year there is an increasing number of outsiders who are interested in professional lectures on subjects that are of an interesting character but are not related in any way to the science taken up in the Museum, and while some of these, owing to their popularity, drew a crowd, we adhere rather strictly to the plans set before us.[36]

While these outsiders may have had considerable expertise in areas that intersected with the Museum's work, unless they had the right credentials or were affiliated with scientific institutions, they were politely turned away.[37] The biggest problem in this regard was that the public's interpretation of what constituted scientific research and the Museum's narrower definition were often at odds, although, as we saw from lecture titles such as "The Romance of the Rhine" and "The Glories of Venice," the Museum was hardly consistent on this policy and did program lectures dealing with the arts and travel. There was also the additional risk that an outsider might deliberately misrepresent his or her talk in a letter to the Museum in order to secure a booking and then embarrass the Museum with an amateurish or unscientific presentation.

As the years went by, the Museum began to compete more directly with popular amusements by organizing special film screenings for New York City's children. Even here, though, the Museum's justification for the screenings was framed by discourses of moral uplift and edification rather than entertainment. George Sherwood wrote New York City's school principals in 1922 with news about a special series of screenings: "Wholesome recreation for children is a serious problem in the city, [and] has led the American Museum of Natural History to arrange a holiday series of motion pictures for the boys and girls of the New York public schools."[38]

Another indication of the Museum's ambivalence about the role of motion pictures within the institution's scientific and civic mission can be seen in its treatment of cameramen-adventurers such as James Barnes and Paul J. Rainey. Though Museum staff members did police the occasional intertitle and certain brief sequences in films screened at the AMNH, at the same time the institution acquired films shot by such entrepreneurs for its permanent collection.[39] The Museum undoubtedly wished to maintain some distance between its image of scientific propriety and the public figure of the swashbuckling,

FIG. 6.2 Valentia Steer's *Romance of the Cinema* (1913),
showing the adventurer-cameraman filming lions in Africa.

safari-hunting cameraman-adventurer[40] as represented in popular fiction of the time (fig. 6.2).[41] Many of the films associated with such figures—safari travelogues with occasional glimpses of local ethnographic interest—were the cinematographic equivalent of the ubiquitous wild-game trophy photographs of the hunter posing before the fresh kill and were unlikely to convey the disinterested air of scientific inquiry sought by Museum officials. Indeed, the motives of financial gain and self-aggrandizement behind the use of film in some of these expeditions were explicitly evoked by film critic Ernest A. Dench in 1915, who noted that "the explorer who decides to combine cinematography with his other work—hobby as he no doubt regards it—does so with the object of recovering his traveling expenses apart from adding a substantial amount to his bank account."[42] On the surface, then, one would assume that such frankly commercial motives would have dissuaded anthropologists and museum officials from endorsing such filmmaking efforts.[43]

However, the Museum did not always insist that all films and lectures closely adhere to the larger institutional mission of scientific education, and in cases where film screenings might be expected to attract large audiences, the Museum responded with uncharacteristic enthusiasm. A closer look at two films shown at the Museum during the teens might be useful, therefore, in illuminating the institution's evolving approach to the problem of ensuring scientific rigor in the context of popularized ethnography; these films are Paul J. Rainey's 1912 film *African Hunt* and Frank E. Moore's 1913 adaptation of Henry Wadsworth Longfellow's poem *Hiawatha*.[44]

Paul J. Rainey's African Hunt: *The Adventurer-Explorer Draws a Mass Audience*

A Cleveland-born millionaire and adventurer who ran his family's estate from offices in New York City, Paul Rainey attracted considerable public attention with the commercial success of his "African Safari" films of 1912 and 1914.[45] Rainey privately financed the $250,000 hunting expedition to Mombassa in 1912, during which he collected scientific materials for the Smithsonian and the New York Zoological Society and shot enough footage to form the basis of two films released a couple of years apart.[46] Rainey achieved his prominence not only within the commercial theater circuit on the East Coast and Midwest but also from his visiting lectures to professional and scientific venues eager to host him and his film. A *Moving Picture World* review of *African Hunt*, which opened with an exclusive engagement at Daniel Frohman's Lyceum Theatre in New York City in April 1912, describes the film as "destined to go down in the archives of many governments as an authentic record in the study of natural history . . . stand[ing] out, head and shoulders over anything of the kind that had heretofore been attempted in Africa."[47] Advertisements in the *Washington Post* for Rainey's 1912 film, which was later incorporated into Rainey's AMNH lecture "Hunting Lions with Hounds," contained endorsements from the National Geographic Society, the Smithsonian Institution, and the American Museum of Natural History.[48] A 1914 *New York Times* article entitled "Praise for Paul Rainey from the Museum" reported President Osborn's salute to Rainey's films as "extremely important scientific records" and his request that Rainey deposit footage from both the 1912 and 1914 expeditions at the Museum where they would be used, Osborn said, "only in educational work."[49] Osborn's simultaneous praise for Rainey's films and his assurances that they would be exhibited only within an educational context suggests a calculated effort to both reassure the public that the Museum did not stand to gain financially from owning a copy of the prints and to assuage any doubts about the pedagogical and scientific value of films shot by a wealthy amateur-adventurer. Rainey's considerable personal wealth might also have played a role in the sympathetic treatment he received at the Museum, since he may have been courted as a potential benefactor. Moreover, given the popular appeal of Rainey's films, Osborn's edict seems an attempt to reassure the public that the Museum's desire to own prints of the film was motivated strictly by educational goals and was unrelated to the sensational nature and commercial value of the films.

African Hunt contains many of the iconographic trademarks of the nature film, a genre, as Greg Mitman argues, that appealed to the growing managerial middle class's "increased leisure and money to pursue the luxuries of country life previously confined to the rich."[50] Shots of native couriers carrying supplies for the traveling party; gruesome images of wildlife slaughter intercut with shots of animals in captivity or in the wild; comic scenes showing white hunters and monkeys; footage of expedition members at the base camp, including tea drinking and personal grooming; and glimpses of indigenous life comprise the subject matter of *African Hunt*.[51] In this regard, detailed tex-

FIG. 6.3 Advertisement for Paul Rainey's *African Hunt* from *Moving Picture World*, November 5, 1913.

tual analysis of the film's individual scenes is less important for our purposes than a consideration of how these cinematic fragments of the expedition and African life were packaged for popular consumption. What comes across from some of the reviews of *African Hunt* is just how mainstream and family entertainment–oriented the film was perceived to be; for example, in the words of one Pittsburgh reviewer: "To the layman they are a source of instruction and entertainment, to the lover of natural history they are a revelation and a source of keenest pleasure, and to the hunter and expert they must be productive of a great deal of heartfelt pleasure."[52] The idea of "something for everyone" had been planted in Rainey's promotional material for the film; in November 1913, for example, his distribution company, Jungle Film Co., bought a two-page spread in *Moving Picture World* to promote the film under the title *Paul J. Rainey's African Hunt* (fig. 6.3). The advertisement reassured theater owners that the film would appeal to

FIG. 6.4 Interior of auditorium at AMNH, 1900. (Neg. no. 349. Courtesy Dept. of Library Services, AMNH)

all classes which makes them forget for the time their stations in life in their absorbing interest in the domestic joys and sorrows of God's obscure four-footed kingdom, which, after all, are much the same as their own. There is something in it that appeals to every mother, that appeals to every father, and, best of all, it appeals to every child.[53]

The advertisement also assured commercial theater owners that a lecturer would not be required since "to obviate the expense . . . the entire film has been comprehensively re-titled."[54] Significantly, despite their extensive inter-titling, Rainey's films were never shown at the Museum without a lecturer present, a point that highlights the institution's sensitivity to maintaining the balance between popular amusement and pedagogical instruction. Despite these rhetorical claims for the diversified class appeal of Rainey's films, the audience most attracted to this genre (and to the Museum) was a solidly middle- and upper-class one, as Mitman rightly observes: "[While] advertisements for *Paul Rainey's African Hunt* underscored nature's alleged power to unify people of different socioeconomic backgrounds . . . the development of a mass market for natural history films would not come until after World War II" (19–20).

Osborn's endorsement of the scientific merit of Rainey's film should also be considered in the context of the public reception of *African Hunt* at the Museum in February 1912. The premier screening attracted one of the largest audiences the institution had ever seen;[55] the auditorium, with a seating capacity of 1,500, was so overcrowded that two additional performances were scheduled for the following month (fig. 6.4). Nevertheless, protesting the indignity of waiting in line only to be turned away from the sold-out screening, some AMNH members canceled their Museum subscriptions.[56] Two and a half thousand people showed up for the additional screenings on March 13, many of them Museum members who had been denied entry to the February screening. Conscious of public and membership interest in Rainey's films, Osborn may have felt that acquiring the films for the Museum might appease disgruntled members or even entice lapsed members to renew their subscriptions.

Carlton Miles, a reviewer of Rainey's 1914 follow-up film to *African Hunt*, which comprised new footage shot by Rainey (as well as old footage) and which was shown in the AMNH lecture entitled "Latest Motion Pictures of African Animals" (with the use of the word "latest" to differentiate the 1914 from the 1912 footage), turned President Osborn's hierarchy of still images, artifacts, and motion pictures on its head, arguing that "when you've carefully traced the smudgy maps of Africa and read paragraphs describing the contour of the country . . . did it convey anything of the actuality to you? Did it awaken within you a desire to see a land in which circus animals roamed without cage or trainer?"[57] For Miles, the verisimilitude of the cinematic image presented the spectator with an economy of representation in which knowledge became synonymous with vision; *tracing* maps and *reading* about non-Western countries and cultures were poor substitutes, in Miles's view, for witnessing the unadulterated real thing. Seeing a moving image of a foreign place and people was the next best thing to being there for Miles and many other reviewers; "from the comfort and security of his orchestra chair," one critic opined, the cinema spectator could vicariously identify with Rainey's hunters.[58] References to the thrill of the hunt without any of its personal risks and expressions of admiration for the bravery of the hunters were ubiquitous tropes in the critical reception of safari films like Rainey's. Likewise, discourses of romanticism, heroism, and unswerving nerve become enduring tropes in popular articles on adventurer-cameramen such as Paul Rainey and Carl Akeley.[59] Wilbur Daniel Steele's essay on British wildlife photographer Cherry Kearton in *McClure's Magazine*, for example, describes the patience involved in securing a shot of wild game as requiring a trancelike concentration:[60]

> Now here is a peculiar phenomenon connected with the taking of animated pictures: once the operator has his eye to the sights, he seems to pass into a state of mesmerism, losing all consciousness of the world about him. . . . Even perspective loses its significance.[61]

Heroic stories in the pages of popular magazines of the adventurer-cameraman hunting down his prey were replicated as frozen vignettes in many museum animal habitat groups that re-created the dramatic encounter between man and beast (although typically effacing the presence of the white hunter from the scene). Like the museumgoer standing before such habitat groups, film spectators and the hunter became one for a fleeting moment, as they looked upon what the hunter had seen as he focused the animal in his sights. Unlike the trophy scene typically found at the end of the wildlife film, the death of the taxidermied animal is denied representation, since the action in the tableaux is frozen the instant before the shot was fired and the animal crumpled to its feet. What we see in the glass case, then, is not death cheated but death permanently suspended, in a moment that appears contingent, but is, in fact, petrified. As Donna Haraway writes:

> The moment seems fragile, the animals about to disappear, the communion about to break. . . . But it does not. The gaze holds. . . . There is no impediment to this vision, no meditation. The glass front of the diorama forbids the body's entry, but the gaze invites his visual penetration. The animal is frozen in a moment of supreme life, and man is transfixed.[62]

The extremely popular safari films made by Rainey and others were entangled in the looking regimes of the habitat groups in contradictory ways; while both evoked the mimetic power of the simulacral, they represented death quite differently. While the moment of death is paradoxically both forever inscribed and suppressed in the habitat diorama (although animals hunting one another for prey is acceptable), the same moment returns again and again in *African Hunt*. Death is the master narrative in both taxidermy and nature films such as Rainey's, for death is the ultimate goal of the hunt.

Hiawatha: *Redeemable Ethnography*

While the commercially obtained films exhibited at the Museum during this period generally served an illustrative function in public lectures, in the case of Frank E. Moore's film adaptation of Longfellow's *Hiawatha*—a joint presentation by the American Scenic and Historical Society and the Museum in April 1913—a reading of the classic poem delivered as the film was being projected replaced the traditional lecture format (fig. 6.5).[63] Though resistant to the use of commercially produced fiction films, Museum officials were so certain of *Hiawatha*'s literary pedigree, ethnological features (including an all–Native American cast), and educational value that they had no qualms screening it. The AMNH had also played a role in the film's production; Moore drew upon the ethnographic expertise of the Museum's assistant curator of the Department of Anthropology, Alanson Skinner, even borrowing Native American costumes and props from the Museum for use in the production.[64] *Hiawatha*'s inclusion in the program could thus be justified because the film illustrated some of the ethnological work taking place in the institution and was validated by anthropologist Alanson Skinner, who had served as a consultant to motion picture producers on other occasions. The idea that Museum audiences would have a chance to see the costumes and props that the institution had lent to the production both in the film and in the Museum's collection may also have appealed to AMNH officials. In a letter to Skinner in the spring of 1913, Moore requested information about Sioux and Ojibwa burial customs, noting that he planned to recruit two hundred Native American extras for the winter scenes. In his reply, Skinner helpfully informed the filmmaker that the deceased body "was deposited in the grave, after which the chief mourner stepped quickly over the grave and hastened home. This is

THE INDIAN PLAYERS

PRESENT

THEIR PASSION PLAY

Hiawatha

A PICTURE MASQUE IN FOUR PARTS
PRODUCED UNDER THE PERSONAL DIRECTION
OF MR. F. E. MOORE

Minnehaha   Hiawatha

AUDITORIUM OF THE MUSEUM
THURSDAY EVENING, APRIL 3
At Quarter past Eight

Auspices: American Scenic and Historic Preservation Society
And American Museum of Natural History

FIG. 6.5 Program for Frank E. Moore's *Hiawatha* at the AMNH, 1913.

common among the Menomini and also found among the Ojibwa. It seems to me that this would do very well for your moving pictures and perhaps would be even more picturesque than the other [scaffold burial method]."[65]

Moore had directed various stage versions of *Hiawatha* for ten years before deciding to "use the resource of the moving picture to represent the drama with a larger personnel, in surroundings more harmonious with Indian life, and at different times of the year more appropriate to the story than were practicable in the acting of the play itself heretofore."[66] In addition to the April 1913 screening, the film was shown at the AMNH the following year, this time as part of a Saturday morning children's lecture series; in the promotional pamphlet for the series, children were reminded that even if the picture is "only a legend" and "not a true Science Story" it is, nevertheless, told by "real Indians" who take us "into the deep wild woods to learn many of the animals Hiawatha might have known."[67] The "real Indian" trope used to justify *Hiawatha*'s inclusion in the Children's Program was also exploited by Alanson Skinner, who, upon resigning from the AMNH in 1916 (perhaps inspired by Moore's success with *Hiawatha*), became a freelance lecturer. A 1919 brochure promoting Skinner's "Wigwam Stories" informed the reader that "although Mr. Skinner was born in Buffalo, he is now a real Indian. A few years ago he was adopted by the Menomini Indians and became a member of the tribe. His Indian name is Sekosa, which means Little Weasel, The One-Who-Never-Comes-Home-Empty. He has sat at the feet of the old chiefs and has heard the ancient stories from their lips."[68] It seems certain that Skinner's Museum experience as a consultant to motion picture professionals must have given him the confidence to break out on his own and try his hand at popular lecturing. Skinner must have had enough show business acumen to know that a promotional hook, such as privileged access to Menomini culture and a "real Indian" identity, would distinguish his lecture program from that of his competitors. However, the fluidity of Skinner's identity—the fact that he could be a "real Indian" in spite of his Caucasian descent—would never have worked in reverse, since, as a result of the power differential at work here, it was unthinkable that a Native American could become a "real" white despite having been acculturated into Western ways.

Although Skinner had illustrated his 1913–14 Museum lectures with moving pictures, he held a low opinion of most commercially produced motion pictures dealing with Native American life. In a letter to the *New York Times* in 1914, for example, Skinner criticized the latest film westerns for being little more than "ethnologically grotesque farces" in which "Delawares are dressed as Sioux, and the Indians of Manhattan Island are shown dwelling in skin tipis of the type used only by the tribes beyond the Mississippi." Skinner berated commercial photoplay producers for their inaccurate and anachronistic representations of contemporary Indian life, arguing that "the majority of modern Indians are dwelling in the same status as their white neighbors, have cut their hair, given up most of their ancient customs, and settled down to a quiet life."[69] Skinner also criticized the enormous liberties taken by commercial producers in their depiction of native cultures; accusing filmmakers of perpetuating offensive stereotypes of Native Americans, Skinner argued that "every film that serves to degrade the Indian adds another weight to the load which the progressive modern Indians . . . are trying to remove from the backs of their less progressive brothers."[70] But Skinner's tone of moral outrage belies the tensions within Skinner's own representations of Native American culture.

Skinner's 1919 talk, "Wigwam Stories" (part of the longer presentation entitled "Inside My Grandfather's Wigwam"), did not include film and was delivered by Skinner in the role of a freelance lecturer rather than a Museum employee.[71] Given Skinner's former AMNH affiliation, speculating on some of the possible reasons why he chose not to use film to illustrate his talks may shed some light on anthropological and museological responses to ethnographic film's role within the illustrated lecture.[72] First and foremost, the cost of renting commercial films may have been prohibitively expensive for Skinner (working as a freelance lecturer, his budget and his venues may have precluded the use of film and he may no longer have had access to the AMMH's modest film collection). Second, Skinner may have felt that his authority as an anthropologist, especially his broad knowledge of Indian culture, dance, and song, was sufficient to capture an audience's attention, unlike nonspecialist lecturers who depended more upon lantern slides and moving pictures to sustain audience interest and ensure ethnographic authenticity. Finally, Skinner's low regard for commercially produced films featuring Native Americans may have discouraged him from using film in his lectures, since it was the same commercial distributors to which he would have turned for film material. Unwilling or unable to shoot his own films, Skinner nevertheless used his pro-

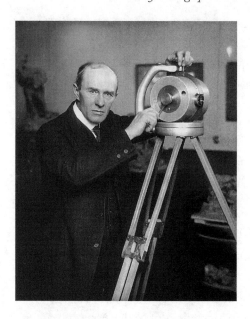

FIG. 6.6 Carl Akeley with original 1916 model of the Akeley camera. (Neg. no. 311839. Courtesy Dept. of Library Services, AMNH)

fessional experience as an anthropologist to differentiate *his* brand of showmanship from that of his inauthentic competitors. If motion pictures seem to have been largely ignored in the public career of AMNH-employee-turned-freelance-lecturer Alanson Skinner, how did the ambivalent status of early cinema at the AMNH play out in the late teens? Despite its undeniable success in helping attract huge audiences to scheduled lectures at the Museum, cinema, and its place in the scientific mission of the institution, continued to pose a challenge for Museum administrators throughout the late teens.

When compared with other major urban museums of science of the period, the relatively late appearance of film at the AMNH, coupled with the Museum's close supervision of the hiring and overseeing of film-lecturers, suggest the institution's ambivalence toward cinema. Unlike the Brooklyn Institute of Arts and Sciences, for example, which showcased Edison's kinetoscope in 1893 and began regularly exhibiting films in 1898, the AMNH integrated motion pictures in its public programs at a more leisurely pace. Our understanding of institutional ambivalence toward cinema at the AMNH can be heightened by considering the role of similar debates over life groups that occurred in the Museum in the first two decades of the twentieth century. While no one at the Museum drew a direct comparison between the signifying practices of diorama groups and motion pictures, ongoing discussions about the role of habitat and life groups must have been an informing context for the AMNH's response to cinema. And yet by 1917 the Museum was resigned to cinema's enduring appeal with audiences, as suggested by AMNH curator Robert Lowie's remarks that the "diversified style of lectures" — those featuring slides *and* motion pictures — were more likely to draw a crowd than nonillustrated lectures. Lowie's concession that "people have come to expect them and I don't think we can say anything about it,"[73] suggests that by the late teens the Museum had moved into a new phase of using cinema both within public programs and sponsored expeditions. In addition, in 1916 the Museum bought an Akeley motion picture camera[74] (fig. 6.6) and began asking certain curators to produce films on natural history.[75]

However, in light of cinema's uncertain status within the AMNH during the medium's first decade, it is not surprising that the curatorial staff and directors lacked a coherent policy on how film could be used within both the public and children's lecture programs. Even after the Museum began sponsoring films made by their curatorial staff, funding was limited, and the films that were made were incorporated into the public programs in sporadic and unsystematic ways. While Museum officials expressed misgivings about employing lecturers who used amateur footage and generally eschewed commercially produced travel films, it is not the case that the AMNH had no dealings whatsoever with commercial distributors. For example, in 1913 the Museum showed the Gaumont-owned Herbert G. Ponting films of Captain Scott's expedition to the South Pole[76] and acknowledged the support of industrial sponsors such as the Canadian Pacific Railway.[77] By 1916 the Museum had acquired enough films to establish a library of motion pictures, and the first loans of prints were made the following year, when two-reel films of Museum expeditions, *Life in the Frozen North* and *Hunting Whales off the Coast of Japan*, were lent to the YMCA for use in Army camps.[78] At the same time that the AMNH became an occasional producer of and regular venue for motion pictures, a small group of anthropologists affiliated with the Museum became interested in exploring the ethnographic value of motion pictures. One of these anthropologists was Pliny Earl Goddard, who shot films of Apache Indians while working as an assistant curator in the Department of Anthropology at the AMNH in the teens and twenties and who wrote a noteworthy article on the ethnographic potential of cinema in the *American Museum Journal* in 1915. Goddard was part of a first generation of ethnographic filmmakers who had one thing in common: professional training in the field of anthropology. It is to their films and intellectual writings on ethnographic cinema that we now turn.

7

Finding a Home for Cinema in Ethnography

THE FIRST GENERATION OF

ANTHROPOLOGIST-FILMMAKERS IN AMERICA

LOOKING BEYOND the museum as exhibition site, this chapter examines the work of five American anthropologists who took up the cause of ethnographic filmmaking during the silent film era: Frederick Starr, Pliny Earl Goddard, M. W. Hilton-Simpson, J. A. Haeseler, and Franz Boas.[1] As lonely proponents of ethnographic cinema within American anthropology during a period when most anthropologists remained publicly indifferent to the scientific potential of the motion picture camera, it is not surprising that the ethnographic filmmaking and writings of these men have gone largely unnoticed in subsequent accounts.[2] With the exception of Goddard, their writings largely explored ethnographic film's relationship to commercial cinema, unsurprising in light of anthropology's tangled and ambivalent relationship to early twentieth-century popular culture. The written work of these anthropologists contains frequent references to commercial cinema and the popular demand for images of native peoples, references that echo Haddon's and Spencer's earlier arguments for ethnographic film's cross-over appeal. Starr wrote about ethnographic film in the rhetorical style of turn-of-the-century travelogue lecturers, and Hilton-Simpson and Haeseler offered aspiring ethnographic filmmakers concrete advice on how to reconcile the interests of anthropology with the imperatives of Hollywood in the production and postproduction stages of ethnographic subjects. In a similar fashion, Boas was as much interested in the ethnographic potential of fictional film as he was in the camera's usefulness as an anthropological research tool. Boas's support for a collaborative ethnographic cinema, combining the financial resources of Hollywood with the ethnographic expertise of professional anthropologists, could also be found in much of the writing on ethnographic film in the trade and popular press. Goddard, however, envisioned ethnographic cinema in terms quite distinct from those of his colleagues, and his writings have an exceptional acuity and prescience as early commentaries on ethnographic cinema.[3]

At the same time, in the absence of a widely shared intellectual and institutional framework for ethnographic film within anthropology, the scattered writings and films of Haddon, Spencer, Goddard, and Boas had little impact on the emergence of visual anthropology. In fact, these early films are largely forgotten, and while a few had limited public release at the time, they failed to receive sustained attention among professional anthropologists. As inexperienced cinematographers working in conditions hostile to motion picture production, these anthropologists were plagued by many of the same challenges that had frustrated Haddon and Spencer some years earlier. Indeed, the technical problems that continued to afflict anthropologist-filmmakers working in the field between 1898 and 1914 suggest how little the technology[4] of nonprofessional cinematography had advanced during this period.[5] In order to explore these issues, this chapter will move chronologically through the filmmaking endeavors of these early pioneers, beginning with University of Chicago anthropologist Frederick Starr.

Frederick Starr's Contributions to Early Ethnographic Film

Born in Auburn, New York, in 1858, Starr obtained a Ph.D. in geology from Lafayette College in Pennsylvania in 1885, and from 1889 to 1891 worked in the Department of Ethnology at the AMNH before joining the faculty at the University of Chicago in 1892.[6] In addition to essays on moving pictures and anthropology for the trade papers *The Show World* in 1907 and *The Nickelodeon* in 1909, Starr published a monograph on the Ainu of Japan as well as an album of photographs on native peoples of the Congo, and contributed frequently to such popular journals and newspapers as the *Atlantic Monthly*, the *Chicago Tribune*, and *Ladies' Home Journal*.[7] In addition, in 1911, Starr shot a number of travelogue films in Japan which were later distributed by the Selig Polyscope

Company. An inveterate traveler and popular public speaker for both professional and lay audiences, Starr defined anthropology in generalist terms;
according to R. Berkeley Miller, Starr did little to advance the theory or practice of ethnography, and as late as 1922 insisted upon evolutionary theories
within anthropology. Writing a colleague in 1911, Starr opined that, "In my
teaching *evolution* is fundamental. It runs through every course I offer. It is
what gives life and value to the work."[8] It was undoubtedly Starr's fascination
with travel and love of public speaking, though, that best accounts for his
interest in moving pictures.

Writing in the *Show World* in 1907, Starr argued that "the best way to learn the
truth about the Congo was through the mediumship of the moving picture
machine." For Starr, cinema's ability to "graphically" depict the "conditions
and scenery of every country on the globe" offered a decisive advantage in
stimulating and educating popular audiences. Cinema enabled spectators to
"readily grasp ideas that would require weeks by the commonly accepted system or plan of instruction," the images represented on the screen "wrapped in
the mind so well that to forget them [was] almost an impossibility."[9] As a lecturer and educator, Starr considered himself responsible for ensuring that "the
listener [got] the benefit of the words of the lecturer as well as the ideas that
may be formed in the mind by watching and studying the views." He took
responsibility for designing the program, ensuring the smooth transition
between stereopticon slides, moving pictures, and phonograph demonstration, and setting the tone of the evening through the coordination of films and
spoken commentary.[10] In all likelihood, before Starr entertained the thought
of using his own films of the Congo in his lectures, he illustrated his talks with
commercially produced travelogues. In fact, Starr confessed that the films he
attempted to make in the Congo in 1906–1907 were ruined by "unfavorable"
climactic conditions.[11] According to Jennifer Peterson, Starr delivered a series
of public lectures illustrated with moving pictures at Chicago's Fine Arts
Building (Music Hall) in April 1909; funded by the Selig Polyscope company,
these films were shot by Starr's camera operator Manuel Gonzales, who
accompanied Starr on several research trips.[12] For Starr, cinema was analogous
to a "moving text-book" which could instruct as well as "provide amusement
for the spectator." Indeed, Starr's description of the cinema as "not only the
greatest impulse of entertainment, but the mightiest force of instruction" and

"the highest type of entertainment in the history of the world" echoes the rhetoric of professional showmen—lecturers such as Lyman Howe and Burton Holmes as well as trade press editorial writers in a motion picture industry hungry for middle-class respectability.[13]

Writing in the *Nickelodeon* two years after the *Show World* article, Starr again lent his scientific authority to the promotional rhetoric of armchair travel by suggesting that ethnographic knowledge was within the reach of both travelers and filmgoers. The nickelodeon patron could thus flit from India, to China, and to Japan without ever leaving the theater. As Starr lyrically put it:

> I have been to the Orient and gazed at water-sellers and beggars and dervishes. I have beheld fat old Rajahs with the price of a thousand lives bejeweled in their monster turbans. . . . I know how the Chinaman lives and I have been through the homes of the Japanese. . . . I have looked upon weird dances and outlandish frolics in every quarter of the globe, and I didn't have to leave Chicago for a moment.[14]

Motion pictures, for Starr, seemed to satisfy an epistephilia that had its roots in the expository mode of the lantern slide lecture; here, knowledge, in the words of Bill Nichols, "provides the viewer a sense of plenitude or self-sufficiency" that often served to buttress Eurocentric attitudes about cultural and racial superiority.[15] In a similar fashion, cinema's defining capability to record movement was linked by Starr to the issue of audience appeal. For Starr, movement was inextricably bound to practical issues of spectatorship—specifically, the problem of sustaining interest among spectators. As Starr explained, it was "far easier to hold the attention of the audience when there [was] a rapid change of pictures" than when the lecture was illustrated with the projection of static slides; there was, Starr argued, "much in the pictures as they come and go to provide amusement for the spectator."[16]

While Goddard and Starr shared an interest in cinema's capacity for verisimilitude, they viewed cinema from distinct vantage points and their articles on ethnographic cinema were written for very different audiences: the middle-class and professional readership of the AMNH's members in the case of Goddard's *American Museum Journal* essay and moving picture industry personnel in the case of Starr's *Show World* and *Nickelodeon* articles. To a large

FIG. 7.1 Portrait of Pliny Earl
Goddard, August 1928. (Neg. no.
263968. *Photo:* H. S. Rice. Courtesy
Dept. of Library Services, AMNH)

extent, Starr approached the idea of ethnographic cinema in a fashion similar
to turn-of-the-century travelogue lecturers who used moving pictures as highlights in lectures that had previously been illustrated by stereopticon slides.
Starr's discursive construction of cinema is thus heavily indebted to the
significatory tropes of the travel genre (dominated by the idea of cinema's
offering the spectator vicarious identification with the lecturer-traveler). In
addition, by endorsing cinema in the motion picture trade press, Starr lent his
weight as a prominent academician to the ongoing battle for respectability
being waged by the fledgling film industry.

Early Ethnographic Film in the American Southwest

The field correspondence of Pliny Goddard and his artist-collaborator
Howard McCormick and the extant film footage shot by McCormick during
his 1912 expedition to the American Southwest are compelling records of the
exigencies of shooting motion pictures in the field in the early part of the
twentieth century. Moreover, Goddard's attempts to negotiate the multifarious factors involved in shooting film in a remote and at times inhospitable

environment are testimony to an early instance of ethnographic filmmaking that has been largely overlooked in traditional histories of the genre. Goddard was born in Maine in 1869, received a doctorate in anthropology from the University of California in 1904, and took up employment at the AMNH in 1909 as an assistant curator of ethnology (fig. 7.1). Goddard's specialty was Native American languages, especially those of the Hopi, Navajo, and Apache, and during his tenure at the AMNH he oversaw the construction and installation of three Native American life groups.[17]

The first Museum-sponsored expedition to the American Southwest to produce films of native ceremonies and industries took place in the summer and early fall of 1912. While Goddard was not physically present during this expedition, he closely supervised McCormick's work from his AMNH office, and it was he alone who commissioned McCormick to shoot moving pictures of the Hopi Indians. An artist who had been hired by the AMNH to research, design, and help install Native American life groups in its exhibition halls, McCormick traveled to the Southwest in the late summer of 1912 to "make sketches and obtain other data for the proposed Pueblo [human life] group" at the Museum. McCormick was accompanied by sculptor Mahonri Young, who was instructed to make no fewer than seven casts of Pueblo peoples for the human life group.[18] Before the expedition, Goddard wrote McCormick inviting him to shoot film of Native Americans during the three-month expedition: "If you care to provide films for taking moving pictures in the Southwest, we shall be glad to have . . . negatives of any of the dances or other ceremonies of the Hopi and also of such industrial processes as the making of baskets, pots, and blankets."[19] Goddard told McCormick that even though the Museum had no available funds to buy film stock at present, McCormick would be reimbursed for money spent on negatives and film processing, providing he shot no more than 2,000 feet of film and incurred costs of less than twenty-five dollars.[20]

The only surviving footage from this expedition is an 8-minute fragment called *Snake Dance of the Ninth Day*, shot at Shipaulovi, Arizona, in September 1912. Given the Snake Dance's status as one of the most widely represented ceremonies of Native American peoples in the Southwest, its inclusion as a filmed subject by McCormick is hardly surprising; as Leah Dilworth argues, "The Snake dance—the event itself as well as the burgeoning representations

FIG. 7.2 Frame enlargement from Snake dance shot by Howard McCormick, Arizona, 1912.

of it—became a spectacle that defined and displayed the cultural differences between the 'primitive' Hopis and 'civilized' Americans."[21] The opening intertitle[22] informs us that the dance we are about to see was substituted for the planned dance because of "the meddling of a Hopi from another village," consequently, "the consent of the Snake Priest was withdrawn and the last dance was not secured."[23] Following two more intertitles announcing the start of the Snake Dance, we see a medium shot of about seven dancers moving in a circle in front of adobe buildings. It is unclear what "meddling" actually meant in this context. Native peoples were often put in extremely awkward positions as a result of the complex negotiations that went into arranging dances for the benefit of the camera: whites occasionally reneged on promises of financial compensation, tribe members sometimes changed their minds about wanting to perform, and reservation superintendents often intervened and either put a stop to filming or imposed themselves as middlemen. Shooting a film was therefore far from straightforward and required a great deal of cooperation on both sides.

McCormick's Snake Dance footage is a fascinating record of a ceremony that was seldom recorded on film within the context of an ethnographic survey (fig. 7.2); writing about his experiences of obtaining the footage, McCormick pointed out that "the Snake Dance has always been hard to get on account of the lateness of the hour. At Shipaulovi I took the last pictures at 6:45p."[24] Compounding logistical problems of filming ceremonial dances that usually took place late in the day were other, ethically charged issues. Hopi men and women were routinely paid to perform for visitors, although on several occasions the offer of money was insufficient compensation for performing the dance solely for the benefit of the camera. For example, McCormick wrote of offering Hopi women ten dollars for a Butterfly dance, but complained that "the girls would not dance so we gave up the idea."[25]

Ceremonial dances thus became valuable commodities within a transactional economy that collapsed symbolic value into use value. Given the widespread practice of native peoples demanding payment from anthropologists or commercial filmmakers for performances in front of a camera, it is useful to consider what impact (if any) the financial agreement may have had on native perceptions of cinema and their situation as imaged subjects. It is also worth bearing in mind that native peoples may have been compensated for their appearance before the camera in nonmonetary ways and that payment in currency was in part an indication of the degree of their acculturation into a cash-based economy.

The meaning of early ethnographic cinema is contingent not only upon different interpretive communities and exhibition sites but is inflected by what native peoples themselves might have thought about the camera, its impact on their ceremonial life, and their interaction with whites. The social significance of ethnographic film for indigenous groups is mediated on a local level by the native peoples themselves, some of whom may have been familiar with cinema from itinerant showmen, and on a global level by cinema's emblematic status as a technology of Western culture. Cinema's instability as a signifier is taken up by David MacDougall, who asks "by what means can we distinguish the structures we inscribe in films from the structures that are inscribed upon them, often without our knowing, by their subjects? And is film in any sense the same object for those who made it, for whom it may have the status of discourse, and for those who in passing have left their physical traces upon it?"[26]

While there is no easy way of determining what cinema might have meant to each of these different constituents in history, there is, as we shall see, evidence that McCormick and possibly the Hopi people themselves were both cognizant of how discourses of authenticity impinged upon the bargaining process that often preceded the procurement of images. Specifically, the Hopi probably knew that anthropologists were willing to pay a higher price for a "real" ceremony, as opposed to tourists who were happy to point and click at whatever came their way.

McCormick was well enough informed of contemporaneous debates concerning the deleterious effect of commercial and tourist photographers and filmmakers on native dances to differentiate between "authentic" dances and less pristine versions. On a number of occasions, McCormick faced the choice of either making do with good-quality footage of what he considered a "fake" Indian dance, altered for the touristic gaze, or sticking with a badly photographed recording of a "less contaminated" dance. For example, when filming a Snake Dance at Oraiba, Arizona, in August 1912, McCormick complained in a letter to Goddard that while the light had been "great," the "dance was not the real thing as they had Snake men acting as Antelope men."[27] That McCormick was even aware of this substitution is noteworthy (given his formal training in visual art, not anthropology), although his experience painting and drawing in the Southwest would clearly have informed his knowledge of Native American life. We should also bear in mind that camera-toting anthropologists were most likely not the first Westerners to gain access to native communities; with some exceptions, other visitors equipped with still and moving picture cameras in search of exotic images of American Indians had almost certainly preceded them. In any event, anthropologists, like tourists and commercial film producers, had to negotiate the right to film with the Indians themselves, and often with reservation superintendents and the Bureau of American Ethnology.

McCormick's sensitivity to issues of authenticity may have been heightened by Goddard's insistence that footage obtained under the auspices of the Department of Anthropology at the AMNH had to be ethnographically accurate. In outlining the Museum's policy on suitable subjects for filming, Goddard encouraged McCormick to procure as many films of Indian industries as he did of Indian ceremonies, since, as Goddard put it: "I really care as much for the industrial ones as I do for the ceremonies, since other people are inclined to take ceremonies and the films are sure to be in existence somewhere."[28] However, recognizing the popular appeal of ceremonial dances for general Museum audiences, Goddard conceded that "the ceremonials will be the proper thing for lectures," thereby anticipating the perennial (if contested) distinction made in ethnographic cinema between films representing aspects of native life intended for an audience of anthropologists and films featuring visually spectacular scenes that are more obviously constructed for general consumption (this dialectic is also present in Goddard's and Starr's reflections on the ethnographic promise of the moving picture camera). While McCormick's efforts to ensure that he was not duped by Hopi Indians who might fob off on him an inauthentic version of a dance must be read in the context of his institutional affiliation—altered dances would not do for an exhibition in a scientific institution—they are also indicative of anthropologists' wider concerns over the accuracy of data gathered in the field. However, it is worth pointing out that McCormick's (and possibly Goddard's) concern about ethnographic authenticity may have waned over the months of the expedition, so that by September 1912 McCormick had few qualms admitting in a letter to Goddard that, as a result of the difficulties he faced both in trying to procure permission to film the Hopi snake dance and cope with the lighting conditions (snake dances traditionally took place late in the day), he was now "ready to shoot the first snake dance that show[ed] its head."[29]

In an article in the AMNH's own *American Museum Journal* in March 1913, McCormick discussed the deleterious effect of Western acculturation on traditional Native American culture, but posed the problem not in relation to what effect this might have on indigenous life, but what effect it would have on the accuracy of McCormick's art: "The Hopi have now adopted white man's dress in their daily life. Automobiles carry the mail to within a few miles of the Hopi villages . . . [and] it will soon be necessary for the artist to reconstruct the customs and habits which may now be seen in their final stage of dissolution."[30] Because McCormick conceived of his painting and photography as small-scale attempts to salvage the vanishing traces of "pure" Indian culture for future generations, he deliberately repressed evidence of many aspects of the contemporary life of his native subjects, specifically those aspects that revealed how Hopi cultural identity was being irrevocably changed by the encroachment of Euro-American technology and settlement. McCormick offered reconstruction as the only means of piecing together accounts of these people's lives; through painting and photographing native people, McCormick could eliminate traces of contact.

Oral history and native memory became key instruments in this process of cultural reconstruction and salvage ethnography; as Margaret Mead would later argue, one of the consequences of the conditions under which anthropologists conducted fieldwork in the early twentieth century was that they had to rely upon the memory of informants to describe aspects of cultural life to which anthropologists no longer had direct access. Because these cultural memories could not be directly visualized (although they could be reconstructed), anthropologists were forced to rely on lexical modes of ethnographic inscription to describe cultural practices — such as war dances, buffalo hunts, and methods of scarification or mutilation — that had long been abandoned. Thus, as Mead explained in 1975, "Relying on words (the words of informants whose gestures we had no means of preserving, words of ethnographers who had no war dances to photograph), anthropology became a science of words."[31] But the issue of access to so-called vanishing cultures was just one of the many constraints placed upon anthropologists such as Goddard as the discipline became professionalized in the early twentieth century. Widespread inertia and what Mead would probably label methodological conservatism were also behind the slow adoption of cinema by anthropologists. Goddard was clearly breaking ranks with prevailing disciplinary practices, then, when he decided to include film among his arsenal of field research techniques in 1914.

Another set of challenges facing McCormick in his 1912 expedition stemmed from the limited amount of available film stock; the Museum had very little money for the purchase of positive film — 500 feet cost about twenty-five dollars in 1912 — and McCormick frequently pleaded for more film in his letters to Goddard. Forced to record time-consuming native crafts such as blanket-weaving and plaque-making in 100-foot rolls, McCormick also complained to Goddard that he found it "impossible to get the various phases of the dances in less than 50 or 100-feet."[32] However, in a subsequent letter McCormick reassured Goddard that, with the experience he had now acquired, he thought he could "take any dance out here with about 200-feet and get the various incidents."[33] Goddard's lack of appreciation of how much film would be required to shoot a specific event indicates his scant technical understanding of the pragmatics of field film production at this stage. Yet Goddard would soon learn firsthand of the practical challenges of field cinematography, when he joined McCormick in the Southwest to shoot film of members of the Apache tribe in 1914.

Filming the Apache: Goddard's 1914 Ethnographic Films

Equipped with an Ensign daylight loading camera with a 3-inch lens, a tripod capable of panning and tilting, a leather carrying case, six 25-foot rolls and nine 100-foot rolls of Ensign film, Goddard and McCormick set off for Arizona in July 1914.[34] Goddard's firsthand experience with the challenges facing the ethnographic filmmaker are suggested in his description of one of the early films he shot of an Apache woman making a basket: "I used 25 feet first and didn't get all I wanted so I put in 100 feet the next time. I hope I didn't cut her head off. I developed a little piece which came out rather poorly."[35] Goddard was keen to receive feedback on some of the early footage he had shipped to the Museum and suggested to his secretary Bella Weitzner that either Museum taxidermist Carl Akeley, curator George Sherwood, or "anyone who knows about films" should assess the quality of the footage and offer advice on how it could be improved.[36] Weitzner reported to Goddard that Akeley had found the films "somewhat blurred and lacked 'snap' " and had wondered whether it was "because of an error in exposure or because of poor developing."[37] Goddard's lack of confidence in his filmmaking and his wish to have someone with experience examine his films suggest how little cinematographic expertise had been diffused among anthropologists since Haddon and Spencer first experimented with moving pictures at the turn of the century. Indeed, Goddard's complaints about his abilities as a camera operator sound very much like Haddon's assessment of his own poor filmmaking efforts years earlier.

Perhaps because of his initial unsatisfactory attempts to shoot the large spontaneous movements of dancers and because Goddard attributed greater ethnographic value to films of native industries than ceremonies, he devoted more time to shooting aspects of material culture as well as food preparation

F I G. 7.3 Still from Goddard's 1914 films of Apache Indians, San Carlos, Arizona. (Neg. No. 242693. Courtesy Dept. of Library Services, AMNH)

(principally chucking and grinding corn) (fig. 7.3).[38] However, Goddard also noted that it would "probably be impossible to get dances," suggesting that he anticipated insurmountable technical challenges in filming the less predictable movements of dancers or feared failing to gain access to restricted ceremonies altogether.[39]

The complex interpersonal transactions involved in filming Indian cultural practices were discussed at some length by Goddard following his attendance at a ceremony involving an adolescent girl that took place over several days in late August 1914. Writing to Weitzner, Goddard expressed disappointment at being unable to film the event, but admitted it would have "produced a panic, probably, and ruined the ceremony."[40] Deeply affected by what he saw, Goddard acknowledged the limitations of traditional anthropological description; for him the ceremony was "really very interesting and beautiful and supplied the feeling and vividness one never really gets from descriptions. I wished many times you could have seen it for it would have repaid you for many weary years spent on the uninteresting side of ethnology."[41]

For Goddard and his predecessor Haddon, cinema, it seemed, promised to capture the affect and intensity of the cross-cultural encounter otherwise lost in the process of translating ethnographic experience into written text. Recalling Haddon's description of the Malu-Bomai ceremony as a "fantasy in red and green," Goddard's emotional tone here suggests the limitations of conventional anthropological writing in conveying the atmosphere of a ceremonial performance. Goddard's reference to the "uninteresting side of ethnology" can also be read as a thinly veiled reference to the curatorial versus fieldwork responsibilities of the museum anthropologist, who was forced to devote much of his (or occasionally her) time to the preparation of exhibits for popular consumption in place of pursuing extended research in the field. Goddard undoubtedly gave primacy to the latter, arguing that the "true subject of ethnology is made up of the habitual movements and activities of a people,"[42] material recoverable only through intensive fieldwork observation (and self-observation in the case of this photograph showing Goddard's shadow in the lower right-hand corner) (fig. 7.4).

Goddard was most impressed by cinema's ability to simultaneously render the positions and movements of lots of people within a crowded frame. Noting that when a field observer attempts to watch "several individuals [who] are engaged in the same undertaking, it becomes impossible for a single observer to follow the movements of each worker," Goddard argued that cinema offered "an excellent method of making a permanent record of the movements of one or . . . several people," a record that could be "scrutinized in detail for as long a time as is desired."[43] Goddard also proposed that the film camera could be used to record "things which would otherwise not be made objective, such as the characteristic coordinations and movements of different people."[44] For Goddard, the camera's mechanical eye could open up a world of visual phenomena otherwise closed to the unaided senses and, through the unique facility of repeatability, offer the ethnographer access to minute details only detectable through repeated viewings.[45]

Despite the fact that Goddard advised readers that "great pains must be taken not to arouse self-consciousness in the subjects being photographed," he nevertheless conceded that a certain amount of "unavoidable self-

FIG. 7.4 Photograph taken by Goddard of Apache woman straining pitch for covering a water basket, 1914. (Neg. no. 242697. Courtesy Dept. of Library Services, AMNH)

consciousness" on the part of native peoples was inevitable. This recognition of the ultimate intersubjectivity of the visual anthropologist's encounter with native informants is perhaps the most strikingly contemporary quality of Goddard's text; as an implicit rejection of nineteenth-century positivist claims regarding the self-sufficiency and objectivity of the photographic image, Goddard's essay displays remarkable sensitivity to the contingencies attending the encounter between Western filmmaker and native peoples.

Goddard's status within museum anthropology undoubtedly had a significant impact upon how his footage was presented to the public. Six months after McCormick's return from the Southwest, the AMNH organized several special screenings of McCormick's films for the public,[46] including a Saturday morning program in the Museum's "Natural History Stories for Children" series.[47] The advertisement for this lecture-screening, entitled

" 'Poonkong' and His People," began with a description of Poonkong: "Down on the high, dry plateaus of Arizona lives Poonkong, who, like Peter Pan, never grew up." Readers were told that, in addition to meeting Poonkong and his twin brother, they would "*attend* the Hopi dances by means of lantern slides and moving-picture films"; spectators would not simply watch Poonkong witness the dances but metaphorically *join* him and his brother (through the conceit of virtual travel) as the film was projected on the screen.[48] For the audience member, entry into the fictional diegesis was mediated by Poonkong, offered as a figure of identification for the young spectators through the reference to Peter Pan. Whether or not a specific Hopi boy pictured in McCormick's film was identified as Poonkong by Goddard in his narration, or whether Poonkong existed purely as a fictive device, is unclear. It is also difficult to ascertain how this fictionalized application of AMNH fieldwork footage escaped President Osborn's tight supervision of the use of motion pictures at the Museum; judging by his other interventions in planning public screenings, it is hard to imagine that Osborn wouldn't have objected to such nonscientific uses of motion pictures. One can only assume that the target audience of the series, children, affected the Museum's decision to allow this sort of film programming.

While it is difficult to reconstruct from the surviving documentation precisely how McCormick's expedition footage was used by the AMNH, it is possible to speculate on the general status of the expeditionary film for anthropologists such as Goddard, who had few qualms interpolating field footage into a range of different educational lecture formats. It is also significant, if unsurprising, that Goddard, as one of the preeminent anthropological authorities on the American Southwest, insisted on assuming total responsibility for the film's public presentations (although McCormick's role as camera operator was acknowledged in a few screenings). It was perhaps inevitable that it was Goddard (the professional anthropologist), rather than McCormick (the artist and cameraman) who typically introduced and contextualized the films, given the Museum's anxieties about science taking a backseat to visual spectacle. Furthermore, Museum administrators seemed to have few problems exhibiting both actuality footage of Native Americans and fictional films featuring Indian characters, albeit in separate lecture-screenings. For example, Frank Moore's fictional *Hiawatha* was shown at the Museum within a month of a special screening of McCormick's Hopi footage for public school teachers. It would seem, then, that the Museum integrated Goddard and McCormick's fieldwork footage fairly casually into the institution's public program.[49] Beyond the scientific credibility of the invited speaker, the institutional setting of the Museum itself was thought to neutralize the amateur and/or commercial contexts of some of the ethnographic films exhibited there. In other words, for the Museum to differentiate between the scientific and nonscientific production contexts of the films it exhibited might have drawn unnecessary attention to the sometimes questionable educational value of some films that were, after all, simultaneously available to audiences in commercial theaters.

Notwithstanding his use of film in public lectures, Goddard believed cinema's greatest contribution to ethnology lay less in its ability to represent the world to popular audiences than in its ability to produce detailed scientific records of cultural difference for trained anthropologists, records that would be more accurate than accounts obtained via written texts, drawings, or photographs. Whereas in the past, Goddard argued, ethnographic fieldwork data had been "*reduced* to writing," drawings, and photographs, moving pictures went far beyond these static media in their ability to represent the "habitual movements and activities" of a people, features of native culture that were, in Goddard's mind, the "true subject matter of ethnology."[50] It was "tolerably difficult to observe and record every significant movement involved in the work of a single individual engaged in such a simple task as making a flint arrow head," Goddard explained, and a moving picture record would enable the anthropologist to "re-examine the complex and collective movements of a dance or native industry *ad infinitum*."[51]

Goddard was not the first anthropologist to single out the infinite repeatability of modern recording devices as one of their greatest assets; in 1890, for example, anthropologist J. Walter Fewkes wrote about the benefits of using a phonograph to record native languages in ways that clearly anticipate Goddard:

There are inflections, gutturals, accents, and sounds in aboriginal dialects which elude the possibilities of phonetic methods of expression. . . . The use of the phonograph among the Passamaquoddies has convinced me that the main characteristics of their language can be recorded and permanently preserved, either for study or demonstration, with this instrument. . . . In the quiet of his study [the anthropologist] can hear the song repeated over and over again as often as he wishes, and can, so to speak, analyze it, and in that way separate the constituent sounds.[52]

Fewkes saw in the phonograph recording a unique capacity to replay the exact sounds the anthropologist heard in the field, with the same tempo, timbre, and inflection as the original utterance, something that a transcription of the song or sentence could never attain. The phonograph's ability both to capture a furtive inflection lost to phonetic transcription and to offer infinite replay of its recorded data link it to Goddard's conception of the motion picture camera as an ethnographic instrument. Goddard celebrated cinema's similar capacity for repeatability, noting that the visual record produced by the moving picture camera could be "scrutinized in detail for as long a time as is desired" and "viewed repeatedly."[53] Implicit in both Fewkes's and Goddard's writings is the idea that a mechanical ear and eye will open up a world of visual and auditory phenomena otherwise closed to the unaided senses, a point prefigured in the experiments of Étienne-Jules Marey and Félix-Louis Regnault.

Goddard, Fewkes, and Regnault all argued for the usefulness of mechanical means of reproduction within a general project of salvage ethnography, the task of recording indigenous cultures threatened with extinction. As a "call to arms," the project of salvage ethnography has often been (and continues to be) seen as the raison d'être of visual anthropology; Margaret Mead in 1975 lamented the fact that "all over the world, on every continent and island . . . precious, totally irreplaceable and forever irreproducible behaviors are disappearing." For Mead, cinematic records of native peoples were "reliable, reproducible, [and] re-analyzable" and could empower communities by encouraging them to "repossess their cultural heritage."[54] Anticipating Mead in several regards, Goddard argued that cinema should be taken up "systematically and energetically" by anthropologists doing fieldwork among what he saw as vanishing Native American cultures, arguing that "after the disappearance of primitive life, film [showing native industries would] be invaluable."[55]

Goddard's sophisticated appreciation of how moving pictures of cultural life could, with close and repeated analysis, render certain details visible (thus increasing the overall legibility of an event) not only harkens back to Marey's and Regnault's hopes for a scientific cinema but anticipates Mead's view of ethnographic film as a repository of raw data of equal value to written field notes. When Mead argued that "as anthropologists, we must insist on prosaic, controlled, systematic filming and videotaping, which will provide us with material that can be repeatedly re-analyzed with finer tools and developing theories" she strikingly echoed Goddard's ideas on the value of repeat viewings which were articulated some sixty years earlier. In addition, Mead's contention that "with properly collected, annotated, and preserved visual and sound materials, we can replicate over and over again and can painstakingly analyze the same materials" recalls Regnault's idea for an interactive ethnographic film archive in which visitors could retrieve a range of audiovisual materials that had been recorded and catalogued by him.[56] This is not to suggest, however, that there are no important figures in the field of visual anthropology between Goddard in the teens and early twenties and Mead in the late 1930s.[57] Two examples of ethnographic filmmaking that provide a window on how moving picture technology was being applied by anthropologists in the mid to late 1920s are the efforts of the Anglo-American team M. W. Hilton-Simpson and J. A. Haeseler in 1923–24, and the 1930 research films of Kwakwaka'wakw dances made by Franz Boas. While the filmmaking endeavors of these individuals lie slightly outside the historical purview of this investigation, their discussion of cinema's utility within both science and the arts makes them useful figures to explore in greater depth.

Ethnography as Cinema: The Films of M. W. Hilton-Simpson and J. A. Haeseler

What distinguished Starr, Goddard, and Hilton-Simpson and Haeseler from other anthropologists who dabbled with film in the teens and twenties was their decision to reflect upon their filmmaking experiences publicly in published articles. When we consider that the place of the visual within anthropology had been largely subordinated to written discourse in fieldwork in the late teens and early twenties, references to visual anthropology are relatively rare and detailed discussions of cinema by trained anthropologists almost unheard of.

Published in the British popular science journal *Discovery* in 1925, Hilton-Simpson and Haeseler's article, "Cinema and Ethnology," is structured in two parts; the first part, written by Hilton-Simpson, describes how film was integrated into his field expedition to Southeast Algeria; the second part, under the subheading "Notes By J. A. Haeseler," covers a number of technical and logistical issues. A professional ethnologist for over twenty years, Hilton-Simpson explained that inertia, coupled with a lack of technical expertise, had previously dissuaded him from seriously considering the "rudiments of cinematography." However, after meeting anthropology professor J. A. Haeseler, who was about to begin production on a series of films that would form the basis of an ethnographic film library, Hilton-Simpson invited Haeseler to join the expedition party and take responsibility for photography and film. In the first part of the article, Hilton-Simpson confesses that he had had no idea just how complex, time-consuming, and unwieldy moving picture technology would be; as he recalled: "The extreme accuracy required to obtain the exact range in 'close-up' photos, the vigilance necessary to prevent curious spectators casting their shadows on the picture from flank or rear during the taking of a protracted scene, the constant anxiety lest the 'targets' may become weary and remove themselves before a shot is complete, are but a few of the minor worries which vex the soul of the cinema photographer."[58]

The notion of the ethnographic camera as a disembodied and panoptic technology is implicit in Hilton-Simpson's account of his filmmaking; for example, Hilton-Simpson wrote of the "utter lack of self-consciousness . . . of the Shawiya of both sexes" in front of the camera, although such claims for the unobtrusiveness of the technology are undercut in Haeseler's subsequent description of the magnetic draw of the unfamiliar apparatus in public places: "No matter where in the world one sets up a cinema camera, one becomes the centre of interest and attracts a crowd that soon runs into scores. Managing this is a task for three vociferous native assistants, and on market days or during ceremonies the conditions are particularly trying."[59] At stake in these conflicting accounts of the anthropologist's camera as itself an object of spectacle is an appeal to the supposed nonreciprocal nature of the wider encounter between ethnographer and human subject. Certain claims for the scientific status of ethnographic motion pictures thus depended on assertions of non-intervention in the profilmic and the utter transparency of the anthropologist's gaze.

Striking in this discussion of ethnographic cinema is explicit acknowledgment of its Janus-faced form, its indebtedness to both the highbrow arena of scientific research and the more prosaic world of popular amusements. Hilton-Simpson wrote that "there are two sides to field work with a [*sic*] cinema, one the purely scientific side, the other the showman's. Success in both fields demands a realization of the needs of each, a thorough grasp of technique and a spirit of compromise." Hilton-Simpson's pragmatic stance on ethnographic filmmaking characterizes anthropologists' attitudes toward a range of early twentieth-century ethnographic forms — from museum exhibits and world's fairs to photography — and suggests something of the future direction of much ethnographic filmmaking, a practice that would find one foot firmly planted in science and the other foot firmly planted in showmanship.[60] For Hilton-Simpson and his generation of anthropologists, the dearth of opportunities for practical training in ethnographic filmmaking meant that they were frequently faced with little alternative to hiring a commercial cinematographer for their fieldwork filmmaking. But as Haeseler complained in 1925, this arrangement often worked better on paper than it did in practice: "It is very difficult to get the ordinary camera man to fit himself into the scientific spirit of an expedition. He is a different *milieu* — that of a showman — and it is from this point of view that he is inclined to regard everything that presents itself. Consequently, unless he is ruled with a rod of iron, told exactly where to take and almost where to place his camera, his results from a scientific point of view will be deficient."[61]

Haeseler's solution to the problem of relying upon nonanthropologists to obtain footage was to urge that anthropologists themselves learn the basics of cinematography before leaving for the field: "If a complete outfit was turned over to him for practice purposes some time before the expedition, he should be able, with the advice of the company selling the camera and the cinema laboratories, to make himself proficient enough to carry out the work."[62] There is little evidence of significant numbers of anthropologists taking up Haeseler's advice; one anthropologist who seemed to was Franz Boas, who later in his career decided to use a motion picture camera to record

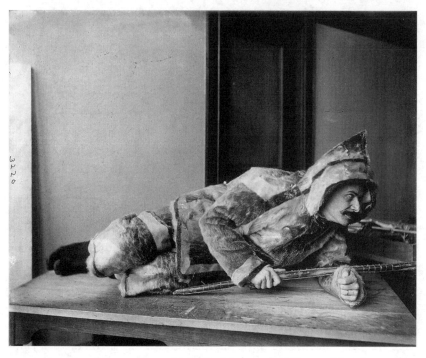

FIG. 7.5 Franz Boas demonstrating position of Inuit harpoon for life group. (Neg. no 3220. Courtesy Dept. of Library Services, AMNH)

Kwakwaka'wakw dances in the Pacific Northwest (fig. 7.5). Boas's belief in the value of visual evidence in the study of native culture motivated the undertaking of his Kwakwaka'wakw movement studies, films he shot at Fort Rupert on Vancouver Island during the winter of 1930–31.[63]

Franz Boas's Behavioral Studies of the Kwakwaka'wakw Indians of Vancouver

On one level, Boas's films are recapitulations of an earlier era of ethnographic filmmaking, when the novelty value of a scene from an exotic culture was the main pretext for setting up a camera. This is especially true in the ceremonial dance recordings that Boas made — some seventeen in total — which are extremely simple in their structure and composition. However, Boas never intended these films of Kwakwaka'wakw ceremonial and daily life to be seen by the public; they were the equivalent of visual field notes. His motivation for making them was driven entirely by their evidentiary status and practical utility, including the fact that Boas could return to them again and again to refresh his memory or to assist him in his interpretive work on the cultural significance of native dance. According to Jay Ruby, Boas's films only make sense if "one believes that behavioral events removed from their normal social and physical contexts retain sufficient validity to reveal patterns of culture"; staged for the camera, these filmic records oscillate between being reflexive documents of the contingencies of ethnographic data collection and glimpses of a petrified Kwakwaka'wakw culture that is synecdochally represented in the ethnographically rich details of the indigenous costumes and dances.[64] At the same time, the sound recording apparatus seen in some of the shots complicates the status of these films as salvage ethnography; the very presence of Western technology in the frame suggests the intrusion of Euro-American culture into the lives of Northwestern Indian tribes and the complex interlocking of indigenous life with Western technology and economic development.[65] As the primary sign-event, the Kwakwaka'wakw performer was all that really mattered to Boas and surrounding details were ignored, providing they didn't impinge upon the integrity of the dance. In many ways, Boas's footage is the visual equivalent of written field notes, consisting, in the words of anthropologist Rosalind Morris, of "numerous sequences of detailed images strung together one after the other with only minimal overt theorization."[66] According to Morris, Boas's filmmaking was part of a process of cultural reconstruction, a tool that "effaces the supposed impurities of cultural change, and thereby elides the reality of cultural contact, colonization, and historical process."[67] In the absence of an expository framework that might help the viewer decode the meaning of the Kwakwaka'wakw's games and ceremonies, Boas's films are reminiscent of Edison's Black Maria kinetographs and his 1898 location films, which are powerfully linked to the idea of ethnographic film as cultural reconstruction.

Boas's decision to record the Kwakwaka'wakw ceremonies and dances can be seen as an extension of his inductive approach to ethnographic data collection and analysis, which he had begun in 1897.[68] Boas believed that film depictions of technological processes, subsistence activities practiced by women (such as basket-weaving), the world of play, and the ceremonial life of the Kwakwaka'wakw would provide him with "adequate material for making a real study," although years of accumulating raw data on the Kwakwa̱ka̱'wakw had yet to yield definitive theoretical breakthroughs, in part due to Boas's "interpretive reticence."[69] Reviewing Boas's contribution to the discipline, Mead observed in 1959 that what Boas wanted was "a real corpus of materials to work on, large bodies of materials which would make possible the cross-checking of each detail."[70]

Offered as "objective" and permanent records that could be subjected to verification by future anthropologists, Boas's films echo Goddard's recommendations for ethnographic cinema, especially regarding film's ability to record the "habitual movements and activities" of native peoples. Boas's interest in the human body as a signifier of cultural norms also recalls the epistemological premise of Félix-Louis Regnault's chronophotography, in which the gesture is seen as an expressive sign system, *le langage par gestes*.[71] Like McCormick's films of the Hopi, Boas's films were also used by the AMNH's staff to design diorama life groups for the Museum; Boas's films include reconstructions of Kwakwa̱ka̱'wakw dances, crafts, games, oratory, and shamanic activities. Boas asked his long-term informant George Hunt and his Kwakwa̱ka̱'wakw wife to demonstrate woodworking techniques, cedar-bark weaving, and long-defunct fishing and gathering practices. Boas left the Kwakwa̱ka̱'wakw film project unfinished (for a number of years the footage was assumed lost), and it wasn't edited into a complete film until anthropologist Bill Holm (who, along with George Quimby, had earlier restored Edward S. Curtis's *In the Land of the Head Hunters*) edited Boas's footage into a 55-minute version entitled *The Kwakiutl of British Columbia* for the Burke Museum in Washington State in 1973.[72]

Most of the second half of *The Kwakiutl of British Columbia* is taken up with seventeen dance sequences; in each of the long or medium long shots, Kwakwa̱ka̱'wakw men and women perform in either traditional costume or in Western attire. Boas's inexperience as a camera operator is obvious from the innumerable jump cuts and incorrect exposures, including parts of "Bird Dance" and "Salmon Dance," performed by George Hunt's daughter Agnes Hunt. As part of the restoration project, Holm interviewed surviving Kwakwa̱ka̱'wakw performers (as he had done in the case of Curtis's film) and added intertitles. Recontextualizing Boas's footage within a native exegesis, *The Kwakiutl of British Columbia* "simultaneously honors Boasian method, with its rigorous attention to material objects and its categorical exploration of behavior, and incorporates the knowledge of contemporary Native 'performers' and exegetes,"according to Rosalind Morris.[73]

It is worth considering how Boas's films compare with the work of Goddard, Spencer, and Haddon and to speculate on how ethnographic cinema may have emerged differently had Boas been interested in film at an earlier stage in his career. The most striking feature of Boas's films when compared to those of the anthropologists working earlier is the similarity of formal choices. Seriously inhibited by the limitations of early film technology (including the lack of panning capability and very short film reels), Haddon and Spencer had little choice but to adopt an observational mode of representation; beyond deciding where to place the camera, they could stop and start it and do little more. During the next three decades, when commercial cinema was undergoing rapid technological and cultural transformations, it is telling that Goddard in 1915 and Boas in 1930 should have grappled with the exigencies of ethnographic film production in remarkably similar ways. Neither Goddard nor Boas, for example, employed a single close-up or medium close-up, and their films are edited into sequences that are virtually indistinguishable from those of films shot in the pre-1907 cinema period. But then when we consider for whom these films were primarily intended and their role as empirical field records in the eyes of these anthropologists, it is hardly surprising that they lack many of the trademarks of narrative cinema, such as camera movement, editing, and close-ups.

The lack of formal innovation in anthropological filmmaking across the first three decades of the twentieth century in part reflects the fact that, with a few exceptions, the moving picture camera never became a standard research tool for anthropological expeditions.[74] At the same time, amateur filmmaking, with its hobbyist and prosaic connotations, also threatened the professional codes of anthropology, so that some anthropologists, fearing that their reputations would be tarnished if they publicly exhibited or identified themselves with badly shot footage that highlighted their inexperience as cinematographers at the expense of their skill as ethnographers, may have thought the challenges of filmmaking too daunting. As Sol Worth argues: "For the most part, anthropologists . . . are professional scientists only when they are employing words. When it comes to the visual mode of articulation and data-gathering, most produce snapshots . . . [or] good (or bad) home movies."[75] Film was rarely considered a viable alternative to the written monograph and, in the eyes of most professional ethnologists, could not carry them any deeper into the world of the Other than a notepad and pencil. The dearth of theoretical writing in the early twentieth century on the place of visual evidence in ethnography meant that Haddon, Spencer, Goddard, and eventually Boas, all experienced similar kinds of problems when they ventured into the field with a motion picture camera.[76] With the exception of Goddard, none of these men contributed to theory-building within visual anthropology (a stiff demand, considering the relative youth of the discipline as a whole), and each seemed to set out with a motion picture camera and phonograph as if for the very first time.

Given Boas's legendary status in the history of American anthropology, one can't help wonder that had he enthusiastically endorsed cinema at an earlier point in his career and perhaps inspired an entire school of budding anthropologists to see the utility of cinema (Margaret Mead being the notable exception here), then ethnographic film may have taken a different course. As it stands, while it is tempting to draw a connection between Boas's flirtations with film and his student Margaret Mead's pivotal role in the emergence of ethnographic cinema in the United States, there is no evidence of Boas ever having discussed his filmmaking with Mead (or vice versa), and we are left to speculate on what connection (if any) there was between the two. That Boas was interested in the ethnographic potential of cinema around the time he shot the Fort Rupert films is evident from his correspondence with Will H. Hays, president of the Motion Picture Producers and Distributors of America. Hays first contacted Boas in January 1933 to request anthropological cooperation on a film project that would document the lives of "primitive peoples" threatened with extinction. Responding favorably to Hays's initial inquiry, Boas agreed to set up an advisory board and brought in Columbia University president Nicholas Murray Butler to validate the project.[77] Boas seemed interested in the collaborative nature of the work and detailed his views on ethnographic film with striking clarity.

Until that date, Boas argued, the scientific potential of commercially produced ethnographic films such as *Nanook of the North*, *Grass* (Merian C. Cooper and Ernest B. Schoedsack, 1925), *Chang*, and *Moana* (Robert Flaherty, 1926) had been underexploited, since the films had not been produced under the supervision of anthropologists. As Boas explained:

> Excellent material is contained in these pictures; nevertheless they might have been made ever so much more interesting if a person had been consulted who knows the social life of the people intimately. . . . I do not mean to imply that a film of this kind should be built up exclusively on scientific principles, but it ought to contain what is really fundamentally characteristic of each culture, bearing in view what is picturesque and attractive to the public.[78]

The idea of collaboration between anthropologists and professional image-makers predates Boas's ruminations on the topic, going back to the use of professional photographers on nineteenth-century scientific expeditions and the 1901 collaboration between the Bureau of American Ethnology and commercial film producers like the Armat Motion-Picture Company to produce films of Native Americans. However, there is less evidence of interest among professional anthropologists in enlisting Hollywood as an ad hoc ethnographer. The notion that commercial films with ethnographic sequences, or what Erik Barnouw calls the "explorer as documentarist" tradition, could be commercially successful while satisfying the standards of scientists and educators recalls an earlier era in ethnographic film production, when the same film titles might be seen in a wide variety of exhibition contexts.[79] There is, however, an ironic twist to Boas's suggestion that commercial explorer-adventurer films would be improved if produced under the governing eye of an anthropologist, as his own films, conversely, might have been more appealing to general audiences had Boas collaborated in the field with a professional cinematographer.

The ethnographic filmmaking and writing of Frederick Starr, Pliny Goddard, M. W. Hilton-Simpson, J. A. Haeseler, and Franz Boas respond to some of the major questions raised in any historical inquiry into cinema's links with anthropology and popular culture during the silent film period. They also attest to the specter of commerce that seems to haunt the filmmaking of this first generation of university-trained anthropologists: Starr's strong ties with the world of popular amusements, Hilton-Simpson and Haesler's resigned attitude toward science and popular culture's being necessary bedfellows, and Boas's radical proposition for anthropologist-Hollywood coproductions leave little doubt about the role of popular amusements as determinants in each of these projects. That all these men (with the exception of Goddard) discussed the relationship of ethnographic cinema to commercial filmmaking, including the ways in which footage procured on anthropological expeditions could be made available for popular consumption, harkens back to an earlier period in anthropology's history when the line between science and entertainment was often blurred. Haeseler, for example, recommended in 1923 that

> if the scientist cares to look beyond the scientific field, with the hope of getting a return on his expenditure, there are a number of commercial cinema companies that buy rights to travel material. There are those who put out magazine reels made up of several subjects, those distributing single-reel subjects, and those exploiting travel feature films.[80]

It would seem that Alfred Cort Haddon's advice to Baldwin Spencer in 1900 about selling Spencer's ethnographic footage to the motion picture trade was prescient. Indeed, Boas saw possibilities for ethnographic cinema that Haddon could not have imagined, including the prospect of professional collaboration with large-scale commercial film productions. (Incidentally, Boas's thoughts on what role native peoples might play in these arrangements or what remuneration they might receive for their cooperation in the filming are not available in the historical record.) Yet for all their radicalism and forward-sightedness, each of these proponents for a nascent ethnographic cinema worked during a period in the history of visual anthropology marked by general hostility or indifference to the value of visual evidence. Against this backdrop, the promise of reciprocity between anthropology and the motion picture industry takes on additional significance; rather than simply sell their footage to the trade, anthropologists would be given prints of ethnographically rich sequences and could serve as consultants on feature films with ethnographic subject matter. Boas's proposal reads, therefore, as a premonition of made-for-television popular ethnography series such as Granada's *Disappearing World* (shown on British television) or the Public Broadcasting System's *National Geographic* specials — programs backed by corporate sponsors but researched and sometimes directed by visual anthropologists. If few of Boas's hopes for professional collaboration between anthropologists and commercial movie-makers materialized during his lifetime, the legacy of this early period of ethnographic filmmaking on contemporary ethnographic film theory and practice cannot be ignored, as will become clear in the next and final chapter.

8

Conclusion

THE LEGACY OF EARLY ETHNOGRAPHIC FILM

All over the world, on every continent and island, in the hidden recesses of modern
industrial cities . . . totally irreplaceable, forever irreproducible behaviors are disappearing,
while the departments of anthropology continue to send fieldworkers out with no equipment
beyond a pencil and a notebook. . . . Why? What has gone wrong?
—MARGARET MEAD (1975)[1]

ATTITUDES AMONG anthropologists toward film have been anything but
unified throughout the history of the discipline. This ambivalence, I have
argued, is the result of cinema's simultaneous appeal to scientific verisimilitude and visual spectacle; of the paradigmatic shifts within anthropology
regarding the status of the visual; and of the logistical and financial challenges
of using cinema in the field. While photography gained substantial institutional acceptance within anthropology from the 1860s through the turn of the
century, cinema was left waiting in the wings and had far fewer opportunities
to make it to center stage in anthropological fieldwork or theorizing. Institutional changes within anthropology, what Asen Balikci describes as anthropology's move from the museum to the university at the turn of the century,
were accompanied by a transformation of anthropological discourse, a shift
from the "descriptive-ethnographic to the analytical-sociological." As a result,
Balikci argues, "records [including visual records] lost their intrinsic value."[2]
The sovereignty of the ethnographic image as the ultimate bearer of scientific
truth in racially based typological models could no longer be vouched for, as
anthropologists realized that even though the visual image "flooded the

observer with concreteness and detail . . . [it] revealed very little in the absence of a surrounding discourse."[3] In the early twentieth century, the privileging of the ethnographic image as evidence of racial difference was replaced by the techniques of the anthropological monograph, which relied less upon photographs than on the anthropologist's writings *in situ*, in pursuit of a more holistic vision of culture. As Margaret Mead aptly put it, "anthropology became a science of words, and those who relied on words have been very unwilling to let their pupils use the new tools, while the neophytes have only too often slavishly followed the outmoded methods that their predecessors used."[4]

Reiterating Mead's assessment of visual anthropology, contemporary ethnographic filmmaker and scholar Lucien Taylor blames what he sees as an antipathy toward visual technologies within anthropology on a deep-seated iconophobia within anthropology. However, if Taylor's argument about visuality's ancillary status within anthropology recapitulates the rationale for the declining status of the visual within anthropology in the teens and twenties, it oversimplifies anthropology's complex attitudes toward visual evidence and fails to take into account other factors shaping anthropologists' attitudes toward cinema, such as cinema's relation to popular culture.[5] Furthermore, Taylor's assertion that the unease among anthropologists about film is "surely part and parcel of an abhorrence of imagery in general, a sentiment that, together with an array of attendant anti-iconic prohibitions, has existed from time immemorial," overgeneralizes the place of visuality in the history of anthropology.[6] While film's status within anthropology has historically been uneasy, the broad assertion that anthropologists have been skeptical of the visual since "time immemorial" needs to be subject to historical scrutiny. Judging by the widespread endorsement of photography among anthropologists in the second half of the nineteenth century, it would seem that the photographic medium was seen by many anthropologists at the time to be uniquely well-suited to meet the demands of the discipline.

Coming to terms with the status of the visual within the history of anthropology is a highly contentious project within contemporary anthropological theory. A number of anthropologists hold views diametrically opposed to Taylor; Johannes Fabian and James C. Faris, for example, argue that rather than being relegated to the margins of the discipline, the visible has always had a powerful hold upon the anthropological imagination. Faris argues that anthropology's near obsession with making the "disappeared" reappear before the lens of the camera was part of a wider urge to visualize cultural difference, part of what Faris sees as anthropology's legacy as a "seeing mechanism," as opposed to a listening device.[7] Fabian's critique of the hegemony of the visual within anthropology is constructed along similar lines, and, for Fabian, anthropology's tendency to detemporalize relations between subject and object is an inevitable by-product of this visual process of knowledge production: "As long as anthropology presents its object primarily as seen, as long as ethnographic observation is conceived primarily as observation and/or representation . . . it is likely to persist in denying the coevalness of the Other."[8]

What are we to make of these recent claims for the privileged status of the visual in anthropology, what Faris sees as anthropology's "naive embrace of scopic technologies," given Taylor's position that visuality remains "merely ancillary" for most anthropologists?[9] In order to make sense of these opposing views, it is important to situate the claims of Faris and Fabian within a postmodernist critique of anthropological authority, a shift that has forced ethnographers to redefine their own position vis à vis their object of study. As James Clifford explains: "[Whereas] ethnography in the service of anthropology once looked out at clearly defined others, defined as primitive, or tribal, or non-Western, or pre-literate, or nonhistorical . . . now ethnography encounters others in relation to itself, while seeing itself as other."[10]

The reflexive turn in anthropology was influenced by theoretical work on reflexivity and cinema since the 1970s by Jay Ruby, David MacDougall, and Faye Ginsburg, among others.[11] With it came a questioning of traditional research techniques, including those recording methods that privilege what the anthropologist *sees* at the expense of other modes of ethnographic enunciation which may, in the words of Paul Stoller, "better solve the problem of voice, authority, and authenticity" in ethnographic inquiry.[12] Stoller argues that a text that mixes ingredients, including "dialogue, description, metaphor, metonymy, synecdoche, irony, smells, sights, and sounds to create a narrative that savors the world of the Other" might bring anthropologists a deeper understanding of cultures than the methods of visual technologies and single-authored monographs.[13] Partisans of a more interpretive anthropology, one that emphasizes a dialogic approach to the study of culture, have attacked traditional anthropology for what they see as its naive faith in the visual as an unimpeachable record of cultural reality. It is little surprise, then, that as part of the reflexive turn in anthropology in the 1980s, the status of the visual as a transmitter of ethnographic knowledge became a popular target for anthropologists who looked to anthropology's nineteenth-century embrace of visual technologies as evidence of a naive belief in the camera's mimeticism.

The historical evidence suggests that, at least in the case of cinema, ambivalence among anthropologists about the role of the visual may be less a case of iconophobia than of "popularphobia," a deep-seated professional anxiety about ethnography's fraught relationship with popular culture.[14] For example, Margaret Mead and Gregory Bateson's films of comparative child-rearing practices in New Guinea and the United States were shunned for popularizing anthropology, despite the fact that Mead viewed her films as objective scientific records of indigenous culture. In her classic essay, "Visual Anthropology in a Discipline of Words," in which she criticized members of the profession for their antipathy toward film, Mead argued that it was

a curious anomaly that those against whom the accusations of being subjective and impressionistic were raised—those, in fact, who were willing to trust their own senses and their own capacity to integrate experiences—have been the most active in the use of instrumentation that can provide masses of objective materials that can be re-analyzed in the light of changing theory. Those who have been loudest in their demand for "scientific" work have been least willing to use instruments that would do for anthropology what instrumentation has done for other sciences—refine and expand the areas of accurate observation.[15]

Mead's defense of the motion picture camera as an objective instrument of scientific investigation, a rhetorical strategy designed to fend off charges of impressionism, is evidence of ethnographic film's paradoxical status as a tool of scientific research and source of cheap amusement. That Mead felt impelled to make a case for ethnographic film on the basis of its superior scientism, its ability to "refine and expand the areas of accurate observation," suggests that cinema was incapable of shaking off pejorative associations of subjectivity and partiality. But even when cinema has been put into the service of anthropological investigation, arguments over the legitimacy of nonprofessionally trained anthropologists making films versus trained professionals have continued unabated. On the one hand, the fear is that nonanthropologists employed to shoot ethnographic moving pictures would lack, in the words of anthropologist Jack Rollwagen, the "conceptual framework necessary to treat the subject matter in a way that is enlightened by anthropological theory, ethnology, and ethnography."[16] As Don Rundstrom explains, "The visual ethnographer needs to develop a 'critical imagistic eye,' that is, a disciplined way of interpreting multi-sensual information within a temporal/spatial framework" when incorporating visual techniques into the enterprise of ethnographic investigation.[17] Despite the struggles for legitimacy waged by generations of ethnographic filmmakers not trained in anthropology, the belief that nonanthropologists lack competence to make ethnographically informed portraits of cultural groups still holds considerable sway among professional anthropologists. On the other hand, the claim that only individuals formally trained in anthropological research techniques can produce images of ethnographic validity has been challenged by many contemporary filmmakers, who argue that ethnographic film practice is historically and discursively too variegated to be limited by rigid taxonomies. Nevertheless, many anthropologists still perceive ethnographic film as the visual equivalent of the anthropological monograph, a mode of communication that can embody anthropological precepts rather than simply illustrate them, to paraphrase Taylor.[18]

In spite of Mead's pessimistic pronouncements on ethnographic film, there have been major developments within the genre since the end of World War II. Jean Rouch, one of the most influential figures in the field of ethnographic film, shot his first film with a 16mm Bell and Howell camera in West Africa in 1946 and went on to pioneer a participatory and reflexive approach to ethnographic filmmaking in such films as *Les maîtres fous* (1955), *Chronique d'un été* (1960), and *Jaguar* (1967).[19] Rouch's filmmaking includes an ethical awareness of the politics of image-making and a shunning of the positivist ethos of scientific "objectivity" in favor of a more dialogical creative approach.[20] However, if Rouch inspired a new generation of ethnographic filmmakers concerned with developing more reflexive, participatory models of filmmaking (including David and Judith MacDougall, John Marshall, Gary Kildea, and Jorge Preloran), the obstacles of technical training, economic demands, and intermittent academic support continue to be substantial challenges for ethnographic filmmakers. Admittedly, these hurdles were considerably more formidable for aspiring ethnographic filmmakers in the teens and twenties, who had few role models, cumbersome equipment, and little institutional support for their work.

Anthropology's encounter with early cinema took place as the young subject matured into a full-fledged academic discipline. Cinema's coincidence with anthropology's professionalization around the turn of the century was not, however, altogether good news for ethnographic film. Due to the low cultural esteem of cinema, scientists were more fearful of the contaminating popular associations of cinema than they were of those of photography (recall that commercially produced photographs circulated freely within anthropological circles and anthropologists often doctored photographic images to emphasize their ethnographic significance). If some anthropologists, including Boas, had few qualms validating commercially produced films of native peoples as "scientific" evidence (providing they had been shot under the supervision of an anthropologist), institutions such as the AMNH initially resisted integrating cinema into their programs, doing little to encourage the use of moving pictures during expeditions or in lectures delivered at the Museum. Responding to this general inertia toward cinema, a 1909 editorial in the *Moving Picture World* argued that

> in each case the traveler or explorer seems to have unaccountably overlooked the claims of the moving picture camera to a place in the equipment. We are at a loss to account for this, unless it be on the ground that people who make it their business to produce stationary photographs are not aware of the enormous public interest which attaches to a moving picture of rarities of scenery and life. Of course, it is far more difficult to successfully use a moving picture camera than it is a snapshot camera. But the difficulties are not so great that they cannot be overcome.[21]

In rebuking anthropologists, scientists, and explorers alike for failing to recognize the widespread public interest in "rarities of scenery and life," the editorial begged a number of questions, including the extent to which moving pictures of native peoples could advance anthropologists' understanding of patterns of culture, the impact of cinematography on anthropological method, the educational role of ethnographic films, and the entertainment value of visual anthropology. Such finger-pointing at anthropologists and explorers for not exploiting the public's interest in motion pictures of native peoples continued unabated; for example, in a 1915 essay entitled "Exploring by Motion Pictures," Harvey N. Hurte argued that "it is the human-interest material that outshines the rest in popularity, and this is what, in my opinion, has been the principally neglected theme down to date."[22] Given the AMNH's lukewarm attitude toward motion pictures, it is not without irony that in 1976 the Museum began hosting one of the world's most prestigious ethnographic film showcases, the Margaret Mead Film and Video Festival, featuring a wide range of ethnographic films and indigenous media from around the world.

It is perhaps fitting that 1908, the year of the first AMNH screening, also marks a turning point in the history of the commercial film industry; in that year the Motion Picture Patents Company (MPPC) was founded and, as Tom Gunning points out, one of the goals of the MPPC was to dignify filmgoing by raising its social standing and making it more appealing to middle-class audiences. Thus, a 1909 MPPC advertisement characterized filmgoing as "Moral, Educational and Cleanly Amusing."[23] This larger context of industry rehabilitation was the discursive backdrop to the AMNH's tardy decision to include motion pictures within its civic and pedagogical remit. The challenge facing AMNH curators charged with hiring suitable film lecturers for public programs was compounded by the fact that on a textual level, films shot by anthropologists were often indistinguishable from those made by commercial cinematographers, especially in regions of the world where tourists and anthropologists jostled for space, such as the heavily trafficked American Southwest. Efforts to discern textual signatures of scientific authority in early ethnographic film are difficult, since ethnographic films shot by anthropologists often cannot be differentiated from those made by commercial producers for popular audiences.

Ethnographic films from the early cinema period are therefore best characterized as modes of enunciation that move freely between commercial genres such as the home movie, scientific demonstration film, observational ethnographic film, and travelogue. In some respects, Patricia Zimmermann's account of amateur-ethnographic travel footage shot in Africa in the 1920s is applicable to early ethnographic film; according to Zimmermann, the films' "incompleteness, their inarticulate representation of the 'primitive,' their failed reconstruction of the . . . anthropological subject, their scattered and repetitive cinematography, their visual disintegration of order and their silencing of all . . . into images of blackness inscribe the chaotic as the primary signifier."[24] Moreover, in many cases there is no extant information on whether a piece of ethnographic film footage was produced as part of scientific research, for commercial release, or by an amateur cinematographer. Likewise, basic information about the identities of the native people being filmed or the date and geographical location of the filming is often absent. Furthermore, given the imperfect state of knowledge about the profilmic event, paying attention to the exhibition site of early ethnographic film as a determinant of a film's ethnographic status can illuminate how meaning may have shifted across distinct venues, since where a film was shown would have had an enormous impact on the kind of meanings it privileged or suppressed.

Reclaiming Early Ethnographic Film

Early ethnographic films have been the subject, and in some cases the raw material, of a number of recent films by anthropologists and independent filmmakers. These early films document the untold stories of the lives of the thousands of native peoples who appeared in front of the camera during the apotheosis of Western colonialism, offering often poignant and elusive illustrations of how the cultures of colonialism, modernity, and tourism swept across the far-flung outposts of empire. This itinerary is vividly recapitulated in Yervant Gianikian and Angela Ricci Lucchi's haunting film *From the Pole to the Equator* (1986), a 96-minute avant-garde meditation on cinema as a "seeing and moving apparatus" constructed from footage shot in the Alps, the South Pole, Africa, Russia, India, and Italy by the Italian cinematographer Luca Comerio (1874–1940) between 1910 and the beginning of World War I. Through its inscription of the modes of representation associated with the travelogue and a host of other ethnographic subgenres, *From the Pole to the Equator* leaves an indelible mark on the spectator, exploiting almost every trope of early ethnographic filmmaking, including the phantom ride, native peoples performing for the camera, processions and marches, scenes of abject imagery associated with the safari, missionary camps, and most memorably, the return gaze. Gianikian and Ricci Lucchi have rephotographed Comerio's original footage, step-printed it into slow motion, and hand-tinted it in a range of tones from bleached sepia to aqua blue, sometimes within the same shot.[25] Combined with a contemporary minimalist musical score, these visual effects transform the profilmic into a multicolored dreamscape, converting Comerio's indexical records of his journeys into a highly aestheticized ethnographic autobiography of an absent subject.[26] Within this reflexive landscape, Comerio's oneiric visions of an imperial world foreground the act of looking and traveling (movement fills the frames: either bodies moving in space or the camera steadily penetrating a mountainous landscape), creating what Scott MacDonald argues is a binocular (or even trinocular) gaze, in which we watch the two filmmakers watching Comerio looking through his viewfinder. This act of seeing is also underscored through the number of irised shots that Comerio employed (particularly in the polar bear hunt sequence toward the beginning of the film):

> Instead of simply allowing us to *see* the Comerio materials, Gianikian and Ricci Lucchi enable us to both *see* them and *see through* them. The result is that we witness the quest of early twentieth-century Italians to penetrate the Third World and to challenge the wilderness, *and* (implicitly) the journey of consciousness that ultimately led to Gianikian and Ricci Lucchi's horror at the events of this period.[27]

However, the extent to which *From the Pole to the Equator* is inevitably read by contemporary viewers as a "cinematic subversion of Luca Comerio's imagery, and the ideology it embodies," as argued by MacDonald, is up for grabs. Even though simple identification with the original footage is problematized as a result of the filmmakers' interventions, the original subject positions still remain available in the Gianikian and Ricci Lucchi film. We are therefore left wondering whether the native peoples represented in *From the Pole to the Equator* are any more or less objectified or fetishized by their filmic resurrection, or whether the spectacle laid bare by the camera's brutal unmasking of the atrocities of the colonial era remains simply a visual spectacle. For example, in a scene depicting Africans walking in a missionary camp, the tempo of their gait is perfectly synchronized with the techno score; wrested of all meaning save their status as bodies performing in sync with the music, the scene takes on an overtly aestheticized quality, stripping these people of any agency save their corporeality. Returning to the colonial archive in a spirit of "nostalgic longing," to borrow from Catherine Russell, the filmmakers may end up fetishizing Comerio's travelogue footage without considering how its legacy as historical evocation is inextricably bound up with its use value as colonial propaganda. While for some viewers the slow motion and aestheticization of Comerio's images may provoke a kind of Brechtian alienation, for other viewers the manipulation of the original footage serves only to further alienate the representations of the native peoples, rerendering them as spectacles of Otherness that can be scrutinized in even more detail, given the optical treatment of the film.

While *From the Pole to the Equator* refuses easy identification with the colonialist viewpoint implicit in Comerio's gaze, the structures of power that gave Comerio the mobility and authority to capture these images remain outside the diegesis and are never interrogated. If the highly formalized nature of Gianikian and Ricci Lucchi's reconstruction of Comerio's footage creates a far more disjunctive sense of what it means to revisit the filmic past than one finds in traditional archival documentaries, where found footage becomes a metonym for historical "truth," the power relations between imagemaker and imaged remain implicit in Gianikian and Ricci Lucchi's film. Moreover, as Russell argues, "the inappropriateness of such a treatment to the scenes of cruelty and subjugation is not only disturbing; it transposes the archive into a fantastic scenario that privileges the pleasure of the image over its role in constructing history and memory."[28] But there *are* occasional moments in *From the Pole to the Equator* when the project of subversion referred to by MacDonald does seem to succeed; transformed into ghostly bodies that float across time and the filmic frame, it is as if the specters of colonialism have returned to haunt us (especially in scenes showing the return gaze), laying bare some of the atrocities of human subjugation in the most painful of lingering looks.

From the Pole to the Equator also raises important ethical questions about the status of archival film for indigenous peoples engaged in contemporary struggles for political and cultural self-determination. In this context, the role of the film archive as the custodian of early ethnographic film is complicated; who gains access to these films, how they are programmed as part of contemporary retrospectives, and what kinds of restrictions are imposed upon them for commercial use and academic research are pressing concerns for curators, archivists, and members of indigenous groups. Moreover, restrictions on the circulation of media works representing native peoples vary significantly; for some indigenous people, for example, "knowledge is a form of property . . . and violating the highly structured rights which restrict general access to information is regarded as theft."[29] Other cultures have elaborate systems of restriction which forbid the unauthorized display or transmission of secret or otherwise restricted material, including the representation of rituals, stories, songs, or dances.[30] This issue is vividly illustrated in the case of Baldwin Spencer's 1901 and 1912 films, which are under the curatorial control of the Department of Aboriginal Studies at the National Museum of Victoria in Melbourne.[31] After consultation with members of the Arrernte people, Museum officials have restricted public viewing of some of the Spencer footage; as part of the research for this book, I was only permitted access to brief excerpts of Spencer's footage (not exceeding a total of three minutes) and could only screen the films for personal research purposes.[32]

The reappropriation and "remediation" of silent film footage by native peoples is part of a broader movement of self-determination, a way of using technologies of representation as "a self-conscious means of cultural preservation and production."[33] But as anthropologist Harald E. L. Prins argues, there is a paradoxical quality to the ways in which primitivism, especially the Noble Savage paradigm, has been used by some native groups; while these stereotypes depend on mythical constructions of cultural difference for meaning, they have nevertheless provided peoples with a model of self-representation which they can exploit for their own political ends.[34] Cultural survival films, such as the noted *Our Lives in Our Hands* (1986) produced by the Mi'kmaq tribe of Maine, use the cinematic medium as a form of native rights advocacy, documenting traditional arts and crafts, strengthening cultural identity, and informing the public of their existence and ongoing struggles.[35] The restoration of Edward S. Curtis's *In the Land of the Head Hunters* into the collaboratively produced *In the Land of the War Canoes* following the 1972 discovery by anthropologists Bill Holm and George Quimby of a badly damaged and incomplete print of the film, is another example of the early ethnographic film archive revitalizing native identity, although as discussed elsewhere in the book, this project does raise important questions about the ultimate effect this kind of restorative work has on the integrity of the original film.[36] Notwithstanding these criticisms, Holm and Quimby's work on *In the Land of the War Canoes* did give contemporary Kwakwaka'wakw the opportunity not only to serve once again as collaborators on the film but to recuperate it as part of *their* history. Working with a group of fifty Kwakwaka'wakw, including a number of surviving cast members, Holm and Quimby added a soundtrack consisting of Kwakwaka'wakw dialogue, chanting, and singing. According to Russell, contemporary Kwakwaka'wakw spectators have tended to ignore the film's ostensible narrative structure in favor of seeing the film as a "living memory of both the traditional practices and the colonial containment activated by the . . . 'photoplay' conventions."[37] The reconstructed film becomes a cultural "document" in several senses of the word: as a home movie for descendants of the performers; as a visual record of traditional cultural practices and material artifacts; as evidence of Curtis's working practices and artistic vision for the film; and as an example of early twentieth-century popular entertainment.

This act of cultural regeneration by native descendants complements a similar kind of recuperative work being done by contemporary Native American film and videomakers, including Victor Masayesva Jr. and Dean Curtis Bear Claw. Masayesva has recontextualized (and, in effect, decolonized) nineteenth-century images of Native Americans in *Itam Hakim, Hopiit* (1985) by filming the photographs in such a way that denies the viewer access to the whole bodies on display. By thwarting our ability to see, Masayesva forces us to reconsider our relationship to the images and what they say about a Western desire to visualize native peoples as mute, racialized bodies. Similarly, in *Ritual Clowns* (1988), Masayesva experiments with narrative as well as technological and formal devices in a film that combines computer animation, archival footage from the early cinema period, aestheticized images of landscape, performance art, and music in order to consider how the sacred figure of the Hopi clown has been misappropriated by anthropologists, while also deploying the clowns to comment on international crises.[38] Finally, in *Imagining Indians* (1992), Masayesva combines interviews of Native American performers about their roles in contemporary big-budget Hollywood westerns, shots of natural landscapes, and dramatic sequences in order to explore the nature of Native

American representation in Hollywood. Through an act of reclamation in these films, Masayesva asks us to reexamine the nature of visuality in photographs and films of Native Americans going back to the nineteenth century and how racialized images of native peoples in both popular and academic culture have captured the imagination of a nation.

Our relationship to images of the past demands a self-consciousness about how these historical representations may be circulated in the present, at a speed and scale previously unimagined, in the forms of broadcasting, satellite transmission, home video, and the Internet. This reflection must address how people's histories and identities are mediated through such visual documents and how these films might be used by native peoples in ongoing efforts of cultural renewal.[39] The issue of how and by whom these early film records of native peoples are currently being used has assumed greater urgency in the last two decades, as Western archivists, media-makers, and the public at large begin to recognize the rights of indigenous peoples to control their own images. Where native peoples were once the object of a scrutinizing gaze, they are now redirecting that gaze at their colonial interlocutors in a form of "reverse ethnography," which, Ginsburg argues, "opens up new questions regarding the production and circulation of media in non-western societies and the ways in which historically objectifying representations of their cultures made by others are resignified not only textually but in production and distribution processes as well."[40]

An example of this resignification of early ethnographic film involved the use of Alfred Cort Haddon's 1898 films of Australian Aborigines to overturn Australia's *terra nullius* law, which denied their land rights claims. Haddon's films were used as evidence of the continuity of indigenous tradition in Australia in litigation brought about by Australian Aborigine Eddie Mabo, who showed the films in court; it was this court case that laid the ground for the 1993 Native Title act, which granted Australian Aborigines land rights.[41] One cannot help noting the historical irony in Mabo's decision to use Haddon's footage in a culturally productive way in this juridical milestone; Haddon's intention in making these films was to document the cultural rituals of a so-called disappearing people, whereas it was precisely the persistence of these practices that won the case for Australian Aborigines in a court of law nearly a century later. Little could Haddon have known that his films would go on to play such a crucial role in Aboriginal politics and self-determination.

Early ethnographic film material may achieve new relevance in other ways as well, including its incorporation in work by contemporary ethnographic filmmakers. Marlon Fuentes, a Filipino-American with a background in visual anthropology and ethnographic film production, has taken up some of these issues in his 1996 "fake documentary" *Bontoc Eulogy*, a film that mines the ethnographic film archive to explore issues of cultural identity and the West's relationship to its imaged Others. *Bontoc Eulogy* uses the occasion of the St. Louis World's Fair of 1904 to explore the ethics of imagemaking, nineteenth-century anthropology's obsession with graphing, dissecting, and photographing the body of the colonial Other, and the historical use-value of archival film as visible evidence. By foregrounding what David MacDougall has referred to as the "encounters" that take place between ethnographic filmmakers and their indigenous subjects, Fuentes resignifies archival photographs and films in order to inscribe Igorot subjectivity into the official histories of the fair and to point to the ongoing relevance of these issues for subject peoples in general.[42] Fuentes uses the archive as a cultural mnemonic to creatively reconstruct Igorot memory of the World's Fair and to explore how multiple subjectivities can be evoked in ephemeral records that tell a very different story of Igorot life at the St. Louis exhibit compared to that in the official record.[43] On one level, the film navigates a set of discursive issues similar to *From the Pole to the Equator*, using archival film of Igorot and other Filipino peoples to question what it means to review these films as indexical records of colonialist control. Like Gianikian and Ricci Lucchi, Fuentes eschews some of the classic elements of the traditional documentary in favor of a more reflexive engagement with the question of how the film archive can recuperate historical memory. But unlike *From the Pole to the Equator*, Fuentes's film has a distinctive autobiographical element; in fact, the film is as much about Fuentes's attempt to come to terms with his hyphenated identity as a Filipino-American as it is a story about his (fictional) grandfather Markod's experiences as a performer in the Philippine enclosure of the 1904 World's Fair.

An example of Fuentes's treatment of early ethnographic footage to signify the past is his use of a 1904 Biograph film shot in the Asia exhibit at the St. Louis World's Fair. Depicting the slow street procession of one hundred or so elaborately costumed Asian musicians, dancers, and actors, *Asia in America*

encodes "Asianness" in typically orientalist ways. The architecture and costuming are a *bricolage* of South Asian iconography (such as the curved detailing
on the roof over the underpass) and Chinese influences (the geometric forms
on the building in the background), and the scene conveys as much (if not
more) about the "imaginative geography" that shapes the West's view of the
Orient as it does the ethnic and cultural realities of the national groups represented in the pageant.[44] Resignified in Fuentes's film, *Asia in America* functions
as historical evidence of the elaborate spectacles of nationalism staged at turn-
of-the-century world's fairs. But as a direct consequence of the faux mise-en-
scène, the film assumes some of the qualities of an early Méliès film, resembling a carnival parade more than a scientific evocation of Asian culture. Even
the Biograph film's title, *Asia in America*, is the perfect metaphor for the looking relations implicit in the text; the film is less about Asia or Asianness than
its imaginary construct through American eyes.

One of Fuentes's proclaimed aims in *Bontoc Eulogy* was to undercut the evidentiary status of the cinematic image;[45] in a kind of historical filtration of the
past through a postmodernist lens, Fuentes creates a multilayered textuality
combining archival actuality footage of the St. Louis World's Fair (mostly of
the architecture and amusements located on the Pike) and so-called tribal peoples of the Philippines (shot in the 1920s) with reconstructions of Markod's
experiences and scenes shot in the present. Two voice-over statements by
Fuentes near the beginning of the film ("Now my memories of life back home
have faded to the point where it is difficult to know where reality ends and
imagination begins," and "You have to remember in order to survive") encap-
sulate the central theme of *Bontoc Eulogy*: how our understanding of cultural
identity in the present can be shaped through reconstructing images of the
past.[46]

In contrast to *From the Pole to the Equator*, *Bontoc Eulogy* powerfully explores
how native subjectivity is erased in filmic and photographic evidence; through
a number of formal and textual devices, Fuentes evokes multiple subjectivities
that challenge official histories of native peoples' experiences of world's fairs.
The opening sequence of the film is a striking evocation of the trading post
scene from Robert Flaherty's *Nanook of the North*, when the character Nanook
(played by Flaherty's guide and friend Allakariallak) pretends not to know
what a phonograph is by biting the record and laughing at the camera. *Bontoc*

Eulogy's opening image (of Fuentes in medium close-up turning the handle of a vintage phonograph) is repeated three times, accompanied by indigenous music from the Philippines in the first two renditions and by native voices in the third. The sequence is most successful, I would argue, at producing a reflexive metacommentary on the process of reconstructing native history and memory, one of *Bontoc Eulogy*'s defining aims.

Blurring past and present, Fuentes juxtaposes the images and voices of the official white culture at the fair with a powerfully evoked native subjectivity. Despite the film's closing written disclaimer that its story, while "inspired by actual events," is not about an actual historical figure, the affective narrative and first-person narration draw us into Fuentes's imaginary past. The story of Markod, Fuentes's fictional grandfather, concludes as Fuentes describes in voice-over how his grandfather may have been among the three Filipinos who died at the fair and whose body parts ended up preserved in specimen jars at the Smithsonian Institution in Washington, D.C. Over images of Fuentes examining the contents of glass display cases filled with dissected human faces and brains, we hear the filmmaker say: "So many objects, identities unknown. Labeled but nameless. Anonymous stories permanently preserved in a language that can never be understood." The film's collage structure succeeds in evoking the experience of objectification of native peoples via the colonialist spectacles of world's fairs and scientific research. When Fuentes's narration refers to Markod's keeping "his rage within" as he was forcibly brought back to the fair after an attempted escape, that rage speaks for untold numbers of native peoples whose voices have never been heard.[47]

Bontoc Eulogy's subversive attitude toward the cinematic document and its mixture of actuality, fiction, and reconstruction are useful reminders of early ethnographic films' sometimes tenuous relationship to the historically real. Moreover, *Bontoc Eulogy*'s use of early ethnographic film as cultural memory, as a retelling of stories that represent native peoples, not just as the victims of colonialism but as historical actors and interlocutors, invites us to explore the disjunction between the illusion of total control exerted by colonial authorities and a recognition of its fragility and discursive complexity. Early ethnographic films have come to serve diverse purposes in our own time, including providing the filmic material for personalized narratives and cultural autobiographies that open up new cultural conversations on the meanings of the

past.[48] In an effort to counter the effect of a century of unequal looking relations, filmmakers like Victor Masayesva Jr., Marlon Fuentes, and Vincent
Monnikendam have turned to the ethnographic film archive as a source of
inspiration, recuperating early ethnographic film as part of an ongoing effort
by indigenous artists to resignify colonialist imagery and to produce meta-
commentaries on the politics of cross-cultural representation. For these artists,
films and photographs are not simply relics of a colonialist era but artifacts
that refract a series of gazes across cultural divides, or what art critic Lucy R.
Lippard calls "the then-present space of the subjects, the then-present, but
perhaps very different, space of the photographer, and the now-present space
of the [reader] in retrospect, as a surrogate for contemporary viewers."[49]
Introducing a collection of essays about Native American photographs written by native peoples, Lippard argues that films and photographs from the
early cinema period

> bring back a storm of colonial emotions, which have to be sorted out
> from more progressive responses. And demythologizing can bring disil-
> lusionment as well—a good thing, since illusions of any kind of "perfec-
> tion" (nobility, impassivity, pantheistic connectedness, or authenticity) are
> obstacles for political freedom for the subjects.[50]

Of course, indigenous media-makers are not the only people interested in
this archival material; a great many of the films have also been used as stock
footage in countless news reports and documentaries, have become part of
early cinema retrospectives, or have been recuperated for political purposes
by cultural activists. The ongoing ability of these early film actualities to satisfy modern curiosity about the past is a question of cultural translation, a matter of getting *their* stories into our lives and of recognizing our lives in their
stories. While filmmakers like Fuentes, Masayesva, and Monnikendam have
drawn attention to the power relations implicit in early ethnographic film,
there has been less interest among traditional historians of visual anthropology in exploring the early cinema archive as a repository of potentially ethno-
graphic-rich filmic material, or situating the few early filmmakers more fully
within their social, historical, or scientific milieux.

This investigation into the imbricated worlds of cinema, anthropology, and turn-of-the-century visual culture has been a reconstructive exercise in more than one sense. Faced with a dearth of published writings on the anthropological uses of the moving picture camera in the pre-1907 period (and only sporadic commentary thereafter), debates over precinematic forms of ethnographic representation have given us important clues for understanding cinema's utility as an ethnographic recording device. By establishing linkages with modes of ethnographic enunciation that anticipated or complemented those of cinema (including the museum life group, the world's fair, the anthropological photograph, and the travelogue), this book has drawn attention to early ethnographic film's complex interactions with both popular and scientific culture.

Unpacking ethnographic film's heterogeneous origins in nineteenth-century visual culture also puts us on a more solid foundation for considering the impact on museums and anthropologists of new digital technologies such as the Internet, interactive multimedia exhibits, the virtual museum, and IMAX films. For example, clues for understanding contemporary museum attitudes toward new media technologies can be found in a number of experimental exhibits proposed (if not always installed) in American and European museums at the beginning of the twentieth century. At one extreme, French scientist Félix-Louis Regnault's turn-of-the-century plan for an encyclopedic ethnographic archive strikingly anticipates contemporary visions of the multimedia museum and Web site.[51] In Regnault's imagined ethnographic museum,[52] anthropologists and members of the general public could retrieve written texts, sound recordings, and still and moving images of indigenous peoples "at the flick of a switch." More than merely a repository of material artifacts such as potter's wheels or looms, Regnault's museum-archive was to be a "laboratory and . . . center of teaching," where scientists could view cinematographic records frame by frame and compare them with films of other cultures.[53]

The sense of déjà vu in current debates over the efficacy of digital media in disseminating ethnographic knowledge suggests that curators and anthropologists are still grappling with the problem of how to reconcile a desire for scientific rigor with the demand for audience appeal. Digital technologies like virtual reality bring with them their own sets of representational, political, and ethical concerns and are as likely to pose as many new questions about how ethnographic imagery is gathered, stored, and disseminated as they are to offer long sought-after solutions to issues of access, authenticity, and accountability. While anthropologists have become more sensitive to the politics of representation and to the ethical dimensions of transnational media-making, these new media technologies will remap the experiences of Self and Other, touch and sight, ethnographic immersion, scientific investigation, and armchair travel. The peoples who have traditionally been the subject of the ethnographic gaze are now, more than ever, inserting themselves into the new media landscape by taking up the tools of production (especially the Web) and organizing within communities and across international borders. David MacDougall's idea of the "ethnographic encounter" is considerably more complex today than it was when he coined the phrase in 1982; in this new millennium, the ethnographic encounter is as much an encounter between the mediated past and the observer in the present, or between electronically linked native peoples located in geographically distinct spaces as it is an encounter between the individual professional ethnographer and native subject.[54] Native peoples are forming virtual communities through such Internet services, including Native Net, which provide indigenous peoples with a forum for discussing the media as well as a range of other issues affecting their communities.[55]

No one can predict with certainty what impact emerging digital technologies may have on questions of anthropological authority or the democratization of ethnographic media; whether or not they radically alter the discursive terrain of ethnographic film will depend on how they are taken up by mediamakers working in a range of economic, social, and cultural settings. Doubtless they will engender some of the same anxieties that troubled anthropologists in the wake of modernity over a century ago. To some extent, the future of ethnographic film is as uncertain now as it was when Alfred Cort Haddon cranked the handle of his Neuman and Guardia camera in 1898, wondering what on earth his colleagues back home would make of his unusual endeavor.

Notes

INTRODUCTION

1. The term is a reworking of Raymond Corbey's evocative phrase "wondrous, disturbing difference," which he uses to characterize the spectacle of otherness on display at turn-of-the-century world's fairs. See Raymond Corbey with Steven Wachlin, "Ethnographic Showcases, 1870–1930," *Cultural Anthropology* 8.3 (Aug. 1993): 364.

2. For more on the idea of "ambivalence" as a theoretical construct and spectatorial response to images of the Other, see Homi K. Bhaba, *The Location of Culture*, 66.

3. Alan Lomax, Irmgard Bartenieff, and Forrestine Paulay, "Choreometrics: A Method for the Study of Cross-Cultural Pattern in Film," *Research Films* 6.6 (1969): 506.

4. Films include *Balinese Character* (1942); *Trance and Dance in Bali* (1951); and from the Character Formation in Different Cultures Series: *Karba's First Years* (1950); *Bathing Babies in Three Cultures* (1951); *First Days in the Life of a New Guinea Baby* (1951); and *Childhood Rivalry in Bali and New Guinea* (1952).

5. Films include *Les maîtres fous* (1955); *Moi, un Noir* (1957); *Chronique d'un été* (1960); *Petit à Petit* (1969); and *Jaguar* (1967).

6. For more on the filmmaking sponsored by the IWF, see Martin Taureg, "The Development of Standards for Scientific Films in German Ethnography," *Studies in Visual Communication* 9.1 (Winter 1983): 19–29.

7. David MacDougall, "The Visual in Anthropology," in Marcus Banks and Howard Morphy, eds., *Rethinking Visual Anthropology*, 292.

8. Anne Mintz, "That's Edutainment," *Museum News* 73.6 (1994): 32.

9. L. A. Gratacap, "The Making of a Museum," *Architectural Record* 9 (Apr. 1900): 399.

10. Quoted in ibid., 301.

11. Frank Woolnough, "Museums and Nature Study," *Museums Journal* 4.8 (Feb. 1905): 265.

12. Quoted in Lisa C. Roberts, *From Knowledge to Narrative: Educators and the Changing Museum*, 22.

13. The Science Museum in London, the AMNH in New York City, and the National Museum of Natural History in Washington have all recently either installed or upgraded their IMAX screens.

14. Author interview with Elaine Charnov, Oct. 14, 1997, New York City.

15. For more on discourses of visuality as configured in the work of twentieth-century anthropologists, see Anna Grimshaw, *The Ethnographer's Eye: Ways of Seeing in Anthropology.*

16. See Martin Jay's *Downcast Eyes* for a discussion of the "denigration of vision" within turn-of-the-century philosophical discourse and the effects this revisionist thinking had on dominant models of perception, knowledge, and visuality. Jay, *Downcast Eyes: The Denigration of Vision in Twentieth-Century French Thought* (Berkeley: University of California Press, 1993).

17. C. A. Bayly, ed., *The Raj and the British, 1600–1947*, 287.

18. Elizabeth Edwards, "Introduction," in Edwards, ed., *Anthropology and Photography, 1893–1923*, 3.

19. Howard Morphy, "The Original Australians and the Evolution of Anthropology," in Morphy and Elizabeth Edwards, eds., *Australia in Oxford*, 60.

20. Ibid. Anthropologist Franz Boas's use of photography in his study of Kwakwaka'wakw (Kwakuitl) Indians of the Northwest Coast in the 1890s is an important case study. See Ira Jacknis, "Franz Boas and Photography," *Studies in Visual Communication* 10.1 (1984): 2–60.

21. MacDougall, "The Visual in Anthropology," 279.

22. Anthony R. Michaelis, *Research Films in Biology, Anthropology, Psychology, and Medicine,* 191–92.

23. For an excellent account of Regnault's chronophotographs, see Fatimah Tobing Rony, *The Third Eye: Race, Cinema, and Ethnographic Spectacle*, 21–73.

24. While there are films showing anthropologists measuring the bodies of native peoples in the 1920s and 1930s and films of native peoples performing routinized movements for the camera (see, for example, entomologist Norman Tindale's 1932 footage shot in Mt. Liebig, Central Australia, in which Australian Aborigines move from a standing to a crouching position, walk, run, jump, and demonstrate how to lift a baby for the camera), these comparative movement studies take place in the field rather than in the controlled conditions of the laboratory. My thanks to Fred Myers for drawing my attention to the Tindale films.

25. See *Pathé Fortnightly Bulletin* 11.23 (July 7, 1913) and 11.25 (July 21, 1913) for descriptions of these films.

26. Jonathan Crary, *Techniques of the Observer: On Vision and Modernity in the Nineteenth Century*, 150.

27. See Rony's book on race and cinema (*The Third Eye*), which examines how

filmmakers constructed the body of the ethnographic Other as a racialized sign in remarkably consistent ways across different periods and styles of ethnographic and Hollywood filmmaking.

28. Adopting a very different methodology to Rony, Jennifer Peterson's work on the travelogue follows the earlier research into the genre by Charles Musser, Tom Gunning, and Theodore X. Barber. According to Peterson, the travelogue offered viewers a unique mode of film spectatorship; producing a new kind of tourist-spectator, travelogues were a way of showing off the world's spoils accessible to the new technologies of transport and image-making, as well as vicariously returning immigrant viewers to their distant homelands through mechanized means. Peterson, "World Pictures: Travelogue Films and the Lure of the Exotic," 30.

29. One of the first film scholars to consider the significance of the travel genre in early cinema was Charles Musser, whose essay, "The Travel Genre in 1903–1904: Moving Towards Fictional Narrative" (in Thomas Elsaesser, ed., *Early Cinema: Space, Frame, Narrative*), framed a number of important issues. Musser's book with Carol Nelson, *High-Class Moving Pictures: Lyman H. Howe and the Forgotten Era of Traveling Exhibition, 1880–1920*, offers a detailed account of the screen practices of the early travelogue and is an invaluable resource for historians of the genre. Rony examines a wide range of ethnographic travelogues — from the films in Albert Kahn's French archive to Burton Holmes, Martin and Osa Johnson, and Edward Curtis — in her chapter, "Gestures of Self-Protection: The Picturesque and the Travelogue," in *Third Eye*, 77–98. Also see the essays in Daan Hertogs and Nico de Klerk, eds., *Uncharted Territory: Essays on Early Nonfiction Film*, esp. Jennifer Peterson, " 'Truth Is Stranger Than Fiction': Travelogues from the 1910s in the Nederlands Filmmuseum," 75–90, and Tom Gunning, "Before Documentary: Early NonFiction Films and the 'View' Aesthetic," 9–24. Dan Streible has also written extensively about early actualities, namely, the boxing film; see his forthcoming book, *Fight Pictures: A History of Prizefighting and Early Cinema*.

A great deal more attention has been devoted to early nonfiction cinema in recent years, fostered in part by a spate of events organized by Domitor, the Nederlands Filmmuseum Archive, and the Giornate del Cinema Muto in Pordenone. On an optimistic note, Gunning points out that "the place of nonfiction filmmaking in early cinema has at least been acknowledged and has begun to be theorized and investigated" ("Before Documentary," 10).

30. Gunning, "Before Documentary," 15.

31. Held over four days at the Nederlands Filmmuseum Archive in July 1998, the workshop programmed an eclectic mix of films representing native as well as European folk cultures shot between the turn-of-the century and the late 1950s. Moderators responded to general themes identified within the individual programs and led discussion among the fifty or so international delegates. As well as early cinema scholars, the

workshop was attended by filmmakers, archivists, anthropologists, and curators. A transcript of the workshop discussion can be found on the Filmmuseum's Web site: www.nfm.nl.

32. Mary Louise Pratt's idea of the "contact zone" in which native and outsider cultures intermingle in improvised and unpredictable ways is a more useful paradigm. According to Pratt, contact zones are "social spaces where disparate cultures meet, clash, and grapple with each other, often in highly asymmetrical relations of domination and subordination" (*Imperial Eyes: Travel Writing and Transculturation*, 4).

33. Luc De Heusch was among the earliest to write about early ethnographic film in "The Cinema and Social Science," Reports and Papers in the Social Sciences, no. 14 (Paris: UNESCO, 1962), reprinted in *Visual Anthropology* 1.2 (1988): 99–156.

34. There are three exceptions: Edward S. Curtis's *In the Land of the Head Hunters* (1914), a fiction film with scenes of ethnographic import, and adaptations of Longfellow's poem *Hiawatha* by Joseph K. Dixon (1908) and Frank E. Moore (1913), which were exhibited commercially and in more elite venues.

35. With the exception of more recent scholars of early nonfiction film, the dominant historiographic model of those few scholars who have written about early ethnographic film involves proposing an a priori definition of the genre which is then used to classify what can and cannot be historically included within the canon. These efforts are often accompanied by attempts to align such definitions with a privileged filmmaker-anthropologist whose work constitutes the defining moment in the history of ethnographic filmmaking. For example, despite being chronologically correct in identifying Regnault as a nascent ethnographic filmmaker (and Regnault, as Rony shows us, is a visionary in terms of his conceptualization of ethnographic film), Emilie de Brigard's nomination of a chronophotographer as the first ethnographic filmmaker privileges a scientific genealogy of ethnographic film above its roots in popular culture. Aside from problems of teleology, identifying a chronophotographer as the "first" ethnographic filmmaker also elides the specific signifying practices and cultural contexts of film as a new imaging technology. De Brigard, "History of Ethnographic Film," in Hockings, ed., *Principles of Visual Anthropology*, 15. De Brigard is also dismissive of what she calls "non-scientific films" (actualities, newsreels, and filmed dances), arguing that "human behavior in documentary and fiction films is subject to directorial distortions to such an extent that the film may be scientifically worthless." De Brigard does see value in thinking about all ethnographic films as artifacts that "reveal cultural patterning," although she qualifies this by arguing that some films are "clearly more revealing than others." De Brigard, ibid., 13.

36. As David MacDougall argues: "Ethnographic film cannot be said to constitute a genre, nor is ethnographic film-making a discipline with unified origins and an established methodology . . . the term has served a largely emblematic function, giving a semblance of unity to extremely diverse efforts in the cinema and the social sciences."

MacDougall, "Ethnographic Film: Failure and Promise," *Annual Review of Anthropology* 7 (1978): 405.

37. For an interesting reading of the meanings of stereocards produced around the construction of the Panama Canal and representing the native peoples of Panama, see Ellen Strain, "Stereoscopic Visions: Touring the Panama Canal," *Visual Anthropology Review* 12.2 (Fall/Winter, 1996–97): 44–58.

38. Tom Gunning, "Film History and Film Analysis: The Individual Film in the Course of Time," *Wide Angle* 12.3 (July 1990): 7–8.

39. This question has recently been explored in Banks and Morphy, eds., *Rethinking Visual Anthropology*, a collection that aims to "rethink the place of visual anthropology in the discipline as a whole, and to . . . disentangle the relationship between visual anthropology, film and photography" (4–5).

1. LIFE GROUPS AND THE MODERN MUSEUM SPECTATOR

1. Henry Fairfield Osborn, "Memorial to the Late Morris Ketchum Jesup," *Science* 31.792 (Mar. 4, 1910): 337–38.

2. Huntley Carter, "How to Promote the Use of Museums by an Institute of Museums," *Museums Journal* (hereafter, *MJ*) 7.6 (Dec. 1907): 195.

3. For more on the layout and exhibiting styles of the "Great Exhibition" of 1851, see Thomas Richards, *The Commodity Culture of Victorian England: Advertising and Spectacle, 1851–1914*, 17–72.

4. For a contemporaneous guide to the American Museum of Natural History, see Fremont Rider, *Rider's New York: A Guide-Book for Travelers*, 277–300.

5. In truth, the museum was already a force to be reckoned with in terms of attendance. In 1909, for example, the museum was open free to the public 365 days and on 179 evenings; up until 1907, the museum had charged a small admission fee to the general public on Mondays and Tuesdays (as these days were reserved for public schools). The gross attendance for 1909 was 1,043,562, and the attendance at public afternoon and evening lectures was 82,718. The number of children attending lecture classes was 10,325. The impressive figures were attributed in part to the phenomenal success of the tuberculosis exhibition at the museum. By comparison, in 1902 the total number of visitors was 461,026, with lecture attendance reaching 76,021. The number of children attending lectures was 4,959. Figures for 1902 in Frank M. Chapman, "Natural History for the Masses," *World's Work* 5 (Nov. 1902): 2769; figures for 1909 in *MJ* 8.10 (Apr. 1909): 367.

6. Franz Boas, "Some Principles of Museum Administration," *Science* 25.650 (June 14, 1907): 921.

7. Lucas, untitled transcript (Apr. 2, 1917), p. 5 (Central Archives, Dept. of Library Services, American Museum of Natural History; hereafter, CA-AMNH).

8. Alfred Goldsborough Mayer, "Educational Efficiency of Our Museums," *North American Review* 177 (Oct. 1903): 564.

9. Such concerns were addressed in a lecture delivered to the Brooklyn Institute in 1899, when Smithsonian National Museum president George Browne Goode reminded his audience of the power of museums to raise standards of public culture, arguing that the museum of the future should be adapted to the needs of all classes, including "the factory operator, the day laborer, the salesman, and the clerk, as much as to those of the professional man and man of leisure." George Browne Goode, "The Museum of the Future" (lecture delivered before the Brooklyn Institute, Feb. 28, 1899), 248.

10. The 1877 building was designed by Calvert Vaux and Jacob Wrey Mould; historian Peter Salwen describes it as "bright red brick with high arched windows, embellished with slender columns and varied stone trim, and topped with a gaily colored roof of red, white, and blue slate" (*Upper West Side Story: A History and Guide*, 60–61). For more on the history of the institution see Lyle Rexer, *The American Museum of Natural History: 125 Years of Expedition and Discovery*, and Douglas J. Preston, *Dinosaurs in the Attic: An Excursion into the American Museum of Natural History*. Receiving its charter from the State of New York, the ground and building of the AMNH belonged to the City of New York which, through the Department of Parks, covered roughly 40 percent of the running costs, the other 60 percent coming from benefactors and members. Attendance at the AMNH was miserably low when the museum first opened on the Upper West Side, due to its remote location in an underdeveloped part of Manhattan, and it was not until the New York Elevated Railroad was extended up Ninth—later Columbus—Avenue in June 1879 that attendance picked up (Salwen, *Upper West Side Story*, 63).

11. The following comparative attendance figures for U.S. museums were offered by F. A. Lucas in a 1908 article published in *Science*: AMNH: 476,133; Smithsonian (Washington, D.C.): 360,547; Field Museum (Chicago): 254,516; Brooklyn Institute of Arts and Sciences (including the Children's Museum): 229,028. The popularity of the AMNH—after the arrival of the elevated train line—can be partially explained by its favorable location on Central Park West in Manhattan; according to Lucas, "The Museum enjoys the best location of any in the country, so far as ease of access is concerned and not unnaturally stands first in the number of its visitors." Cited in Lucas, "The Work of Our Larger Museums as Shown by their Annual Reports," *Science* 27.679 (Jan. 3, 1908): 35.

12. Following a series of disputes with the first AMNH president (Morris K. Jesup) over the museum's exhibition policy, Boas handed in his resignation on May 23, 1905.

13. Morris K. Jesup, cited in Henry M. Leipziger, "Address to President, Ladies, and Gentlemen," AMNH *Annual Report for 1899* (1900): 42.

14. The term "rational amusement" was first coined by the British writer Thomas Greenwood in his book *Museums and Art Galleries*. Greenwood argued that the first objec-

tive of any museum should be to "provide rational amusement of an elevating character to the ordinary visitor" (4). The term was subsequently borrowed by numerous museum writers in the late nineteenth century, including Jesup.

15. Bennett, *Birth of the Museum*, 33.

16. Ibid., 30.

17. Francis Arthur Bather, "Presidential Address to the British Museum's Association Aberdeen Conference," *MJ* 3.3 (Sept. 1903): 76.

18. Bennett, *Birth of the Museum*, 6.

19. Francis Arthur Bather, "Dr. Myer on Some European Museums," *MJ* 2.11 (May 1903): 326. Myer was referring specifically here to the public habit of spitting down the hot-air gratings in museums rather than into their pocket handkerchief.

20. Bennett, *Birth of the Museum*, 28.

21. Henry Fairfield Osborn, "The Museum of the Future," *American Museum Journal* (hereafter, *AMJ*) 11.7 (Nov. 1911): 224

22. Donna Haraway's account of adventurer-taxidermist Carl Akeley's role in designing habitat groups for the AMNH illustrates Osborn's philosophy on habitat groups and draws attention to Akeley's obsession with typology in selecting suitable specimens for the installations. Akeley was concerned both with perfection as a normative criterion (which, incidentally, could only be found in the male of the species) and with the "character" of the selected animal, which was also important in assessing perfection. See Haraway, "Teddy Bear Patriarchy: Taxidermy in the Garden of Eden, New York City, 1908–1936," in *Primate Visions: Gender, Race, and Nature in the World of Modern Science*, 26–58.

23. Anna Billings Gallup, "The Children's Museum as an Educator," *Popular Science Monthly* 72 (Apr. 1908): 373.

24. John Maclauchlan, "Presidential Address, Dundee Meeting of Museum Association," *MJ* 7.1 (July 1907): 9.

25. See Neil Harris, "Museums, Merchandising, and Popular Taste: The Struggle for Influence," in Ian M. G. Quimby, ed., *Material Culture and the Study of American Life*, 140–74, for a discussion of the consonance between the exposition, museum, and department store.

26. Wolfgang Schivelbusch, *The Railway Journey: The Industrialization of Time and Space in the 19th Century*, 189.

27. For a fascinating discussion of how the British Museum's Assyrian artifacts (exhibited in the museum in 1850) were both emulated and commodified in British popular culture following the enormous success of the Assyrian artifacts exhibit, see Frederick N. Bohrer, "The Times and Spaces of History: Representation, Assyria, and the British Museum," in Daniel J. Sherman and Irit Rogoff, eds., *Museum Culture: Histories, Discourses, Spectacles*, 197–222. As a number of commentators have pointed out, it was common practice for nineteenth-century department store owners to embellish their displays of

merchandise with precious artifacts and fine art; Neil Harris notes that John Rodman Wanamaker tastefully hung paintings in his Philadelphia store in the 1880s and 1890s and included museum reproductions in window displays (Harris, "Museums, Merchandising," 152).

28. Of course, not all museums were imposing edifices; some occupied very modest dwellings, such as the Pitt Rivers Museum in rural Dorset, England, which consisted of a one-story brick building.

29. Bennett, *Birth of the Museum*, 43; William H. Holmes, "Classification and Arrangement of the Exhibits of an Anthropological Museum," *Journal of the Anthropological Institute of Great Britain and Northern Ireland* (hereafter, *JAI*), n.s., 2 (1902): 360. In 1891, British amateur collector and scientist A.H.F.L. Pitt-Rivers recommended a rotunda as the most effective architectural design for a museum, since the "concentric circles of a circular building adapt themselves, by their size and position, for the exhibition of the expanding varieties of an evolutionary arrangement." Rivers, "Typological Museums, as Exemplified by the Pitt Rivers Museum at Oxford, and His Provincial Museum at Farnham, Dorset," *Journal of the Royal Society of Arts* (Dec. 18, 1891): 117.

30. Bennett, *Birth of the Museum*, 44.

31. Each issue of the *AMJ*, sent free to members, contained an illustrated "Guide Leaflet" which focused on one collection. In addition, bound copies of the guides were put next to the exhibits in the galleries. Booklets were also produced in conjunction with certain collections and aimed to serve as substitutes for personal guides. Frank M. Chapman, "Natural History for the Masses," 2769.

32. "Collections from Africa," in the *General Guide to the Exhibition Halls of the AMNH* (1911): 48–9. Five hundred objects collected from the Congo Free State were given to the AMNH in 1907 by King Leopold II of Belgium. According to Enid Schildkrout and Curtis A. Keim, "many of these artifacts were exhibited alongside zoological trophies in the Museum's African Hall, which opened to the public in 1910" (*African Reflections: Art From Northeastern Zaire*, 50). See their chapter, "Collecting the Congo: The American Museum of Natural History Congo Expedition, 1909–1915," for background information on the African Hall exhibit (47–67).

33. Robert H. Lowie, "Industry and Art of the Negro Race," *AMJ* 11.1 (Jan. 1911): 15.

34. "The Spectator," *Outlook* 92 (May 29, 1909): 273. The author describes the group of museum attendees as being in a state "bordering on collapse, dragging their weary limbs through rooms full of things in which they had not the faintest spark of interest."

35. Ibid.

36. Alfred A. Wallace, "Museums for the People," *Macmillan's Magazine* 19 (1869): 250. Wallace's description of the museum spectator as continually distracted by the promise of upcoming visual delights is reminiscent of contemporary theorizations of postmodern spectatorship in which television viewers' consumption of cable services such as

MTV or via channel surfing is characterized by a delayed gratification and an expectation that what comes next will somehow satisfy (although only ever temporarily) scopophilic and auditory needs.

37. Greenwood, *Museums and Art Galleries*, 29.

38. Ibid.

39. Stephen Greenblatt, "Resonance and Wonder," in Ivan Karp and Steven D. Lavine, eds., *Exhibiting Cultures: The Poetics and Politics of Museum Display*, 49.

40. Bather, "Presidential Address," 79.

41. Boas, "Some Principles," 922.

42. Letter to Jesup from Boas, Apr. 29, 1905 (Boas Papers, *American Philosophical Society*, 299).

43. Boas, "Some Principles," 922.

44. Letter from Boas to Jesup, Jan. 1, 1897 (Boas file 1894–1905, Department of Anthropology, AMNH [hereafter, DA-AMNH]).

45. Boas, "Some Principles," 924.

46. Ibid., 921.

47. For a fascinating debate on life groups from the British perspective, see Dr. Hoyle, "Egyptological Collections," *MJ* 8.5 (Nov. 1908): 152–62. While generally enthusiastic to the idea of groups, some British critics, including Alfred Cort Haddon, blamed their high cost as the key reason why so few museums had adopted these "popular" or "synthetic" display methods.

48. Holmes, "Classification and Arrangement," 360.

49. Mark B. Sandberg, "Effigy and Narrative: Looking into the Nineteenth-Century Folk Museum," in Leo Charney and Vanessa R. Schwartz, eds., *Cinema and the Invention of Modern Life*, 321.

50. Haraway, *Primate Visions*, 29.

51. Letter to Jesup from Putnam, Nov. 6, 1894, p. 8 (Putnam file, DA-AMNH). In addition to recommending that data be collected from living American Indians, Putnam also stressed the urgency of collecting skeletons, crania, and "casts of the soft parts of the body" such as the brain and nervous system which, Putnam argued, had "so much to do with a full understanding of man's characters and special abilities and adaptation to peculiar conditions of life" (10).

52. Martin Meisel, *Realizations: Narrative, Pictorial, and Theatrical Arts in Nineteenth-Century England*, 45. For more on tableaux and *tableaux vivant*, see 45–51.

53. Meisel used the example of Aaron Hill's MEROPE (1749–1750) in which the audience, having "been treated to a vigorous verbal description of the butchery and its setting" is shown the aftermath of the sacrificial ax killing (*Realizations*, 47).

54. Ibid.

55. For more on nineteenth-century pictorial realism in theatrical staging techniques,

see A. Nicholas Vardac, *From Stage to Screen: Theatrical Origins of Early Film—David Garrick to D. W. Griffith*, esp. chs. 2, 3, and 4.

56. Mary Chapman, " 'Living Pictures': Women and *Tableaux Vivant* in Nineteenth-Century American Fiction and Culture," *Wide Angle* 18.3 (part 2) (July 1996): 24.

57. For more on taxidermy in relation to habitat groups, see Karen Wonders, "The Art of Taxidermy, 1800–1900," in Wonders, *Habitat Dioramas: Illusion of Wilderness in Museums of Natural History*, 23–45.

58. See, for example, the family group cooking in front of the hut (reminiscent of the Pygmy life group shown in figure 1.6.) in the film *Revelations from the Land of the Burning Sand (The Mysteries of the Dark Continent)* (France, 1926), housed at the Nederlands Filmmuseum Archive).

59. Dolf Sternberger, *Panoramas of the Nineteenth Century*, 13, cited in Karen Wonders, "The Illusionary Art of Background Painting in Dioramas," *Curator* 33.2 (1990): 91. For an interesting discussion of the optical techniques and exhibition of dioramas in Great Britain in the early nineteenth century, see R. Derek Wood, "The Diorama in Great Britain in the 1820s," *History of Photography* 17.3 (Autumn 1993): 284–95. Also see chs. 10 to 15 of Richard D. Altick's *The Shows of London* for a detailed history of panoramas and dioramas.

60. Quoted in Helmut and Alison Gernsheim, *L. J. M. Daguerre*, 2d ed. (New York: Dover, 1968), 11, cited in Wonders, "The Illusionary Art," 92.

61. S. A. Barrett, "Photographic and Panoramic Backgrounds: Anthropological Groups," *Museum Work* 1 (June 1918–May 1919): 76. The life masks were also used to prepare a series of busts for the AMNH's Races of Man exhibit, while the paintings, in addition to giving information regarding skin tone, were also intended for exhibition in the Races of Man gallery (76). The process of obtaining life masks demanded considerable cooperation from the native participant, as the author of "The Museum's Collection of Life Casts" noted in 1912: "Formerly the man who allowed a plaster model of his head to be taken was subjected to considerable discomfort, which resulted in a cast in which features were so distorted that it could serve only as a basis from which the sculptor modeled the finished bust; but since the paraffin method has been in use the cast can be gained without distress to the subject, therefore the expression remains true to life and all measurements are accurate" (*AMJ* 12.1 (Jan. 1912): 29). The man responsible for producing the facial life casts at the AMNH was Casper Mayer; writing to Boas from the field in 1897, Mayer said that "the Indians did not want plaster on their faces in the beginning but after a while they agreed." Letter to Boas from Mayer (Mayer file 1897, DA-AMNH).

62. Sandberg, "Effigy and Narrative," 331.

63. Ibid.

64. The system of anchoring the ethnographic meaning of physical objects through

accompanying visual representations such as photographs was advocated as early as 1893 by British anthropologist Everard im Thurn, who recommended that the artifacts should always be featured alongside a photograph, preferably depicting the native object in its original context. E. F. im Thurn, "Anthropological Uses of the Camera," *JAI* 22 (1893): 195. I discuss im Thurn's contributions to anthropological photography in chapter 3.

65. Holmes, "Classification and Arrangement," 357.

66. Mayer, "Educational Efficiency," 567.

67. Holmes, "Classification and Arrangement," 355.

68. A number of writers at the time singled out the AMNH for its excellent label-writing. Sherman Langdon, for example, wrote in 1906 that "everything is concrete, and above all human, in its appeal. We are tricked into reading sentence after sentence, and then wild horses would not drag us from examining specimens so fetchingly advertised." Langdon, "The New Museum Idea," *World's Work* 12.3 (July 1906): 7711.

69. Holmes, "Classification and Arrangement," 258, 271.

70. Letter from Boas to Frederick Ward Putnam Nov. 7, 1896, cited in Ira Jacknis, "Franz Boas and Exhibits: On the Limitations of the Museum Method of Anthropology," in George W. Stocking Jr., ed., *Objects and Others: Essays on Museums and Material Culture*, 101 (emphasis in original).

71. Boas, "Some Principles," 925.

72. Ibid., 923.

73. Everett Wallace Smith, "Natural Science for the Every-Day Man," *Outlook* 89.4 (May 23, 1908): 183. A sense of unease over the uncanny quality of the human replicant, especially over spectators' scopophilic fascination with the body and *tout ensemble* Otherness of the represented, has resurfaced throughout the history of ethnographic filmmaking and is also present in psychoanalytic accounts of the cinematic apparatus explored by cinema theorists such as Christian Metz and Jean-Louis Baudry. Christian Metz, *The Imaginary Signifier*; and Jean-Louis Baudry, "Ideological Effects of the Basic Cinematic Apparatus," trans. Alan Williams, *Film Quarterly* 28.2 (Winter 1974–55); reprinted in Gerald Mast, Marshall Cohen, and Leo Braudy, eds., *Film Theory and Criticism*, 302–312.

74. Letter from Boas to Frederick Ward Putnam, July 11, 1896, cited in Jacknis, "Boas and Exhibits," 102.

75. Boas to Putnam, ibid.

76. Ibid., 100. Boas was concerned that attention to scientific detail and precise information would become marginalized through the popularization of science, which for him was an endeavor to "bring out the sublimity of truth and the earnest efforts that are needed to acquire it." For Boas, "every kind of inaccuracy should be most carefully avoided, and attempts to make all problems appear childishly simple by the elimination

of everything that is obscure should not be tolerated." Boas therefore advocated displaying objects in front of neutral backgrounds in the hope that some subject would grab the attention of the visitor and convey additional information either via the label or surrounding specimens. For an extended discussion of the interrelationship of these goals, see Boas, "Some Principles," 921–33.

77. Mrs. Roesler, "The Work of an Instructor in the American Museum of Natural History," *MJ* 8.9 (Mar. 1909): 306.

78. For more on these debates as they played out in Scandinavia, see Sandberg, "Effigy and Narrative," 326–27.

79. "Art in a Natural History Museum with Special Reference to Mural Decorations in the Indian Halls," *AMJ* 7.3 (Mar. 1913): 101.

80. AMNH *Annual Report* (1911), 23.

81. The spectacularizing tendencies of the natural history museum life group exhibit were, in some ways, exacerbated by the use of narrativizing techniques that were considered by many crucial to the dissemination of ethnographic meaning in the life group; in 1903, Alfred Goldsborough Mayer compared the entire contents of a museum exhibition to a narrative, with individual specimens analogized as "sentences composing the story," and as late as 1918, S. A. Barrett argued that life groups told "stories of truly aboriginal life before its contamination with the whites." Euro-American contact with the tribe represented was not, however, totally eclipsed from the display; in order to insert the group within a history of native-white interaction, a scene depicting an early historical event showing white settlers or explorers in contact with the tribe was placed above the display case. According to Barrett, this technique "forms a very pleasing auxiliary to the group and teaches a very valuable additional lesson." Mayer, "Educational Efficiency," 564, and Barrett, "Photographic Backgrounds," 76–77.

82. Frederic A. Lucas, "The Story of Museum Groups: Part II," *AMJ* 14.2 (Feb. 1914): 7, 10.

83. That life groups were concerned with distinctly modern methods of museological display is suggested in a 1906 article published in *MJ* from 1906. According to the author, "the old sash-framed cases which were obsolete have nearly all disappeared and in their place are handsome cases of the newest type, in which zoological specimens, in groups, with their natural surroundings are seen to the greatest advantage, and which it is hoped convey correct ideas to the observer." "National Museums: British Museum," *MJ* 5.12 (June 1906): 78.

84. George A. Dorsey, "The Anthropological Exhibits at the American Museum of Natural History," *Science* 25.641 (Apr. 12, 1907): 588.

85. Henry L. Ward, "The Anthropological Exhibits in the American Museum of Natural History," *Science* 25.645 (May 10, 1907): 745.

86. William Ryan Chapman, "Arranging Ethnology: A.H.F.L. Pitt Rivers and the

Typological Tradition," in Stocking, ed., *Objects and Others*, 43.

87. Ward, "Anthropological Exhibits," 745.

88. Maurice A. Bigelow, "Educational Value of the American Museum," *AMJ* 11.7 (Nov. 1911): 234.

89. For a later discussion of the defects of the habitat group, see Frank Tose, "Comments Upon the Habitat Groups in the California Academy of Sciences," *Museum News* 8.10 (Nov. 15, 1929): 7–8.

90. "Art in a Natural History Museum," 99.

91. Haraway, *Primate Visions*, 40.

92. Charles Waterton, *Essays on Natural History Chiefly Ornithology* (1838), cited in Stephen Bann, *The Clothing of Clio: A Study of the Representation of History in Nineteenth-Century Britain and France*, 17.

93. For another contemporaneous discussion of taxidermy and its attendant difficulties see W. P. Pycraft, "Some Common Errors in the Representation of Stuffed Birds in Museums," *MJ* 3.9 (Mar. 1904): 288–93, and (anonymous author) "Taxidermy at Darmstadt," *MJ* 4.5 (Nov. 1904): 167–68.

94. Haraway, *Primate Visions*, 44.

95. Ibid., 30.

96. Bann, *The Clothing of Clio*, 17.

97. Lucas, "Story of Museum Groups I," 13.

98. Pitt-Rivers, "Typological Museums," 116.

99. A primitive forerunner of the habitat group was the ornamental arrangement of birds on a bush in a glass case, a popular centerpiece in Victorian homes before making its appearance in museums. A. E. Parr proposes that these "conversation pieces" may have suggested the idea of the habitat group to curators, although he notes that they initially took the form of what he calls a "semi-habitat" group, which did not create the illusion of the bird's larger environment (as later habitat groups did) but simply reproduced a "small, rectangular section of nature entirely removed from its normal surroundings." These groups could be viewed from three, or even four sides, since they did not use background painting to form an integrated whole with the foreground and gave no impression of distance. A. E. Parr, "The Habitat Group," *Curator* 2.2 (1959): 107; also see Parr's essay, "Dimensions, Backgrounds, and Uses of Habitat Groups," *Curator* 4.3 (1961): 199–215, for a detailed discussion of the relationship between foreground and background in habitat groups.

100. Parr, "Habitat Group," 113.

101. Lucas, "Story of Museum Groups II," 61.

102. Sandberg, "Effigy and Narrative," 322.

103. The Swede Artur Hazelius is often credited as being one of the earliest proponents of the life group. Hazelius began collecting Swedish ethnographic materials in

1872, and in 1878 exhibited wax figures in dramatic tableaux or "living pictures" at the Universal Exposition in Paris. In 1891 he created an open-air museum in Sweden called Skansen that contained reconstructions of buildings and scenes from Swedish folklife. Docents dressed in costumes would mingle with members of the public. For background information on Hazelius and the visual logic of the folk museum, especially issues of corporeality and narrativity, see Sandberg, "Effigy and Narrative," 320–61. Also see Edward P. Alexander, "Artur Hazelius and Skansen: The Open Air Museum," in *Museum Masters: Their Museums and Their Influence*, 241–75.

104. Marina Warner, "Waxworks and Wonderlands," in Lynne Cook and Peter Wollen, eds., *Visual Display: Culture Beyond Appearances*, 187. Born Marie Gresholtz in 1760, Madame Tussaud was the niece of the Swiss physician Philippe Curtius, who began teaching the art of waxworks (ceroplastics) in Paris in 1766. Tussaud learned the craft from her uncle (180).

105. Ludmilla Jordanova, "Objects of Knowledge: A Historical Perspective on Museums," in Peter Vergo, ed., *The New Museology*, 35–36.

106. Giuliana Bruno, *Streetwalking on a Ruined Map: Cultural Theory and the City Films of Elvira Notari*, 61. For Bruno, the analytic desire inscribed into the spectacle of the eighteenth-century anatomy lesson is present in the language of film and its spectatorial codes and "strongly instantiated in early cinematic forms, which were obsessed with investigating and performing acts upon the body" (ibid.).

107. The museum grew from Peale's efforts to exhibit his paintings in a portrait gallery. Following the suggestion of a friend to exhibit some natural history specimens Peale happened to own, the museum ended up displaying collections of art, natural history, technology, and science. Information from Sidney Hart and David C. Ward, "The Waning of an Enlightenment Ideal: Charles Willson Peale's Philadelphia Museum, 1790–1820," in Lillian B. Miller and David C. Ward, eds., *New Perspectives on Charles Willson Peale*, 220. Also see David R. Brigham, *Public Culture in the Early Republic: Peale's Museum and Its Audience*; and Edward P. Alexander, "Charles Willson Peale and His Philadelphia Museum: The Concept of a Popular Museum," in *Museum Masters*, 45–77, for background information on Peale's museum.

108. Reverent Manasseh Cutler quoted in Charles Coleman Sellers, *Charles Willson Peale* (New York: Scribner's, 1969), 221. Literary theorist Susan Stewart notes that in addition to the vast collection of paintings and occasional waxwork, Peale was also interested in embalming and wanted to find ways of using " 'powerful antisepticks' to preserve the remains of great men, thereby keeping their bodies from becoming the 'food of worms' and making them available for memorial reverence." Stewart, "Death and Life, in that Order, in the Works of Charles Willson Peale," in John Elsner and Roger Cardinal, eds., *The Cultures of Collecting*, 212–13.

109. According to Bazin, "The guiding myth . . . inspiring the invention of cinema,

is the accomplishment of that which dominated in more or less vague fashion all the techniques of the mechanical reproduction of reality in the nineteenth century, from photography to the phonograph, namely an integral realism, a recreation of the world in its own image, an image unburdened by the freedom of interpretation of the artist or the irreversibility of time. . . . Every new development added to the cinema must, paradoxically, take it nearer and nearer to its origins. In short cinema has not yet been invented!" Bazin, "The Myth of Total Cinema," in Bazin, *What Is Cinema?* 2:21, ed. Hugh Gray; also see "The Ontology of the Photographic Image" in the same volume (9–16).

110. Walter Benjamin, "The Work of Art in the Age of Mechanical Reproduction," in Hannah Arendt, ed., *Illuminations*, 217–52.

111. Marina Warner's account of the waxwork evokes the similar apparatical pleasure of an early "cinema of attractions," since part of the appeal of the celebrity waxwork stems from the irrevocable hold it exerts over our imaginations and its hierarchical placement of affect and spectacle over cognitive and narrative comprehension: "The subjects are drained of semantic and narrative particularity while simultaneously crammed and heaped with visual and tactile specifications. Story cedes to spectacle . . . encouraging the mythic imagination of the visitor to make up for the semantic emptiness" (Warner, "Waxworks," 196–97). While Warner's point of reference here is the practice of displaying waxworks of historical personages or celebrities in noncontextual settings, her argument concerning the haptic and phantasmatic qualities of the waxwork is equally applicable to the human life group.

112. Haraway, *Primate Visions*, 29.

113. Cultural historian Vanessa R. Schwartz has explored this fascination with lifelike attractions in the context of turn-of-the-century Parisians' patronage of the public morgue, the wax museum, and panoramas. Schwartz describes visitors' enthusiastic excursions to the morgue in order to gaze at unidentified cadavers as a form of public voyeurism, in which a sensational interest in real events was justified as a form of civic duty. Indeed, the morgue was even more fascinating than the wax museum because of the double signification of the exhibits (actual bodies as opposed to representations of the dead) and, as Schwartz points out, because "like the newspapers, the morgue re-presented a spectacularized Parisian life." Schwartz, "Cinematic Spectatorship Before the Apparatus: The Public Taste for Reality in Fin-de-Siècle Paris," in Linda Williams, ed., *Viewing Positions: Ways of Seeing Film*, 93.

114. Anne Friedberg, *Window Shopping: Cinema and the Postmodern*, 68.

115. Sandberg, "Effigy and Narrative," 337.

116. Tom Gunning, "An Aesthetic of Astonishment: Early Film and the (In)Credulous Spectator," *Art and Text* 34 (Spring 1989): 33–34.

117. Sandberg, "Effigy and Narrative," 333.

118. Langdon, "The New Museum Idea," 7711.

119. Friedberg, *Window Shopping*, 2.

120. Ibid., 37.

121. Ibid., 2.

122. The genealogy of promenade theater can be traced to medieval staging techniques in which the life of Christ and other biblical narratives were performed in different locations within a church. The performance sites were set up on each side of the central nave, constituting the separate scenes of the play. Referred to as either mansions, houses, or booths, these liturgical dramas later moved outside the church and utilized either static or perambulating staging techniques (the latter was more common in England). In the static design, audiences would be seated either in a straight line in front of the action or grouped on a platform with the action all around them (an early form of theater-in-the-round). In the perambulating form, the action moved to the spectators since each emblematic setting was mounted on a two-story pageant or cart that paraded through a town or village where the actors repeated the play at each stopping place in front of a group of spectators. The audience remained at each location and viewed the drama unfolding over an entire day. For background reading on these staging practices, see William Tydeman, *The Theatre in the Middle Ages* (Cambridge: Cambridge University Press, 1978), and Glynne Wickham, *The Medieval Theatre* (Cambridge: Cambridge University Press, 1987). A homology between theatrical spectatorship and museum-going is suggested by museum historian and theorist Susan M. Pearce when she says that "each [museum] exhibition is a production, like a theatrical production, and like a play, it is a specific work of culture with game rules of its own" (*Museums, Objects, and Collections: A Cultural Study*, 136–37).

123. Boas to Frederick Ward Putnam, 1896 (Frederick Ward Putnam Papers, Harvard University Archives, Pusey Library, Cambridge, Mass.), cited in Jacknis, "Boas and Exhibits," 102.

124. Wallace, "Museums for the People," 247, and Everett Wallace Smith, "Natural Science," 184.

125. Bather, "Presidential Address," 82.

126. Barrett, "Photographic Backgrounds," 77.

127. Carl Akeley, "The New Akeley Hall Planned by Carl E. Akeley," *AMJ* 14.5 (May 1914): 183.

128. Akeley to Henry Fairfield Osborn, Mar. 29, 1911, cited in John Michael Kennedy, "Philanthropy and Science in New York City: The American Museum of Natural History, 1868–1969" (Ph.D. diss., Yale University, 1968), 49.

129. Haraway, *Primate Visions*, 29.

130. Herbert Adams Gibbons, *John Wanamaker*, 2 vols. (New York: Harper, 1926), 238–42, cited in Simon J. Bronner, ed., *Consuming Visions: Accumulation and Display of Goods in America, 1880–1920*, 233.

131. Simon J. Bronner, "Object Lessons: The Work of Ethnological Museums and Collections," in Bronner, ed., *Consuming Visions*, 233.

132. Ibid., 233–34.

133. The author of "Art in a Natural History Museum" went so far as to claim that "in large part the province of telling the cultures and lives of the people represented in any hall must be relegated to mural decorations on the large wall spaces," since in the case of life groups, the installation "tends to lose in artistic value." Will S. Taylor's "The Salmon Fishers" mural from the North Pacific Series (1913) and E. M. Deming's panel groups for the Plains Indian Hall (1913) are two noted examples discussed in this article.

2. SCIENCE AND SPECTACLE: VISUALIZING THE OTHER AT THE WORLD'S FAIR

1. F. W. Putnam, "Introduction," in *Portrait Types of the Midway Plaisance*, i.

2. Mary Bronson Hartt, "The Play-Side of the Fair," *World's Work* II, no. 4 (Aug. 1901): 1097.

3. Robert W. Rydell, "The Culture of Imperial Abundance: World's Fairs in the Making of American Culture," in Bronner, ed., *Consuming Visions*, 195–96.

4. For a cultural studies approach to the study of world's fairs that links the fairs to some of the broader historical tensions of their times, see Robert W. Rydell, John E. Findling, and Kimberly D. Pelle, eds., *Fair America: World's Fairs in the United States*.

5. As Rydell notes, substantial collections in the following museums were derived from world's fairs, with some institutions even owing their existence to world's fairs: Museum of Man, San Diego; the Field Museum of Natural History, Chicago, and the Museum of Science and Industry, Chicago; the Commercial Museum, Philadelphia; and many of the Smithsonian Institution's museums. Rydell, "Culture of Imperial Abundance,," 210–11.

6. Ibid., 193.

7. Prior to its professionalization as an academic discipline encompassing the fields of physical anthropology, archaeology, linguistics, and cultural anthropology, anthropology was conceived of as "an overarching science that embraced diverse yet interrelated lines of inquiry and encouraged interest and support of a wide range of men and women" (Curtis M. Hinsley, "Amateurs and Professionals in Washington Anthropology, 1879–1903," in John V. Murra, ed., *American Anthropology: The Early Years*, 39). Anthropology's sprawling roots were reflected in the backgrounds of the members of the Anthropological Society of New York, who would meet in the homes of the city's elite to share published and unpublished accounts of their latest forays into the world of the ethnographic Other. In this setting, geographers, lawyers, doctors, historians, archaeologists, travel writers, members of the clergy, and even literary critics could

claim knowledge about the world and its distinct cultures. United by a desire to participate in a "larger, perhaps universal quest" for the "secrets of man's origins," extensive
training and specialized knowledge was not considered an impediment to participation.
Otis T. Mason, "What Is Anthropology?" (Saturday Morning Lecture, Smithsonian
Institution, Mar. 18, 1882), 5, cited in Hinsley, "Amateurs and Professionals," 39.

8. William Ordway Partridge, "The Educational Value of World's Fairs," *Forum* 33
(Mar. 1902): 125.

9. R. Reid Badger, *The Great American Fair*, 104, cited in Burton Benedict et al.,
Anthropology of World's Fairs, 49.

10. Benedict, *Anthropology*, 116.

11. Despite the proclaimed scientific and pedagogical aims of these exhibits, by inviting Western visitors to make objectified comparisons between white and nonwhite physical types and have their measurements taken, they risked pandering to existing preju-
dices. Melissa Banta and Curtis M. Hinsley, *From Site to Sight: Anthropology, Photography,
and the Power of Imagery*, 61.

12. George Brown Goode, "First Draft of a System of Classification for the World's
Columbian Exposition," cited in Robert W. Rydell, *All the World's a Fair: Visions of Empire
at American International Expositions, 1876–1916*, 45; Arthur Goodrich, "Short Stories of
Interesting Exhibits," *World's Work* 2.4 (Aug. 1901): 1054.

13. Corbey, "Ethnographic Showcases," 360. As Barbara Kirshenblatt-Gimblett
argues, the "gallery of nations" trope has served as an organizing principle for a wide
range of literary works since the sixteenth century (particularly books on world reli-
gions, costumes, manners, and customs) and was easily appropriated by designers of
ethnographic exhibitions and in turn by ethnographic cinema. Barbara Kirshenblatt-
Gimblett, "Objects of Ethnography," in Karp and Lavine, eds., *Exhibiting Cultures*, 399.

14. Of course, as evidence of a determinant visual and physiognomic structure, the
ethnographic "type" was also closely bound up with theories of biological determinism
and was, in Deborah Poole's view, a crucial "strategy for disciplining the scientific gaze."
According to Poole, "the transformation in racial thinking that took place during the
early decades of the nineteenth century from a genealogical or historical paradigm of
racial identity to the objectifying discourse of biologically determined racial types was
conditioned by this visual discourse of type." Deborah Poole, *Vision, Race, and Modernity:
A Visual Economy of the Andean Image World*, 103.

15. Corbey, "Ethnographic Showcases," 364.

16. See, for example, Paul Greenhalgh, *Ephemeral Vistas: The Expositions Universalles,
Great Exhibitions, and World Fairs, 1851–1939*, 92; Corbey, "Ethnographic Showcases," 344;
and Brian Street, "British Popular Anthropology: Exhibiting and Photographing the
Other," in Edwards, ed., *Anthropology and Photography*, 122.

17. Dean MacCannell, *The Tourist: A New Theory of the Leisure Class*, 91–107, cited in
Kirshenblatt-Gimblett, "Objects of Ethnography," 407–408.

18. Kirshenblatt-Gimblett, "Objects of Ethnography," 415, 420.

19. Corbey, "Ethnographic Showcases," 364.

20. Steven Mullaney, "Strange Things, Gross Terms, Curious Customs: The Rehearsal of Cultures in the Late Renaissance," *Representations* 3 (Summer 1983): 48.

21. Ibid.

22. Kirshenblatt-Gimblett, "Objects of Ethnography," 397.

23. For a discussion of the use of gendered colonial metaphors in this configuration, see Ella Shohat, "Gender and the Culture of Empire: Towards a Feminist Ethnography of the Cinema," *Quarterly Review of Film and Video* 131.1–3 (Spring 1991): 45–84.

24. George Catlin, *Proposal*, cited in Roslyn Poignant, "Surveying the Field of View: The Making of the RAI Photographic Collection," in Edwards, ed., *Anthropology and Photography*, 51.

25. Rosemarie Garland Thomson, "Introduction: From Wonder to Error—A Genealogy of Freak Discourse in Modernity," in Thomson, ed., *Freakery: Cultural Spectacles of the Extraordinary Body*, 4–5.

26. P. T. Barnum, *Selected Letters of P. T. Barnum*, ed. and with an introduction by A. H. Saxon (New York: Columbia University Press, 1983), 226.

27. According to Thomson, Barnum gathered an astonishing array of "corporeal wonders, from wild men of Borneo to fat ladies, living skeletons, Fiji princes, albinos, bearded women, Siamese twins, tattooed Circasians, armless and legless wonders, Chinese giants, cannibals, midget triplets, hermaphrodites, spotted boys and much more" (Thomson, "Introduction," *Freakery*, 5).

28. "Out of the Ashes," *Chicago Tribune*, June 6, 1883, 8. Barnum's Ethnological Congress shared more than a structural affinity with the living villages at world's fairs; reviving the Ethnological Congress in 1893, two years after Barnum's death, Barnum's partner William Bailey recruited native peoples who had appeared at the Chicago World's Fair. See Robert Bogdan, *Freak Show: Presenting Human Oddities for Amusement and Profit*, 185. For contemporaneous responses to Barnum's "Congress of Nations" and "Ethnological Congress," see Bluford Adams, *E. Pluribus Barnum: The Great Showman and the Making of U.S. Popular Culture*.

29. The term "enfreakment" is from David Hevey, *The Creatures That Time Forgot: Photography and Disability Imagery*, 53, cited in Thomson, ed., *Freakery*, 10.

30. James W. Cook Jr., "Of Men, Missing Links, and Nondescripts: The Strange Career of P. T. Barnum's 'What is It?' Exhibition," in Thomson, ed., *Freakery*, 140.

31. George W. Stocking Jr., "What's in a Name? The Origins of the Royal Anthropological Institute (1837–71)," *Man* 6 (1971): 373.

32. Benedict, *Anthropology*, 46.

33. Annie E. S. Coombes, *Reinventing Africa: Museums, Material Culture, and Popular Imagination in Late Victorian and Edwardian England*, 63.

34. Descriptions used in the captions accompanying photographs in *Midway Types: A Book of Illustrated Lessons About the People of the Midway Plaisance, World's Fair, 1893*.

35. Otis T. Mason, "Anthropology in Paris During the Exposition of 1889," *American Anthropologist* 3 (Jan. 1890): 31.

36. J. Q. Smith to Secretary of the Interior, Apr. 29, 1876, cited in Robert A. Trennert Jr., "A Grand Failure: The Centennial Indian Exhibition of 1876," *Prologue* 6.2 (Summer 1974): 126.

37. The "Wild Men of Borneo" were in fact Hirma and Barney Davies, two mentally and physically handicapped white children from Ohio who had been the main attraction in a dime museum run by one of Barnum's competitors. In a commercialized masquerade of their deformities, their act required them to "talk strange gibberish" and "scurry about . . . snapping and snarling, adorned with chains." According to Bogdan, the exhibition evolved into an elaborate story about the origins of the "Wild Men." In 1878, for example, spectators could buy a sixteen-page pamphlet describing the capture of "Waino" and "Plutano" on the rocky coast of Borneo in 1848. As well as furnishing vivid details of their capture, the booklet also contained accurate information about climate, geography, fauna, and flora. This seamless blending of fact and fiction typified the promotional techniques used in popular constructions of "savages"; in the case of the "Wild Men," Darwinian theories of evolution were summoned to explain their "marvelous prehensile power" and part human/part ape dexterity. Bogdan, *Freak Show*, 122–24.

38. James D. McCabe, *The Illustrated History of the Centennial Exhibition Held in Commemoration of the One Hundredth Anniversary of American Independence*, 302–15, cited in Rydell, *All the World's a Fair*, 34.

39. James Mooney to W. J. McGee, Sept. 27, 1898, Bureau of American Ethnology papers, cited in Ira Jacknis, "In Search of the Imagemaker: James Mooney as an Ethnographic Photographer," *Visual Anthropology* 3.2 (1992): 183.

40. The Chicago World's Fair drew the largest crowd of all the American fairs held during this era; more than 25 million Americans out of a national population of 70 million visited the grounds. While anthropologists such as Frederick Ward Putnam attested to the ethnological value of the Javanese, Samoan, and Dahomeyan villages located on the Midway, guidebooks for the exposition recommended that visitors should only pay the Midway a visit after having first exhausted their time in the White City and national exhibits.

41. By way of preempting the insalubrious appeal of the Midway, the planners gave the Department of Ethnology jurisdiction over the space, although from all accounts this had little impact on visitors' perceptions of the Midway. Rather than let Putnam oversee the installation of the concessions and exhibits on the Midway, Exposition planners hired a 21-year-old San Francisco entrepreneur named Sol Bloom, who had signed

up a troop of "dancers, acrobats, glass-eaters and scorpion swallowers" at the Paris Exposition in 1889, to take charge of the Midway. Sol Bloom, *The Autobiography of Sol Bloom*, 107, cited in Benedict, *Anthropology*, 49.

42. Rydell, *All the World's a Fair*, 62–63. Although Bloom and Putnam worked separately throughout the planning stage, the net result of their efforts was, in Rydell's words, "an alliance between entertainment and anthropology replicated in subsequent fairs." While Bloom "had no quarrel with Putnam's scientific capabilities," he later claimed that putting Putnam in charge of the exhibits would have been "tantamount to making Albert Einstein manager of Barnum and Bailey's Circus" (ibid., 63).

43. Marianna G. van Rensselaer, "At the Fair," *Century Magazine* 46 (May 1893): 12–13, cited in Robert W. Rydell, "The World's Columbian Exposition of 1893: Racist Underpinnings of a Utopian Artifact," *Journal of American Culture* 1 (1978): 257.

44. Meg Armstrong, " 'A Jumble of Foreignness': The Sublime Musayums of Nineteenth-Century Fairs and Expositions," *Cultural Critique* 23 (Winter 1992–93): 208.

45. Denton J. Snider, *World's Fair Studies*, 255–57.

46. Ella Shohat and Robert Stam, *Unthinking Eurocentrism: Multiculturalism and the Media*, 108.

47. However, Tom Gunning has argued that rather than buttress the ideological work taking place in the official St. Louis World's Fair (1904), the Midway had the effect of demystifying and desublimating the pretension of the official exposition. Gunning, "The World as Object Lesson: Cinema Audiences, Visual Culture, and the St. Louis World's Fair, 1904," *Film History* 6.4 (Winter 1994): 431–32.

48. Armstrong, " 'A Jumble of Foreignness,' " 207.

49. For a discussion of some of the reasons behind the divergent attitudes toward the Chinese and Japanese at the 1893 exposition, see Neil Harris, "All the World a Melting Pot? Japan at American Fairs, 1876–1904," in Harris, *Cultural Excursions: Marketing Appetites and Cultural Taste in Modern America*, 29–55. Also see Rydell, *All the World's a Fair*, 30–31 and 49–52.

50. Frederick Ward Putnam, *World's Columbian Exposition: Plan and Classification*, 8–9, cited in Rydell, *All the World's a Fair*, 63. In addition to his role as director of Division M, which included overseeing the Midway's ethnological concessions as well as the official anthropological exhibits, Putnam continued as head of Harvard's Peabody Museum of American Archaeology and Ethnology and served as permanent secretary of the American Association for the Advancement of Science. For an interesting discussion of some of the challenges Putnam faced organizing the anthropology exhibit, see Ralph W. Dexter, "Putnam's Problems Popularizing Anthropology," *American Scientist* 54.3 (1966): 315–32.

51. T. R. MacMechan, "Down 'The Pike': The 'Boulevard of Gaiety' at the St. Louis Exposition," *Pacific Monthly* 12 (July 1904): 30.

52. William Dean Howells, "A Sennight of the Centennial," *Atlantic Monthly* 38 (July 1876): 97, cited in Rydell, *All the World's a Fair*, 14. Indeed, As Rydell points out, Native Americans participating in the 1876 exposition were subject to frequent abuse and ridicule from fairgoers and treated as "apocalyptic threats to the values embodied in the White City" (Rydell, *All the World's a Fair*, 63).

53. W. J. McGee, "Strange Races of Men," *World's Work* 3.4 (Aug. 1904): 5188.

54. Curtis M. Hinsley, "Anthropology as Science and Politics: The Dilemmas of the Bureau of American Ethnology, 1879–1904," in Walter R. Goldschmidt, ed., *The Uses of Anthropology*, 17. For example, in 1853, Smithsonian philologist William W. Turner optimistically offered anthropology as an instrument for both the organized religious conversion of the "heathen Indian," and the eradication of white ignorance and prejudice toward Native Americans. Despite the perennial appeal of the allochronic Other as anthropological subject, the impact of modern Europeans upon primitive cultures (and vice versa) became an ongoing preoccupation of anthropologists. Within an ascendant positivist epistemology, such "scientific" knowledge about Native Americans provided a legitimizing tool for anthropology at a time when concerns over assimilation, reservation policy, and the closing of the frontier became urgent matters of popular and political debate. Ibid., 19.

55. Otis T. Mason, "Summary of Progress in Anthropology," *Annual Reports of the Smithsonian Institution for the Year Ending July 1893*, 605.

56. Edward B. McDowell, "The World's Fair Cosmopolis." *Frank Leslie's Monthly* 36 (Oct. 1893): 415–16.

57. Ibid.

58. Christopher A. Vaughan, "Ogling Igorots: The Politics and Commerce of Exhibiting Cultural Otherness, 1898–1913," in Thomson, ed., *Freakery*, 219.

59. Ibid., 224. For a discussion of earlier displays of Filipinos at world's fairs, see Vaughan, "Ogling Igorots," 21. For an analysis of the Philippine Reservation and how it was photographed, see "The Philippine Reservation: Igorots, Bagobos, and 'The Missing Link,' " in Eric Breitbart, *A World on Display: Photographs from the St. Louis World's Fair, 1904*, 51–69. Breitbart also examines the representation of American Indians, Ainu, and Pygmy peoples at the St. Louis World's Fair, dealing with such issues as authenticity, reconstruction, and the indexicality of the images produced as part of the exposition.

60. Rydell, *All the World's a Fair*, 172.

61. National Archives and Records Administration (hereafter, NARA), Washington, D.C., Record Group (RG) 350, file 9640/3, cited in Vaughan, "Ogling Igorots," 224–25.

62. Vaughan, ibid., 173.

63. NARA, RG 350, file 9640/18, cited in ibid., 225; Frederick Starr, cited in memorandum from Clarence Edwards to William P. Wilson, July 6, 1904, Record of the Bureau of Insular Affairs, RG 350, General Classified Files, no. 9640-22, cited in Rydell, *All the World's a Fair*, 174.

64. "Igorrotes [*sic*] Not to Wear Breeches," *St. Louis Globe-Democrat*, July 15, 1904, 1, cited in Rydell, ibid., 174.

65. Vaughan, "Ogling Igorots," 225–26.

66. This view was promulgated by G. S. Johns, editor of the *St. Louis Post-Dispatch*, July 3, 1904, 1, and endorsed by Frederick Starr in a memo to William P. Wilson, cited in Rydell, *All the World's a Fair*, 174.

67. Contracts were generally worked out with scientists and showmen such as Xavier Pene specifying the content of the ethnological exhibits, ensuring that evolutionist theories were an integral part of the overall display, and that the people exhibited were "genuine" representatives of their race.

68. *Darkest Africa: Real African Life in a Real African Village* (souvenir guide), n.p., in Buffalo Historical Society, "Scientific Exhibits," vertical file cited in Rydell, *All the World's a Fair*, 146.

69. *French Exposition*, Earl's Court, Daily Program (Oct. 7, 1890), cited in Coombes, *Reinventing Africa*, 97; McDowell, "The World's Fair Cosmopolis," 415. The Dahomeyans were considered by most contemporary critics to be at the very bottom of the evolutionary ladder and elicited consistently negative reactions. Writing in the *Chautauquan* (Chautauqua, New York), John C. Eastman argued that the "Dahomans" (*sic*) were "more closely allied with the cruel and superstitious practices of savagery than any other country represented on the Midway." Their women were "as fierce if not fiercer than the men," and they had to be watched "day and night for fear they may use their spears for other purposes than a barbaric embellishment of their dances"; cited in "Village Life at the World's Fair," *The Chautauquan* 17 (1893): 603–604.

70. F. Hopkinson Smith, "The Picturesque Side," *Scribner's* 14.5 (Nov. 1893): 608.

71. My thanks to Robert Stam for drawing my attention to this tension.

72. Smith, "Picturesque Side," 608.

73. Ibid.

74. Kirshenblatt-Gimblett, "Objects of Ethnography," 428.

75. Rony, *Third Eye*, 43.

76. Rydell, "Culture of Imperial Abundance," 198.

77. Rony, *Third Eye*, 40.

78. Ibid., 43.

79. Many contemporary cinema scholars have pointed out the links between the figure of the nineteenth-century *flâneur* and the spectator of early cinema, especially as the nickelodeon joined other new urban heterotopias. See, for example, Miriam Hansen, *Babel and Babylon: Spectatorship in American Silent Film*; Bruno, *Streetwalking on a Ruined Map*; Anne Friedberg, *Window Shopping: Cinema and the Postmodern*; and Leo Charney and Vanessa R. Schwartz, eds., *Cinema and the Invention of Modern Life*.

80. Curtis M. Hinsley, "The World as Marketplace: Commodification of the Exotic

at the World's Columbian Exposition, Chicago, 1893," in Karp and Lavine, *Exhibiting Culture*, 356.

81. J. A. Mitchell, "Types and People at the Fair," *Scribner's* 14.2 (Aug. 1893): 186.

82. Tom Gunning, "From the Kaleidoscope to the X-Ray: Urban Spectatorship, Poe, Benjamin, and *Traffic in Souls* (1913)," *Wide Angle* 19.4 (1997): 29.

83. Possessing characteristics antithetical to the *flâneur*, the *badaud* gives up the "elbow room so essential for the *flâneur*, and allows himself to be jostled and absorbed by the crowd, a part of it rather than its observing decipherer" (ibid.).

84. Sophia A. Walker, "An Art Impression of the Exposition," *Independent* 53 (July 18, 1901): 1678, cited in Neil Harris, *Cultural Excursions*, 59.

85. See Rony, *Third Eye*, 39–41, for a discussion of the permeable boundaries between Self and Other at world's fairs.

86. Hartt, "The Play-Side," 1097.

87. Michel Foucault, "Of Other Spaces," *Diacritics* (Spring 1986): 25–26.

88. Ibid., 26.

89. Lumière shot several films of the 1900 Paris Universal Exposition, including one showing spectators getting on and off the moving sidewalk.

90. See Ellwood Parry, *The Image of the Indian and the Black Man in American Art, 1590–1900*, 87–91, for a discussion of John Banvard's famous panorama from 1846, which traveled to Louisville, Boston, New York, and finally, Europe, where it drew large crowds at the Egyptian Hall in London. On an enormous length of canvas, Banvard created one continuous view extending from the mouth of the Missouri River to New Orleans; at times the panorama detoured from the river to represent views of Indian life such as a Sioux war dance, a buffalo hunt, and the "City of the Dead" funeral ceremony in which bodies of the deceased were laid on platforms or in the branches of trees. Unlike the 360-degree circular diorama, Banvard's landscape was linear, which, in Parry's words, had the more "dramatic effect of moving and developing through time, like the unfolding plot of a story." The canvas unrolled in a two-dimensional plane across the back of a stage (where the machinery could be concealed), and each segment of the river-bank was seen from one direction only. Contemporaneous reviews of the panorama indicate that while audiences were impressed by the picturesque landscape, it was the views of native peoples that were considered the most impressive and popular. Wood engravings of the panorama were published in *People's and Howitt's Journal* in 1849 (87–89).

91. Gunning, "World as Object Lesson," 436.

92. For more on Hale's Tours, see Raymond Fielding, "Hale's Tours: Ultrarealism in the Pre-1910 Motion Picture," in John Fell, ed., *Film Before Griffith*, 116–30.

93. For more on panoramas, see Stephen Oettermann, *The Panorama: History of a Mass Medium*; Richard Altick, *The Shows of London*; and Vanessa Schwartz, *Spectacular Realities: Early Mass Culture in Fin-de-Siècle France*, 149–76.

94. Altick, *The Shows of London*, 460–61 and 465, cited in Benedict, *Anthropology*, 56.

95. Emmanuelle Toulet, "Cinema at the Universal Exposition, Paris, 1900," *Persistence of Vision* 9 (1991): 17.

96. Ibid., 18 and 20.

97. Benedict, *Anthropology*, 56.

98. Annie Coombes argues that such conveyances "cultivated at one and the same time, both a sense of the availability and containability of those societies represented." In the same way, she continues, the ethnological villages "successfully fostered a feeling of geographical proximity, while the sense of 'spectacle' was calculated to preserve the cultural divide." Coombes, "Museums and the Formation of National and Cultural Identities," *Oxford Art Journal* 11.2 (1988): 59.

99. Coombes, *Reinventing Africa*, 69.

100. Ibid. Coombes is here referring to the Stanley and African Exhibition, which opened at the Victoria Gallery in Regent Street, London, on March 24, 1890. She says that the "entrance to the exhibition was through a 'pallisade of . . . tree stems . . . ornamented with skulls' which led into a simulated explorer's camp, surrounded by a composite landscape supposedly representative of the key features of Central African territory, as 'discovered' by the European" (quoted in *The Stanley and African Catalogue of Exhibits* [1890], 9).

101. *Midway Types*, n.p.

102. *Official Guide to the World's Columbian Exposition*, 40–41. This outdoor exhibit was located on the bank of the South Pond in the southeastern portion of the fairgrounds, in between the Anthropology Building to the south and the INDIAN SCHOOL at the top of the South Loop. Both the CLIFF DWELLERS and the ESQUIMAUX VILLAGE charged a 50-cents entrance fee (entrance to the exposition was also 50 cents). The CLIFF DWELLERS consisted of an exact replica of Battle Rock mountain in the MacEimo valley of Colorado (made out of timber, iron, and stone and painted to "imitate nature." It was then covered with "forced growth of moss and vines"). Once inside, "the visitor may see all over the walls of the canyon real cactus, sage-brush, and other vegetation transplanted from their native clime. Opening from the cave are mysterious caverns and niches in the exact form of the original. These contain utensils and ornaments found on the original site, and a mummy, supposed to be one of the ancient Cliff Dwellers" (ibid., 42).

103. Miles Orvell, *The Real Thing: Imitation and Authenticity in American Culture, 1880–1940*, xvi.

104. Ibid., 13.

105. Frederick Ward Putnam, draft of speech, Sept. 21, 1891 (Frederick Ward Putnam Papers, Harvard University Archives, Pusey Library, Cambridge, Mass.), cited in Hinsley, "The World as Marketplace," 347.

106. Rydell, "The Culture of Material Abundance," 193.

107. Jeffrey Steele, "Reduced to Images: American Indians in Nineteenth-Century Advertising," in Elizabeth Bird, ed., *Dressing in Feathers: The Construction of the Indian in American Popular Culture*, 46.

108. See, for example, *Sham Battle at the Pan-American Exposition* (Edison, 1901), featuring American Indians; *Japanese Village* (Pan-American Exposition; Edison, 1901); *Asia in America, St. Louis Exposition* (Biograph, 1904); and *Scenes in the Swiss Village at Paris Exposition (nos. 1 and 2)*, filmed by Edison at the 1900 Universal Exposition in Paris.

109. As their titles suggest, the second and third films consist of demonstrations of whip-snapping and leap-frogging; in the former the performance is staged in front of two tents, a wigwam, and painted background of an Arctic landscape. In *Esquimaux Leap Frog* an Inuit man with a white flag directs the leap-froggers, who occasionally stumble as they complete their jumps.

110. Biograph films of Native Americans were shown daily in the "United States Government Department of the Interior Exhibit" at the St. Louis World's Fair. For example, dances by Pueblo and Crow Indians living on reservations were shown as well as films of Navahos and other tribes making native crafts such as basket-weaving (see Gunning, "World as Object Lesson," 439).

111. The Touaregs (aka Tuaregs) are a nomadic people of the central and western Sahara and along the Middle Niger from Timbuktu (Tombouctou) to Nigeria who have preserved their Hamitic speech but have adopted the Muslim religion. At the end of the Touaregs sequence in the print of the film housed at the Library of Congress (an incomplete U.S. release), there is footage shot on location at the edge of the Bedja Hadendoa desert in North Africa. It is unclear whether this film was originally shown after *The Touaregs in Their Country*. It contains shots of white tourists mounting camels, a fight between two men (at the end of which a crowd of bystanders joins in), a "Spear Dance by the Arabs of the Bicharyn Tribe," and separate shots of young Bicharyn girls and boys who find it very hard to stand still for the camera.

112. I borrow this term from Thomas Elsaesser, who draws a distinction between witting and unwitting evidence; he defines the former as "what the film intends to say," and the latter as "what it says in spite of itself—evidence like clothes and historic buildings that might appear, or labels, brand names, machinery, and so on." Elsaesser, "Locations: Evidence, Fantasy, Response," in Daan Hertogs and Nico de Klerk, eds., *Nonfiction Film from the Teens*, 34.

113. But as soon as the camera records the Touaregs' performing, their status as live performers is inexorably changed because, in the strict ontological sense, once a performance is repeated, it is " 'different.' " As Peggy Phelan explains: "Performance honors the idea that a limited number of people in a specific time/space frame can have an experience of value which leaves no visible trace afterward. Writing about it [or filming it] necessarily cancels the 'tracelessness' inaugurated within this performative promise." Phelan, *Unmarked: The Politics of Performance*, 146, 148–49.

114. Gunning, "World as Object Lesson," 423.

115. For example, as director of the Kwakwaka'wakw (Kwakuitl) village featuring Northwest Coast peoples at the 1893 Chicago World's Fair, Boas hired Chicago photographer John H. Grabill to photograph various dances that would be sold to the public. Boas justified this commercial endeavor by arguing to the fair's administrators that public sales of copies of the photographs would be profitable. Boas also promised to give copies of the photographs to the Kwakwaka'wakw singers and dancers. See Jacknis, "Boas and Photography," 6.

116. Rydell, "Culture of Imperial Abundance," 125; Martin Heidegger, "The Age of the World Picture," in *The Questions Concerning Technology and Other Essays*, trans. William Lovitt.

117. Gunning, "From the Kaleidoscope to the X-Ray," 32.

118. See Breitbart, *A World on Display*. Over 750 professional photographers were accredited by the press bureau of the St. Louis World's Fair (1904); in addition, thousands of tourists would have taken photographs of the ethnographic peoples living at the Fair (ibid., 11).

3. KNOWLEDGE AND VISUALITY
IN NINETEENTH-CENTURY ANTHROPOLOGY

1. Edward B. Tylor, "Dammann's Race Photographs," *Nature* (Jan. 6, 1876): 184.

2. Crary, *Techniques of the Observer*, 3.

3. Christopher Pinney, "Classification and Fantasy in the Photographic Construction of Caste and Tribe," *Visual Anthropology* 3.2 (1990): 260.

4. For an overview of Flower's career as a curator, see the tribute to "Sir William Flower, K.C.B." in *MJ* 3.2 (Aug. 1903): 59–62.

5. W. H. Flower, 'President's Address," *JAI* 11 (1882): 184.

6. For a discussion of anthropological photography within the British colonial context, see "Photographing the Natives" in James R. Ryan, *Picturing Empire: Photography and the Visualization of the British Empire*, 140–82.

7. Elizabeth A. Williams, *The Physical and the Moral: Anthropology, Physiology, and Philosophical Medicine in France, 1750–1850*, 237. For a history of photography's relationship to portraiture, race, colonialism, and the social sciences, see John Pultz, *Photography and the Body*, 13–36.

8. Elizabeth C. Agassiz and Louis Agassiz, *A Journey in Brazil* (Boston: Ticknor and Fields, 1868), 276–77, cited in Banta and Hinsley, *From Site to Sight*, 58. For an insightful discussion of Zealy's photographs, see Alan Trachtenberg, *Reading American Photographs: Images as History, Mathew Brady to Walker Evans*, 53–60.

9. Letter from Joseph Henry to Lewis V. Bogy, Feb. 20, 1867, Office of Indian Affairs, RG 75, "letters sent (miscellaneous)," National Archives and Records Administration,

Washington D.C., cited in Paula Richardson Fleming and Judith Luskey, *The North American Indians in Early Photographs* (New York: Dorset, 1986), 22–23.

10. Tylor, "Dammann's Race Photographs," 184.

11. James Urry, *"Notes and Queries in Anthropology* and the Development of Field Methods in British Anthropology, 1870–1920," *Proceedings of the Royal Anthropological Institute of Great Britain and Northern Ireland* (1972): 45.

12. David Tomas, "Tools of the Trade: The Production of Ethnographic Observation on the Andaman Islands, 1858–1922," in George W. Stocking, Jr., *Colonial Situations: Essays on the Contextualization of Ethnographic Knowledge*, 87.

13. *Notes and Queries* (1874 ed.), n.p., cited in David Green, "Classified Subjects: Photography and Anthropology—The Technology of Power." *Ten-8* 14 (1984): 34. According to James Urry, many of the papers published in the *JAI* in the 1870s reflected the influence of *Notes and Queries* upon the authors and their research methods (Urry, "*Notes and Queries*," 47).

14. The geopolitical context of British anthropology was quite different to that of America; whereas American anthropologists enjoyed relatively easy access to their ethnographic subjects living on reservations in the American West via transcontinental railways and could stay for relatively short periods of time, British ethnographers had to travel long distances by sea in order to gain access to their colonies, so that once they reached their destination they tended to stay longer among peoples who, in some instances, had very little experience of Western contact. In addition, unlike Britain's colonial subjects, Native Americans were often considered an undifferentiated military enemy by the government (and sections of the population), which meant that ethnographic research was never completely divorced from politics. George W. Stocking Jr., *The Ethnographer's Magic and Other Essays in the History of Anthropology*, 354.

15. C. Read, "Prefaratory Note," *Notes and Queries*, 3rd ed. (1899), 87.

16. A. C. Haddon, "Photography and Folklore," *Folklore* 6 (1895): 222.

17. Ibid.

18. The 1899 edition of *Notes and Queries* offered the most detailed advice on anthropometric photography. When producing portraits (both head and profile), Haddon recommended that "the lens should be on a level with the face, and the eyes of the subject looking straight from the head should be fixed on a point at their own height from the ground. . . . When the whole nude is photographed, front, side and back views should be taken; the heels should be close together and the arms hanging straight down the side of the body; it is best to photograph a metric scale in the same plane as the body of the subject. It is desirable to have a soft, fine grained, neutral-tinted screen to be used as a background. This screen should be sufficiently light in colour to contrast well with the yellow and brown skins." Haddon, "Photography," *Notes and Queries in Anthropology* (1899 ed.), 239.

19. Lucile E. Hoyme, "Physical Anthropology and Its Instruments: An Historical Study," *Southwestern Journal of Anthropology* 9 (1953): 410. One of the earliest instruments specifically designed for somatic measurement was the "anthropometron," invented in 1663, although artists had earlier developed canons summarizing the relative sizes of parts of the body using dividers or rods of standard length to measure the body.

20. Tomas, "Tools of the Trade," 91.

21. W. Y. Turner, "On the Ethnology of the Motu," *JAI* 7 (1878): 472–73.

22. Ibid. (emphasis added).

23. E. H. Man, "A Brief Account of the Nicobar Islands," *JAI* 15 (1886): 440.

24. Letter from Thomas Henry Huxley to Lord Granville, Dec. 8, 1869, Huxley Manuscripts, Imperial College of Science and Technology, London, cited in Frank Spencer, "Some Notes on the Attempt to Apply Photography to Anthropometry During the Second Half of the Nineteenth Century," in Edwards, *Anthropology and Photography*, 99–100. For a discussion of anthropometry and race, see Stephen Jay Gould, *The Mismeasure of Man*.

25. Pinney, "Classification and Fantasy," 272–73. Due to the highly invasive nature of the procedure, it was only performed upon individuals either incarcerated at the Straits Penal Colony (where Indians, Malays, and Sri Lankans were imprisoned) and at Breakwater Prison in South Africa. Elizabeth Edwards, "Photographic 'Types': The Pursuit of Method," *Visual Anthropology* 3 (1992): 247.

26. In the frontal position the subject was instructed to stand with heels together and right arm outstretched with the palm of the hand turned toward the camera, while in the profile pose, "the subject was presented to the camera with the arm bent in a manner that did not interrupt the contours of the trunk," a factor of greater significance in the case of female subjects where there was a possibility that the arm might "interfere with the contour of the breast which is very characteristics in some races." Huxley to Granville, Dec, 8, 1869, cited in Spencer, "Some Notes," 100.

27. Ibid., 99–100.

28. J. H. Lamprey, "On a Method of Measuring the Human Form for the Use of Students of Ethnology," *Journal of the Ethnological Society of London* 1 (1869): 85.

29. David Spurr, *The Rhetoric of Empire: Colonial Discourse in Journalism, Travel Writing, and Imperial Administration*, 23.

30. W. H. Flower, cited in Christopher Pinney, "Colonial Anthropology in the 'Laboratory of Mankind,'" in Bayly, ed., *The Raj and the British*, 253.

31. For more on the relationship between discourses of visuality and racial classification in nineteenth-century anthropology, see Rony, *Third Eye*, 21–43.

32. For an analysis of how the methods of anthropometric photography found application in nineteenth century criminology studies conducted by the French police official Alphonse Bertillon and Francis Galton, see Sekula, "The Body and the Archive," 18–55.

33. "Current Notes on Anthropology" (anonymous author), ed. Daniel G. Brinton, *Science* 22.564 (Nov. 24, 1893): 281.

34. Pinney, "Colonial Anthropology," 257.

35. H. H. Risley, "Ethnology and Caste," *The Imperial Gazetteer of India* (Oxford, 1909:288), cited in Pinney, "Colonial Anthropology," 257. Pinney notes that Risley was a central figure in colonial anthropological surveys of India between 1890 to 1910, holding such important positions as census commissioner and honorary director of the Ethnological Survey of the Indian Empire (ibid.).

36. Pinney, "Colonial Anthropology," 258.

37. For more on Muybridge's work, see Marta Braun, *Picturing Time: The Work of Etienne-Jules Marey (1830–1904)*, 228–54; Linda Williams, *Hard Core* (London: Pandora, 1990), 37–57; Charles Musser, *The Emergence of Cinema: The American Screen to 1907*, 48–54; and Pinney, "Colonial Anthropology," 258.

38. Braun, *Picturing Time*, 237. Braun argues that the aesthetic and narrative elements of Muybridge's photographs overwhelm the production of analytically verifiable data, since "the unsystematic and incongruent aspects of Muybridge's photographs effectively obscure any knowledge of the underlying laws governing the mechanics of movement." While I agree that Muybridge's reliance upon such techniques as insertion, expansion, contraction, and substitution of photographic images were motivated by a desire to ensure an overall illusion of internal consistency and to offer a dramatic and aesthetic sequence of images, I think that Braun's argument that Muybridge's photographs "effectively obscure *any* knowledge of physiology or the mechanics of movement" is too strong. Marey's research was grounded in the natural sciences, whereas Muybridge had no comparable scientific training. Braun, *Picturing Time*, 237 (emphasis added).

39. Steve Neale, *Cinema and Technology: Image, Sound, Color*, 36, cited in Cartwright, *Screening the Body*, 34.

40. Marey's research enjoyed great influence in the development of physical education, gymnastics, and army training in France, and some of his experiments addressed the purported neurological degeneration caused by shocks of urban life in fin-de-siècle Paris (Braun, *Picturing Time*, 109). As an offshoot of his research into normal and pathological locomotion, Marey also chronophotographed elephants and water buffaloes borrowed from a Parisian zoo and Arabian horsemen in traditional dress. The inclusion of these exotic subjects in Marey's research suggests that even men of science were not indifferent to the lure of the orient as an iconographic sign. After Marey's death in 1904, his associates conducted chronophotographic experiments with French colonial subjects from North Africa and prisoners from Biskra in Algeria, work sponsored by the French ministries of Labor and Public Instruction and part of a larger campaign initiated by the War Ministry to conscript native soldiers. For more information on experiments conducted in the wake of Marey's death, see Braun, *Picturing Time*, 320–48.

41. Spencer, 'Some Notes," 102. Spencer points out that it took until the 1890s for anthropologists to agree upon standard methods of measuring the living body. This led to the Monaco Agreement for the unification of craniometric and cephalometric measurements of 1906 (ibid., 106*n*3).

42. Pinney, "Classification and Fantasy," 247.

43. Ibid., 284.

44. An Oxford graduate, im Thurn was curator of the British Guiana Museum who later became a district magistrate and administrator in the colony. After being appointed governor of Fiji and High Commissioner of the Western Pacific, he became president of the Royal Anthropological Institute (1919–20) during his retirement. In 1883, im Thurn published a book of his experiences in Guiana entitled *Among the Indians of Guiana, Being Sketches, Chiefly Anthropological, from the Interior of British Guiana.* A collection of his writings were published posthumously in 1934: im Thurn, *Thoughts, Talks, and Tramps: A Collection of Papers.* See Donald Taylor, " 'Very Loveable Human Beings': The Photography of Everard im Thurn," in Edwards, *Anthropology and Photography*, 187–92.

45. Im Thurn, "Anthropological Uses," 184.

46. Flower, "President's Address," 186. The most notorious example of the preservation of anatomical specimens is the case of Saartjie Baartman (Sarah Bartman), referred to as the "Hottentot Venus." Baartman was brought to England as a physiognomic "freak" in the eighteenth century where she died at the age of twenty-five. Her buttocks and genitalia were dissected by the French physician George Cuvier and are still housed at the Musée de l'Homme in Paris. For analyses of the "Hottentot Venus," see Shohat and Stam, *Unthinking Eurocentrism*, 108, 322–33; Sander Gilman, "Black Bodies, White Bodies: Toward an Iconography of Female Sexuality in Late Nineteenth-Century Art, Medicine, and Literature," *Critical Inquiry* 12 (Autumn 1985): 205; Altick, *The Shows of London*, 268–72; and Carmel Schrire, "Native Views of Western Eyes," in Pippa Skotnes, ed., *Miscast: Negotiating the Presence of the Bushmen*, 343–54.

47. For example, French anthropologist Paul Tropinard argued that while "anatomical truth" should be the criterion in studies upon the skeleton, there were insufficient numbers of them in museums. Consequently, "living people alone [could] supply the number indispensable to arrive at any degree of certainty." According to Tropinard, "all our efforts should therefore tend to perfect the methods of operating upon the living, and to simplify them, so as to render them accessible to all—travellers, officers of the navy, recruiting agents, schoolmasters, etc." Tropinard, "Observations upon the Methods and Processes of Anthropometry," *JAI* 10 (1881): 217, 213.

48. Michel Foucault, *Discipline and Punish: The Birth of the Prison.*

49. Christopher Pinney, "The Parallel Histories of Anthropology and Photography," in Edwards, *Anthropology and Photography*, 78.

50. Taylor, " 'Very Loveable Human Beings,' " 188.

51. Taylor argues that im Thurn's intervention should be viewed more as a rationali-

zation or justification of his earlier approach to photography rather than as a manifesto, since by the time he wrote "Anthropological Uses of the Camera" in 1893, he had more or less stopped taking photographs (ibid., 188).

52. Im Thurn, "Anthropological Uses," 184, 186; Taylor, " 'Very Loveable Human Beings,' " 188.

53. Marta Macintyre and Maureen MacKenzie, "Focal Length as an Analogue of Cultural Distance," in Edwards, ed., *Anthropology and Photography*, 162.

54. Most of Mooney's photographic training came from John Hilliers and, after 1898, De Lancey Gill, although he relied upon the Kodak manuals when he was in the field. Mooney also shot landscapes and architecture because of their "special social or religious significance" and as important backgrounds in portrait photographs (Jacknis, "In Search of the Imagemaker," 185, 196). For a discussion of Mooney's ethnology and career at the Bureau of American Ethnology (BAE), see Hinsley, *The Smithsonian and the American Indian: Making a Moral Anthropology in Victorian America*, 207–24.

55. Jacknis, "In Search of the Imagemaker," 190. This practice of paying subjects was not uncommon, and native peoples often drove hard bargains with anthropologists, commercial photographers, and tourists.

56. Jacknis, "In Search of the Imagemaker," 193, 196.

57. Ibid., 202.

58. Common mistakes in Mooney's photographs include out-of-focus images, distracting backgrounds, the camera being held too far away from the subject, miscalculated exposure time, or Mooney's own shadow with tripod-mounted camera in the foreground of the image. Mooney sent all his exposed glass plates back to the Smithsonian for developing, an arrangement that resulted in many of them being damaged in transit (ibid., 186, 189).

59. Jacknis, "In Search of the Imagemaker," 186–87.

60. Rudolph Arnheim, "On the Nature of Photography," *Critical Inquiry* 1.1 (Sept. 1974): 150.

61. Roland Barthes, *Camera Lucida*, trans. Richard Howard, 13.

62. Agassiz and Agassiz, *A Journey in Brazil* (1868), 276–77, cited in Banta and Hinsley, *From Site to Sight*, 58.

63. This is not to infer that native beliefs were nothing but a ruse; Dakota Indians, for example, called photographers "shadow catchers," considering the act of taking a photograph of a person as tantamount to controlling that person's soul. Banta and Hinsley, *From Site to Sight*, 58.

64. Man, "A Brief Account," 440.

65. Pinney, "Anthropology and the Colonial Image," 282.

66. The man trembling in front of the camera was a member of the Long-Glat tribe (Carl Lumholtz, *Through Central Borneo*, 263); the woman with tears in her eyes from the

Bukats (ibid., 217). Raja Bear, from the Kampong tribe, took enormous pride in his appearance, making "altogether a splendid subject for the camera" (ibid., 229–30).

67. Banta and Hinsley, *From Site to Sight*, 29–30.

68. M. V. Portman, "Photography for Anthropologists," *JAI* 25 (1896): 81, cited in Tomas, "Tools of the Trade," 93 (emphasis in original). Portman rephotographed some of the images he had taken of the Andamans, using the background grid recommended by Lamprey. Copies of Portman's huge photographic and statistical survey were sent to the British Museum and the Indian Government. Pinney, "Anthropology and the Colonial Image," 285–86.

69. For a discussion of the forms of objectification and exchange associated with the *carte-de-visite*, see Poole, *Vision, Race, and Modernity*, esp. chs. 4 and 5. Also see Christraud M. Geary and Virginia-Lee Webb, *Delivering Views: Distant Cultures in Early Postcards*.

70. Walter Benjamin, *Passagen-Werk* (Arcades Project), vol. 5, 831 [Y4, 4], cited in Susan Buck-Morss, *The Dialectics of Seeing: Walter Benjamin and the Arcades Project*, 136.

71. Poignant, "Surveying the Field," 54.

72. Shohat and Stam, *Unthinking Eurocentrism*, 108.

73. George Catlin, *North American Indians, Being Letters and Notes on Their Manners, Customs, Written During Eight Years Travel Amongst the Wildest Tribes of Indians in America* 1:293, quoted in Robert Berkhofer, *The White Man's Indian: Images of the American Indian from Columbus to the Present*, 89 (emphasis in original).

74. Pinney, "Classification and Fantasy," 282.

75. Edwards, "Introduction," 7.

76. Joanna Cohan Scherer, "You Can't Believe Your Eyes: Inaccuracies in Photographs of North American Indians," *Studies in the Anthropology of Visual Communication* 2.2 (1975): 675. For more on the cultural construction of Native Americans within early American photography and practices of distortion, see Scherer, "The Public Faces of Sarah Winnemucca," *Cultural Anthropology* 3.2 (May 1988): 178–204, and Margaret B. Blackman, "Posing the American Indian," *Natural History* 89.10 (Oct. 1980): 68–74.

77. Alison Devine Nordström, "Photography of Samoa: Production, Dissemination, and Use," in Casey Blanton, ed., *Picturing Paradise: Colonial Photography of Samoa, 1875 to 1925*, 21.

78. Alison Devine Nordström lecture given in conjunction with "Picturing Paradise: Colonial Photography of Samoa, 1875 to 1925" exhibit at the Metropolitan Museum of Art, New York, May 1995. See the catalogue accompanying the show as published by Daytona Beach (Fla.) Community College, 1995.

79. Neil Harris points out that the emergence of the half-tone engraving as a major reproductive method for publishers of mass-illustrated material between the late 1880s and early 1890s solved a problem that had plagued printers for quite some time, namely, how to develop a photomechanical method for reproducing images in the form of a

printing block that could be applied to the same paper that was used for type-print. Harris, "Iconography and Intellectual History: The Halftone Effect," in John Higham and Paul K. Conkin, eds., *New Directions in American Intellectual History*, 197.

80. Catherine A. Lutz and Jane L. Collins, *Reading National Geographic* (Chicago: University of Chicago Press, 1993), 27–28. Lutz and Collins also point out that the board policy at the journal during this period demanded that images "be subordinate to, and illustrative of, the text" and were constrained by magazine editor Gilbert Hovey Grosvenor's principles "of fairness, veracity, and positive outlook"—in other words, aesthetically pleasing, realistic representations that "embodied certain conventions of highbrow forms of art." Grosvenor had been hired to build circulation and popularize the magazine in 1899 (27).

81. Iskander Mydin, "Historical Images—Changing Audiences," in Edwards, *Anthropology and Photography*, 250.

82. Jacknis, "Boas and Photography," 6, cited in Banta and Hinsley, *From Site to Sight*, 106.

83. Pinney, "Classification and Fantasy," 281–82.

84. Ibid.

85. See Barthes's influential essay "The Rhetoric of the Image" for a discussion of how captions anchor the connotative meaning of images. Barthes, *Image, Music, Text*, trans. by Stephen Heath, 32–51.

86. Christopher Pinney, "The Lexical Spaces of Eye-Spy," in Peter Crawford and David Turton, eds., *Film as Ethnography*, 27.

87. Context is no less important, however, in photography. While it may take the form of captioning that appears on, or on the back of, the photograph, it can also be provided by the personal album, a museum archive box, and the interrelationship between illustrations and text in a published article or book.

88. André Gaudreault, "Les traces du montage dans la production Lumière," in Dujaidin, Galdies, Crerstenkorn, and Sequin, eds., *L'aventure de Cinematographe*, 299–306. My thanks to Tom Gunning for drawing my attention to this important point.

89. Barthes, *Camera Lucida*, 27. Subsequent page numbers are cited in the text.

90. Ibid., 89.

91. Corbey, "Ethnographic Showcases," 364.

92. Félix-Louis Regnault was not, however, the only scientist to write about the role of cinematography in the natural and social sciences. For example, the German biologist Oswald Polimanti emphasized the exactitude with which cinema reproduced ethnographic detail over verbal records, even suggesting that as raw data, anthropological research films could allow other scientists to discover new phenomena or even interpret moving pictures as raw data differently. Oswald Polimanti, "Der Kinematograph in der biologischen und medizinischen" (Wissenschaft), *Naturwissenschaftliche Wochenschrift* 26.49 (1911): 770, cited in Taureg, "The Development of Standards," 23.

Similarly taken with the objectivity of the *cinematographe*, another German scientist, H. Lehmann, regarded the camera as an "almost completely accurate copy of the human eye," and, like Marey, felt that cinema's greatest value lay in its ability to enlarge upon human vision by enabling scientists to examine very quick or slow movements and to measure velocity and distance through frame-by-frame analysis. H. Lehmann, *Die Kinemtaographie, ihre Grundlagen und ihre Anwendungen*, 306, cited in Taureg, ibid., 23.

93. Rony, *Third Eye*, 57. Regnault differentiated between the *cinematographe*, a scientific cinema which filmed successive movements and decomposed them into a series of photographic images, and the *cinematoscope*, a commercial cinema that recomposed movement to produce "an animated spectacle" (ibid., 47), a qualification that, for Regnault, may have come from the benefit of hindsight since his two major articles on ethnographic cinema were written between 1922 and 1923: Regnault "L'évolution du cinéma," *La revue scientifique* (1922): 79–85, cited in Rony, ibid., 231*n*9, and "Films et museés d'ethnographie," *Comptes rendus de l'association francaise pour des sciences* 2 (1923): 680–81, cited in Rony, ibid., 231*n*11.

94. Étienne-Jules Marey, preface to *La photographie animée* by Charles-Louis Eugene Trutat, ix, in Braun, *Picturing Time*, 255. Paradoxically, Marey's interest in the differential between images as opposed to the illusion of continuous movement generated by film projection was, as Lisa Cartwright points out, what distinguished chronophotography from cinematography. Cartwright, *Screening the Body*, 38.

95. Noël Burch, "Primitivism and the Avant-Gardes: A Dialectical Approach," in Philip Rosen, *Narrative, Apparatus, Ideology*, 484.

96. Étienne-Jules Marey, *La chronophotographie*, 26–27, cited in Braun, *Picturing Time*, 196.

97. Marey, *Movement* (New York: Appleton, 1895), 311, cited in Braun, *Picturing Time*, 174. In 1891 the acclaimed French photographer Albert Londe anticipated Marey's later comments on cinema when he said that "leaving aside the curiosity aspect that enables us to reproduce various scenes, there is no doubt that seeing these scenes leaves us in exactly the same position as we are before the model itself." Albert Londe, *La photographie moderne, traite pratique de la photographie et de ses applications a l'industrie et a la science*, 2d ed. (Paris: G. Masson), 726, cited in Noël Burch, *Life to Those Shadows*, 13.

98. Despite his lack of interest in commercial uses of moving pictures, Etienne-Jules Marey developed a portable electric gun camera (*fusil electrique*) which he presented at the 1900 Universal Exposition in Paris. The camera was powered by a lightweight generator or battery carried by an assistant and employed a band of 35mm film twenty meters long. Unlike other cameras at the time which were fixed on a tripod, this model was held and operated like a gun, although, as Michel Frizot notes, Marey's design was never taken up by other manufacturers. Michel Frizot, *La Chronophotographie*, 124, cited in Braun, *Picturing Time*, 195.

4. THE ETHNOGRAPHIC CINEMA OF ALFRED CORT HADDON
AND WALTER BALDWIN SPENCER

1. Charles Urban, "The Cinematograph in Science and Education: Its Value in Surgical Demonstrations," *Moving Picture World* (hereafter, *MPW*) 1.25 (Aug. 24, 1907): 388.

2. Thomas Clegg, "Education by Kinematograph: Future Prospects," *MPW* 6.9 (Mar. 5, 1910): 331.

3. Information cited in Pat Laughren and Chris Long, "Australia's First Films (Part 6): Surprising Survivals," *Cinema Papers* 7 (1993): 34. In a July 28 diary entry, C. S. Myers mentioned that "cameras and phonograph apparatus constitute the bulk of our baggage." C. S. Myers Journal entry, July 28, 1898, p. 92 (1898–99) ADD 8073, Haddon Collection at Cambridge University Library (hereafter, HC-CUP). For a detailed breakdown of the equipment and its costs, see Newman and Guardia invoices in box 13, file 3, HC-CUP.

4. Films shot by Austrian anthropologist Dr. Rudolf Pöch during his 1904–1906 expedition to German, British, and Dutch New Guinea and to New South Wales are notable exceptions. In his writings, if not in his practice, Pöch was an early advocate of what came to be known as observational ethnographic film. Pöch argued that a camera should simply be set up in a public place and allowed to record native life with minimum intervention from the filmmaker-anthropologist. However, as Rony points out, Pöch's commitment to an observational style of filming is belied in the films themselves, which often show Pöch in colonial garb replete with rifle posing alongside self-conscious native peoples. Pöch nevertheless recognized the fact that his vision of an omniscient ethnographic camera-eye could never be practically achieved due to the camera's monocular perspective. Rony, *Third Eye*, 66.

Pöch's ethnographic filmmaking was discussed in *Moving Picture World* in 1907, when an anonymous reviewer wrote that "it was very difficult [for Pöch] to get a good quality of cinematographic exposure, for in the [native] dances and some of the movements which the explorer desired to record, the natives were always moving about considerable distances and he had to follow with his machine" ("New Finds Among Primitive Peoples," *MPW* 1.4 [Dec. 14, 1907]: 663). Also see Rudolf Pöch, "Reisen in den Jahren, 1904–1906," *Zeitschrift für Ethnologie* (1907): 382–400, and Paul Spindler, "New Guinea, 1904–1906," *Science and Film* 8.1 (Mar. 1959): 10–14, both cited in Rony, *Third Eye*, 66.

5. MacDougall, "The Visual in Anthropology," 289.

6. George W. Stocking Jr., *After Tylor: British Social Anthropology, 1888–1951*, 99; and Stocking, *Ethnographer's Magic*, 21.

7. Stocking, *After Tylor*, 101.

8. Stocking, *Ethnographer's Magic*, 22–23. According to Stocking, the expedition rep-

resented a turning point in the careers of several of the anthropologists; MacDougall and Myers went on to become leaders in psychology while Seligman and Rivers were distinguished field anthropologists of their generation (28).

9. Stocking, *After Tylor*, 109.

10. It is telling that in a recent anthology published to celebrate the expedition's centenary, Haddon's filmmaking is only really mentioned in passing and then in the context of his field photography. See Edwards, "Performing Science: Still Photography and the Torres Strait Expedition," in Anita Herle and Sandra Rouse, eds., *Cambridge and the Torres Strait: Centenary Essays on the 1898 Anthropological Expedition*.

For more on the history of the Torres Strait Islanders' encounter with the institutions of colonialism, see R. B. Beckett's essay, "Haddon Attends a Funeral: Fieldwork in the Torres Strait, 1888, 1898," in Herle and Rouse, eds., ibid., 23–49, and his book *Torres Strait Islander: Custom and Colonialism* (Cambridge: Cambridge University Press, 1987). A documentary celebrating the centenary of the 1898 Cambridge expedition was made for the BBC2 *Horizon* series. In it, the renowned psychologist-director Dr. Jonathan Miller retraced Haddon's journey to the Torres Strait. For a critique of the film, see Jude Philip, "Expectations—*Dr. Miller and the Islander*," *Anthropology Today* 14.2 (Apr. 1998): 16–18.

11. Emilie de Brigard's essay "The History of Ethnographic Film" is the most frequently cited reference, although she only devotes a paragraph to Haddon's filmmaking. According to Stocking, the Torres Strait Expedition was noted less for its accumulation of empirical data—much of which was secondhand—than as a symbol of a new era in ethnographic enterprise (Haddon is credited with introducing the term *fieldwork* into anthropology). There is, however, as Stocking points out, some disparity between this multidisciplinary model of fieldwork and the more recent anthropological model of participant observation, the "lone ethnographer" model of inquiry which Rivers formalized in his 1912 revision of *Notes and Queries*. Stocking, *Ethnographer's Magic*, 24.

12. Jay Ruby, *Picturing Culture: Explorations of Film and Anthropology*, ix.

13. Anthony Wilkin's personal collection of photographs taken during the expedition are housed at the Metropolitan Museum of Art in New York. While there is some overlap with Haddon's collection, archived at the Cambridge Museum of Archaeology and Anthropology, there are also differences. My thanks to Anita Herle for information on the expedition's photographs.

14. In Laughren and Long's view, the convoluted threading pattern of the Newman and Guardia camera may have caused the film to jam under the tropical conditions. Laughren and Long, "Australia's First Films," 34.

15. Letter to Fanny Haddon from Haddon, Sept. 4, 1898 (box 12, file 1, HC-CUL).

16. Haddon, cited in Laughren and Long, "Australia's First Films," 34.

17. Ibid., 35. The four and a half minutes of film shot during the expedition—complete, in Laughren and Long's opinion—is housed at the National Film and Television

Archive in London (the films were copied from Cambridge University's Museum of Archaeology and Anthropology in 1967, which still holds the copyright). Prints are also owned by the Australian Institute of Aboriginal and Torres Strait Islander Studies Film Unit in Canberra and by Ian Dunlop at Film Australia in Lindfield.

18. A. C. Haddon, "Introduction," *Reports of the Cambridge Anthropological Expedition to the Torres Straits* 6:xiv. Haddon admitted that when carrying out physical examinations, "the men had to be given tobacco and the children sweets as rewards of merit for having their eyesight tested, while at the same time an appeal to their vanity was very efficacious" (quoted in Joseph Jastrow, review of Haddon's *Reports of the Cambridge Anthropological Expedition*, vol. 2, *Physiology and Psychology*, in *Science* 15.384 [1902]: 742).

19. In a July 16, 1898, diary entry, Myers referred to Joe Brown as the "best singer on the island . . . generally giving the lead and general stimulus to the singing of the other men who came with him." Dance and semireligious songs were recorded onto seven cylinders. On another occasion (Aug. 15, 1898), Myers referred in his diary to photographing a dead body (possibly a baby) and using his phonograph to record the sound of the wailing mother. C. S. Myers Journal (1898–99) ADD 8073, HC-CUP.

20. For background information on Haddon's interest in the Malu initiation rites and the negotiations leading up to the performance of the Malu-Bomai ceremony, see Anita Herle, 'The Life-Histories of Objects: Collections of the Cambridge Anthropological Expedition to the Torres Strait," in Herle and Rouse, eds., *Cambridge and the Torres Strait*, 90–94. In this dance, the senior mentor (*zogo-le*) utters "the sacred words and sings the chant about Malu in front of the initiates (*kersi*)" (92).

21. Laughren and Long, "Australia's First Films," 35–36. With the exception of the film demonstrating fire-making, which was shot on Sept. 5, 1898, all the remaining films were shot on Sept. 6. Given the limited exposure these films have received and their significance as some of the earliest examples of ethnographic filmmaking, I will provide a measure of textual description of each film; this detail is essential I believe if we are to appreciate what Haddon was trying to accomplish with a motion picture camera. After describing each of the five short films, the discussion will focus upon Haddon's first film of the climax of the Malu-Bomai ceremony (the *zogo-le* dance).

22. Haddon's decision to shoot footage of fire-making and ceremonies accords with the advice he proffered in the 1899 *Notes and Queries*, in which he urged the recording of such ancient customs before they died out, thus linking his filmmaking to a broader mission of salvage ethnography. Edgar Thurston, who went on to become the superintendent of ethnography for southern India, in 1900 carried out a similar comparative photographic study of fire-making to Haddon's. His composition of three Nayadis using a rubbing stick to start a fire is almost identical to Haddon's cinematograph view of the same process (see Bayly, ed., *The Raj and the British*, 296–97).

23. See Herle, "The Life-Histories of Objects," 91, for a detailed description of the masks. The following information on the Malu-Bomai ceremony is taken from Herle.

24. C. S. Myers journal entry, July 28, 1898, in Myers Journal, HP-CUL.

25. Alfred Cort Haddon, *Head-Hunters: Black, White and Brown*, 46.

26. Herle, "The Life-Histories of Objects," 95.

27. Edwards, "Performing Science," 110.

28. As Herle and Rouse point out in their introduction to *Cambridge and the Torres Strait*, at the time of the expedition the spelling of Torres was plural whereas the correct current spelling is singular (1).

29. Haddon, *Head-Hunters*, 48.

30. Herle, "The Life-Histories of Objects," 93.

31. According to Edwards, "The *appearance* of the 'primitive' in performance of primitivist tropes such as dance, clothing, tattoo [in the photographs], is played out for the camera, despite the fact that the coastal villages were heavily missionized by this date and that the Expedition party . . . visited in the company of colonial officers and missionaries." Edwards, "Performing Science," 113 (emphasis in original).

32. Edwards, "Performing Science," 116.

33. Ibid., 110.

34. As defined by *Merriam-Webster's Collegiate Dictionary* (10th ed., 1994).

35. Antonia Lant, "Haptical Cinema," *October* 75 (1995): 71. Burch first explores the idea of haptic cinema in "Primitivism and the Avant-Gardes," 483–506.

36. Frances Hubbard Flaherty, *The Odyssey of a Film-Maker: Robert Flaherty's Story* (Putney, Vt.: Threshold, 1984), 58, cited in Michael Taussig, *Mimesis and Alterity: A Particular History of the Senses* (New York: Routledge, 1993), 200. Flaherty's book was first published by the University of Illinois Press in 1960.

37. Laura U. Marks, "Video Haptics and Erotics," *Screen* 32.4 (Winter 1998): 332–33.

38. On Regnault's chronophotography, see Rony, *Third Eye*, 21–73.

39. For a detailed explication of Gunning's groundbreaking theorization of the "cinema of attractions," see the following essays by him: "The Cinema of Attractions: Early Film, Its Spectator and the Avant-Garde," in Elsaesser, ed., *Early Cinema*, 56–62; "An Aesthetic of Astonishment," 114–33; and " 'Now You See It, Now You Don't': The Temporality of the Cinema of Attractions," in Richard Abel, ed., *Silent Film*, 71–84.

40. Edwards, "Performing Science," 120.

41. Ibid., 121.

42. Ibid., 122.

43. C. S. Myers journal entry, June 4, 1898, p. 63, in Myers Journal, HC-CUL.

44. Letter to Haddon from J. S. Bruce, Dec. 26, 1902 (box 9, file 101, HC-CUL).

45. Letter from Haddon to Fanny, July 26, 1898 (box 12, file 1, HC-CUL).

46. Noël Burch, "Charles Baudelaire Versus Doctor Frankenstein," *Afterimage* 8–9 (1981): 16.

47. In addition to his own photographs in the multivolume account of the expedition, Haddon also included engravings and photographs made by other researchers of

artifacts such as masks, headdresses, and combs, suggesting that he had few qualms publishing images made by other photographers.

48. Dr. Hoyle, "Egyptological Collections," 158. Despite arguing that this was "without doubt, the very best way of arranging a collection so far as the instruction of the public was concerned," Haddon was aware of the prohibitively high cost of constructing illusionistic groups. Anticipating the role of corporate sponsorship within the museum, Haddon suggested that curators should "try and persuade rich Corporations or individuals to start one or two cases" (quoted in ibid., 158).

49. Letter from Haddon to Spencer, 1900, in Spencer Papers, Pitt-Rivers Museum, Oxford, cited in Ian Dunlop, "Ethnographic Filmmaking in Australia: The First Seventy Years (1898–1968)," *Studies in Visual Communication* 9 (Winter 1983): 11.

50. *The Scotsman* (May 12, 1900), n.p. (clipping in Haddon file in HC-CUP).

51. Leonard Donaldson, *The Cinematograph and the Natural Sciences*, 43–44.

52. *Daily Telegraph*, Feb. 15, 1905, n.p. (clipping in box 13, file 1024, HC-CUP). Myers provided a live drumbeat accompaniment to the films. Of course, Haddon may very well have exhibited his films on other occasions, but there is no extant record of the screening or event. Haddon was certainly active as a lecturer during this period and could well have shown his films in museums. During the fall of 1903, for example, Haddon gave a course of free lectures on "Animal Life in a Fresh-water Aquarium" at the Horniman Museum in connection with the Technical Education Board of the London County Council. "General Notes," *MJ* 3.5 (Nov. 1903): 168.

53. Stocking, *After Tylor*, 88–89.

54. Ibid. According to Spencer's biographers D. J. Mulvaney and J. H. Calaby, Gillen suffered a lifelong obsession with gambling and playing the stock market, a pastime that led him to sell most of his ethnographic collection to the National Museum of Victoria. Mulvaney and Calaby, *"So Much That Is New"—Baldwin Spencer, 1860–1929: A Biography*, 164.

55. Stocking, *After Tylor*, 90–91.

56. Mulvaney and Calaby, *"So Much That Is New,"* 174–75.

57. For more on Spencer's photographs, see Ron Vanderwal, ed., *The Aboriginal Photographs of Baldwin Spencer*.

58. Ibid., 166.

59. Spencer had first shown interest in using a motion picture camera in 1900, when he wrote to Haddon telling him that he had contacted Charles Urban's Warwick Trading Co. in London asking them to send him a Bioscope machine. Spencer asked Haddon for advice on how much film to purchase since, he confessed, he had "no experience in this line and can get no help out here." Letter to Haddon from Spencer, Dec. 1, 1900 (box 1, file 3, HP-CUL).

60. Spencer used moving pictures again in a 1912 expedition to tropical Northern Australia, and he donated both the 1912 and the 1901 footage to the National Museum

of Victoria in 1916. The 1912 footage was shot around Oenpelli, Flora River, and on Bathurst Island. Spencer was now able to attach a panning head to his tripod so he could follow his subjects as they moved. Like the 1901 films, Spencer mostly concentrated on shooting Aboriginal ceremonies. The longest sequence was filmed on Bathurst Island where he filmed part of a Pukamuni ceremony involving Tiwi mortuary rights in which carved posts are erected around the graves of a dead person (information in Dunlop, "Ethnographic Filmmaking," 12). Seven thousand feet of 35mm film shot by Spencer from both expeditions were transferred from the original nitrate to safety stock in 1966. According to Dunlop, the footage is remarkably well-preserved and was never edited. Rights to the footage from this and the 1901 expedition are still held by the Department of Aboriginal Studies at the National Museum of Victoria, Melbourne, although the film is housed at the National Film and Sound Archive in Canberra. A 34-minute compilation entitled *Aborigines of Central and Northern Australia, 1901, 1912* was produced by Ian Dunlop in 1966 for a Retrospective of Australian Ethnographic Film at the 1967 Festival dei Popoli in Florence. The film contains eight sequences from the 1901 expedition and five from 1912. I shall focus exclusively on the 1901 expedition.

61. Mulvaney and Calaby argue (in *"So Much That Is New,"* 194) that had Spencer been able to afford a second assistant, the expedition could have collected more ethnographic material and been spared the burden of carrying heavy film and sound recording equipment across difficult terrain (Mounted Trooper Harry Chance cost the expedition approximately £200).

62. The following list of phonograph paraphernalia referred to by Gillen in his April 4th diary entry provides some sense of how much equipment was taken on the expedition: "phonograph recorder reproducer, spare diaphragms, spare gaskets, wax for repairing diaphragm, 24 cylinder records, oil, oil-can, chip brush, rubber horn tube, flexible speaking tube, winding handle, horn stand and horns" in Francis James Gillen, *Gillen's Diary: The Camp Jottings of F. J. Gillen on the Spencer and Gillen Expedition Across Australia, 1901–1902*, 19. According to Australian filmmaker Arthur Cantrill, Spencer bought 3,000 feet of negative film stock in 150-foot rolls (20 rolls, which came to a total of £50). Cantrill, "The 1901 Cinematography of Walter Baldwin Spencer," in Claire Dupré la Tour, André Gaudreault, and Roberta Pearson, eds., *Cinema at the Turn of the Century* (1999), 327–28. An older and expanded version of this paper was published with the same title in *Cantrill's Film Notes* 37–38 (1982): 26–42. For clarity's sake, I shall refer to each essay only by date of publication.

63. Letter from Haddon to Spencer, 1900, cited in Dunlop, "Ethnographic Filmmaking," 11 (emphasis in original).

64. Ibid.

65. Letter from Spencer to Haddon, Dec. 1, 1900 (box 1, file 3, HP-CUP).

66. Letter from Gillen to Spencer, Dec. 4, 1900, cited in John Mulvaney, Howard

Morphy, and Alison Petch, eds., *My Dear Spencer: The Letters of F. J. Gillen to Baldwin Spencer.*

67. Mulvaney and Calaby, *"So Much That Is New,"* 197. Gillen recommended that Spencer contact Davidson of Reeves and Co. in Adelaide for assistance. Letter #86 from Gillen to Spencer, Dec. 11, 1900, in Mulvaney, Morphy, and Petch, eds., *My Dear Spencer.*

68. Cantrill (1999): 328. According to Mulvaney and Calaby (*"So Much That Is New,"* 199), four cylinders survive in the National Museum of Victoria and eleven are in the possession of the South Australian Board for Anthropological Research.

69. Spencer exhausted the last fifty feet of film stock on May 11. Carefully sewing the exposed film up in calico, Spencer sent the film and camera back to Melbourne for developing. Despite the careful packing, 8 out of the 36 films were cracked and ruined during the journey. Spencer, *Wanderings in Wild Australia* 2:361. The film was developed by the Salvation Army's Limelight Department, one of the few facilities with a laboratory capable of processing the footage (under Capt. J. Perry, moving pictures had been pioneered as part of Australian missionary work). While there are no records of the film processing, Gillen referred to a bill for £83 16s. 8d. for processing 2,000 feet, two-thirds of the total amount of film shot during the expedition (Mulvaney and Calaby, *"So Much That Is New,"* 218). Along with similarly inclined Protestant churches, the Salvation Army was at the forefront of pioneering the uses of new technologies such as the phonograph and cinematograph and was responsible for producing a large number of films about Australian Aborigines from 1898 onwards. Michael Leigh, "Curiouser and Curiouser," in Scott Murray, ed., *Back of Beyond: Discovering Australian Film and Television,* 80 (my thanks to David MacDougall for this reference). For more on the Salvation Army and early cinema in Australia, see Chris Long, "Screening the Salvation Army," *Cinema Papers* 97–98 (Apr. 1994): 34–66.

70. Walter Baldwin Spencer and Frank J. Gillen, *Across Australia,* 218.

71. Spencer, *Wanderings,* 360. Another difficulty Spencer discussed was the tendency to vary the speed at which he turned the handle on the camera according to the rapid or slow movements of the performers; as he recalled: "To be a successful cinematographer, with the machine that I used in these early days, you had to suppress your feelings, and rise or fall to the mentality of an experienced barrel organ grinder, who, I then realized, must train him or herself to become utterly oblivious to what, I think, is called tempo, if he or she is to be a success." Cantrill states that on the basis of Spencer's own estimate that each roll of film lasted three minutes, Spencer must have been cranking the camera a little slower than sixteen frames per second (Cantrill [1999]: 328).

72. Spencer, *Wanderings,* 359.

73. Ibid., 374. Another problem Spencer had to contend with was the film slipping off the cogs (which was only discovered after opening the camera in the darkroom).

74. Spencer and Gillen, *Across Australia,* 231.

75. Spencer, *Wanderings*, 374.

76. The first preparation shot, which lasts 45 seconds, is a medium long shot depicting a group of eight men applying face and body makeup for the ceremony while two men stand at frame left. As the shot continues, a few men get up to stand at either side of the frame before moving toward the center. The second preparation shot (1 min., 45 sec. long) is a closer view of the same group; the only person now standing is an old man who rhythmically beats two boomerangs together.

77. Spencer and Gillen, *Across Australia*, 240.

78. Cantrill (1982): 28.

79. Ibid. Spencer and Gillen also worked collaboratively to procure the best range of perspectives of a ritual with one of them responsible for taking wide shots of the event and another moving in for closer shots (Mulvaney, Morphy, and Petch, eds., *My Dear Spencer*, 45).

80. Spencer and Gillen, *Across Australia*, 245.

81. Alfred Cort Haddon, "The Ethnography of the Western Tribes of Torres Straits," *JAI* 19 (1889): 298.

82. Cantrill (1982): 35.

83. Ibid., 28.

84. Gillen, *Gillen's Diary*, 72.

85. Spencer and Gillen, *Across Australia*, 231.

86. Stocking, *After Tylor*, 91.

87. In a diary entry for April 3, 1901, the first occasion the moving picture camera was used, Gillen stated that "we find that our kine films are not long enough to take in a whole ceremony; they should be 300ft instead of 150ft" (Gillen, *Gillen's Diary*, 18).

88. Cantrill (1982): 31.

89. Mulvaney and Calaby, *"So Much That Is New,"* 196.

90. Gillen, *Gillen's Diary*, 165, 258.

91. Cantrill (1982): 28. According to Mulvaney and Calaby, Spencer sent Syme almost 50,000 words for his newspaper column. The photographs published in *The Leader*, affiliated with *The Age*, also appeared in Spencer's book *Across Australia*.

92. Gillen, *Gillen's Diary*, 130.

93. Cantrill (1999): 333.

94. Mulvaney and Calaby, *"So Much That Is New,"* 217.

95. Profits from the lecture went to the University of Melbourne. Spencer was by no means a novice at delivering public lectures on his ethnographic research. In the wake of the Horn Expedition, Spencer gave over sixty lectures before wide-ranging societies and organizations including the Royal Geographical Society, which met in Melbourne's Town Hall, science club students, and Queen's Club socials where his slides were featured alongside such attractions as pianoforte and arias. His lectures were illustrated

with "limelight views" (lantern slides) of Central Australian geography, natural history, and Australian Aborigines. Mulvaney and Calaby, *"So Much That Is New,"* 181.

96. Ibid., 217. The university used the £208 0s. 6d. raised by the lectures to purchase apparatus for the eight science laboratories.

97. Cantrill (1999): 333.

98. Letter from Lorimer Fison to Spencer, May 1902 (#13), in Baldwin Spencer correspondence collection, Pitt Rivers Collection, Oxford.

99. Cantrill (1982): 37

100. Mulvaney and Calaby, *"So Much That Is New,"* 217.

101. Spencer and Gillen, *Across Australia*, 267, cited in Cantrill (1999): 332.

102. Cantrill (1982): 38.

103. Cantrill (1999): 334.

104. See Andrew Markus, *Governing Savages*, for background information on the racist treatment of Australian Aborigines by white Australians.

105. Marilyn Strathern makes a similar argument in relation to the popular reception of British armchair anthropologist James Frazer's *The Golden Bough*; according to Strathern, Frazer "did not have to create the context in which his ideas could take shape and thus promote as an organizing device an image (such as Darwin's metaphor of kinship among living things drawn from some other domain). Indeed, by the 1900s, many of Frazer's ideas were unremarkable." Strathern, "Out of Context: The Persuasive Fictions of Anthropology," *Current Anthropology* 28.3 (June 1987): 257.

106. He also exhibited his films in 1913 in England and again in 1915 in response to popular demand for lectures illustrated with still and moving images and sound recordings of native peoples. Letter from Spencer to Haddon, Nov. 11, 1915 (box 1, file 3, HC-CUL).

107. Ibid. Following Haddon's and Spencer's lead, a number of other scientists working in Australia used moving pictures in the teens and twenties. The Swedish entomologist and collector Eric Mjoetberg used film during his 1913 Cape York, Queensland, expedition, while Brooke Nicholls, a dentist, shot footage of southwest Queensland and northeastern South Australian Aborigines in conjunction with Kodak. Nicholls's 3-minute films produced for the commercial cinema were largely burlesque in style and racist in content; focusing on the Australian Aborigine's alterity and curiosity value, these shorts became staples of the commercial cinema by the 1920s and were often underwritten by such film companies as Gaumont, Pathé, and Australian Gazette. Francis Birtles and Frank Hurley were two of the most well-known adventurer-filmmakers who took advantage of this arrangement (Leigh, "Curioser," 81).

108. With regard to the challenges of fieldwork filmmaking, it is noteworthy that the scientific community *was* to some extent interested in the technical advances which would make cinematography more adaptable to fieldwork. For example, a 1900 article

in *La Nature* reported recent attempts in France to reduce the size, weight, and cost of the cinematograph. The article cited the Gaumont Company's development of a more portable camera, which was expected to have a "great influence upon the popularization of the photography of motion by permitting amateurs to perform all the necessary operations themselves and with an inexpensive and simple equipment." It also pointed out that the camera did not have a winch handle but a clockwork movement which gave the apparatus "greater mobility" since it allowed it to be hand-held. This automatic function meant that the operator could appear in front of the camera while filming the scene. However, the author noted that at the current price of $6 for film negative for recent camera models (and an additional $6 to develop the film), a potential cinematographer was "apt to look at it twice before selecting a subject, and the more so in that a positive will afterward have to be made." Cited in "A Pocket Chronophotographic Apparatus," *Scientific American Supplement* (Dec. 22, 1900): 20890.

109. Albert Britt, "Hunting for the Movies," *Outing* 73.6 (Mar. 1919): 290. Of course these problems would persist until the 1960s, until lightweight professional-standard equipment finally became available for ethnographic filmmakers.

110. Jacknis, "In Search of the Imagemaker," 206.

111. The source for the terms *emic* and *etic* comes from Kenneth L. Pike, "Language in Relation to a Unified Theory of the Structure of Human Behavior, Part I. II. III." My thanks to Faye Ginsburg and Fred Myers for tracking this information down.

112. Rosalind C. Morris, *New Worlds from Fragments: Film, Ethnography, and the Representation of Northwest Coast Cultures*, 17.

113. Ibid., 60.

5. "THE WORLD WITHIN YOUR REACH": POPULAR CINEMA AND ETHNOGRAPHIC REPRESENTATION

1. Publicity brochure for Lyman Howe's 29th Semi-Annual Tour, Wilkes-Barre, PA (1909), in Lyman Howe clipping file, Billy Rose Theater Collection, New York Public Library (hereafter, BRTC-NYPL).

2. Charles Lowe, *Four National Exhibitions in London and their Organizers*, 56. The Four National Exhibitions Show was scheduled in connection with Queen Victoria's Golden Jubilee. The cast for "Buffalo Bill's Wild West Show" included 141 American Indians, 25 cowboys, 2 women riders, 125 American ponies, 30 buffalo, 15 elk, and other livestock (*New York Times*, Mar. 31, 1887, n.p., cited in William E. Deahl Jr., "A History of Buffalo Bill's Wild West Show, 1883–1913" (Ph.D. diss., Southern Illinois University, 1974), 60–61.

3. The "reality effect" of watching films of "Buffalo Bill's Wild West Show" was considerably less than entering the performers' arena on the grounds of a show, although

this didn't dissuade Edison and Biograph from shooting films of Buffalo Bill parades in 1898 and 1902 (respectively). *Parade of Buffalo Bill Wild West Show*, nos. 1 and 2 (Edison, 1898) and *Buffalo Bill's Wild West Parade* (Biograph, 1902), both housed at the Library of Congress (hereafter, LOC).

The National Film and Television Archive (hereafter, NFTA) in London also owns *Colonel Buffalo Bill Cody* (c. 1900, #601860A), which shows the Colonel on his horse on what looks like a racetrack. Spectators are seen standing in an enclosure on either side of the track. We also see an Indian horse race before returning to a final shot of Buffalo Bill.

4. According to Charles Musser, members of "Buffalo Bill's Wild West Show" visited the Black Maria studio at least four times during the fall (Musser, *Emergence of Cinema*, 78). Musser argues that patterns of kinetoscope production and exhibition inherited a great deal from nineteenth-century photographic and phonographic practices; akin to the sound recording studio that blocked out extraneous sound, at the Black Maria studio the subject was photographed against a visually stark black background, a feature clearly indebted to the chronophotography of Eadweard Muybridge and Étienne-Jules Marey.

5. See, for example, Edwards, ed., *Anthropology and Photography, 1860–1920*, and Laurel Kendall, Barbara Mathé, and Thomas Ross Miller, *Drawing Shadows to Stone: The Photography of the Jesup North Pacific Expedition, 1897–1902*.

6. For an interesting discussion of the fascination with Native American subjects in early westerns, see Richard Abel, " 'Our Country/Whose Country?' The 'Americanization' Project of Early Westerns," in Edward Buscombe and Roberta Pearson, eds., *Back in the Saddle Again: New Essays on the Western*, 77–95.

7. Despite the pioneering work of Margaret Mead and Gregory Bateson in the late 1930s, the term *ethnographic film* didn't come into use until after World War II. See de Brigard, "History of Ethnographic Film," 13–43. There is no book-length project devoted to the history of ethnographic film, although Rony's *Third Eye* does a good job of surveying a wide range of ethnographic filmmaking practices from the work of French physicist Félix-Louis Regnault in the precinema period to *King Kong* in the 1930s. For a useful, if incomplete, catalog of international ethnographic filmmaking starting in the early cinema period, see Pierre-L. Jordan, *Premier Contact—Premier Regard*.

8. As Lee Grieveson has argued, cinema functioned as a disciplinary apparatus in a number of important ways, through regulating social and moral behavior as well as spurring juridical controls over the distribution and circulation of films. See Grieveson, "Fighting Films: Race, Morality, and the Governing of Cinema, 1912–1915," *Cinema Journal* 38.1 (Fall 1998): 40–72, and "Policing the Cinema: *Traffic in Souls* at Ellis Island, 1913," *Screen* 38.2 (Summer 1997): 149–71.

9. Both of these kinetograph films are extant and can be viewed at the Museum of Modern Art Film Study Center.

10. See Kinetoscope Company, *Price List of Films* (May-June 1895), 3, and Edison Manufacturing Company, *Edison Film* (Mar. 1900), 19, both cited in Charles Musser, *Before the Nickelodeon: Edwin S. Porter and the Edison Manufacturing Company*, 50.

11. Antonia Dickson, "Wonders of the Kinetoscope," *Frank Leslie's Monthly* 39.2 (Feb. 1895): 250.

12. Antonia Dickson's description of Edison's human menagerie might also suggest why anthropologists adopted a guarded attitude toward early cinema, since moving pictures threatened to turn ethnological subjects into sideshow attractions reminiscent of the American Indians and Australian Aborigines exhibited at Barnum's American Museum in New York City and the "Zulus," "Nubians," and "Afghans" featured in Barnum's "Ethnological Congress."

13. " 'Wild West' Kinetoscoped," *East Orange Gazette* 22.21 (Sept. 27, 1894): 3. For another local account of the event, see "Indians Before the Kinetoscope," *Orange Chronicle* 26.1339 (Sept. 27, 1894): 4. My thanks to George Tselos at the Edison Historical Site, Orange, N.J., for giving me copies of these reviews.

14. My thanks to Tom Gunning for pointing this out. According to Alice Beck Kehoe, the counterclockwise movement of the Ghost Dance symbolized the "ingathering of all people in the embrace of Our Father, God, and in his earthly deputy Jack (Pauite) Wilson. As the people move in harmony in the dance around the path of the son . . . so they must live and work in harmony" (Kehoe, *The Ghost Dance: Ethnohistory and Revitalization*, 7). The Ghost Dance movement, which was a peaceful, spiritual form of resistance to white oppression, began in the 1870s. Deemed threatening by the government, it was contained in the 1890s after the massacre at Wounded Knee where the U.S. Army launched an attack on the Sioux; ninety-eight unarmed men and 200 women and children were killed. Thomas F. Gossett, *Race: The History of an Idea*, 236.

15. The idealized concept of the Noble Savage was applied primarily to American Indians, and by extension to Polynesians and native peoples of West Africa transported as slaves to the New World. Ellwood Parry, *The Image of the Indian*, 35.

16. However, as Julie Schimmel points out, beginning in the 1840s, paintings representing Indians in a generally favorable light were challenged by two other subject categories: scenes representing conflict with whites and images of the "vanishing" or "doomed" Indian. While the doomed-Indian genre declined in popularity in the late 1860s and 1870s, it reemerged in painting and fiction after the Plains wars of the 1880s. Schimmel, "Inventing the Indian," in William H. Treuttner, ed., *The West as America: Reinterpreting Images of the Frontier, 1820–1920*, 159.

17. It is possible that the Indian dancer who gestures defiantly at the camera in Edison's *Sioux Ghost Dance* is the Sioux performer American Horse. A photograph of him taken by Gertrude Kasebier around 1900–1901 appears in Fleming and Luskey, eds., *The North American Indians*, plate 1 (p. 215).

18. Phelan, *Unmarked*, 148.

19. This film is a virtual remake of Edison's *Moki Snake Dance* (1901). Both films employ a very similar profilmic space; internal white spectators view the proceedings from behind what looks like a rope barricade (the print is obscure at this moment), although their obvious pleasure at viewing the ceremonial dances (there is a pan showing men smoking cigars and joking with one another and another shot revealing women onlookers), and from being image-makers themselves (we see a still camera being operated in one medium shot of the onlookers), is given more prominence than in Edison's film. Despite the jump cuts, awkward framing, and minimal camera movement, we are nonetheless occasionally afforded closer and more dramatic views of the snake dancers than in Edison's films, something we might expect from a film made twelve years later.

20. Burton Holmes lecture brochure, 1900, n.p., collection of the Art Reference Library, Brooklyn Museum of Art.

21. Description of "Moki Land" lecture in brochure for Burton Holmes's seventh film season at the Brooklyn Institute of Arts and Sciences (Jan. 6, 1900), n.p. "Moki Land" was one of the first series of films to be integrated into the lecture, projected, we are told, "at moments when movement is essential to complete and vivify the impressions produced by spoken words and colored illustrations." Prior to this, "chronomatograph views" were shown as a "separate appended feature of the entertainment."

22. George Wharton James, "The Hopi Snake Dance," *Outing* 36 (June 1900): 303.

23. George Wharton James, "The Snake Dance of the Hopis," *Camera Craft* 1.1 (Nov. 1902): 10 (emphasis added). Indians themselves were officially protesting the presence of cameras and, in the same year James wrote his article, the Hopi restricted photographers to a certain area to prevent interference with the ceremonies. After seeing a congressional room full of photographs of religious ceremonies during a trip to Washington, D.C., and upon realizing that the photographs were being used by officials to discredit their religion, the Hopi forbade cameras altogether in 1910; in 1911 photography was further outlawed in the pueblos.

24. Jesse Walter Fewkes, "Notes on Tusayan, Snake, and Flute Ceremonies," in the *Nineteenth Annual Report of the Bureau of American Ethnology* (1897–98) (Washington, D.C.: GPO, 1900), 978.

25. Ibid.

26. Lucy R. Lippard, ed., *Partial Recall*, 29. According to art historian Lucy Lippard, entrepreneurial tourists even went so far as to "suggest changes in the ceremonies in order to make them more photogenic" (ibid.). After years of imposing tighter and tighter restrictions on the presence of Western photographers at ceremonies, a decision was made to ban all outsiders from the overexposed Walpi Snake Dance in 1915. Ironically, at the same time as Indians fought for control of their ceremonial life, the dances came under attack from such officials as the commissioner of Indian Affairs,

Charles Burke, who in 1921 made certain ceremonial dances "Indian Offenses." However, as Lippard notes, in response to public and legal opposition, the bureau had backed down by 1928 (30).

27. Jaune Quick-To-See Smith, introduction to first national Native American photography exhibition, *Contemporary Native American Photography*, n.p., cited in Lippard, ed., *Partial Recall*, 22.

28. According to Musser, the three films that make up the 1898 Native American series, *Circle Dance*, *Buck Dance*, and *Wand Dance, Pueblo Indians*, were shot in Denver, Colorado, around the Festival of Mountain and Plain celebrated during the first week of October (Musser, *Before the Nickelodeon*, 108). Four of the five films of the 1901 series are known to have been shot in Walpi, Arizona. The 1898 films were copyrighted at the LOC on Feb. 24, 1898. Of the three 1898 films, the one that offers the clearest view of the dance is *Wand Dance, Pueblo Indians* (the extreme long shot of *Circle Dance* and the visually congested frame of *Buck Dance* make the dancers' movements harder to decipher). The medium long shot film features a small group of identically dressed Pueblo Indian dancers performing around a drummer who stands in the center of the frame. Three Pueblo girls sit facing the camera in the extreme foreground, with their backs to the performers, while a handful of Indian participants occupy spaces in the background and edges of the frame.

29. Marshall Deutelbaum, "Structural Patterning in the Lumière Films," in Fell, ed., *Film Before Griffith*, 299–310.

30. Fred J. Balshofer and Arthur C. Miller, *One Reel a Week* (Berkeley: University of California Press, 1967), 40, cited in Eileen Bowser, *The Transformation of Cinema, 1907–1915*, 176.

31. According to Kemp Niver, Edison offered exhibitors a "lecture synopsis" for each of the five Native American films shot during the 1901 series, which either accompanied each film or could be obtained directly from Edison's New Jersey studio. While the synopsis is no longer extant, it probably provided information about the location, tribe, and even cultural meanings of the dances, although the latter information may have been deemed too esoteric for popular audiences. Kemp Niver, *Early Motion Pictures: The Paper Print Collection in the Library of Congress*, 48.

32. Curtis began filming Native Americans in 1900 when he visited members of the Blackfoot tribe in Montana. In 1904 he shot footage of a Yabachi Snake Dance which the *Seattle Times* called an "exact and lifelike picture of a dance that, in its reality, had never been seen by light of day, or had been looked upon by the eyes of a white man." *Seattle Times*, May 22, 1904, n.p., cited in Mick Gidley, "From the Hopi Snake Dance to 'The Ten Commandments': Edward S. Curtis as Filmmaker," *Studies in Visual Communication* 8.5 (Summer 1982): 71.

33. Christopher Lyman, *The Vanishing Race and Other Illusions: Photographs of Indians by*

Edward Curtis, 69. This reversal was identified by contemporary Native Americans view-ing films shot by Curtis that appear in the documentary *Shadowcatcher* (Phoenix Films, 1975).

34. Philip Rosen, "Document and Documentary: On the Persistence of Historical Concepts," in Michael Renov, ed., *Theorizing Documentary*, 62–64.

35. The other four titles in the series are: *Native Women Coaling a Ship at St. Thomas, B.W.I.*; *Native Women Coaling a Ship at St. Vincent*; *Native Women Washing a Negro Baby in Nasau, B.I.*; and *Native Women Washing Clothes at St. Vincent, B.W.I.* Images of people of color working as "coalers" and of children diving for money were popular subjects in early cinema. For example, W. K. L. Dickson recalled shooting a film he called "Madeira Boys Diving for Pennies" and of coalers working as part of his voyage as a war corre-spondent to South Africa. Dickson's description of the coalers suggests that part of the impetus for obtaining these scenes was to represent peoples of color as subservient sub-jects performing heavy labor: "First we took a panoramic view of the bay, then a picture of a coaling scene—a horde of black devils half naked, carrying huge sacks of coal on their backs, and performing the most extraordinary antics while screaming some wild chant to each other." W. K. L. Dickson, *The Biograph in Battle*, 24.

36. Abbé Joseph Joye, a Jesuit priest from Switzerland, amassed a private collection of some 1,200 early films before his death in 1919. When the collection was discovered in 1975, an arrangement was made between the Cinematographe Suisse and the National Film Archive in London for the NFA to repair, identify, and transfer copies of Joye's films. Joye collected a wide range of early films, many of which were ethnographic in content. The untitled film discussed is identified as Rone C962.

37. Hair-braiding was (and continues to be) a popular motif in commercial ethno-graphic films; see, for example, *Madagaskar: Manners and Customs of the Sakalavas* (Pathé, 1910), which is an interesting parallel to the Joye film. In this film a woman sitting on the ground outside a hut facing the camera gets her long hair braided by another woman who sits in profile to the camera. This scene ends with a close-up of the woman's face smiling at the camera (as in the Joye film). Like the Joye film, this shot is also followed by one showing a man shaving another man's head with a piece of glass or pottery. Unlike the women's scene, though, this one is taken from a higher angle and represents the Madagascan man as a more threatening force to be reckoned with as he looks up and glowers at the camera.

38. David MacDougall, "Unprivileged Camera Style," *Royal Anthropological Institute Newsletter* 50 (June 1982): 9.

39. The print of the film housed at the National Film and Television Archive, London, has German intertitles.

40. Lippard, ed., *Partial Recall*, 26.

41. Catherine Russell, "Beyond Authenticity: The Discourse of Tourism in Ethno-

graphic and Experimental Film," *Visual Anthropology* 5 (1992): 134–35.

42. Livio Belloï, "Lumière and His View: The Cameraman's Eye in Early Cinema," *Historical Journal of Film, Radio, and Television* 15.4 (1995): 463 (emphasis in original).

43. Ibid., 464, 463. Several titles shot as part of Edison's 1898 Mexican series—especially *Repairing Street Scenes in Mexico, Mexico Street Scene,* and *Surface Transit, Mexico*—illustrate Belloï's analysis of the Lumière views. In each of the Edison films, the camera penetrates a space which contains a great deal of kinetic energy—people working, pedestrians crossing streets, or people disembarking from a trolley. These films function, therefore, as micro-ethnographies of the impact of modern forms of mass transportation on native culture, since in *Mexico Street Scene* and *Surface Transit, Mexico* we see bourgeois Mexicans as well as poorer people with mules negotiating a route through the busy urban space.

44. For reference to the kind of unwanted attention garnered by a motion picture camera, see Theodore Waters, "Out with a Moving Picture Machine," *Cosmopolitan* 40.3 (Jan. 1906): 256.

45. For an example of apparent interest tinged with nonchalence, see *African Caravan* from the Joye Collection (c. 1910; catalogued as Joye X7).

46. David MacDougall, *Transcultural Cinema,* 100.

47. For a discussion of the complicating effects of the return gaze, see Peterson, " 'Truth Is Stranger Than Fiction,' " 83.

48. Fatimah Tobing Rony, "Those Who Squat and Those Who Sit: The Iconography of Race in the 1895 Films of Félix-Louis Regnault," *Camera Obscura* 28 (May 1992): 273.

49. According to Pratt, contact zones are "social spaces where disparate cultures meet, clash, and grapple with each other, often in highly asymmetrical relations of domination and subordination." Pratt, *Imperial Eyes,* 4.

50. Ibid., 6–7.

51. Australian Aborigine Don Featherstone's film *Babakiueria* (1988) is an example of what Ella Shohat and Robert Stam call "media jujitsu" (derived from the Brazilian "anthropophagic" movement that uses the techniques of the oppressor to counter European domination). In Shohat's and Stam's words, "media jujitsu . . . steals elements of the dominant culture and redeploys them in the interests of oppositional praxis." In *Babakiueria,* the white discovery of Australia is reversed as Australian Aborigines subject white cultural institutions to the same forms of objectification experienced by Aboriginal peoples. Furthermore, the return gaze in cinema is also coded along generic lines, being an acceptable mode of enunciation in comedy but more problematic in dramatic works. Of course, the Shakespearean soliloquy attests to the longevity of direct address as a mode of dramatic enunciation and the fact that it wasn't always perceived as having a rupturing effect on diegetic coherence. Shohat and Stam, *Unthinking Eurocentrism,* 328. Also see Faye Ginsburg's extensive treatment of this subject in

"Culture/Media: A (mild) Polemic," *Anthropology Today* 10.2 (Apr. 1994): 5–15, as well as Ginsburg, "Aboriginal Media and the Australian Imaginary," *Public Culture* 5 (1993): 557–78, and Ginsburg, "The Parallax Effect: The Impact of Indigenous Media on Ethnographic Film," in Jane Gaines and Michael Renov, eds., *Visible Evidence*, 156–75.

52. According to Jon Gartenberg, the panning movement had become more conventionalized by 1904, and rather than simply moving the camera to the right or left in a shot, the camera operator paid great attention to the start and end points of the camera movement, a technique used to great effect in *Market Scene in Old Cairo*. Jon Gartenberg, "Camera Movement in Edison and Biograph Films, 1900–1906," *Cinema Journal* 19.2 (Spring 1980): 14.

53. For a wonderful example of native peoples being offered direction from offscreen, see *Die Beabbeiting der Wolle* (The processing of wool; 1912), in which a man's hand juts in and out of the frame instructing a woman on how to move. The film can be seen at the NFA (614918A).

54. Benjamin, "The Work of Art in the Age of Mechanical Reproduction," 234.

55. "Picturesque Java" (Pathé, 1907), *Film and Views Index*, vol. 2; and *A Primitive Man's Career to Civilization* (Warwick, 1911), reviewed in *The Bioscope* (Jan. 19, 1911): 31.

56. "Howe's Picture Festival Takes the Audience into Many Interesting and Unique Places," *Philadelphia Enquirer*, Sept. 15, 1908, n.p. (in Howe clipping file, BRTC-NYPL).

57. X. Theodore Barber, "The Roots of Travel Cinema: John L. Stoddard, E. Burton Holmes, and the Nineteenth-Century Travel Lecture," *Film History* 5 (1993): 82. For more on travel cinema, see Charles Musser, "The Travel Genre"; Jennifer Peterson, "World Pictures"; and Calvin Pryluck, "The Itinerant Movie Show and the Development of the Film Industry," *Journal of the University Film and Video Association* 35.4 (Fall 1983): 11–22.

58. Musser, *Emergence of Cinema*, 223.

59. Evidence of the commercial importance of actuality films can be found in the efforts within the early film industry to produce a taxonomy of nonfiction types, including scenic, travel, educational, and industrial. However, even before these proto-genres emerged, the outbreak of the Spanish-American War in February 1898 (just as interest in cinema as a novelty amusement began to wane) occasioned one of the earliest attempts by the industry to use the fledgling medium as a propaganda vehicle. Public demand for the "Wargraph machine" (which referred to both staged and authentic images of the war as exhibited in New York City vaudeville houses) did a great deal to boost cinema attendance.

60. For a discussion of the origins of the travel lecture, see X. Theodore Barber, "Phanstasmagorical Wonders: The Magic Lantern Ghost Show in Nineteenth-Century America," *Film History* 3 (1989): 73–86, and Barber, "The Roots of Travel Cinema," 68–84.

61. For a fascinating discussion of virtual voyages at world's fairs, see Gunning, "The World as Object Lesson," 435–38.

62. Lauren Rabinovitz, "Temptations of Pleasure: Nickelodeons, Amusements Parks, and the Sights of Female Sexuality," *Camera Obscura* 23 (May 1990): 85.

63. Ibid.

64. "Fine Entertainment," *Toledo Blade*, Dec. 9, 1910, n.p; "Howe's Pictures," *San Antonio Light*, Sept. 20, 1913, n.p. (both in Howe clipping file, BRTC-NYPL).

65. Musser offers two reasons for Howe's continued success: the commercial methods and network of contacts he established as a phonograph exhibitor and the technical excellence of his shows. Musser and Nelson, *High-Class Moving Pictures*, 67.

66. Ibid., 54, 179.

67. Evidence of the broad-based class appeal of Howe's films is suggested in a review from 1903, in which the author notes that the films were chosen "with nice discretion so as to amuse the various classes of people who attend these performances" ("Mr. Howe's New Pictures," *Wilkes-Barre Record*, Mar. 28, 1903), 7.

68. Flier for "Lyman H. Howe's Lifeorama: The Epitome of Moving Pictures," Apr.-May 1909 (BRTC-NYPL). Film subjects included Wilbur Wright's airplane demonstrations; footage of Sicily before and after the recent earthquake; "Russia: The Life of the Czar"; and "The Runaway Train." A series entitled "Egypt Past and Present" "possessed a peculiar fascination," readers were told, "because Egypt is unsurpassed in pictorial possibilities." Among the films screened during the series were shots of an Arab market and cemetery in Cairo; departure of pilgrims for Mecca; the pyramids of "Gizeh"; the Sphinx; and peasant life in Egypt.

69. Unattributed quote in flier for "Lyman H. Howe's Lifeorama," ibid.

70. According to Musser, Holmes was the first travel lecturer to exhibit his own films in conjunction with a course of lectures. During the summer of 1897, Holmes's lantern operator, Oscar Depue, purchased a 6omm motion picture camera from Léon Gaumont in Paris and shot films of Venice, Milan, and France. Holmes originally screened moving pictures at the end of his lectures, but starting in 1899–1900 he integrated films shot in Hawaii, the Philippines, and Japan throughout the talk. Musser, *Emergence of Cinema*, 221–22.

71. Hansen, *Babel and Babylon*, 98.

72. Nico de Klerk, "Print Matters: Film-Archival Reflections," in Hertogs and de Klerk, eds., *Nonfiction Film*, 69.

73. See Musser's discussion of the practices of traveling exhibitor Burton Holmes in *High-Class Moving Pictures*, 82.

74. Genoa Caldwell's edited collection of Burton Holmes's writing—chronological descriptions of his experiences as a traveler and photographer—which also contains a large number of extraordinary photographs shot by Holmes between 1886 and 1938, offers us fascinating insight into Holmes's lecturing style. Genoa Caldwell, ed., *The Man Who Photographed the World: Burton Holmes Travelogues, 1886–1938*.

75. *Brooklyn Institute of Arts and Sciences Bulletin* (hereafter, *BIASB*) 6.4 (Feb. 1911): n.p.

76. Despite these similarities, there could be important differences between the speaking positions of authors of travel novels and the makers of ethnographic travelogues; in the case where the lecturer-filmmaker was present to contextualize the screening, his or her prominent subjective explication of events was in marked contrast to the suppressed voice of the travel writer. In addition, the occasional presence of the lecturer on the screen as well as in the auditorium created a doubling effect in which the filmmaker's diegetic persona mutually reinforced his live performance.

77. Mary Louise Pratt, "Scratches on the Face of the Country: Or, What Mr. Barrow Saw in the Land of the Bushmen," *Critical Inquiry* 12.1 (Autumn 1985): 127.

78. Ibid., 128.

79. The rhetoric of a quick response to a service or product is probably borrowed from general advertising techniques which pressured consumers into buying through a "limited time offer" appeal. My thanks to Jim Latham for pointing this out.

80. Pratt, "Scratches," 120.

81. Johannes Fabian, *Time and the Other: How Anthropology Makes Its Object*, 33.

82. Pratt, "Scratches," 120.

83. Malek Alleloula, *The Colonial Harem*, 120.

84. Ibid., 4.

85. Reviewing the same film, the *Pittsburgh Leader* evoked a far more serene picture of a land "rich in mystery and weirdly beauty [*sic*]." The various attractions portrayed "on the canvas" included the "historic sphinx" and the pyramids of Gaza as well as "beautiful and unique views of the lives of the natives." "Howe's Wonderful Pictures," *Pittsburgh Leader*, July 12, 1906 (Howe clipping file, BRTC-NYPL). Howe had been exhibiting *From Cairo to Khartoum* since 1903.

86. *MPW* 1.23 (Aug. 10, 1907): 362.

87. For another review of *From Cairo to Khartoum*, see "Mr. Howe's New Pictures" in the *Wilkes-Barre Record*, Mar. 28, 1903, 7.

88. Review of "Japan, Land of Flowers," *Brooklyn Eagle*, Jan. 6, 1900, n.p. (Holmes clipping file, BRTC-NYPL; emphasis added).

89. Dan Streible's work on early boxing films deftly illustrates this point. See "Fake Fight Films," in la Tour, Gaudreault, and Pearson, eds., *Cinema at the Turn of the Century*, 55; "Female Spectators and the Corbett-Fitzsimmons Fight Film," in Aaron Baker and Todd Boyd, eds., *Sports, Media, and the Politics of Identity*, 16–47; and "A History of the Boxing Film, 1894–1915: Social Control and Reform in the Progressive Era," *Film History* 3.3 (1989): 235–58. Streible's book-length study of prizefighting and early cinema is forthcoming (2002) from Smithsonian Institution Press: *Fight Pictures: A History of Prizefighting and Early Cinema*.

90. For an excellent example of the admixture of actuality and staged footage in early cinema, see Philip Rosen's discussion of Pathé's *Policeman's Tour of the World* (1906) in

"Disjunction and Ideology in a Preclassical Film: *A Policeman's Tour of the World*," *Wide Angle* 12.3 (1990): 20–36.

91. Streible, "Fake Fight Films," 56. According to Streible (ibid., 55), between 1897 and 1910 an equal number of ringside and restaged boxing films were produced for the U.S. market.

92. Hartman, "Lyman H. Howe," unidentified newspaper clipping (Lyman Howe file, BRTC-NYPL).

93. Occasionally, promotional materials are supplemented by personal records kept by camera operators, lecturers, and other individuals associated with a film.

94. Description from *Pathé Weekly* 107 (Nov. 15, 1909; emphasis added).

95. Walker Percy, "The Loss of the Creature," in David Bartholomae and Anthony Petrosky, eds., *Ways of Seeing: An Anthology for Writers*, 424–45.

96. Jonathan Culler, "The Semiotics of Tourism," *American Journal of Semiotics* 1 (1981): 127–40.

97. Martin Loiperdinger in "A Change of Programme," Session 5 of Hertogs and De Klerk, *Nonfiction Film*, 53.

98. Friedberg, *Window Shopping*, 2.

99. *MPW* 1.25 (Aug. 24, 1907): n.p.

100. "Interesting Travel with Lyman Howe: Moving Pictures of World's Scenes at State Armory," *(Rochester, N.Y.) Times*, Sept. 20, 1912, n.p. (Howe clipping file, BRTC-NYPL).

101. "Teaching by Pictures," *MPW* 7.1 (June 2, 1910): 19.

102. "Howe's Pictures," *San Antonio Light*, Sept. 20, 1913, n.p. (Howe clipping file, BRTC-NYPL).

103. "The Cult of the Motion Picture: Their Importance as Recorders of Historical Events and the Tricks of Their Manufacture," *MPW* 3.10 (Sept. 5, 1908): 177. The use of the word "cult" in the title of this article is a reminder of the phenomenal mass appeal of moving pictures during the nickelodeon boom; "cult," "nickel madness," "dippy over the movies" were just some of the expressions freely evoked to describe the popularity of motion pictures.

104. "Howe Pictures at the Nixon," *Pittsburgh Leader*, June 22, 1909, n.p. (Howe clipping file, BRTC-NYPL); and "Usefulness of Moving Pictures," *MPW* 7.6 (Feb. 19, 1910): 247.

105. "Fine Entertainment," *Toledo Blade*, Dec. 9, 1910 (Howe clipping file, BRTC-NYPL). Musser notes that during the 1899–1900 period, Howe had at least five people producing his show. In addition to a pianist-manager and projectionist, he had three people responsible for sound effects, a sound-effects artist who doubled as a monologist, and two locally hired effects-makers. Musser and Nelson, *High-Class Moving Pictures*, 97.

106. "Howe's Lifeorama," Dec. 1, 1905 (unidentified clipping: Howe clipping file, BRTC-NYPL).

107. "How the Sounds Are Made That Add Realism to the Scenes on the Screen," *Pittsburgh Leader*, July 10 1908 (Howe clipping file, BRTC-NYPL).

108. "Long Line Besieges Office to See Howe's Travel Wonders," *Pittsburgh Courier*, May 19, 1914 (Howe clipping file, BRTC-NYPL). Other reviewers were less enthusiastic about the sound effects; writing in the *Pittsburgh Post*, one reviewer found them "distracting and irritating," May 20, 1913 (Howe clipping file, BRTC-NYPL).

109. For a revisionist reading of the issue of sound in early cinema, see Rick Altman, "The Silence of the Silents," *Musical Quarterly* 88.4 (1996): 648–718. In this important article, Altman counters the perceived historiographic wisdom that films were rarely, if ever, shown in silence.

110. Ibid., 651. According to Altman, "If ever a claim qualified for the status of received opinion in the field, the notion that silent cinema was never silent would be it" (658).

111. Howe and Holmes often deliberately undercranked some of their landscape films in order to create the sensation of out-of-control movement. Tom Gunning uses the example of Howe's *The Runaway Train* in which overcranking of the projector caused a film taken from a train going down the Alps to plunge down inclines and across bridges ("An Unseen Energy Swallows Space: The Space in Early Film and Its Relation to American Avant-Garde Film," in Fell, ed., *Film Before Griffith*, 364). Of course, local exhibitors could also create similar effects through undercranking and overcranking.

112. For a discussion of the uses of both licensed commercial releases and films shot by Depue in Holmes's "Two Ways Round the World" lecture, see *MPW* 10.6 (Nov. 11, 1911): 6. While praising the slides, the author is highly critical of the poor quality of some of Holmes's films, complaining that the prints were dark, rainy, and contrasty.

113. One cannot but notice the gendered and ethnic composition of skilled workers employed by white, male industry representatives such as Holmes. White, male hegemony in the nascent motion picture industry inculcates all aspects of production and exhibition.

114. *BIASB* 2.3 (Feb. 13, 1909): n.p. Evidence of the gendered and class-based appeal of Holmes's lectures can be gleaned from a feature in *Ladies' Home Journal* on Holmes's recent tour to Japan. Such issues as Japanese art, industrial development, and the Americanization of Japan are covered in the article in a flowery style that may have paralleled the proselytizing of the travelogue lecturer: "There is no new Japan: there is only old Japan, outwardly effecting in pure self-protection a transformation; likening herself in outward seeming to the stronger threatening Western world, but inwardly remaining true to her old ideals, keeping her inner life in harmony with that Eastern concept of life that is not and never can be understood by us in the West." The article is a rich source of orientalist themes and discourses, although it is unclear whether the anonymous informant is, in fact, Holmes himself. "Around the World with Burton Holmes: What

the New Japan Really Means," *Ladies' Home Journal* (Nov. 1908), n.p. (Holmes clipping file, BRTC-NYPL).

115. Klerk, "Print Matters," 70.

116. "Ford's Opera House," *Baltimore American*, Aug. 30, 1910 (Howe clipping file, BRTC-NYPL).

117. "Mr Howe's New Pictures," *Wilkes-Barre Record*, Mar. 28, 1903, 7.

118. "Garrick Travel Pictures," *Detroit Journal*, May 25, 1914 (Howe clipping file, BRTC-NYPL). For a discussion of racist discourse in turn-of-the-century popular culture, see Wayne M. Mellinger and Rodney Beaulieu, "White Fantasies, Black Bodies: Racial Power, Disgust, and Desire in American Popular Culture," *Visual Anthropology* 9.2 (1997): 117–47.

119. Both films can be viewed at the LOC's Motion Picture, Broadcasting, and Recorded Sound Division.

120. Bhaba, *The Location of Culture*, 66.

121. Peterson, "World Pictures," 7.

122. Peterson, " 'Truth Is Stranger Than Fiction," 84.

123. See Lant, "Egypt in Early Cinema."

124. "Takes and Possibilities in the Moving Picture Business as Reviewed by an Outsider," *MPW* 3.7 (Aug. 15, 1908): 121.

125. Louis Reeves Harrison, "Photoscenes of Travel," *MPW* 14.1 (Oct. 5, 1912): 21.

126. Harrison, "Photoscenes of Travel," 21.

127. George W. Stocking Jr., "Anthropology as Kulturkampf: Science and Politics in the Career of Franz Boas," in Goldschmidt, ed., *Uses of Anthropology*, 37.

128. Samuel Pierpoint Langley, "Minutes of the Meeting of the Board of Regents of the Smithsonian Institution," Jan. 27, 1904 (Smithsonian Institution Archives).

129. For an insightful analysis of the discursive construction of Jewish groups by Boas and how this work was enmeshed in larger debates concerning Jewish racial and ethnic identity, see Barbara Kirshenblatt-Gimblett, "Erasing the Subject: Franz Boas and the Anthropological Study of Jews in the United States, 1903–1942" (unpublished paper presented to the American Anthropological Association, 1986).

130. Charles Urban, "The Cinematograph in Science and Education," *MPW* 1.21 (July 27, 1907): 324. An important figure in the industry up until World War I, Urban was particularly interested in scientific film, and his British-based firm, the Warwick Trading Co., was renowned for its documentary and news films. For a useful snapshot of Urban's career, see Stephen Herbert and Luke McKernan, eds., *Who's Who of Victorian Cinema*, 144–45.

131. Bureau of American Ethnology (BAE) *Annual Report* 23 (1901–1902), xvi. Phillips's proposal to Professor W. J. McGee was for the BAE to front the costs of a motion picture camera, film, and traveling expenses (at a maximum of $400). Phillips approached

the BAE on the recommendation of the Armat Motion-Picture Company of Washington, D.C., who felt that Phillips would be an excellent choice to make films of Native Americans on the basis of his prior experience taking Indian photographs and shooting some film. Other than supplying the camera free of charge, it is unclear what role the Armat Motion-Picture Company played in this project; what we do know is that by May of the following year, some of Phillips's films which he had shot the previous summer had still not been processed by Armat, much to Phillips's annoyance. See O. P. Phillips correspondence file in BAE Records at the National Anthropological Archives (NAA), National Museum of Natural History (NMNH), Washington, D.C. My thanks to Photograph Archivist Paula Richardson Fleming for locating this file for me.

132. BAE *Annual Report* 23 (1901–1902), xvi.

133. Letter to W. J. McGee, May 28, 1901 (in Phillips correspondence file, NAA, NMNH). Part of Phillips's determination to get the BAE to agree to fund the project was his desire to procure a copy of the films for a series of popular lectures he had planned on Native Americans. Realizing that he couldn't possibly fund his own filmmaking trip to Arizona, or that if he did, it would be with an "inferior camera and much less film," Phillips had initially approached Armat with the idea but the company had turned it down, suggesting Phillips approach the BAE. Phillips was therefore offering his services free of charge as long as he could get a copy of the films.

134. For an interesting discussion of issues of accuracy in early westerns representing Native Americans, see Abel, " 'Our Country/Whose Country?' " 77–95.

135. Selig had already won the cooperation of the Commissioner of Indian Affairs, a fact that might have influenced the BAE's decision to back the project. Information in e-mail correspondence from Andy Smith to John Homiak in Wanamaker File, Human Studies Film Archive, NMNH, Washington, D.C.

136. U.S. Bureau of Indian Affairs, *Annual Report of the Commissioner for Indian Affairs (1917)*, 40, cited in Gidley, "From the Hopi," 78. Of course, Biograph films of Yellowstone Park and Native Americans shot in 1904 and shown at the St. Louis World's Fair were made "under the auspices of the U.S. Department of Interior," an early example of a government agency turning to a commercial manufacturing company to produce actualities. See Kemp R. Niver, comp., *Biograph Bulletins, 1896–1908*, 145–47. My thanks to Tom Gunning for reminding me of this.

137. See "Moving Pictures Aid Mission Work," *MPW* 5.20 (Nov. 13, 1909): 678, for a brief discussion of the work of a home mission by the Rev. Dr. Jacob Sallade in Philadelphia.

138. Clegg, "Education by Kinematograph," 331.

139. F. Laurent, in *Le Cinéma* (May 24, 1912), n.p., cited in Burch, *Life To Those Shadows*, 53.

140. Ibid., 52.

141. For the same series, Barnes also wrote: *The Motion Picture Comrades Along the Orinoco; Or, Facing Perils in the Tropics*; *The Motion Picture Comrades' Great Venture; Or, On the Road with the Big Round Top*; and *The Motion Picture Comrades Aboard a Submarine; Or, Searching for Treasures Under the Sea*, all published in 1917. On the inside cover of each volume, readers are told that the "object of these books is to place before the reader the unusual experiences of a party of boys who succeed in filming a number of interesting scenes. . . . [They] describe with remarkable accuracy the methods employed to obtain many of the wonderful pictures which may be seen on the screen."

142. Gunning, "An Aesthetic of Astonishment," 40.

143. "Moving Pictures as an Educator," *MPW* 3.21 (Nov. 21, 1908): 397.

144. De Brigard, "History of Ethnographic Film," 20. Worcester lectured with the films at the American Museum of Natural History in the spring of 1914. The lecture blurb stated that Worcester ("known as the 'Great White Father' of the wild tribes") had "opportunities paralleled by none of obtaining vivid and realistic photographs and motion pictures of the inhabitants and of natural life." Members Courses lecture announcement for Feb. 5, 1914 (in AMNH Spring Course 1914 file, Special Collections Dept., AMNH).

145. For a discussion of the kinds of anxieties cinema engendered for colonial administrators and expatriates during the 1920s and 1930s, see Brian Larkin, "White Prestige and the Immoral, Subversive Problem of Film: Moral Panic and Colonial Authority."

146. This epithet was the title given to the first Domitor (International Association to Promote the Study of Early Cinema) conference held in Quebec City in 1990 ("An Invention of the Devil? Religion and Early Cinema"). Organized to explore the textual strategies used in early films about religious subjects, the social and cultural meanings of religious films, and the relationship between the state, film production, and the church in various national contexts, the conference provided a useful forum for understanding cinema's discursive construction as an "invention of the devil." The proceedings were published in Roland Cosandey, André Gaudreault, and Tom Gunning, eds., *An Invention of the Devil: Religion and Early Cinema*.

147. "Making the Devil Useful," *English Journal* 2 (Dec. 1913): 658. A sample of articles attacking noneducational cinema for its imputed immorality (amongst other related issues) includes: "Public Opinion as a Moral Censor," *MPW* 1.10 (May 11, 1907): 147–48; J. E. Wallace Wallin, "The Moving Picture in Relation to Education, Health, Delinquency, and Crime," *Pedagogical Seminary* 17.2 (June 1910): 129–42; and Edward Lyttelton, "Note on the Educational Influence of the Cinematograph," *Hibbert Journal* (July 1913): 851–55. According to Lyttelton, the "influence of moving pictures [was] prejudicial to learning in the same way as the reading of snippets of information in half-penny newspapers, only to a much greater degree" (854). A sample of articles in support of cinema's contribution to education include: Urban, "The Cinematograph," 324;

"Moving Pictures as an Educator," *MPW* 3.21 (Nov. 21, 1908): 397; "Education by Cinematograph," *The Bioscope* (Jan. 26, 1911): 7–9; and Clegg, "Education by Kinematograph," 331.

148. Review in *MPW* 5.2 (July 10, 1909): 49. Pathé was one of the most prolific producers of ethnographic films between 1905 and 1913, making films in Japan, India, and North Africa. As Richard Abel has shown, Pathé was not only a key player in the maturation of the developing American cinema industry—between 1905 and 1909 it was the leading supplier of films—but developed a reputation for producing films of exceptional quality across a number of genres. For an excellent account of Pathé's operations in the United States, see Richard Abel, "The Perils of Pathé, or the Americanization of Early American Cinema," in Charney and Schwartz, eds., *Cinema and the Invention of Modern Life*, 183–226; also see Abel, *The Ciné Goes to Town: French Cinema, 1896–1914*, and *The Red Rooster Scare: Making Cinema American, 1900–1910*.

149. "Weekly Comment on the Shows," *MPW* 4.7 (Feb. 13, 1909): 169.

150. *MPW* 1.24 (Aug. 17, 1907): 373. *MPW*'s readers were left in little doubt as to the racial inferiority of the Veddahs, as the remainder of the review attests: "They are of dwarfish stature, their habits are extremely degraded, and they are devoid of any sort of organization. The Veddahs dwell in caves, or in the depths of the forest, subsisting on vermin, reptiles, or whatever animal they contrive to capture with their rude weapons. They are not able to count, neither have they any idea of time. They cannot distinguish colors, and differ from all other known races in that they never laugh, and do not possess even the rudest form of musical instrument" (373).

151. "Another Lost Opportunity" (editorial), *MPW* 5.16 (Oct. 16, 1909): 5.

152. A huge box-office hit, Martin and Osa Johnson's *Simba* (1928) was just one of several adventure films that used actuality footage within a fictional narrative. Other films to do so include Cooper and Schoedsack's *Chang* (1927) and Osa and Martin Johnson's *Congorilla* (1932).

153. Susan Applegate Krouse, "Photographing the Vanishing Race," *Visual Anthropology* 3 (1990): 215.

154. According to anthropologist Susan Applegate Krouse, the hand-colored film was shown to schoolchildren in Wanamaker's stores in Philadelphia and New York, although only the script and photographs are extant. Dixon cast Crow Indians rather than members of the Ojibwa tribe (upon whom the legend is based). Scenes shot include "Hiawatha tended by Mokomis, his meeting with his father, the wooing and wedding of Minnehaha, her death, and Hiawatha's final journey" (Krouse, "Photographing the Vanishing Race," 215). Over 3,000 feet of film and 125 colored slides were shot during the expedition, and a special screening of the expedition films was organized in Washington, D.C., for President Taft. The screening took place on April 20, 1910. According to a report in the *Nickelodeon*, two sets of the film were to be preserved in government

archives "for the benefit of future generations of Americans who will not be able to see Indians . . . [because] in time the red man will be extinct" ("Wanamaker Aids Indians' History," *Nickelodeon* 3.9 (Apr. 30, 1910): 234).

155. The temporary camp was set up every third weekend in August and contained sweat and purification lodges; 1,200 Crows attended the camp in 1908 (Dean Bear Claw interview with John Homiak, American Indian Department, Smithsonian Institution, Washington D.C., Mar. 13, 1990). Dixon, his son Rollin, and photographer James Bartlett Rich took over 1,600 photographs and shot ten reels of film during the expedition; some processing was done in darkrooms set up in the field, although many of the enlargements were developed by Kodak (Krouse, "Photographing the Vanishing Race," 215).

Footage Dixon shot of the Crow camp, Crow Fair, and Custer reenactment came to light in 1982 and can be viewed at the Human Studies Film Archive (HSFA) in Washington, D.C. According to former HSFA curator Wendy Shay, the 1,120 feet of film found in a Montana basement were out-takes discarded by Dixon because of poor framing and exposure. Both positive and negative footage was haphazardly arranged on several reels. Shay matched the scenes, eliminated some of the duplicated footage, edited the film from its original 34 minutes to 18 minutes, and organized the scenes in roughly the same order in which they were photographed (which culminated with the reenactment of the Custer battle).

156. "Wanamaker Aids Indians' History," *Nickelodeon* 3.9 (Apr. 30, 1910): 224.

157. Joseph K. Dixon, *Wanamaker Primer on the North American Indian*, 44.

158. See Lyman (*Vanishing Race*, 62–112) for a discussion of Curtis's photographic practices. For general information on the manipulation and stereotyping of Native Americans in late nineteenth- and early twentieth-century photography, see Blackman, "Posing the American Indian," 68–74; Scherer, "You Can't Believe Your Eyes," 67–79; and Scherer, "The Public Faces of Sarah Winnemucca," 178–204.

159. Letter from Roosevelt to Harriman, Mar. 2, 1905 (in file 4.2.004, Stuart Culin Archival Collection, Art Reference Library, Brooklyn Museum).

160. A. F. Muhr, "E. S. Curtis and His Work," *Photo-Era* (July 1907): 12.

161. Joseph K. Dixon, *The Purpose and Achievements of the Rodman Wanamaker Expedition of Citizenship to the North American Indian* (pamphlet). N.p.: Summer and Autumn 1913), 1 (Department of Library Services, AMNH; hereafter, DLS-AMNH).

162. Quoted in Bill Holm and George Quimby, *Edward S. Curtis in the Land of the War Canoes: A Pioneer Cinematographer in the Pacific Northwest*, 32.

163. Promotional statement by the Continental Film Company (without source documentation), cited in Holm and Quimby, *Edward S. Curtis*, 113.

164. Ibid., 59.

165. Susan Applegate Krouse, "Filming the Vanishing Race," in Martin Taureg and

Jay Ruby, eds., *Visual Explorations of the World: Selected Papers from the International Conference on Visual Communication*, 260.

166. "Films of Custer Massacre," *Nickelodeon* 2.5 (Nov. 1909): 154. We are told that more than 400 Indians and two companies of national guardsmen took part in the reenactment and, according to Gen. C. H. Englesby, who was in attendance, the fight "was more spectacular than the regular performances given at the [Crow Fair] exposition."

167. Ibid.

168. Ernest A. Dench, *Making the Movies*, 92–94.

169. Sander Gilman, *Difference and Pathology: Stereotypes of Sexuality, Race, and Madness*, 17, 21.

170. The *Biograph Bulletin*'s description of the Sioux Indian featured in *The Redman and the Child* (Biograph, 1908) betrays no hint of the fact that the "magnificent type of aboriginal American" was played by the famous white actor Charles Insee. Conforming to the ideology of the romantic savage and illustrating the recurring white fetishization of the body of the Native American male, the *Bulletin*'s emphasis on the static qualities of the image also recalls Curtis's photographic technique, especially his fondness for shooting his subjects against the light in order to render them a silhouette: "What a magnificent picture he strikes as he stands there, his tawny skin silhouetted against the sky, with muscles turgid and jaws set in grim determination." *Bulletin* 156 (July 1908), quoted in Eileen Bowser, *Biograph Bulletins, 1908–1912*, 5. For a description of Curtis's technique, see "Ethnology in Action," the anonymous review of *In the Land of the Head Hunters* from *The Independent* (Jan. 11, 1915): 72.

171. *MPW* 6.11 (Apr. 30, 1910): 690.

172. *MPW* 6.20 (May 21, 1910): 830.

173. Lyman, *Vanishing Race*, 60.

174. Holm and Quimby, *Edward S. Curtis*, 32.

175. Uncited Curtis reference in Gidley, "From the Hopi," 75.

176. "Ethnology in Action," *The Independent* (Jan. 11, 1915): 72.

177. Edward S. Curtis, "The Continental Film Company" (1912), cited in Holm and Quimby, *Edward S. Curtis*, 113.

178. W. Stephen Bush, " 'In the Land of the Head-Hunters,' " *MPW* 22.12 (Dec. 19, 1914): 1695.

179. Ibid.

180. Vachel Lindsay, *The Art of the Moving Picture*, 115. For more on Lindsay's contribution to a discourse of orientalism and exoticism in the formation of the motion picture industry, see Nick Browne, "Orientalism as an Ideological Form: American Film Theory in the Silent Period," *Wide Angle* 11, no. 4 (1989): 23–31.

181. Lindsay, *Art of the Moving*, 114.

182. Ibid., 115.

183. Ibid., 121.

184. Dixon delivered three daily lectures in conjunction with the films and photographs, which were exhibited in the John Rodman Wanamaker Collection in the redwood booth in the Palace of Education at the 1915 exposition. A production still of Chief Two Moons from Dixon's 1908 film *Hiawatha* was used to illustrate *The Blue Book: A Comprehensive Official Souvenir View Book of the Panama-Pacific International Exposition at San Francisco, 1915*, 92.

185. The aim of the expedition was to photograph and film "The Last Great Indian Council." Fifteen tribes attended the council, which took place in September 1909. Cooperating fully with Dixon, the Indians supplied their own native dress, tepees, bows, and other paraphernalia and spent several weeks setting up camp, riding across the prairie, and talking in council. Krouse, "Photographing the Vanishing Race," 220.

186. Program for "The Last Great Indian Council: The Farewell of the Chiefs," lecture given by Joseph K. Dixon at the AMNH on October 24, 1912 (DLS-AMNH). An exhibition of Dixon's photographs had been installed in the West Assembly Hall of the AMNH. All quotations are from this document unless stated otherwise.

187. *MPW* 8.10 (Mar. 11, 1911): 58.

188. *MPW* 8.11 (Mar. 18, 1911): 600.

189. For a discussion of Native American representation in the silent period and beyond, see Gretchen M. Bataille and Charles L.P. Silet, eds., *The Pretend Indians: Images of Native Americans in the Movies*.

190. "The Make-Believe 'Indian' " (editorial), *MPW* 8.9 (Mar. 4, 1911): 473.

191. Ibid.

192. W. Stephen Bush, "Moving Picture Absurdities," *MPW* 9.10 (Sept. 16, 1911): 733. "Licensed Indians" refers to films produced by members of the Motion Picture Patents Company, a cartel created by Edison and other leading production companies in 1909 to raise profits and create barriers to entry. The Independents were formed by the American Mutoscope and Biograph Company and George Kleine. See Musser, *Before the Nickelodeon*, for a discussion of MPPC (438–42, 379–82) and the Independents (442–45).

193. Alanson Skinner, "Red Men in 'Movies,' " *New York Times*, June 3, 1914, 12, quoted in Kevin Brownlow, *The War, the West, and the Wilderness*, 329. Despite Skinner's scorn for ethnographic liberty-taking, he had, on previous occasions, served as a consultant for commercial filmmakers.

194. C. H. Claudy, "Too Much Acting," *MPW* 8.9 (Feb. 11, 1911): 288.

195. Ira Jacknis, "George Hunt, Kwakiutl Photographer," in Edwards, ed., *Anthropology and Photography*, 144. For a more detailed biographical account of Hunt's work, see Jacknis, "George Hunt, Collector of Indian Specimens," in Aldona Jonaitis, ed., *Chiefly Feasts: The Enduring Kwakiutl Potlatch*, 177–224.

196. Jacknis, "George Hunt, Kwakuitl Photographer," 145.

197. Lyman, *Vanishing Race*, 118.

198. Working with a cast of fifty Kwakwa̱ka'wakw, including a number of surviving cast members from the original Curtis film, Holm and Quimby added a soundtrack consisting of Kwakwa̱ka'wakw dialogue, chanting, and singing. Catherine Russell argues that Kwakwa̱ka'wakw spectators tended to ignore the film's ostensible narrative structure in favor of viewing the film as both a "living memory of both the traditional practices and the colonial containment activated by the rigorous framing and the 'photoplay' conventions." Catherine Russell, "Playing Primitive: 'In the Land of the Headhunters' and/or 'War Canoes,' " *Visual Anthropology* 8 (1996): 70.

199. Russell, "Playing Primitive," 56. The transformation of "Head Hunters" into "War Canoes" has been anything but a smooth process in terms of the kinds of debates generated in response to Holm and Quimby's restoration. Upon finding an original version of Curtis's film in the private collection of Hugo Zeitler housed at the Chicago Field Museum, University of Chicago professor Brad Evans critiqued Catherine Russell's reading of the film, especially her criticism of its narrative incoherence and "cinema of attractions" style. (Russell had based her reading of the film on Holm and Quimby's reedited version rather than the original print found by Evans and saw the film as an exemplary instance of what she calls "experimental ethnography.") Defending Curtis's abilities as a filmmaker, Evans places the blame for the film's confusing narrative structure squarely at the feet of Holm and Quimby, arguing that "the editing of the restored version disguises the narrative coherence of Curtis's original, the new soundtrack betrays its dramatic intentions, and the new intertitles deaden its linguistic flair" (Brad Evans, "Commentary: Catherine Russell's Recovery of the *Head-Hunters*," *Visual Anthropology* 11, no. 3 [1998]: 224; see also Russell's response to Evans in the same issue [241–42]). For a slightly revised version of Russell's *Head-Hunters* essay that originally appeared in *Visual Anthropology*, see ch. 5 of Russell's book *Experimental Ethnography: The Work of Film in the Age of Video*, 98–118.

200. This phrase is borrowed from Ella Shohat, "Imagining Terra Incognita: The Disciplinary Gaze of Empire," *Public Culture* 3.2 (Spring 1991): 42. For an excellent discussion of cinema's role within the colonial imagination and how discourses of Eurocentrism, gender, and empire intersect to construct "visual embodiments of gendered and eroticized tropes" (9), see Shohat and Stam, *Unthinking Eurocentrism*, esp. chs. 3 and 4.

201. T. A. Church, " 'Beasts of the Jungle': A Two-Part Educational and Scenic Feature of the Highest Quality by the Supreme Features Corporation," *MPW* 21.3 (Sept. 26, 1914): 1817.

202. "From Durban to Zululand" (Edison, 1913), *The Kinetogram*, Nov. 15, 1913, 8.

203. Review of *In Africa*, *MPW* 6.7 (Apr. 30, 1910): 690.

204. Charles Urban, "The Cinematograph in Science and Education," *MPW* 1.24 (Aug. 17, 1907): 373.

6. EARLY ETHNOGRAPHIC FILM AT
THE AMERICAN MUSEUM OF NATURAL HISTORY

1. Langdon, "The New Museum Idea," 7711.

2. "The Spectator," *The Outlook* 92 (May 29, 1909): 273.

3. Michel Foucault, *The Archaeology of Knowledge*, 4, cited in Eilean Hooper-Greenhill, *Museums and the Shaping of Knowledge*, 10.

4. John R. Saunders, "Development of Educational Services, 1869–1956," AMNH *Annual Reports (1955–56)*, 14.

5. Kirshenblatt-Gimblett, "Objects of Ethnography," 394.

6. Ibid.

7. AMNH *Annual Report for 1898*, 26 (hereafter, AMNH annual reports will be cited as AR-AMNH).

8. "Museum Illustrated Lectures of Paris," *AMJ* 1.7–8 (Feb.-Mar. 1901): 102.

9. AR-AMNH (1900), 42–43.

10. Roy Chapman Andrews, *Under a Lucky Star: A Lifetime of Adventure*, 46.

11. Raymond Ditmars, *The Making of a Scientist* (New York: Macmillan, 1937), 23.

12. George Sherwood, *AMJ* 11.3 (1911): 245.

13. AR-AMNH (1915), 48.

14. In Great Britain, another issue tended to dominate discussion of illustrated lectures, namely, lecturers exhibiting commercially produced slides of objects not displayed in the museum at which the lecturer was appearing. Discussing a lecture series given at Leeds Museum in 1905, one author noted that "the slides used in the lectures are from the real objects lectured upon," a point reiterated later on in a description of children's lectures: "The slides used in the lecture are from the real objects which are also described in the syllabus." Henry Crowther, "The Museum as Teacher of Nature-Study," *MJ* 5.1 (July 1905): 11–12.

15. Frederic A. Lucas, "The Work of Our Larger Museums," 35. It was noted in the 1898 annual reports that the use of photographs in illustrating the AMNH's collections had increased (24).

16. Sherwood cited in untitled transcript (Apr. 2, 1917), p. 5 (Central Archives, Dept. of Library Services, American Museum of Natural History; hereafter, CA-AMNH).

17. Frank Woolnaugh, "Museums and Nature Study," *MJ* 4.8 (Feb. 1905): 268.

18. *AMJ* 8.3 (Mar. 1908): 46.

19. Letter To George Sherwood from Dr. Hugh Smith, Nov. 1909 (file 878, CA-AMNH). Writing in 1914, Herbert Grau described the Miles Brothers Film Exchange and the Miles brothers themselves as "one of the earliest moving-picture concerns in the country and active factors in every phase of the industry from the outset of the evolution." Herbert Miles was operating vaudeville theaters out in the West in 1905 and was

one of the first exhibitors to operate a storefront nickel theater. Herbert Grau, *The Theatre of Science*, 17. For a more detailed account of the Miles Brothers firm, see Musser, *Emergence of Cinema*.

20. Letter to George Sherwood from Claude Bennett, Mar. 15, 1911 (file 903, CA-AMNH).

21. Letter to Sherwood from Bennett, Feb. 1, 1911, in ibid. In a letter to the Museum in February 1911, Bennett boasted of having delivered his lecture before the Brooklyn Institute of Arts and Sciences, the National Geographic Society, local theaters, chautauquas, and educational institutions, in each case being sensitive to the need to change the lecture and films to "suit the occasion and bring out the latest developments in the work."

22. Letter to Hugh Smith from Frederic A. Lucas, Dec. 1, 1913 (file 1906–20, CA-AMNH).

23. While the precise identification of ethnographic subject matter is complicated by the fact that few of these films are extant, and by the common practice of using stock footage obtained from commercial rental agencies as opposed to titled films to illustrate lectures and talks, the following examples of lecture titles allude to or indicate the presence of native peoples in the films: "Travels in Europe and the Far East" (Roy Chapman Andrews, 1911); "Travels in South America" (L. Hussakof, 1911); "Jungle Scenes in Africa, India, and Borneo" (Cherry Kearton, 1913); "The Indians of the Southwest: Their Daily Lives and Ceremonies" (Pliny Goddard, 1913); "Africa, Egypt, Algiers, Interior, South Africa" (Dr. Fisher, 1913); "The Indians of New York State" (Alanson Skinner, 1913); "Among the Wild Tribes of the Philippine Islands" (Dean C. Worcester, 1914); "Mexico and Her People" (Frederick Monson, 1914); and "Blackfoot Indian Life" (E. M. Deming, 1915).

24. Letter to Frank E. Kleinschmidt from President Osborn, Apr. 1, 1912 (box 903 [Spring Course, 1912], CA-AMNH).

25. *MPW* 22 (Oct. 17, 1914): 399. The film purportedly received the "best endorsements from scientific societies, theater managers and press." Exhibitors renting the film from the Arctic Film Co. could get a copy of the "lecture, press matters, lobby photos—enlarged photos, [and] lantern slides" (ibid). A review of the film in the *MPW* described the representation of the Inuit peoples as follows: "The portrayal of the lives of the natives has in it much of novelty. The huts of a few Eskimos hanging to the barren rocks of a little island had never been photographed before and make an interesting spectacle." *MPW* 19 (Feb. 21, 1914): 956.

26. Anonymous review in the *Philadelphia Telegraph*, May 21, 1912, n.p. (Kleinschmidt clipping file, BRTC-NYPL).

27. Kearton was Teddy Roosevelt's cinematographer for the films he shot in Africa in 1909. For more on Kearton, see "With Roosevelt in Africa," *The Bioscope* (Apr. 14, 1910): 58; "Cherry Kearton and His Work," *MPW* 7.11 (Sept. 10, 1910): 567–68; "Cherry

Kearton," *MPW* 7.14 (Oct. 1, 1910): 739; and Wilbur Daniel Steele, "The Moving-Picture Machine in the Jungle," *McClure's Magazine* 40 (Jan. 1913): 329–37. According to Ernest A. Dench, Kearton netted $50,000 from profits of his big-game hunting trips (see Dench, *Making the Movies*, 119). For a discussion of Kearton's experiences as a photographer, see his books *Wildlife Across the World* and *Photographing Wildlife Across the World*.

28. Letter to James Barnes from George Sherwood, Sept. 27, 1915 (box 903 [1914–24], CA-AMNH). A review of the film from *The Independent* had praised it for its relatively fresh approach to African wildlife films, which were beginning to saturate the market; what particularly impressed this reviewer was the attention given to native peoples, including "the dances, the wrestling, the sham fights, [and] the killing of a lion by spearmen" ("The Dark Continent Illuminated," *The Independent* 82 [May 17, 1915]: 305). The expedition party traveled 3,000 miles from Mombassa to Boma.

29. Nancy Leys Stepan, "Race and Gender: The Role of Analogy in Science," *Isis* 77 (1986): 261.

30. J. Hillis Miller, *Illustration*, 61–62; Roland Barthes, "The Photographic Message," in *Image, Music, Text*, 15–31.

31. Miller, *Illustration*, 102.

32. Letter to Barnes from Osborn, fall 1914 (box 903 [1914–24], CA-AMNH).

33. Letter to Sherwood from President Osborn, Dec. 27, 1918 (box 903 [1914–24], CA-AMNH).

34. Letter to Sherwood from President Osborn, Jan. 16, 1920 (box 903 [1914–24], CA-AMNH).

35. Roger Cardinal, "Pausing Over Peripheral Detail," *Framework* 30.21 (1986): 127.

36. The transcript of the 75-minute meeting, which took place on Apr. 3, 1917, provides a window on institutional attitudes toward motion pictures. The twelve participants discussed the problem of dwindling attendance, the repetition of lectures (some AMNH members had transferred their membership from the Museum to an Extension Course given at Columbia University in New York City), the constituent features of an effective lecture, children's lectures, and promotion of lectures in Museum publications and special announcements. (Untitled transcript [Apr. 3, 1917], p. 5, CA-AMNH).

37. See, for example, letter from Elmer F. Botsford, managing director of the Joseph Ladue Gold Mining & Development Co. of Yukon, Alaska, who wrote the Museum in 1901 offering to show his slides (in excess of 200) "where many could see them." Botsford had spent four summers in Alaska visiting "Indians, Esquimos, mining camps, fishing villages, canneries" as well as some remote islands, and had give talks for the "benefit of Churches, schools, Institutes, Scientific Societies, etc." Putnam file, Department of Anthropology, American Museum of Natural History (hereafter, DA-AMNH).

38. Letter from George Sherwood, the AMNH's curator of public education, to the Principals of the Public Schools, Dec. 19, 1922 (CA-AMNH).

39. A complete set of the films taken during the Barnes-Kearton and Paul Rainey

expeditions formed the nucleus of a film reference library that the American Museum established in 1914; both sets of films were donated by the filmmakers to the Museum. Announcement appeared in AR-AMNH (1914): 53.

40. Several of these individuals were members of the Explorers Club of New York, which also exhibited films shot by its members in the teens. For more on the club, see Susan Gilbert, "The Explorers Club" (Master's thesis, New York University, 1992).

41. For a contemporaneous discussion of the key players involved in gentlemen-adventurer film expeditions, see the chapter "Topicals and Travel" in Valentia Steer's *Romance of the Cinema*, 84–104 (my thanks to Antonia Lant for showing me this book). An example from this period is Elmer Tracey Barnes's *The Motion-Picture Comrades in African Jungles*, the second in a four-part series of "Motion Picture Comrades" titles.

42. Dench, *Making the Movies*, 118–19. The bravado and self-aggrandizement typical of popular accounts of these cameramen's exploits is evoked in Wilbur Daniel Steele's description of Kearton's wildlife cinematography as "natural history made interesting," a magical blending of "romance" and "science" (Steele, "Moving-Picture Machine," 329), and in Steers's aptly titled book *Romance of the Cinema*, where the reader is told that Rainey's cameraman John C. Hemment took significant risks while filming yet "coolly stood and worked the handle of his camera as a rhinoceros charged down on him" (Steer, ibid., 93).

43. See Donna Haraway's critique of Carl Akeley's career as a taxidermist and game hunter for the AMNH in "Teddy Bear Patriarchy: Taxidermy in the Garden of Eden, New York City, 1908–1936," in *Primate Visions*, 26–58.

44. For a discussion of the role of film at the AMNH between 1930 and 1950, see Greg Mitman, "Cinematic Nature: Hollywood Technology, Popular Culture, and the American Museum of Natural History," *Isis* 84 (1993): 637–61.

45. It is unclear whether the 1914 footage has survived. A copy of the 1912 six-reel *African Hunt* is held at the Library of Congress, but there is no record of subsequent footage.

46. Greg Mitman, *Reel Nature: America's Romance with Wildlife on Film*, 18. For more on Rainey and *African Hunt*, see ibid., 16–20

47. "The Paul Rainey African Pictures," *MPW* 12.3 (Apr. 20, 1912): 214. An animated film of Paul Rainey's adventures in Africa entitled *Cartoon of Mr. Paul Rainey's African Hunt* (1912; producer unknown) testifies to Rainey's public profile in the teens. About a white explorer who fears he is going to be eaten by cannibals only to be pursued by an amorous African woman, the film is an extremely racist portrayal of Africans as over-sexed cannibals. A print is on deposit at the Library of Congress.

48. There is also some controversy over authorship. Hemment is routinely credited as cameraman for the 1912 expedition, although correspondence between Rainey and the Museum suggests otherwise. When Hemment offered to project the film for the

repeat screenings of *African Hunt* during the "Hunting Lions with Hounds" lecture in March 1912 ("to be a 'link' connecting the pictures with their creation"), Rainey sent a telegram to the Museum insisting that Hemment had not taken the pictures and had "stupendous nerve" making this claim. Museum naturalist-taxidermist Carl Akeley was eventually invited to introduce the film. Museum officials were also very annoyed with Hemment's behavior in the projection booth during the February screening; Hemment was apparently talking very loudly, and the Museum wrote Rainey saying they would use their own projectionist in future screenings. Letter to Rainey from Sherwood, Mar. 6, 1912 (box 903 [Spring 1912], CA-AMNH).

49. "Praise for Paul Rainey from the Museum," *New York Times*, June 20, 1914, n.p. (Paul Rainey clipping file, BRTC-NYPL).

50. Mitman, *Reel Nature*, 11.

51. In Rainey's film, native peoples oscillate between being attractions in their own right and intermediary figures situated somewhere in-between the white hunters and the wild game.

52. Film review of screening at the Lyceum Theatre, Pittsburgh, in the *Pittsburgh Post*, June 3, 1913, n.p. (Rainey clipping file, BRTC-NYPL).

53. *MPW* 18.7 (Nov. 15, 1913): 770–71.

54. The potential economic return for theater owners was also highlighted in the ad: "The record of this picture amply demonstrates that it is in a class by itself . . . as an entertainer, as a money getter, and as a return attraction. Ninety-five per cent of the American public has never had the joy of seeing this natural history phenomenon. It is now up to you. Profit by the box office proofs [*sic*] of this splendid attraction" (ibid.).

55. The film was also a surprise commercial success in New York City. An article from the *Star Pictorial* from June 1912 (Rainey clipping file, BRTC-NYPL, n.p.) states that the film ran at the Lyceum Theatre as a "sort of stop gap," with the theater manager assuming that *African Hunt* would attract some interest but not heavy patronage. But the film drew large audiences, and ticket prices, which were normally ten cents, ran as high as one dollar. Profits for the film during its eight-week run totaled $5,249.58. The fourth, fifth, and sixth weeks attracted the largest audiences, with the weekly take in the fifth week exceeding $1,000 ($1,025.43).

56. The Museum was a little taken aback by the mass appeal of the Rainey films and the difficulty many of its members experienced trying to procure tickets. An explanation and apology were published in the next issue of the *AMJ*. The phenomenal success of special film exhibitions was discussed at the heads of department meeting (1917) mentioned earlier (see note 36) when Sherwood referred to the first exhibition of prizma (color) motion pictures at the Museum the same year. More than 3,000 spectators turned up for the screening, and two additional screenings for that evening were hastily added. Despite the Museum's efforts to accommodate member demand for the color films, sev-

eral people canceled their membership in protest at being denied admission. Transcript of meeting (box 903 [Spring 1917], CA-AMNH).

The Museum had experienced an event of similar proportions in March 1910 when Comdr. Robert E. Peary gave a lecture about Scott's expedition to the North Pole entitled "The Discovery of the North Pole," which was illustrated by moving pictures. While the Museum routinely issued four tickets to each of its 2,500 members, on this occasion it reduced the number to two in anticipation of the high demand for Peary tickets. The complaints of one disgruntled member are symptomatic of a wider fear about modern urban culture and mass audiences, since the usually refined middle-class Museum audience was on this occasion transformed into an unruly mob: "I was surprised and humiliated . . . by the unparalleled discourtesy of which the institution was guilty. . . . First the members were subjected to the greatest inconvenience until the doors were opened, and when the keys eventually turned, being lined up like so many cattle before a barrier of benches. The consequence of this was that, the instant the benches were removed, the entire throng started a wild stampede for seats. . . . [I] am firmly convinced that the spectacle . . . was one more likely to arouse disgust than pleasure" (letter to Director, Mar. 12, 1910). The member, Mr. E. Mansbach, was reassured in the Museum's reply that "in the future when arrangements are made for men of this kind to meet our Museum, a method must be devised that will provide more satisfactorily for the comfort of all" (letter dated Mar. 30, 1910) (both letters in box 903 [1909–11], CA-AMNH).

57. Carlton Miles, "Rainey Hunt at the Metropolitan: Wonderful Views of Animal Life in Africa Shown on the Screen," (publication unknown), Aug. 4, 1914, n.p. (Rainey clipping file, BRTC-NYPL).

58. Anonymous review in the *Washington Star*, Sept. 1, 1914, n.p. (Rainey clipping file, BRTC-NYPL).

59. Rainey's films gave spectators the opportunity to experience what Bill Nichols calls the "endangered gaze." The ethical code embedded in this looking relation is that of an "ethics of courage . . . that stresses our relationship to the camera and filmmaker" and makes us acutely aware of the personal danger the camera operator may be facing in procuring the footage. Bill Nichols, *Representing Reality*, 84.

60. British wildlife photographer Cherry Kearton and his brother were major suppliers of the natural history museum market; writing in *MJ* in 1905, Frank Woolnaugh noted that "real" images of wildlife could now be obtained with most lectures "greatly indebted to the two Keartons." Woolnaugh, "Museums and Nature Study," 268.

61. Steele, "The Moving-Picture Machine," 330–31.

62. Haraway, *Primate Visions*, 30.

63. Professional lecturer Robert Stuart Pigott was hired to read the poem, and his recollection of the recitation was not entirely favorable. *Hiawatha* was shown in four parts,

and responding to an invitation from Sherwood to read the poem again in a repeat screening of the films (for a fee of $25 and travel expenses), Pigott replied: "When I gave the reading the first time, I was at the disadvantage of using an unedited set of films and no rehearsal, depending almost entirely upon my sense of time to keep up with the strange operator. Fortunately, he, or rather they, knew the business and even Mr. Moore said we synchronized perfectly, but the strain on me was more than I care to undergo except in an emergency." Letter to Sherwood from Pigott, Oct. 8, 1914 (box 903 [1914–24], CA-AMNH).

64. Items lent to Moore by the AMNH's anthropology curator Clark Wissler in September 1912 included birch-bark vessels and dishes, wooden utensils, decorated mats, wooden flutes, cotton shirts, woven bags, skin bags, beaded girdles, leggings, quivers, moccasins, horse-hair headdresses, stone spear-points, and arrow points (Moore file, DA-AMNH).

65. Letter from Alanson Skinner to Frank E. Moore, Feb. 3, 1913 (DA-AMNH).

66. Publicity pamphlet for Frank E. Moore's film *Hiawatha* (described as a "Picture Masque in Four Parts" in the program), first screened at the Museum on April 3, 1913. The film played for two weeks and an extra Saturday at the Berkeley Theatre in New York City at the end of April. At some point soon after these screenings, Moore sold the New York City rights for the film to the Unique Feature Film Company. Moore file (DA-AMNH).

67. Description in "Stories for Members' Children" brochure, Nov. 21, 1914 (box 903 [1914–1924], CA-AMNH).

68. Brochure announcement for Mar. 1, 1919, lecture (box 903 [1914–1924], CA-AMNH).

69. Alanson Skinner, "Red Men in 'Movies,' " *New York Times*, June 3, 1914, 12, quoted in Brownlow, *The War, the West, and the Wilderness*, 329.

70. Skinner, "Red Men in 'Movies,' " 12.

71. The lectures Skinner delivered included "The Indians of New York State" (Nov. 12, 1913), "Inside the Indian's Wigwam" (Mar. 23, 1914), and "Hiawatha's People" (Oct. 23, 1914).

72. The provenance of motion pictures used to illustrate most lectures at the AMNH is unclear, a common problem in identifying films used to illustrate ephemeral events such as lectures. Films may have been obtained from any number of sources: the lecturer's own amateur footage (unlikely in the case of Skinner, who did not use film in his freelance lecturing); a commercial distribution company; or stock footage shot by a Museum employee for lecture exhibition.

73. Lowie, untitled transcript (Apr. 3, 1917), p. 5 (CA-AMNH).

74. The first AMNH-sponsored expedition to use an Akeley camera was the Asiatic Zoological Expedition, which left New York on March 17, 1916. See Roy Chapman

Andrews, "The Asiatic Zoological Expedition of the American Museum of Natural History," *AMJ* 16.2 (Feb. 1916): 105–106. In addition to the motion picture camera, color photography was used.

75. Akeley had first shot motion pictures in 1910 during an African elephant hunt sponsored by the AMNH, although he failed to secure vital footage because of the camera's restricted mobility. Attempts to solve the technical shortcomings of conventional cameras in America were largely unsuccessful until Akeley invented his 1916 "Akeley," which was lighter than regular cameras and could be used more effectively on location. Andrews, *Under a Lucky Star*, 122–22.

76. *AMJ* 13.7 (1913): 328.

77. Some of the other rental agencies used by the Museum in the late teens and twenties include the Community Motion Picture Company; Beseler Educational Film Co.; Educational Films Corp. of America; General Film Company; Carler Cinema; Variety Films Corporation; and William L. Shery Feature Film Co., all located in New York City. The Museum also obtained films from the Department of Street Cleaning of the City of New York, and the Shredded Wheat Co. All the companies named herein were thanked in the *Annual Report for 1912* for "generously allowing" the AMNH to use their slides and moving picture films in lectures on industries. AR-AMNH (1912), 42.

78. By 1924 the journal of the American Association of Museums (*The Museum News*) was regularly reporting on the uses of film within museums. Agencies like the Bureau of Mines would lend their films without charge to museums; commercial companies, seeing an opportunity for free marketing, also offered films of their manufacturing processes. For information on the Bureau of Mines, see *Museum News* 2.8 (Aug. 15, 1908): 3; and on films made by the Lenox, Incorporated, potteries company, see *Museum News* 2.14 (Nov. 15, 1924): 3. That film had reached a certain level of acceptance in museums can be deduced from an advertisement for an Akeley camera featured in *Museum News*. The ad's copy read: "The Power of the Moving Picture is so far-reaching that no museum or institution can afford to further be without them. There is no medium equal for propaganda, to enlist public interest in support of your institution and its various activities, and at the same time no better material for lectures." *Museum News* 1.2 (May 15, 1924): 6.

7. FINDING A HOME FOR CINEMA IN ETHNOGRAPHY: THE FIRST GENERATION OF ANTHROPOLOGIST-FILMMAKERS IN AMERICA

1. Jay Ruby, for example, claims that Boas was "perhaps the first social scientist anywhere to use the motion picture camera to generate data in natural settings (as opposed to a laboratory) in order to study gesture, motor habits, and dance as manifestations of culture" in "Franz Boas and the Early Camera Study of Behavior," *Kinesis Report* 3.1 (1980): 7.

2. There is no mention of ethnographic film in the *American Anthropologist*, the *Journal of the Anthropological Institute of Great Britain and Northern Ireland*, or in a cross-section of scientific journals published during this period. Searches of every issue of these English-language journals, along with *Folklore*, *Science*, *Scientific American*, and *American Museum Journal*, have only unearthed Starr's and Goddard's discussions of ethnographic cinema before 1915.

3. Goddard's films were incorporated into the AMNH's public lecture series in sometimes unexpected ways and, as far as can be ascertained, were not used by Goddard in the manner he prescribed in his published article on the films. See Pliny E. Goddard, "Motion Picture Records of Indians: Films That Show the Common Industries of the Apache." *AMJ* 15.4 (Apr. 1915): 185–87.

4. For a general sense of the difficulties experienced by natural-history filmmakers (including using a telephoto lens, camera vibration, and accurate focusing), see Roy Chapman Andrews, "Hunting Deer in the Adirondacks," *AMJ* 15.8 (Dec. 1915): 409–14, and Norman McClintock, "The Telephoto Lens in Cinematography," *AMJ* 18.1 (Jan. 1917): 5–63.

5. As Patricia Zimmermann has noted, throughout this period "amateur-film equipment seems to have been a technical oddity for hobbyists to follow rather than a large social practice or art involving great numbers of people." Zimmermann, *Reel Families: A Social History of Amateur Film*, 17–18.

6. For background information on Starr and his career at the University of Chicago, see R. Berkeley Miller, "Anthropology and Institutionalization: Frederick Starr at the University of Chicago, 1892–1923." *Kroeber Anthropological Society Papers* 51–52 (1978): 49–60.

7. Frederick Starr, "The Congo in Moving Pictures," *Show World* 1.3 (July 13, 1907): 1 (my thanks to Antonia Lant for giving me a copy of this article). See also Jennifer Peterson, "World Pictures," 235–38, for a discussion of Starr's cinema. Also see the following articles and books by Starr: "Anthropology at the World's Fair," *Popular Science Monthly* 48 (1893): 610–21; *The Ainu Group at the St. Louis Exposition* (1904); "The World Before Your Eyes," *MPW* 4.5 (Feb. 20, 1909): 194–95; "Prof. Starr's Valuable Contribution," *Nickelodeon* 1.3 (Mar. 1909): 64; and *Congo Natives: An Ethnographic Album* (1912). An identical version of Starr's *MPW* essay is reprinted in *The Bioscope* several months later (July 8, 1909, 48), but with the author cited as Montaign Alexander Pylle rather than Starr. Whether this is a case of trade press plagiarism or a pseudonym for Starr, the author changed certain words (such as "Chicago" for "London") although the credit for the piece states that it is being published by the proprietors of the Recreation Theatre, London, in the form of a four-page leaflet to promote their travelogues.

Congo Natives contains photographs taken as part of Starr's 1906–1907 expedition to the Congo (the expedition in which he unsuccessfully tried to use a moving picture camera). Starr's interest in the native peoples of this region was triggered by the outdoor ethnological exhibit at the St. Louis World's Fair. In addition to collecting over 3,500 objects for the AMNH, Starr also took over 700 photographs and made sound recordings. The photographs that appear in the album are stylistically quite diverse, ranging from anthropometric-type poses of "head deformations" to relatively candid shots.

8. Letter from Starr to Harold Amos Logan (Aug. 7, 1911) in Department of Anthropology archival materials at the Field Museum of Natural History, cited in Miller, "Anthropology and Institutionalization," 52 (emphasis in original).

9. Starr, "The Congo in Moving Pictures," 1.

10. Ibid.

11. Starr had used an outdated Selig Polyscope camera to shoot film during the expedition.

12. Frederick Starr Papers, cited in Peterson, "World Pictures," 236.

13. Starr, "The Congo in Moving Pictures," 1.

14. Starr, "Prof. Starr's Valuable Contribution," 64.

15. Nichols, *Representing Reality*, 31.

16. Starr, "The Congo in Moving Pictures," 1.

17. Obituary for Pliny E. Goddard, *Natural History* 28.4 (1928): 441–42.

18. McCormick was given a $500 advance by the Museum, and $250 from the Director's Fund was made available for McCormick's and Young's expenses. Letter to McCormick from Clark Wissler, June 15, 1912, and letter from F. Lucas to Wissler, June 13, 1912 (both in file 566, Central Archives, Dept. of Library Services, American Museum of Natural History; hereafter, CA-AMNH).

19. Letter to McCormick from Goddard, July 22, 1912 (file 566, Department of Anthropology, AMNH; hereafter, DA-AMNH).

20. Ibid.

21. Leah Dilworth, *Imagining Indians in the Southwest: Persistent Visions of a Primitive Past*, 22. For more on the impulses behind avid collectors of Native American artifacts, see Shepard Krech III and Barbara A. Hail, eds., *Collecting Native America, 1870–1960*.

22. Intertitles are used frequently in the 8-minute film, providing information about the dance as it unfolds; for example, we are told that, "The Snake Priests enter and form a line opposite the Antelopes," that "One of each pair of Snake Priests takes a snake in his mouth," and that one priest in each pair carries a feather with which to soothe the snakes (the snakes remain in the mouths of the Hopi for the duration of the dance). At the end of the dance, the head Snake Priest forms a circle on the ground with cornmeal and all the snakes (over fifty) are thrown into it and covered with cornmeal so that they can inform the gods that they were treated with kindness.

23. Intertitle in *Hopi Indians of the Southwest* compilation film, covering footage shot between 1912 and 1925; film 192, housed in the Special Collections Department of the AMNH.

24. Letter to Goddard from McCormick, Sept. 8, 1912 (file 566, DA-AMNH).

25. Letter to Goddard from McCormick, Sept. 6, 1912 (file 566, DA-AMNH). During his solo trip to Kean's Canyon, Arizona, to shoot moving pictures in the fall of 1914, McCormick mentioned being prepared to pay $30 for a daylight ceremony of a Yabichi dance which a Mr. Hubbell was hoping to arrange for him. Unfortunately, when McCormick wrote Goddard for permission to pay this amount, Goddard replied that he didn't think the Museum had that money to spend on dances. Letter to McCormick from Goddard, Oct. 6, 1914 (file 566, DA-AMNH).

26. David MacDougall, "Whose Story Is It?," in Lucien Taylor, ed., *Visualizing Theory: Selected Essays from V.A.R., 1990–1994*, 29.

27. Letter to Goddard from McCormick, Aug. 26, 1912 (file 566, DA-AMNH).

28. Letter to McCormick from Goddard, Sept. 2, 1912 (file 111, DA-AMNH).

29. Letter to Goddard from McCormick, Sept. 14, 1912 (file 566, DA-AMNH).

30. Howard McCormick, "The Artist's Southwest," *AMJ* 13.3 (Mar. 1913): 125. McCormick's lyrical, sentimentalizing tone continues throughout the article: "These people adjusted so perfectly to their surroundings, furnish for the artist the human interest for his pictures. In their daily life and many ceremonies they reflect the colors of skies, the shapes of the clouds and mesas and fill both with the innumerable supernatural logic" (124–25).

31. Margaret Mead, "Visual Anthropology in a Discipline of Words," in Hockings, ed., *Principles of Visual Anthropology*, 5.

32. Letter to Goddard from McCormick, Sept. 8, 1912 (file 566, DA-AMNH). McCormick also refers to shooting film of Hopis grinding corn, putting sinew on a bow and feathers on an arrow, and making and attaching a flint arrowhead.

33. Letter to Goddard from McCormick, Sept. 8, 1912 (file 566, DA-AMNH). In the same letter, McCormick listed the following subjects and film lengths: "Hautsella Snake Dance" (600 feet), "Shipaulovi Snake Dance" (500 feet), "Basket Weaving at Oraiba" (100 feet), "Basket Weaving at Mishougouri" (100 feet), "Navajo Rug Maker" (100 feet), "Flute Ceremony" (400 feet), a total of 1,900 out of 2,000 feet of film endorsed by the Museum (file 566, DA-AMNH).

34. Goddard rarely mentioned McCormick in his correspondence with Anthropology Department secretary Bella Weitzner, other than occasional references to McCormick's painting studies for Museum habitat groups. When McCormick left for Kean's Canyon, Arizona, in September of 1914, he took the moving picture camera with him. Letter to Clark Wissler from Goddard, Sept. 13, 1914 (file 111, DA-AMNH).

35. Letter to Weitzner from Goddard, Aug. 14, 1914 (file 111, DA-AMNH).

36. Ibid.

37. Letter to Goddard from Weitzner, Sept. 2, 1914 (file 111, DA-AMNH).

38. Goddard's first experiences with the motion picture camera in the field were not

altogether successful; in letters to the AMNH he complained repeatedly of the heat's buckling the metal lining of his light meter or fogging up the film stock, and of the "considerable" camera vibration. Four years before his death in 1928, Goddard set out once again to the Southwest, this time to shoot film among the Hopi and Navajo peoples. While these films survive, there is no evidence of any published discussion of them and Goddard's own letters to the Museum from the field relate mainly to practical matters of filmmaking.

39. Letter to Weitzner from Goddard, Aug. 20, 24, 1914 (file 111, DA-AMNH).

40. Letter to Weitzner from Goddard, Aug. 29, 1914 (file 111, DA-AMNH).

41. Ibid.

42. Goddard alludes to this debate in the opening paragraph of his *AMJ* article, "Motion Picture Records," 185.

43. Goddard, "Motion Picture Records," 185.

44. Ibid.

45. Of course, while cinema's potential as a diagnostic tool for the close analysis of unconscious or routinized movement had been explored by Étienne-Jules Marey and Félix-Louis Regnault, the subject also found room for discussion in the commercial trade press. In a *Moving Picture World* article on the use of film in clinical research at Philadelphia General Hospital in 1909, the author described experiments conducted on patients suffering from nervous disorders: "the varied gaits, movements, and expressions were vividly reproduced, and there was an added advantage in the pictures since the camera, which is quicker than the eye, recorded faithfully the finer movements which would escape unaided study, but which could be readily observed when projected on the animated screen." "Another Lost Opportunity" (editorial), *MPW* 5.16 (Oct. 16, 1909): 5.

While there are isolated examples of the motion picture camera's being used to record movement and gait along the lines recommended by Regnault and the *Moving Picture World* article, most of these studies involved filming subjects in laboratory conditions or in controlled settings rather than in the field. Goddard, on the other hand, recorded movements within the social setting with far less staging.

46. Having said this, Museum records suggest that Goddard's footage was awaited with excited anticipation by Museum officials such as George Sherwood and Clark Wissler, who repeatedly inquired as to when the films would be ready (letter to McCormick from Goddard, Sept. 2, 1912, file 566, DA- AMNH). Several special events were hosted at the Museum in the spring of 1913. For example, McCormick's films were exhibited in a February lecture entitled "The Indians of the Southwest: Their Daily Lives and Ceremonies," while on May 26, 1913, two films (*Ceremonies of the Hopi Indians* and *Snake Dance of the Hopi Indians*) from the same expedition were shown during a special event organized for members of the Monday Club. The 8:00 P.M. to 8:45 P.M. screening of the films was followed by a lecture given by Goddard and a private exhibition of a

series of Alaskan painting, as well as the chance to view a recently opened installation of New York, Plains, and Southwest Indian customs and industries.

47. These short films are incorporated into *Hopi Indians of the Southwest*, a compilation film that includes footage shot in 1912 and 1925; a print of the film (film 192) is housed in the Special Collections Department at the AMNH. The film is in extremely poor condition, having suffered nitrate damage.

48. Booklet description of Story Number 4, " 'Poonkong' and His People," presented by Pliny E. Goddard on March 22, 1913, in the AMNH's "Natural History Stories for Children" series (CA-AMNH; emphasis added). It would appear from the story description that identical footage was shown during this event and the meeting of the Monday Club (Snake Dance, Flute Ceremony, and footage of basket-making, pottery, and weaving).

49. It would also seem that these films were not used in any special way within the Anthropology Department, and there is no evidence of Goddard's analyzing his fieldwork footage in the manner outlined in his 1915 article.

50. Goddard, "Motion Picture Records," 185.

51. Ibid. (emphasis in original).

52. J. Walter Fewkes, "On the Use of the Phonograph in the Study of the Languages of American Indians," *Science* 15.378 (May 2, 1890): 267–68.

53. Goddard, "Motion Picture Records," 185.

54. Mead, "Visual Anthropology," 4, 9.

55. Goddard, "Motion Picture Records," 187.

56. Mead, "Visual Anthropology," 10.

57. Margaret Mead and Gregory Bateson first began using photography and film to explore questions of cultural difference in a three-year expedition to Bali and New Guinea between 1936 and 1939. In 1942, Mead published a photographic ethnography, and around 1950 she assembled another photographic study and a series of six films. For more on Mead's and Bateson's photography and their ethnographic film, see Ira Jacknis, "Margaret Mead and Gregory Bateson in Bali: Their Use of Photography and Film," *Cultural Anthropology* 3, no. 2 (May 1988): 160–77; and Sol Worth, "Margaret Mead and the Shift from 'Visual Anthropology' to the 'Anthropology of Visual Communication,' " *Studies in Visual Communication* 6.1 (1980): 15–22.

58. M. W. Hilton-Simpson and J. A. Haeseler, "Cinema and Ethnology," *Discovery* 6 (Jan. to Dec. 1925): 326. De Brigard refers to this article in relation to budgets for ethnographic films in "History of Ethnographic Film," 17*n*2.

59. Hilton-Simpson and Haeseler, "Cinema and Ethnology," 328.

60. Ibid., 325.

61. Ibid., 328. Similarly, in Haeseler's scheme of things the commercial cinematographer is ill-equipped to edit the raw footage as he is "almost sure to cut the scenes so short

that one gets but a little glimpse of them on the screen." Haeseler therefore advised that the editing and writing of intertitles be completed by an anthropologist, as these required "a general background and knowledge that is not the common possession of the camera man" (329).

62. Hilton-Simpson and Haeseler, "Cinema and Ethnology," 329.

63. For background information on Boas's Northwest Coast ethnology, see Ronald P. Rohner and Evelyn C. Rohner, "Franz Boas and the Development of North American Ethnography," in Ronald P. Rohner, *The Ethnography of Franz Boas: Letters and Diaries of Franz Boas Written on the Northwest Coast from 1886 to 1931*, viii–xxx.

64. According to Ruby, Boas may have recorded the songs and dances with Laban's notation ("Labanotation," in Ruby) in mind (Rudolf Laban was interested in applying his notation system to non-Western dance forms), although there is no evidence of Boas having been in contact with Laban or attempting to undertake such an analysis. Ruby, "Franz Boas," 9.

65. This is in stark contrast to his earlier photographs in which all traces of Indian acculturation were erased from the image through retouching. Boas also photographed Kwakwaka'wakw men and women against white sheets that doubled as studio backdrops. For more on Boas's photography, see Jacknis, "Boas and Photography," 2–60.

66. Rosalind Morris, "*The Kwakuitl of British Columbia*," in *New Worlds from Fragments*, 43. Even Bill Holm, the anthropologist who in 1973 reconstructed and edited Boas's original 1930 film, found it nearly impossible to interpret the image track (ibid., 59).

67. Morris, ibid., 64.

68. Boas first began conducting ethnological research as part of the Jesup North Pacific Expedition (1897–1902), which he conceived and organized. The aim of the expedition was to investigate the origin of the American Indian. Three thousand photographs and wax sound recordings were made during the expedition. For a discussion of the background to the expedition and its use of photography, see Kendall, Mathé, and Miller, *Drawing Shadows to Stone*. This is the catalog for the show of the same name that was installed at the AMNH in the fall and spring of 1997–98.

69. Rohner, *The Ethnography of Franz Boas*, 293–94, cited in Ruby, "Franz Boas," 9; Morris, *New Worlds from Fragments*, 62..

70. Margaret Mead, *An Anthropologist at Work*, 16, cited in Asen Balikci, "Visual Anthropology: The Legacy of Margaret Mead," 2.

71. Rony, *Third Eye*, 57.

72. Morris, *New Worlds from Fragments*, 56. According to Morris, editing would have made little difference to the quality of the films as they are pretty raw and unaccomplished even at the production stage. For example, the image is often out of focus, the camera shaky, and the framing inconsistent (65–66).

73. Ibid., 62.

74. Of course, there are lots of notable exceptions during the teens and twenties, including the following films shot by anthropologists: *In Borneo: In the Land of the Head-Hunters* (Carl Lumholtz, 1914–1917); Matthew Stirling's New Guinea Expedition film *By Aeroplane to Pygmyland* (1926), sponsored by the Smithsonian Institution and the Dutch Committee for Scientific Research (in collaboration with photographer Richard K. Peck, 1926); Frederick Wulsin's *Travel Footage of Africa* (c. 1927); and Melville J. Herskovits film study conducted in West Africa (1931). All these films are housed at the Human Studies Film Archive in Washington, D.C. My point is simply that despite the flurry of interest in ethnographic film in the late 1920s, these films were never considered part of an anthropological film canon and have been largely ignored by visual anthropologists. It is also interesting that these anthropologists did not take it upon themselves to institutionalize film as an ethnographic tool, and it was left to Margaret Mead, Jean Rouch, and John Marshall in the postwar period to argue the case for an ethnographic cinema. Ironically, it is *Nanook of the North* (Flaherty, 1922), a film made by a nonanthropologist, that traditionally launches the ethnographic film canon. For more on Lumholtz's filmmaking, see Alison Griffiths, " 'We Partake, as it Were, of His Life': The Status of the Visual in Early Ethnographic Film," in John Fullerton and Astrid Söderbergh Widding, eds., *Moving Images: From Edison to the Webcam*, 91–110.

75. Worth, "Margaret Mead," 196–97.

76. Recall that Spencer and Goddard did shoot films for a second time (Spencer in 1912 and Goddard in 1922), although these efforts remained marginal to their careers as anthropologists.

77. Ira Jacknis, "The Picturesque and the Scientific: Franz Boas's Plan for Anthropological Filmmaking," *Visual Anthropology* 1.1 (1987): 60.

78. Letter to Hays from Boas, Mar. 24, 1933, in ibid., 61. Boas also recommended that copies of existing films could be reedited by "competent ethnologists" so that sequences of ethnographic value could be assembled and used in teaching in schools, colleges, and universities.

79. Erik Barnouw, *Documentary: A History of the Non-Fiction Film*, 50. Also see chapters 5 and 6 of Rony's *Third Eye* for a discussion of how this genre was exploited by Hollywood in the 1920s and 1930s.

80. Haeseler did recommend, however, that the "needs and demands" of commercial film companies should not impinge upon the scientific goals of the expedition; in other words, the anthropologist-filmmaker might have to shoot additional footage for commercial release while in the field and, at the very least, make a separate print for commercial distribution as prints run through projectors several times may lose their value as scientific records since they could be damaged by scratches. Hilton-Simpson and Haeseler, "Cinema and Ethnology," 330.

8. CONCLUSION: THE LEGACY OF EARLY ETHNOGRAPHIC FILM

1. Mead, "Visual Anthropology," 3–12.

2. Balikci, "Visual Anthropology," 13.

3. MacDougall, "The Visual in Anthropology," 289.

4. Mead, "Visual Anthropology," 5.

5. Lucian Taylor, "Iconophobia: How Anthropology Lost It at the Movies." *Transition* 69 (1992): 66.

6. Ibid., 68.

7. James C. Faris, "A Political Primer on Anthropology/Photography," in Edwards, ed., *Anthropology and Photography*, 257.

8. Fabian, *Time and the Other*, 151, 153.

9. Taylor, "Iconophobia," 69.

10. James Clifford, "Introduction: Partial Truths," in Clifford and George E. Marcus, eds., *Writing Culture: The Poetics and Politics of Ethnography*, 23.

11. See, for example, Jay Ruby, "The Image Mirrored: Reflexivity and the Documentary Film," *Journal of the University Film Association* 29.1 (Fall 1997): 3–11; David MacDougall, "Beyond Observational Cinema," in Hockings, ed., *Principles of Visual Anthropology*, 109–23; and Faye Ginsburg, "Culture/Media: A (Mild) Polemic," and "Shooting Back: From Ethnographic Film to the Ethnography of Media" (295–322), in Toby Miller and Robert Stam, eds., *A Companion to Film Theory*.

12. Paul Stoller, *The Taste of Ethnographic Things: The Senses in Anthropology*, 50.

13. Ibid., 32, 27.

14. My thanks to Faye Ginsburg for her input on this issue.

15. Mead, "Visual Anthropology," 9–10.

16. Jack R. Rollwagen, "The Role of Anthropological Theory in 'Ethnographic' Filmmaking," in Rollwagen, ed., *Anthropological Filmmaking*, 295.

17. Don Rundstrom, "Imaging Anthropology," in Rollwagen, ed., *Anthropological Filmmaking*, 317.

18. Taylor, "Iconophobia," 80.

19. For more on Rouch's filmmaking, see Paul Stoller, *The Cinematic Griot: The Ethnography of Jean Rouch*.

20. Rouch has called his work "science fiction," a term that acknowledges "the constructed nature of 'truth' in ethnographic representations . . . [and] is a means by which the distinction between an 'objective' science and a 'subjective' art can be dissolved." Jeanette DeBouzek, "The 'Ethnographic Surrealism' of Jean Rouch," *Visual Anthropology* 2 (1989): 304.

21. "Another Lost Opportunity" (editorial), *MPW* 5.16 (Oct. 16, 1909): 5.

22. Harvey N. Hurte, "Exploring by Motion Pictures," *Picture-Play Weekly* 1.6 (May 15, 1915): 16.

23. Tom Gunning, "From the Opium Den to the Theatre of Morality: Moral Discourse and the Film Process in Early American Cinema," *Art and Text* 30 (Sept.-Nov. 1988): 32

24. Patricia Zimmermann, "Our Trip to Africa," *Afterimage* 17.8 (Mar. 1990): 4.

25. Joel Katz, "From Archive to Archiveology," *Cinematograph* 4 (1992): 101–102. For an interesting discussion of the formal properties of the film, particularly the filmmaker's manipulation of the images, see Scott MacDonald's essay on *From the Pole to the Equator* in *Avant-Garde Film Motion Studies*, 112–21.

26. As an official Italian photographer, what Comerio chose to shoot was probably influenced by what he felt would satisfy audience demand for images of wild-game hunts and exotic-looking peoples and the political careers of government officials who wanted credit for the riches of overseas imperialist expansion.

27. MacDonald, *Avant-Garde Film Motion Studies*, 116–17 (emphasis in original).

28. Russell, *Experimental Ethnography*, 62.

29. Eric Michaels, "A Primer of Restrictions on Picture-Taking in Traditional Areas of Aboriginal Australia," *Visual Anthropology* 4 (1991): 260.

30. Ibid., 261.

31. For a helpful perspective on the political exigencies of anthropological research conducted among Australian Aboriginal people, see Fred Myers, "The Politics of Representation: Anthropological Discourse and Australian Aborigines," *American Ethnologist* 13 (1986): 138–53.

32. In keeping with Arrernte tradition, some of the ceremonies represented in the films cannot be shown to women.

33. Ginsburg, "Mediating Aboriginal Modernities," 5. As Ginsburg points out, the Inuit have been very successful in lobbying for their own satellite television service, the Inuit Broadcasting Corporation, which has "played a dynamic and even revitalizing role for the Inuit" and other Arctic peoples.

34. Harald E. L. Prins, "The Paradox of Primitivism: Native Rights and the Problem of Imagery in Cultural Survival Films," *Visual Anthropology* 9 (1997): 244.

35. Ibid., 254.

36. See Evans, "Commentary," 221–42; Russell's response to Evans's criticisms can also be found in this same issue of *Visual Anthropology* 11.3 (1998): 241–42.

37. Russell, "Playing Primitive," 70.

38. For Faye Ginsburg, "the video is an example of the acerbic, ritually cleansing role of humor, parody, reversals, and prophesy in Southwest Native American cultures; it is simultaneously about and part of the construction of contemporary indigenous identities." Ginsburg, "Visual Anthropology and Reverse Ethnographies: Revisioning Theory and Practice for the Millennium" (unpublished paper, July 1996), 8.

39. Edward Said has pointed out that "only recently have Westerners become aware

that what they have to say about the history and the cultures of 'subordinate' peoples is challengeable by the people themselves, people who a few years back were simply incorporated, culture, land, history, and all, into the great Western empires, and their disciplinary discourses." Said's admonition coincides with a growing awareness of the politics of producing, circulating, and viewing images of native peoples, a sensitivity that has had an enormous impact on how media-makers now view their ethnographic subjects. Said, *Culture and Imperialism*, 195.

40. Ginsburg, "Mediating Australian Modernities," 6.

41. Ibid. For more on the Mabo case, see M. A. Stephenson and Suri Ratnapala, *Mabo—A Judicial Revolution: The Aborigine Land Rights Decision and Its Impact on Australian Law* (St. Lucia: University of Queensland Press, 1993), and Ken Ruthven, general editor, *After Mabo: Interpreting Indigenous Traditions* (Carlton, Victoria: Melbourne University Press, 1993). My thanks to Faye Ginsburg for drawing my attention to the Mabo case.

42. MacDougall, "Unprivileged Camera Style," 10.

43. For a discussion of the how the Philippine exhibit functioned as a "showcase for America's colonial triumph," see Benito M. Vergara, Jr., *Displaying Filipinos: Photography and Colonialism in Early Twentieth-Century Philippines*, 111–50.

44. Edward Said, *Orientalism*, 8.

45. "Fake Documentary: Biography/Autobiography" Symposium featuring Marlon Fuentes (AMNH, Nov. 1996).

46. According to Elaine Charnov of the AMNH and Jake Homiak of the Human Studies Film Archive, some audiences have failed to read the film as a fictional narrative and have asked Fuentes questions about his grandfather in the question and answer period. At the film's 1996 New York premiere at the Margaret Mead Film and Video Festival, it was programmed under the heading "Fake Documentary: Biography/ Autobiography," and despite the disclaimer in the closing credits about the film being "inspired by actual events," the film has gone on to win documentary awards on the basis of its research into the conditions experienced by Filipino exiles who performed at St. Louis. Homiak question to Fuentes at AMNH's "Fake Documentary" symposium (Nov. 1996) (author interview with Elaine Charnov, Oct. 14, 1997, New York City).

47. The idea of giving voice to native peoples is most effectively articulated in the "African Voices" exhibit at the National Museum of Natural History in Washington, D.C., which opened in mid-December 1999. Using sound and image to re-create a far more culturally dynamic and multifarious image of Africa than is usually seen in natural history museums, the permanent exhibit explores such themes as Africa's relationship to the global economy and wealth and market life in Africa. The exhibit thus succeeds in giving voice to the native peoples of this vast continent in innovative and thought-provoking ways. It can be previewed on the NMNH's Web site, www.mnh.si.edu/african-voices.

48. For a discussion of similar kinds of repositioning of archival photographic imagery by contemporary artists, especially how the fragmentary nature of photography relates to anthropological practice, see Elizabeth Edwards, "Beyond the Boundary: A Consideration of the Expressive in Photography and Anthropology," in Banks and Morphy, eds. *Rethinking Visual Anthropology*. 53–79. Also see Edwards's *New Histories: Photographs, Anthropology, and Museums* (2001).

49. Lippard, ed., *Partial Recall*, 35.

50. Ibid., 18.

51. Félix-Louis Regnault, "La chronophotographie dans ethnographie," *Bulletins et mémoires de la Société d'anthropologie de Paris*, vol. 1, 5th ser. (Oct. 4, 1900): 422, cited in Peter Bloom, "Pottery, Chronophotography, and the French Colonial Archive," paper presented at the Screen Studies Conference (Glasgow, June 1993), 4. According to Paolo Chiozzi, the first archivist of ethnographic film was a Parisian banker named Albert Kahn, who between 1916 to 1919 established the Centre de Documentation Sociale and the Archive du Palente in Paris. The archives included 140,000 meters of film and 72,000 autochrome photographs. According to Chiozzi, Kahn had two major goals in mind: to understand the profound social and cultural transformations taking place in the world through preserving records of human activities from cultures that were disappearing, and to make accessible documents providing direct observation of the evolutionary process to scholars and policymakers. Chiozzi, "What Is Ethnographic Film? Remarks About a Debate." *SVA Review* (Spring 1990): 26.

52. Regnault's proposed museum-archive suggests the idea of a parallel universe of vanished objects and peoples that can be summoned up at will; just as Frederick Starr could vicariously experience the ocular and olfactory delights of the Orient without leaving his Chicago theater, so too could Regnault's researcher travel back in time to view threatened peoples and extinct customs. Regnault recommended that sound recordings, chronophotographs, and moving pictures containing ethnographic scenes of scientific interest be deposited and preserved at a national museum supported by a statute similar to that which requires that copies of new publications be submitted to the Bibliotheque Nationale. Bloom, "Pottery," 5

53. Regnault, "Le rôle du cinéma en ethnographie," *La nature* 2866 (Oct. 1, 1931): 306, cited in Rony, *Third Eye*, 62.

54. MacDougall, "Unprivileged Camera Style," 10. For more on the new discursive spaces of media flow, see Arjun Appadurai's influential article, "Disjuncture and Difference in the Global Cultural Economy," *Public Culture* 2.2 (1990): 7.

55. Ginsburg, "Visual Anthropology," 10.

Filmography

Annabelle's Serpentine Dance (Edison, 1894)
Black Diamond Express (Edison 1894)
Buffalo Bill (Edison, 1894)
Buffalo Dance (Edison, 1894)
Coochee-Coochee Dance (Edison, 1896)
Indian War Council (Edison, 1894)
May Irwin Kiss (Edison, 1894)
Sioux Ghost Dance (Edison, 1894)
L'Arroseur Arrosé (Lumière, 1895)
Buck Dance (Edison, 1898)
Circle Dance (Edison, 1898)
Eagle Dance, Pueblo Indians (Edison, 1898)
Films of Mer Islanders and Australian Aborigines (Alfred Cort Haddon, 1898)
Indian Day School (Edison, 1898)
Kanakas Diving for Money (nos. 1 and 2) (Edison, 1898)
Mexico Street Scene (Edison, 1898)
Native Daughters (Edison, 1898)
Parade of Buffalo Bill Wild West Show (nos. 1 and 2) (Edison, 1898)
Parade of Chinese (Edison, 1898)
Repairing Street Scenes in Mexico (Edison, 1898)
Surface Transit, Mexico (Edison, 1898)
Wand Dance, Pueblo Indians (Edison, 1898)
War Dance, Pueblo Indians (Edison, 1898)
Scenes in the Swiss Village at Paris Exposition (Edison, 1900)
Swiss Village No. 2 at the Paris Exposition (Edison, 1900)
Carrying out the Snakes (Edison, 1901)
Esquimaux Game of Snap-the-Whip (Edison, 1901)

Esquimaux Leap-Frog (Edison, 1901)

Esquimaux Village (Edison, 1901)

Films of Arrernte Peoples of Central Australia (Walter Baldwin Spencer, 1901)

Indian Dances and Customs (Edison, 1901)

Japanese Village (Edison, 1901)

Line Up and Teasing the Snakes (Edison, 1901)

The March of Prayer and Entrance of Dancers (Edison, 1901)

Moki Snake Dance by Wolpi Indians (Edison, 1901)

Panoramic View of Moki-Land (Edison, 1901)

Parade of Snake Dancers Before the Dance (Edison, 1901)

Sham Battle at the Pan-American Exposition (Edison, 1901)

Wand Dance, Pueblo Indians (Edison, 1901)

Buffalo Bill's Wild West Parade (Biograph, 1902)

Club Swinging, Carlisle Indian School (Biograph, 1902)

Hindoo Fakir (Edison, 1902)

Loading Cattle in India (Edison, 1902)

Schoolroom in Sudan (Edison, 1902)

Arabian Jewish Dance (Edison, 1903)

Egyptian Boys in Swimming Race (Edison, 1903)

Egyptian Fakir with Monkey (Edison 1903)

Egyptian Market Scene (Edison, 1903)

Market Scene in Old Cairo, Egypt (Edison, 1903)

Native Women Coaling a Ship and Scrambling for Money (Edison, 1903)

Native Women Coaling a Ship at St. Thomas, B.W.I. (Edison, 1903)

Native Women Coaling a Ship at St. Vincent, B.W.I. (Edison, 1903)

Native Women Washing a Negro Baby in Nasau, B.W.I. (Edison, 1903)

Native Women Washing Clothes at St. Vincent, B.W.I (Edison, 1903)

Asia in America, St. Louis Exposition (Biograph, 1904)

Moqui Indian Rain Dance (Biograph, 1904)

French Types (Pathé, 1905)

In India: Marriage of the Nephew of the Maharaj of Tagore (Pathé, 1905)

Hauling Sugar Cane, Hawaii (Edison, 1906)

In Living Hawthorne (William Alfred Gibson and Millard Johnson, 1906)

Kanaka Fishermen Casting a "Throw Net" Hilo, Hawaiian Islands (Edison, 1906)

Lifeorama: The Epitome of Moving Pictures (Lyman Howe, 1906)

Native Canoes (Edison, 1906)

Policeman's Tour of the World (Pathé, 1906)

Pounding Poi (Edison, 1906)

Shearing Sheep, Hawaii (Edison, 1906)

Surf Scenes in Waikiki Honolulu (Edison, 1906)

From Cairo to Khartoum (Urban Eclipse, 1907)

Jamaican Negroes Doing a Two-Step (Edison, 1907)

Picturesque Java (Pathé, 1907)

A Trip Through the Holy Land (Urban Eclipse, 1907)

An African Village (Kleine, 1908; excerpted from *The Touaregs in Their Country*)

The Call of the Wild (Biograph, 1908)

Hiawatha (Joseph K. Dixon, 1908)

Indian Communication: Sign Language of the North American Indian (Joseph K. Dixon, 1908–1913)

The Redman and the Child (Biograph, 1908)

The Touaregs in Their Country (Pathé, 1908)

The Country Doctor (Biograph, 1909)

The Mended Lute (Biograph, 1909)

Tunisian Industries (Pathé, 1909)

African Caravan (from the Joye Collection: Joye X7, c. 1910)

Chuncho Indians of the Amazon River, Peru (Edison, 1910)

Die Mauerische Topfer [*The Moroccan Potter*] (c. 1910; producer unknown; film no. 603582A, NFTA London)

Fighting the Iriquois in Canada (Kalem, 1910)

Madagaskar: Manners and Customs of the Sakalavas (Pathé, 1910)

[Untitled footage] (from Joseph Joye Collection: C962, 1910)

Eskimos in Labrador (Edison, 1911)

In and Around Havana, Cuba (Edison, 1911)

Picturesque Colorado (Rex Motion Picture Co., 1911)

A Primitive Man's Career to Civilization (Warwick, 1911)

African Hunt (Paul J. Rainey, 1912)

Benares and Agra, India (Edison, 1912)

Burma, Rangoon, India (Edison, 1912)

Cartoon of Mr. Paul Rainey's African Hunt (1912)

Cashmere (Edison, 1912)

Ceremonies of the Hopi Indians (McCormick, 1912)

Snake Dance of the Hopi Indians (McCormick, 1912)

Hunting Big Game with a Cinematograph in Alaska and Siberia (Frank E. Kleinschmidt, 1912)

Picturesque Darjeeling, India in Himalayan Mountains (Edison, 1912)

Scenes in Delhi, India (Edison, 1912)

Snake Dance of the Ninth Day (Howard McCormick, 1912)

Camping with the Blackfeet (Edison, 1913)

The Cliff Dwellers (Kalem, 1913)

From Durban to Zululand (Edison, 1913)

Hiawatha (Frank E. Moore; Unique Feature Film Co., 1913)

Indian and Ceylonese Types (Eclair, 1913)

The Oasis of El-Kantara (Eclair, 1913)

The Other Side of the World (Frederick Monsen, 1913)

Quaint Spots in Cairo, Egypt (Edison, 1913)

The Pyramids and the Sphinx, Egypt (Edison, 1913)

Arctic Hunt (Frank E. Kleinschmidt, 1914)

From Coast to Coast Through Central Africa (James Barnes, 1914)

In Borneo: In the Land of the Head-Hunters (Carl Lumholtz, 1914–1917)

In the Land of the Head Hunters (Edward Sheriff Curtis, 1914)

Birth of a Nation (D. W. Griffith, 1915)

Hunting Whales off the Coast of Japan (American Museum of Natural History, 1917)

Lawrence of Arabia (Lowell Thomas, 1917)

Life in the Frozen North (American Museum of Natural History, 1917)

A Vanishing Race: Scenes Among the Blackfoot Indians of Northern Montana (Edison, 1917)

On the Edge of the Desert (France, 1920)

Nanook of the North (Robert Flaherty, 1922)

Street Images (Great Britain, 1923; production company unknown)

Grass (Merian C. Cooper and Ernest B. Schoedsack, 1925)

By Aeroplane to Pygmyland (Matthew Stirling, 1926)

Moana (Robert Flaherty, 1926)

Revelations from the Land of the Burning Sand (The Mysteries of the Dark Continent) (France, 1926)

Chang (Merian C. Cooper and Ernest B. Schoedsack, 1927)

Travel Footage of Africa (Frederick Wulsin, c. 1927)

Simba: King of the Wild Beasts (Martin and Osa Johnson, 1928)

The Kwakuitl of British Columbia (Franz Boas, 1930; edited version by Bill Holm under this title, 1973)

Congorilla (Martin and Osa Johnson, 1932)

King Kong (Merian C. Cooper and Ernest B. Schoedsack, 1933)

Balinese Character (Margaret Mead and Gregory Bateson, 1942)

Karba's First Years (Margaret Mead and Gregory Bateson, 1950).

Bathing Babies in Three Cultures (Margaret Mead and Gregory Bateson, 1951)

First Days in the Life of a New Guinea Baby (Margaret Mead and Gregory Bateson, 1951)

Trance and Dance in Bali (Margaret Mead and Gregory Bateson, 1951)

Childhood Rivalry in Bali and New Guinea (Margaret Mead and Gregory Bateson, 1952)

Les maîtres fous (Jean Rouch, 1955)

The Hunters (John Marshall, 1956)

Moi, un Noir (Jean Rouch, 1957)

Chronique d'un été (*Chronicle of a Summer*) (Jean Rouch, 1960)

N/um Tchai (John Marshall, 1966)

Jaguar (Jean Rouch, 1967)

Bitter Melons (John Marshall, 1968)

Petit à Petit (Jean Rouch, 1969)

Shadow Catcher (T. C. McLuhan, 1975)

N!ai: The Story of a !Kung Woman (John Marshall, 1979)

Familiar Places (David and Judith MacDougall, 1980)

Lorang's Way (David and Judith MacDougall, 1980); *A Wife Among Wives* (1982); and *The Wedding Camels* (1980) (Part of Turkana Conversations Trilogy)

Takeover (David and Judith MacDougall, 1980)

Three Horseman (David and Judith MacDougall, 1980)

Reassemblage (Trinh T. Minh-ha, 1982).

Stockman's Strategy (David and Judith MacDougall, 1984)

Itam Hakim, Hopiit (Victor Masayesva Jr., 1984)

Naked Spaces — Living Is Round (Trinh T. Minh-ha 1985)

From the Pole to the Equator (Yervant Gianikian and Angela Ricci Lucchi, 1986)

Our Lives in Our Hands (Mi'kmaq tribe of Maine, 1986)

Babakiueria (Don Featherstone, 1988)

Ritual Clowns (Victor Masayesva Jr., 1988)

To Hold Our Ground (John Marshall, 1990)

Photo-Wallahs (David and Judith MacDougall, 1991)

Imagining Indians (Victor Masayesva Jr., 1992)

Mother Dao, The Turtle Like (Vincent Monnikendam, 1995)

Bontoc Eulogy (Marlon Fuentes, 1996)

Bibliography

In the bibliography, the following abbreviations are used:

AMJ   *American Museum Journal*
JAI   *Journal of the Anthropological Institute of Great Britain and Northern Ireland*
MJ   *Museums Journal*
MPW   *Moving Picture World*

PRIMARY SOURCES

Akeley, Carl. "The New Akeley Hall Planned by Carl E. Akeley." *AMJ* 14.5 (May 1914): 183.

Andrews, Roy Chapman. "The Asiatic Zoological Expedition of the American Museum of Natural History." *AMJ* 16.2 (Feb. 1916): 105–106.

———. "Hunting Deer in the Adirondacks," *AMJ* 15.8 (Dec. 1915): 409–14.

———. *Under a Lucky Star: A Lifetime of Adventure.* Garden City, N.Y.: Blue Ribbon Books, 1945.

"Another Lost Opportunity" (editorial). *MPW* 5.16 (Oct. 16, 1909): 5.

"Art in a Natural History Museum with Special Reference to Mural Decorations in the Indian Halls." *AMJ* 13.3 (Mar. 1913): 99–102.

Balfour, Henry. "The Relationship of Museums to the Study of Anthropology." *JAI* 34 (1904): 18.

Barnes, Elmer Tracey. *The Motion-Picture Comrades in African Jungles.* New York: New York Book Co., 1917.

———. *The Motion Picture Comrades Aboard a Submarine; Or, Searching for Treasures Under the Sea.* New York: New York Book Co., 1917.

———. *The Motion Picture Comrades Along the Orinoco; Or, Facing Perils in the Tropics*. New York: New York Book Co., 1917.

———. *The Motion Picture Comrades' Great Ventures; Or, On the Road with the Big Round Top*. New York: New York Book Co., 1917.

Barrett, S. A. "Photographic and Panoramic Backgrounds: Anthropological Groups." *Museum Work* 1 (June 1918–May 1919): 75–78.

Bather, Francis Arthur. "Presidential Address to the British Museum's Association Aberdeen Conference, 1903." *MJ* 3.3 (Sept. 1903): 71–94.

———. "Dr. Myer on Some European Museums." *MJ* 2.11 (May 1903): 319–29.

Bigelow, Maurice A. "Educational Value of the American Museum." *AMJ* 11.7 (Nov. 1911): 234.

Blue Book, The: A Comprehensive Official Souvenir View Book of the Panama-Pacific International Exposition at San Francisco, 1915. San Francisco: View Books, 1915.

Boas, Franz. "The Aims of Ethnology" (1888). Reprinted in Boas, *Race, Language, and Culture*, 626–38.

———. "Museums of Ethnology and Their Classification." *Science* 9.229 (June 24, 1887): 612–14.

———. "The Occurrence of Similar Inventions in Areas Widely Apart." *Science* 9.224 (May 20, 1887): 485–86.

———. *Race, Language, and Culture*. New York: Free Press, 1940.

———. "Some Principles of Museum Administration." *Science* 25.650 (June 14, 1907): 921–33.

Britt, Albert. "Hunting for the Movies." *Outing* 73.6 (Mar. 1919): 290–93, 338–39.

Bumpus, Hermon C. "The Museum as a Factor in Education." *The Independent* 61 (Aug. 2, 1906): 269–72.

Bush, W. Stephen. " 'In the Land of the Head Hunters.' " *MPW* 22.12 (Dec. 19, 1914): 1695.

———. "Moving Picture Absurdities." *MPW* 9.10 (Sept. 16, 1911): 733.

Carter, Huntley. "How to Promote the Use of Museums by an Institute of Museums." *MJ* 7.6 (Dec. 1907): 193–204.

Catlin, George. *North American Indians, Being Letters and Notes on Their Manners, Customs, Written During Eight Years Travel Amongst the Wildest Tribes of Indians in America*. 2 vols. Edinburgh: John Grant, 1848; rpt., New York: Dover, 1973.

———. *Proposal*. Museum of Mankind. 3 pages. Catlin Ephemera Collections, City of Westminster Libraries, 1850.

Chapman, Frank M. "Natural History for the Masses." *World's Work* 5 (Nov. 1902): 2761–70.

Church, T. A. " 'Beasts of the Jungle': A Two-Part Educational and Scenic Feature of the Highest Quality by the Supreme Features Corporation." *MPW* 21.3 (Sept. 26, 1914): 1817.

Claudy, C. H. "Too Much Acting." *MPW* 8.9 (Feb. 11, 1911): 288–89.

Clegg, Thomas. "Education by Kinematograph: Future Prospects." *MPW* 6.9 (Mar. 5, 1910): 331–32.

Crowther, Henry. "The Museum as Teacher of Nature-Study." *MJ* 5.1 (July 1905): 5–14.

"Current Notes on Anthropology" (anonymous author), ed. Daniel G. Brinton, *Science* 22.564 (Nov. 24, 1893): 281.

De Cardi, C. N. "Ju Ju Laws in the Niger Delta." *JAI*, n.s., 2, (1899): 51–64.

Dench, Ernest A. *Making the Movies*. New York: Macmillan, 1915.

Dickson, Antonia. "Wonders of the Kinetoscope." *Frank Leslie's Monthly* 39.2 (Feb. 1895): 245–50.

Dickson, W. K. L. *The Biograph in Battle*. London: Unwin, 1901.

Ditmars, Raymond L. "The Anthropological Exhibits at the American Museum of Natural History." *Science* 25.641 (Apr. 12, 1907): 27–28.

———. "Educational Motion Pictures in Natural History." *AMJ* 15.1 (Jan. 1915): 27–28.

Dixon, Joseph K. *The Purpose and Achievements of the Rodman Wanamaker Expedition of Citizenship to the North American Indian* (pamphlet). N.p.: Summer and Autumn, 1913.

———. *The Vanishing Race: The Last Great Indian Council*. New York: Doubleday, Page, 1913.

———. *Wanamaker Primer on the North American Indian*. Philadelphia: Wanamaker Originator, 1909.

Donaldson, Leonard. *The Cinematograph and the Natural Sciences: The Achievements and Possibilities of Cinematography as an Aid to Scientific Research*. London: Ganes, 1912.

Dorsey, George A. "The Anthropological Exhibits at the American Museum of Natural History," *Science* 25.641 (Apr. 12, 1907): 588.

D. W. H. "The Columbian Exposition." *The Nation* 57.1474 (Sept. 28, 1893): 225.

"Education by Motion Pictures." *The Kinetogram*, Dec. 1, 1909, 14.

Fewkes, J. Walter. "On the Use of the Phonograph in the Study of the Languages of American Indians." *Science* 15.378 (May 2, 1890): 267–68.

Flower, W. H. "President's Address." *JAI* 11 (1882): 184–94.

Gallup, Anna Billings. "The Children's Museum as an Educator." *Popular Science Monthly* 72 (Apr. 1908): 371–79.

Galton, Francis. "Composite Types," *JAI* 8 (1879): 132–41.

Gaudreault, André. "Les traces du montage dans la production Lumière." In Philippe Dujaidin, André Galdies, Jacques Crerstenkorn, and Jean-Claude Sequin, eds., *L'aventure de Cinematographe*, 299–306. Lyon: Aleas, 1999.

Gillen, Francis James. *Gillen's Diary: The Camp Jottings of F. J. Gillen on the Spencer and Gillen Expedition Across Australia, 1901–1902* (1902). Rpt., Adelaide: Libraries Board of South Australia, 1968.

Goddard, Pliny E. "Motion Picture Records of Indians: Films That Show the Common Industries of the Apache." *AMJ* 15.4 (Apr. 1915): 185–87.

Goode, George Brown. "The Museum of the Future." Lecture delivered before the Brooklyn Institute, Feb. 28, 1889. Reprinted in the *Annual Report of the Board of the Regents of the Smithsonian Institution, United States House of Representatives*, 243–62. New York: Arno Press, 1980.

———. "First Draft of a System of Classification for the World's Columbian Exposition." Smithsonian Institution Archives (Record Unit 70, box 37, pp. 650–52).

Grau, Herbert. *The Theatre of Science*. New York: Benjamin Blom, 1914.

Greenwood, Thomas. *Museums and Art Galleries*. London: Simpkin, Marshall, 1888.

Haddon, Alfred Cort. "The Ethnography of the Western Tribes of the Torres Straits." *JAI* 19 (1889): 297–440.

———. *Head-Hunters: Black, White and Brown*. London: Methuen, 1901.

———. "Photography." *Notes and Queries on Anthropology* (1899 ed.), 235–40.

———. "Photography and Folklore." *Folklore* 6 (1895): 222–24.

Harrison, Louis Reeves. "Photoscenes of Travel." *MPW* 14.1 (Oct. 5, 1912): 21.

———. *Reports of the Cambridge Anthropological Expedition to the Torres Straits*. 6 vols. Cambridge: Cambridge University Press, 1901–1935.

Hartt, Mary Bronson. "The Play-Side of the Fair." *World's Work* 2.4 (Aug. 1901): 1097.

Hilton-Simpson, M. W. and J. A. Haeseler. "Cinema and Ethnology." *Discovery* 6 (Jan. to Dec. 1925): 325–30.

Holmes, William H. "Classification and Arrangement of the Exhibits of an Anthropological Institute of Great Britain and Northern Ireland." *JAI*, n.s., 2 (1902): 353–72.

Hore, Edward C. "Twelve Tribes of Tanganyika." *JAI* 12 (1883): 2–21.

Howells, William Dean. "A Sennight of the Centennial." *Atlantic Monthly* 38 (July 1876): 97.

Hoyle, Dr. "Egyptological Collections." *MJ* 8.5 (Nov. 1908): 152–62.

Hurte, Harvey N. "Exploring by Motion Pictures." *Picture-Play Weekly* 1.6 (May 15, 1915): 16–17.

"Igorrrotes [*sic*] Not to Wear Breeches." *St. Louis Globe-Democrat*, July 15, 1904, 1.

Im Thurn, E. F. *Among the Indians of Guiana, Being Sketches, Chiefly Anthropological, from the Interior of British Guiana* (1883). Rpt., New York: Dover, 1967.

———. "Anthropological Uses of the Camera." *JAI* 22 (1893): 184–203.

———. *Thoughts, Talks, and Tramps: A Collection of Papers*. London: Oxford University Press, 1934.

James, George Wharton. "The Hopi Snake Dance." *Outing* 36 (June 1900): 303.

———. "The Snake Dance of the Hopis." *Camera Craft* 1.1 (Nov. 1902): 3–10.

———. "The Study of Indian Faces." *Camera Craft* 8.1 (1906): 12–18.

Jastrow, Joseph. Review of A. C. Haddon's *Reports of the Cambridge Anthropological Expedition to the Torres Straits*, vol. 2, *Physiology and Psychology*. *Science* 15.384 (1902): 742–44.

Kearton, Cherry. *Photographing Wildlife Across the World*. London: Arrowsmith, 1923.

———. *Wildlife Across the World*. London: Hodder and Stoughton, 1914.

"The Kinetoscope Stereopticon." *Scientific American* (Oct. 31, 1896): 331.

Lamprey, J. "On a Method of Measuring the Human Form for the Use of Students of Ethnology." *Journal of the Ethnological Society of London* 1 (1869): 84–85.

Langdon, Sherman. "The New Museum Idea." *World's Work* 12.3 (July 1906): 7711.

Lehmann, H. *Die Kinemtaographie, ihre Grundlagen und ihre Anwendungen*. Leipzig: B. G. Teubner, 1911.

Leipziger, Henry M. "Address to President, Ladies, and Gentlemen." AMNH *Annual Report for 1899*, 44. New York: AMNH, 1900.

Lindsay, Vachel. *The Art of the Moving Picture*. New York: Macmillan, 1915.

Lowe, Charles. *Four National Exhibitions in London and Their Organizers*. London: Unwin, 1892.

Lowie, Robert H. "Industry and Art of the Negro Race." *AMJ* 11.1 (Jan. 1911): 15.

Lucas, Frederic A. "The Story of Museum Groups: Part I." *AMJ* 14.1 (Jan. 1914): 3–15.

———. "The Story of Museum Groups: Part II." *AMJ* 14.2 (Feb. 1914): 51–66.

———. "The Work of Our Larger Museums as Shown by their Annual Reports." *Science* 27.679 (Jan. 3, 1908): 35.

Lumholtz, Carl. *Through Central Borneo*. New York: Scribner's, 1920; rpt., New York: Oxford University Press, 1991.

Lyttelton, Edward. "Note on the Educational Influence of the Cinematograph." *Hibbert Journal* (July 1913): 851–55.

Maclauchlan, John. "Presidential Address, Dundee Meeting of Museum's Association." *MJ* 7.1 (July 1907): 4–17.

MacDonald, James. "East Central African Customs." *JAI* 22 (1893): 99–122.

MacMechan, T. R. "Down 'The Pike': The 'Boulevard of Gaiety' at the St. Louis Exposition." *Pacific Monthly* 12 (July 1904): 30.

"Making the Devil Useful." *English Journal* 2 (Dec. 1913): 658–60.

Man, Edward Horace. "A Brief Account of the Nicobar Islands." *JAI* 15 (1886): 428–51.

Marey, Étienne-Jules. *La chronophotographie*. Paris: Gauthier-Villars, 1899.

———. Preface to *La photographie animée* by Charles-Louis Eugene Trutat. Paris: Gauthier-Villars, 1899.

Mason, Otis. T. "Anthropology in Paris During the Exposition of 1889." *American Anthropologist* 3 (Jan. 1890): 27–36.

———. "Summary of Progress in Anthropology." *Annual Report of the Smithsonian*

Institution for the Year Ending July 1883. Washington, D.C.: Smithsonian Institution, 1894.

———. "What Is Anthropology?" Saturday Morning Lecture, Smithsonian Institution, Mar. 18, 1882. Washington, D.C.: Smithsonian Institution, 1882.

Mayer, Alfred Goldsborough. "Educational Efficiency of Our Museums." *North American Review* 177 (Oct. 1903): 564–67.

McCabe, James D. *The Illustrated History of the Centennial Exhibition Held in Commemoration of the One Hundredth Anniversary of American Independence*. Philadelphia: National Publishing, 1876.

McClintock, Norman. "The Telephoto Lens in Cinematography." *AMJ* 18.1 (Jan. 1917): 5–63.

McCormick, Howard. "The Artist's Southwest." *AMJ* 13.3 (Mar. 1913): 119–34.

McDowell, Edward B. "The World's Fair Cosmopolis." *Frank Leslie's Monthly* 36.4 (Oct. 1893): 407–16.

McGee, W. J. "Fifty Years of American Science." *Atlantic Monthly* 82.491 (Sept. 1898): 320.

———. "Medical Kinematography—A Great Discovery." *MPW* 7.9 (Aug. 27, 1910): 456.

———. "Strange Races of Men." *World's Work* 8.1 (Aug. 1904): 5185–88.

Midway Types: A Book of Illustrated Lessons About the People of the Midway Plaisance, World's Fair, 1893. Chicago: American Engraving Co., 1894.

Miles, Carlton. "Rainey Hunt at the Metropolitan: Wonderful Views of Animal Life in Africa Shown on the Screen." (Publication unknown), Aug. 4, 1914, n.p.

Mitchell, J. A. "Types and People at the Fair." *Scribner's* 14.2 (Aug. 1893): 186.

Mooney, James. *The Ghost-Dance Religion and the Sioux Outbreak of 1890* (1890). Rpt., Lincoln: University of Nebraska Press, 1991.

Morton, Samuel G. *Crania Americana; Or, A Comparative View of the Skulls of Various Aboriginal Nations on the Varieties of the Human Species*. Philadelphia, 1839.

"Moving Pictures as a Cure for Insanity." *MPW* 6.10 (Mar. 12, 1910): 376.

"Moving Pictures at Local Clinic." *MPW* 11.1 (Jan. 29, 1912): 286.

"Moving Pictures Cure Mental Diseases." *MPW* 5.16 (Oct. 16, 1909): 5.

"Moving Picture Is an Uplifter: How It Reaches the Multitudes." *MPW* 6.21 (May 28, 1910): 887.

Muhr, A. F. "E. S. Curtis and His Work." *Photo-Era* (July 1907): 9–13.

Muller, F. Max. "Anthropology Past and Present." *Science* 18.452 (Oct. 2, 1891): 190.

"Novel Uses for Moving Pictures." *MPW* 1.3 (Mar. 23, 1907): 39–40.

Official Guide to the World's Columbian Exposition. Chicago: Columbian Guide Company, 1893.

Osborn, Henry Fairfield. "Memorial to the Late Morris Ketchum Jesup." *Science* 31.792 (Mar. 4, 1910): 337–38.

————. "The Museum of the American People." *AMJ* 14.6–7 (Oct-Nov. 1914): 219–20.

————. "Museums of the Future." *AMJ* 11.7 (Nov. 1911): 223–26.

"Out of the Ashes." *Chicago Tribune*, June 6, 1883, 8.

Partridge, William Ordway. "The Educational Value of World's Fairs." *The Forum* 33 (Mar. 1902): 121–26.

"Pictures at the Masonic." *Louisville Post*, May 5, 1908, n.p.

Pitt-Rivers, A.H.L.F. "Typological Museums, as Exemplified by the Pitt Rivers Museum at Oxford, and His Provincial Museum at Farnham, Dorset." *Journal of the Royal Society of Arts* 40 (Dec. 18, 1891): 115–22.

Pöch, Rudolf. "Reisen in den Jahren, 1904–06." *Zeitschrift für Ethnologie* (1907): 382–400.

"A Pocket Chronophotographic Apparatus." *Scientific American Supplement* (Dec. 22, 1900): 20890.

Polimanti, Oswald. "Der Kinematograph in der biologischen und medizinischen" (Wissenschaft). *Naturwissenschaftliche Woschenschrift* 26.49 (1911): 769–74.

Portman, M. V. "Photography for Anthropologists." *JAI* 25 (1896): 75–85.

Putnam, Frederick Ward. "Introduction." *Portrait Types of the Midway Plaisance*. Chicago, 1893.

————. *World's Columbian Exposition: Plan and Classification*. Chicago: Chicago World's Columbian Exposition, Dept. of Publicity and Promotion, 1892.

Pycraft, W. P. "Some Common Errors in the Representation of Stuffed Birds in Museums." *MJ* 3.9 (Mar. 1904): 288–93.

Read, C. "Prefaratory Note." *Notes and Queries on Anthropology*. 3d ed. (1899): 87–99.

Regnault, Félix-Louis. "La chronophotographie dans l'ethnographie." *Bulletins et mémoires de la Société d'anthropologie de Paris*, vol. 1, 5th ser. (Oct. 4, 1900): 421–22.

————. "L'évolution du cinéma." *La revue scientifique* (1922): 79–85.

————. "Exposition ethnographique de l'Afrique occidentale au Champs-De-Mars à Paris Sénégal et Soudan francais." *La nature* 1159 (Aug. 17, 1895): 185–86.

————. "Films et museés d'ethnographie." *Comptes rendus de l'association francaise pour l'avancement des sciences* 2 (1923): 680–81.

————. Le rôle du cinéma en ethnographie." *La nature* 2866 (Oct. 1, 1931): 304–306.

Rensselaer, Marianna G, van. "At the Fair." *Century Magazine* 46 (May 1893): 12–13.

"Review of *A Trip Through Holy Land*." *MPW* 1.14 (June 8, 1907): 219.

Rider, Fremont. *Rider's New York: A Guide-Book for Travelers*. New York: Henry Holt, 1916.

Roesler, Mrs. "The Work of an Instructor in the American Museum of Natural History." *MJ* 8.9 (Mar. 1909): 303–13.

"Sir William Flower, K.C.B." *MJ* 3.2 (Aug. 1903): 59–62.

Skinner, Alanson. "Red Men in 'Movies.'" *New York Times*, June 3, 1914, 12.

Smith, Everett Wallace. "Natural Science for the Every-Day Man." *The Outlook* 89.4 (May 23, 1908): 183–91.

Smith, F. Hopkinson. "The Picturesque Side." *Scribner's* 14.5 (Nov. 5, 1893): 608.

Smith, Harlan I. "Man and His Works: The Anthropological Buildings at the World's Columbian Exposition." *American Antiquarian* 15.2 (Mar. 1893): 117.

Smithsonian Institution. *Annual Report for 1877*. Washington, D.C.: Smithsonian Institution, 1878.

Snider, Denton J. *World's Fairs Studies*. Chicago: Sigman, 1895.

"The Spectator at the World's Fair." *The Outlook* 109 (Apr. 14, 1915): 895–97.

Spencer, Walter Baldwin. *Wanderings in Wild Australia*. 2 vols. London: Macmillan, 1928.

Spencer, Walter Baldwin and Frank J. Gillen. *Across Australia*. London: Macmillan, 1912.

Starr, Frederick. *The Ainu Group at the St. Louis Exposition*. Chicago: Open Court, 1904.

———. "Anthropology at the World's Fair." *Popular Science Monthly* 48 (1893): 610–21.

———. ."The Congo in Moving Pictures." *The Show World* 1.3 (July 13, 1907): 1.

———. *Congo Natives: An Ethnographic Album*. Chicago: Lakeside Press, 1912.

———. "Prof. Starr's Valuable Contribution." *The Nickelodeon* 1.3 (Mar. 1909): 64.

———. "The World Before Your Eyes." *MPW* 4.5 (Feb. 20, 1909): 194–95.

Steele, Wilbur Daniel. "The Moving-Picture Machine in the Jungle." *McClure's Magazine* 40 (Jan. 1913): 329–37.

Steer, Valentia. *Romance of the Cinema*. London: Arthur Pearson, 1913.

"Surgery Taught by Moving Pictures." *MPW* 7.1 (July 12, 1910): 30.

"Too Near the Camera." *MPW* 8.12 (Mar. 25, 1911): 633–34.

Tose, Frank. "Comments Upon the Habitat Groups in the California Academy of Sciences." *Museum News* 8.10 (Nov. 15, 1929): 7–8.

Tropinard, Paul. "Observations upon the Methods and Processes of Anthropometry." *JAI* 10 (1881): 212–24.

Turner, W. Y. "On the Ethnology of the Motu." *JAI* 7 (1878): 472–73.

Tylor, Edward B. "Dammann's Race Photographs." *Nature* (Jan. 6, 1876): 184.

Urban, Charles. "The Cinematograph in Science and Education." *MPW* 1.21 (July 27, 1907): 324.

———. "The Cinematograph in Science and Education." *MPW* 1.24 (Aug. 17, 1907): 373.

———. "The Cinematograph in Science and Education: Its Value in Surgical Demonstrations." *MPW* 1.25 (Aug. 24, 1907): 388–89.

U.S. Bureau of Indian Affairs. *Annual Report of the Commissioner for Indian Affairs (1917)*. Bureau of Indian Affairs, Washington, D.C.: GPO, 1918.

"Visiting the Centennial." *Public Record*, Aug. 8, 1876, 2

Walker, Sophia A. "An Art Impression of the Exposition." *Independent* 53 (July 18, 1901): 1678.

Wallace, Alfred A. "Museums for the People." *Macmillan's Magazine* 19 (1869): 244–50.

Wallin, J. E. Wallace. "The Moving Picture in Relation to Education, Health, Delinquency, and Crime." *Pedagogical Seminary* 17.2 (June 1910): 129–42.

Ward, Henry L. "The Anthropological Exhibits in the American Museum of Natural History." *Science* 25.645 (May 10, 1907): 745–46.

Waters, Theodore. "Out with a Moving Picture Machine." *Cosmopolitan* 40.3 (Jan. 1906): 251–59.

Waterton, Charles. *Essays on Natural History Chiefly Ornithology* (1838), cited in Stephen Bann, *The Clothing of Clio*, 17.

Woolnough, Frank. "Museums and Nature Study." *MJ* 4.8 (Feb. 1905): 265–71.

SECONDARY SOURCES

Abel, Richard. *The Ciné Goes to Town: French Cinema, 1896–1914*. Berkeley: University of California Press, 1994.

———. "Early Fiction Now and Then: 'Phantom Viewing in the Archives.'" *Aura* 2.3 (1996): 4–11.

———. "'Our Country/Whose Country?' The 'Americanization' Project of Early Westerns." In Buscombe and Pearson, eds., *Back in the Saddle Again*, 77–95.

———. "The Perils of Pathé, or the Americanization of Early American Cinema." In Charney and Schwartz, eds., *Cinema and the Invention of Modern Life*, 183–226.

———. *The Red Rooster Scare: Making Cinema American, 1900–1910*. Berkeley: University of California Press, 1999.

Abel, Richard, ed. *Silent Film*. New Brunswick: Rutgers University Press, 1996.

Adams, Bluford. *E. Pluribus Barnum: The Great Showman and the Making of U.S. Popular Culture*. Minneapolis: University of Minnesota Press, 1997.

———. "'A Stupendous Mirror of Departed Empires': The Barnum Hippodromes and Circuses, 1874–1891." *American Literary History* 8.1 (Spring 1996): 34–56.

Alexander, Edward P. *Museum Masters: Their Museums and Their Influence*. Nashville: American Association of State and Local History, 1983.

Alleloula, Malek. *The Colonial Harem*. Minneapolis: University of Minnesota Press, 1986.

Allen, Robert C. *Vaudeville and Film, 1895–1915: A Study in Media Interaction*. New York: Arno Press, 1980.

Altick, Richard D. *The Shows of London*. Cambridge: Belknap Press of Harvard University Press, 1978.

Altman, Rick. "The Silence of the Silents." *Musical Quarterly* 88.4 (1996): 648–718.

Ames, Michael M. *Museums, the Public, and Anthropology: A Study in the Anthropology of Museums.* Vancouver: University of British Columbia Press, 1986.

Appadurai, Arjun. "Disjuncture and Difference in the Global Cultural Economy." *Public Culture* 2.2 (1990): 1–24.

Armstrong, Meg. " 'A Jumble of Foreigness': The Sublime Musayums of Nineteenth-Century Fairs and Expositions." *Cultural Critique* 23 (Winter 1992–93): 199–250.

Arnheim, Rudolph. "On the Nature of Photography." *Critical Inquiry* 1.1 (Sept. 1974): 149–61.

Badger, R. Reid. *The Great American Fair.* Chicago: Nelson Hall, 1979.

Bal, Mike. "Telling, Showing, Showing Off." *Critical Inquiry* 18.3 (Spring 1992): 556–94.

Balikci, Asen. "Visual Anthropology: The Legacy of Margaret Mead." Paper presented at the annual meeting of the American Anthropological Association, Washington, D.C., 1985.

Banks, Marcus and Howard Morphy, eds. *Rethinking Visual Anthropology.* New Haven: Yale University Press, 1997.

Bann, Stephen. *The Clothing of Clio: A Study of the Representation of History in Nineteenth Century Britain and France.* London and New York: Cambridge University Press, 1984.

Banta, Melissa and Curtis M. Hinsley. *From Site to Sight: Anthropology, Photography, and the Power of the Image.* Cambridge, Mass.: Peabody Museum Press, 1986.

Barber, X. Theodore. "Phantasmagorical Wonders: The Magic Lantern Ghost Show in Nineteenth-Century America." *Film History* 3.2 (1989): 73–86.

———. "The Roots of Travel Cinema: John L. Stoddard, E. Burton Holmes, and the Nineteenth-Century Illustrated Travel Lecture." *Film History* 5 (1993): 68–84.

Barkan, Elazar and Ronald Bush, eds. *Prehistories of the Future.* Stanford: Stanford University Press, 1995.

Barnouw, Erik. *Documentary: A History of the Non-Fiction Film.* London: Oxford University Press, 1974.

Barthes, Roland. *Camera Lucida.* Trans. Richard Howard. New York: Hill and Wang, 1981.

———. *Image, Music, Text.* Trans. Stephen Heath. New York: Hill and Wang, 1977.

Bartholomae, David and Anthony Petrosky, eds. *Ways of Seeing: An Anthology for Writers.* 3d ed. Boston: Bedford Books (St. Martin's), 1993.

Basso, Keith H. "History of Ethnological Research." In Alfonso Ortig, ed., *Handbook of North American Indians* 9:14–21. Washington, D.C.: Smithsonian Institution Press, 1979.

Bataille, Gretchen M. and Charles L. P. Silet, eds. *The Pretend Indians: Images of Native Americans in the Movies.* Ames: Iowa State University Press, 1980.

Baudelaire, Charles. *The Painter of Modern Life and Other Essays.* New York: Da Capo, 1986.

Baudry, Jean-Louis. "Ideological Effects of the Basic Cinematic Apparatus," trans. Alan Williams. *Film Quarterly* 28.2 (Winter 1974–75). Reprinted in Gerald Mast, Marshall Cohen, and Leo Braudy, eds., *Film Theory and Criticism*, 302–12. 4th ed. New York: Oxford University Press, 1992.

Bayly, C. A., ed. *The Raj and the British, 1600–1947*. London: National Portrait Gallery, 1990.

Bazin, André. "The Myth of Total Cinema," 17–23, and "The Ontology of the Photographic Image," 9–16, in Bazin, *What Is Cinema?*, vol. 2. Edited by Hugh Gray. Berkeley: University of California Press, 1967.

Beckett, R. B., ed. *John Constable's Correspondence*. Suffolk Records Society 12 (1968).

Belloï, Livio. "Lumière and His View: The Cameraman's Eye in Early Cinema." *Historical Journal of Film, Radio, and Television* 15.4 (1995): 461–74.

Benedict, Burton et al. *The Anthropology of World's Fairs: San Francisco's Panama Pacific International Exposition of 1915*. Berkeley and London: Lowie Museum of Anthropology in association with Scolar Press, 1983.

Benelli, Dana. "Jungles and National Landscapes: Documentary and the Hollywood Cinema in the 1930s." Ph.D. diss., University of Iowa, 1991.

———. "*S.O.S. Iceberg* and *King Kong*: Hollywood Re-Writes the Travelogue-Expedition Documentary." Paper presented to the Society for Cinema Studies Conference, Ottawa, 1997.

Benjamin, Walter. "The Work of Art in the Age of Mechanical Reproduction." In Hannah Arendt, ed., *Illuminations*, 217–52. New York: Schocken, 1969.

Bennett, Tony. *The Birth of the Museum*. New York: Routledge, 1995.

Berkhofer, Robert F., Jr. *The White Man's Indian: Images of the American Indian from Columbus to the Present*. New York: Knopf, 1978.

Bhaba, Homi K. *The Location of Culture*. London: Routledge, 1994.

Bird, S. Elizabeth, ed. *Dressing in Feathers: The Construction of the Indian in American Popular Culture*. Boulder, Colo.: Westview, 1996.

Blackman, Margaret B. "Posing the American Indian: Early Photographs Often Clothed Reality in Their Own Stereotypes." *Natural History* 89.10 (Oct. 1980): 68–74.

Blanton, Casey, ed. *Picturing Paradise: Colonial Photography of Samoa, 1875 to 1925*. Daytona Beach, Fla.: Southeast Museum of Photography, 1995.

Bloom, Peter. "Pottery, Chronophotography, and the French Colonial Archive." Paper presented at the Screen Studies Conference (Glasgow, June 1993).

Bloom, Sol. *The Autobiography of Sol Bloom*. New York: Putnam, 1948.

Bogdan, Robert. *Freak Show: Presenting Human Oddities for Amusement and Profit*. Chicago: University of Chicago Press, 1988.

Bohrer, Frederick N. "The Times and Spaces of History: Representation, Assyria, and the British Museum." In Sherman and Rogoff, eds., *Museum Culture: Histories, Discourses, Spectacles*, 197–22.

Bowser, Eileen. *Biograph Bulletins, 1908–1912*. New York: Farrar, Straus and Giroux, 1973.

———. *The Transformation of Cinema, 1907–1915*. Berkeley: University of California Press, 1990.

Brand, Dana. *The Spectator and the City in Nineteenth-Century American Literature*. New York: Cambridge University Press, 1991.

Braun, Judy. "The North American Indians Exhibits at the 1876 and 1893 World's Expositions: The Influence of Scientific Thought on Popular Attractions." Master's thesis, George Washington University, 1975.

Braun, Marta. *Picturing Time: The Work of Etienne-Jules Marey (1830–1904)*. Chicago: University of Chicago Press, 1992.

Breitbart, Eric. *A World on Display: Photographs from the St. Louis World's Fair, 1904*. Albuquerque: University of New Mexico Press, 1997.

Brigham, David R. *Public Culture in the Early Republic: Peale's Museum and Its Audience*. Washington, D.C.: Smithsonian Institution Press, 1995.

Bronner, Simon J., ed. *Consuming Visions: Accumulation and Display of Goods in America, 1880–1920*. New York: Norton, 1989.

Browne, Nick. "Orientalism as an Ideological Form: American Film Theory in the Silent Period." *Wide Angle* 11.4 (1989): 23–31.

Brownlow, Kevin. *The War, the West, and the Wilderness*. New York: Knopf, 1979.

Bruno, Guiliana. *Streetwalking on a Ruined Map: Cultural Theory and the City Films of Elvira Notari*. Princeton: Princeton University Press, 1993.

Buck-Morss, Susan. *The Dialectics of Seeing: Walter Benjamin and the Arcades Project*. Cambridge: MIT Press, 1993.

Burch, Noël. "Charles Baudelaire Versus Doctor Frankenstein." *Afterimage* 8–9 (1981): 4–21.

———. *Life to Those Shadows*. Berkeley: University of California Press, 1990.

———. "Primitivism and the Avant-Gardes: A Dialectical Approach." In Philip Rosen, ed., *Narrative, Apparatus, Ideology*, 483–506. New York: Columbia University Press, 1986.

Burrow, J. W. "Evolution and Anthropology in the 1860s: The Anthropological Society of London, 1863–71." *Victorian Studies* 7.2 (1963): 137–54.

Buscombe, Edward and Roberta Pearson, eds. *Back in the Saddle Again: New Essays on the Western*. London: British Film Institute (BFI), 1998.

Cahn, Iris. "The Changing Landscape of Modernity: Early Film and America's 'Great Picture' Tradition." *Wide Angle* 18.3 (July 1996): 85–100.

Caldwell, Genoa, ed. *The Man Who Photographed the World: Burton Holmes Travelogues, 1886–1938*. New York: Abrams, 1977.

Cantrill, Arthur. "The 1901 Cinematography of Walter Baldwin Spencer." *Cantrill's Film Notes* 37–38 (1982): 26–42.

———. "The 1901 Cinematography of Walter Baldwin Spencer." In La Tour, Gaudreault, and Pearson, eds., *Cinema at the Turn of the Century*, 327–35.

Carson, Diane, Linda Dittmar, and Janice R. Welsch, eds. *Multiple Voices in Feminist Film Criticism*. Minneapolis: University of Minnesota Press, 1994.

Cartwright, Lisa. *Screening the Body: Tracing Medicine's Visual Culture*. Minneapolis: University of Minnesota Press, 1995.

Chapman, Mary. " 'Living Pictures': Women and *Tableaux Vivant* in Nineteenth-Century American Fiction and Culture." *Wide Angle* 18.3 (part 2) (July 1996): 22–52.

Chapman, William Ryan. "Arranging Ethnology: A.H.L.F. Pitt Rivers and the Typological Tradition." In Stocking, ed., *Objects and Others*, 15–48.

Charney, Leo and Vanessa R. Schwartz, eds. *Cinema and the Invention of Modern Life*. Berkeley: University of California Press, 1995.

Chiozzi, Paolo. "Reflections on Ethnographic Film with a General Bibliography." Trans. by Denise Dresner. *Visual Anthropology* 2 (1989): 1–84.

———. "What Is Ethnographic Film? Remarks About a Debate." *SVA Review* (Spring 1990): 26–28.

Clifford, James. "Introduction: Partial Truths." In Clifford and Marcus, eds., *Writing Culture*, 1–26.

———. "On Ethnographic Allegory." In Clifford and Marcus, eds., *Writing Culture*, 98–121.

Clifford, James and George E. Marcus, eds. *The Predicament of Culture: Twentieth-Century Ethnography, Literature, and Art*. Cambridge: Harvard University Press, 1988.

———. *Writing Culture: The Poetics and Politics of Ethnography*. Berkeley: University of California Press, 1986.

Cook, James W., Jr. "Of Men, Missing Links, and Nondescripts: The Strange Career of P. T. Barnum's 'What is It?' Exhibition." In Thomson, ed., *Freakery*, 139–57.

Cook, Lynne and Peter Wollen, eds. *Visual Display: Culture Beyond Appearances*. Seattle: Bay Press, 1995.

Coombes, Annie E.S. "Museums and the Formation of National and Cultural Identities." *Oxford Art Journal* 11.2 (1988): 57–68.

———. *Reinventing Africa: Museums, Material Culture, and Popular Imagination in Late Victorian and Edwardian England*. New Haven: Yale University Press, 1994.

Corbey, Raymond with Steven Wachlin. "Ethnographic Showcases, 1870–1930." *Cultural Anthropology* 8.3 (Aug. 1993): 338–69.

Cosandey, Roland, André Gaudreault, and Tom Gunning, eds. *An Invention of the Devil: Religion and Early Cinema*. Sainte-Foy/Lausanne: Les Presses de l'Université Laval/Éditions Payot Lausanne, 1992.

Crary, Jonathan. *Suspensions of Perception: Attention, Spectacle, and Modern Culture.* Cambridge: MIT Press, 1999.

———. *Techniques of the Observer: On Vision and Modernity in the Nineteenth Century.* Cambridge: MIT Press, 1991.

Crawford, Peter I. and David Turton, eds. *Film as Ethnography.* Manchester, Eng.: Manchester University Press, 1992.

Culler, Jonathan. "The Semiotics of Tourism." *American Journal of Semiotics* 1 (1981): 127–40.

Deahl, William E., Jr. "A History of Buffalo Bill's Wild West Show, 1883–1913." Ph.D. diss., Southern Illinois University, 1974.

DeBouzek, Jeanette. "The 'Ethnographic Surrealism' of Jean Rouch." *Visual Anthropology* 2 (1989): 301–15.

De Brigard, Emilie. "The History of Ethnographic Film." In Hockings, ed., *Principles of Visual Anthropology,* 13–43.

De Certeau, Michel. *The Writing of History.* Trans. Tom Conley. New York: Columbia University Press, 1988.

De Klerk, Nico. "Print Matters: Film-Archival Reflections." In Hertogs and de Klerk, eds., *Nonfiction Film from the Teens,* 67–72.

Deutelbaum, Marshall. "Structural Patterning in the Lumière Films." In Fell, ed., *Film Before Griffith,* 299–310.

Dexter, Ralph W. "Putnam's Problems Popularizing Anthropology." *American Scientist* 54.3 (1966): 315–32.

Dilworth, Leah. *Imagining Indians in the Southwest: Persistent Visions of a Primitive Past.* Washington, D.C.: Smithsonian Institution Press, 1996.

Dunlop, Ian. "Ethnographic Filmmaking in Australia: The First Seventy Years (1898–1968)." *Studies in Visual Communication* 9 (Winter 1983): 11–18.

Edwards, Elizabeth. "Beyond the Boundary: A Consideration of the Expressive in Photography and Anthropology." In Banks and Morphy, eds., *Rethinking Visual Anthropology,* 53–79.

———. "Introduction." In Edwards, ed., *Anthropology and Photography,* 3–17.

———. *New Histories: Photographs, Anthropology, and Museums.* New York: Reig, 2001.

———. "Performing Science: Still Photography and the Torres Strait Expedition." In Anita Herle and Sandra Rouse, eds., *Cambridge and the Torres Strait: Centenary Essays on the 1898 Anthropological Expedition.* Cambridge: Cambridge University Press, 1998.

———. "Photographic 'Types': The Pursuit of Method." *Visual Anthropology* 3 (1992): 235–58.

Edwards, Elizabeth, ed. *Anthropology and Photography, 1860–1920.* New Haven and London: Yale University Press in association with the Royal Anthropological Institute, 1992.

Elsaesser, Thomas, ed. *Early Cinema: Space, Frame, Narrative*. London: BFI, 1990.

Elsner, John and Roger Cardinal, eds. *The Cultures of Collecting*. Cambridge: Harvard University Press, 1994.

Evans, Brad. "Commentary: Catherine Russell's Recovery of the *Head-Hunters*." *Visual Anthropology* 11.3 (1998): 221–42.

Ewers, John C. "Fact and Fiction in the Documentary Art of the American West." In John F. McDermott, ed., *The Frontier Re-Examined*, 79–95. Urbana: University of Illinois Press, 1967.

Fabian, Johannes. *Time and the Other: How Anthropology Makes Its Object*. New York: Columbia University Press, 1983.

Falconer, John. "Photography in Nineteenth-Century India." In Bayly, ed., *The Raj and the British*, 264–76.

Faris, James C. "A Political Primer on Anthropology/Photography." In Edwards, ed., *Anthropology and Photography*, 253–63.

Fell, John ed. *Film Before Griffith*. Berkeley: University of California Press, 1983.

Fleming, Paula Richardson and Judith Luskey, eds. *The North American Indians in Early Photographs*. London: Phaidon, 1988.

Foucault, Michel. *The Archaeology of Knowledge*. London: Tavistock, 1974.

——. *Discipline and Punish: The Birth of the Prison*. New York: Pantheon, 1977; pbk., New York: Vintage, 1979.

——. "Of Other Spaces." *Diacritics* 6.1 (Spring 1986): 22–27.

Fowler, Don D. and Catherine S. "Anthropology and the Numa: John Wesley Powell's Manuscripts on the Numic Peoples of Western North America, 1868–1880." *Smithsonian Contributions to Anthropology* 14 (1971).

Franz, Charles. "Relevance: American Ethnology and the Wider Society, 1900–1940." In Helm, ed., *Social Contexts of American Ethnology, 1840–1984*, 83–119.

Friedberg, Anne. *Window Shopping: Cinema and the Postmodern*. Berkeley: University of California Press, 1993.

Frizot, Michael. *La Chronophotographie*. Beaune: Association des Amis de Marey et Ministère de la Culture, 1984.

Gaines, Jane. "White Privilege and Looking Relations: Race and Gender in Feminist Film Theory." In Carson, Dittmar, and Welsch, eds., *Multiple Voices in Feminist Film Criticism*, 176–90.

Gartenberg, Jon. "Camera Movement in Edison and Biograph Films, 1900–1906." *Cinema Journal* 19.2 (Spring 1980): 1–16.

Geary, Christaud M. and Virginia-Lee Webb. *Delivering Views: Distant Cultures in Early Postcards*. Washington, D.C.: Smithsonian Institution Press, 1998.

Gidley, Mick. "From the Hopi Snake Dance to 'The Ten Commandments': Edward S. Curtis as Filmmaker." *Studies in Visual Communication* 8.5 (Summer 1982): 70–79.

Gilbert, Susan. "The Explorers Club." Master's thesis, New York University, 1992.

Gilman, Sander. *Difference and Pathology: Stereotypes of Sexuality, Race, and Madness*. Ithica: Cornell University Press, 1985.

Ginsburg, Faye. "Aboriginal Media and the Australian Imaginary." *Public Culture* 5 (1993): 557–78.

———. "Culture/Media: A (Mild) Polemic." *Anthropology Today* 10.2 (Apr. 1994): 5–15.

———. "Mediating Aboriginal Modernities." University College London Daryl Forde Lecture, Mar. 18, 1998.

———. "The Parallax Effect: The Impact of Indigenous Media on Ethnographic Film." In Jane Gaines and Michael Renov, eds., *Visible Evidence*, 156–175. Minneapolis: University of Minnesota Press, 2000.

———. "Shooting Back: From Ethnographic Film to the Ethnography of Media." In Toby Miller and Robert Stam, eds., *A Companion to Film Theory*, 295–322. New York: Blackwell, 1999.

———. "Visual Anthropology and Reverse Ethnographies: Revisioning Theory and Practice for the Millennium." Unpublished paper, July 1996.

Ginsburg, Faye, Lila Abu Lughod, and Brian Larkin, eds. *Media Worlds: Anthropology on New Terrain*. Berkeley: University of California Press (forthcoming, 2002).

———. *The Social Practice of Media: Anthropological Interventions*. Berkeley: University of California Press (forthcoming, 2002).

Ginzburg, Carlo. "Checking the Evidence: The Judge and the Historian." *Critical Inquiry* 18.1 (Autumn 1991): 79–92.

Goldschmidt, Walter R., ed. *The Uses of Anthropology*. Washington, D.C.: American Anthropological Association, 1979.

Gossett, Thomas F. *Race: The History of an Idea*. Dallas: Southern Methodist University Press 1963.

Gould, Stephen Jay. *The Mismeasure of Man*. New York: Norton, 1981.

Green, David. "Classified Subjects: Photography and Anthropology—The Technology of Power." *Ten-8* 14 (1984): 30–37.

———. "Veins of Resemblance: Photography and Eugenics." *Oxford Art Journal* 2 (1985): 3–16.

Greenblatt. Stephen. *Marvelous Possessions: The Wonder of the New World*. Oxford: Clarendon Press, 1991.

———. "Resonance and Wonder." In Karp and Lavine, eds., *Exhibiting Cultures*, 42–56.

Greenhalgh, Paul. *Ephemeral Vistas: The Expositions Universelles, Great Exhibitions, and World Fairs, 1851–1939*. Manchester: Manchester University Press, 1988.

Griffiths, Alison. " 'We Partake, as it Were, of His Life': The Status of the Visual in

Early Ethnographic Film." In John Fullerton and Astrid Söderbergh-Widding, eds., *Moving Images: From Edison to the Webcam*, 91–110. Sydney: John Libbey, 1999.

Grimshaw, Anna. *The Ethnographer's Eye: Ways of Seeing in Anthropology*. Cambridge: Cambridge University Press, 2001.

Gunning, Tom. "An Aesthetic of Astonishment: Early Film and the (In)Credulous Spectator." *Art and Text* 34 (1989): 31–45. Reprinted in Linda Williams, ed., *Viewing Positions*, 114–33.

———. "Before Documentary: Early NonFiction Films and the 'View' Aesthetic." In Hertogs and de Klerk, eds., *Uncharted Territory*, 9–24.

———. "The Cinema of Attractions: Early Film, Its Spectator and the Avant-Garde." In Elsaesser, ed., *Early Cinema*, 56–62.

———. "Film History and Film Analysis: The Individual Film in the Course of Time." *Wide Angle* 12.3 (July 1990): 4–19.

———. "From the Kaleidoscope to the X-Ray: Urban Spectatorship, Poe, Benjamin, and *Traffic in Souls* (1913)." *Wide Angle* 19.4 (1997): 25–61.

———. "From the Opium Den to the Theatre of Morality: Moral Discourse and the Film Process in Early American Cinema." *Art and Text* 30 (Sept.-Nov. 1988): 30–40.

———. " 'Now You See It Now You Don't': The Temporality of the Cinema of Attractions." In Abel, ed., *Silent Film*, 71–84.

———. "An Unseen Energy Swallows Space: The Space in Early Film and Its Relation to American Avant-Garde Film." In Fell, ed., *Film Before Griffith*, 355–66.

———. " 'The Whole World Within Reach': Travel Images Without Borders.' " In Carol Trayner Williams, ed., *Travel Culture: Essays on What Makes Us Go*, 25–38. Westport, Conn.: Praeger, 1998).

———. "The World as Object Lesson: Cinema Audiences, Visual Culture, and the St. Louis World's Fair, 1904." *Film History* 6.4 (Winter 1994): 422–44.

Hansen, Miriam. *Babel and Babylon: Spectatorship in American Silent Film*. Cambridge: Harvard University Press, 1991.

Haraway, Donna. *Primate Visions: Gender, Race, and Nature in the World of Modern Science*. New York: Routledge, 1989.

Harris, Marvin. *The Rise of Anthropological Theory: A History of Theories of Culture*. New York: HarperCollins, 1968.

Harris, Neil. *Cultural Excursions: Marketing Appetites and Cultural Tastes in Modern America*. Chicago: University of Chicago Press, 1990.

———. "Iconography and Intellectual History: The Halftone Effect." In Higham and Conkin, eds., *New Directions in American Intellectual History*, 196–211.

———. "Museums, Merchandising, and Popular Taste: The Struggle for Influence." In Quimby, ed., *Material Culture and the Study of American Life*, 140–74.

Hart, Sidney and David C. Ward. "The Waning of an Enlightenment Ideal: Charles Willson Peale's Museum, 1790–1820." In Miller and Ward, eds., *New Perspectives on Charles Willson Peale*, 219–35.

Heidegger, Martin. "The Age of the World Picture." In *The Questions Concerning Technology and Other Essays*, 115–54. Trans. William Lovitt. New York: Garland, 1977.

Heider, Karl. *Ethnographic Film*. Austin: University of Texas Press, 1986.

Helm, June, ed. *Social Contexts of American Ethnology, 1840–1984*. Proceedings of the American Ethnological Society. Washington, D.C.: American Anthropological Association, 1985.

Herbert, Stephen and Luke McKernan, eds. *Who's Who of Victorian Cinema*. London: BFI, 1996.

Hertogs, Daan and Nico de Klerk, eds. *Nonfiction Film from the Teens*. Amsterdam: Stichting Nederlands Filmmuseum, 1994.

———. *Uncharted Territory: Essays on Early Nonfiction Film*. Amsterdam: Stichting Nederlands Filmmuseum, 1997.

Hevey, David. *The Creatures That Time Forgot: Photography and Disability Imagery*. New York: Routledge, 1992.

Higham, John and Paul K. Conkin, eds. *New Directions in American Intellectual History*. Baltimore: Johns Hopkins University Press, 1979.

Hinsley, Curtis M. "Amateurs and Professionals in Washington Anthropology, 1879–1903." In John V. Murra, ed., *American Anthropology: The Early Years (1974 Proceedings of the American Ethnological Society)*, 36–68. St. Paul: West, 1976.

———. "Anthropology as Science and Politics: The Dilemmas of the Bureau of American Ethnology, 1879–1904." In Goldschmidt, ed., *Uses of Anthropology*, 15–50.

———. "From Shell-Heaps to Stelae: Early Anthropology at the Peabody Museum." In Stocking, ed., *Objects and Others*, 49–74.

———. *The Smithsonian and the American Indian: Making a Moral Anthropology in Victorian America*. Washington, D.C.: Smithsonian Institution Press, 1981.

———. "The World as Marketplace: Commodification of the Exotic at the World's Columbian Exposition, Chicago, 1893." In Karp and Lavine, eds., *Exhibiting Cultures*, 344–65.

Hoberman, Jim. Review of *From the Pole to the Equator*. *Village Voice*, May 26, 1987, 70.

Hockings, Paul, ed. *Principles in Visual Anthropology*. The Hague: Mouton Press, 1975.

Holm, Bill and George Irving Quimby. *Edward S. Curtis in the Land of the War Canoes: A Pioneer Cinematographer in the Pacific Northwest*. Seattle: University of Washington Press, 1980.

Hooper-Greenhill, Eilean. *Museums and the Shaping of Knowledge*. London: Routledge, 1993.

Hoyme, Lucile E. "Physical Anthropology and Its Instruments: An Historical Study." *Southwestern Journal of Anthropology* 9 (1953): 408–29.

Hunt, Lynn. *New Cultural History*. Berkeley: University of California Press, 1984.

Jacknis, Ira. "Franz Boas and Exhibits: On the Limitations of the Museum Method of Anthropology." In Stocking, ed., *Objects and Others*, 75–109.

―――. "Franz Boas and Photography." *Studies in Visual Communication* 10.1 (1984): 2–60.

―――. "George Hunt, Collector of Indian Specimens." In Jonaitis, ed., *Chiefly Feasts*, 177–224.

―――. "George Hunt, Kwakuitl Photographer." In Edwards, ed., *Anthropology and Photography*, 143–51.

―――. "In Search of the Imagemaker: James Mooney as an Ethnographic Photographer." *Visual Anthropology* 3.2 (1992): 179–212.

―――. "Margaret Mead and Gregory Bateson in Bali: Their Use of Photography and Film." *Cultural Anthropology* 3.2 (May 1988): 160–77.

―――. "The Picturesque and the Scientific: Franz Boas's Plan for Anthropological Filmmaking." *Visual Anthropology* 1.1 (1987): 59–64.

Jonaitis, Aldona, ed. *Chiefly Feasts: The Enduring Kwakiutl Potlatch*. New York and Seattle: American Museum of Natural History in association with the University of Washington Press, 1991.

Jones, Sally L. "The First But Not the Last of the 'Vanishing Indians': Edwin Forest and Mythic Re-creations of the Native Population." In Bird, ed., *Dressing in Feathers*, 13–28.

Jordanova, Ludmilla. "Objects of Knowledge: A Historical Perspective on Museums." In Vergo, ed., *The New Museology*, 22–40.

―――. *Sexual Visions: Images of Gender in Science and Medicine Between the Eighteenth and Twentieth Centuries*. Madison: University of Wisconsin Press, 1989.

Jordan, Pierre-L. *Premier Contact—Premier Regard*. Marseilles: Musées de Marseilles, 1992.

Karp, Ivan and Steven D. Lavine, eds. *Exhibiting Cultures: The Poetics and Politics of Museum Display*. Washington, D.C.: Smithsonian Institution Press, 1990.

Katz, Joel. "From Archive to Archiveology." *Cinematograph* 4 (1992): 96–103.

Keil, Charlie. "Steal Engines and Cardboard Rockets: The Status of Fiction and Nonfiction in Early Cinema." *Persistence of Vision* 9 (1991): 37–45.

Keil, Charles and Shelley Stamp, eds. *Cinema's Transitional Era: Audiences, Institutions, Practices* (forthcoming).

Kehoe, Alice Beck. *The Ghost Dance: Ethnohistory and Revitalization*. New York: Holt, Rinehart, and Winston, 1989.

Kendall, Laurel, Barbara Mathé, and Thomas Ross Miller. *Drawing Shadows to Stone: The Photography of the Jesup North Pacific Expedition, 1897–1902*. New York and Seattle: American Museum of Natural History in association with the University of Washington Press, 1997.

Kennedy, John Michael. "Philanthropy and Science in New York City: The American Museum of Natural History, 1868–1969." Ph.D. diss., Yale University, 1968.

Kirshenblatt-Gimblett, Barbara. *Destination Culture: Tourism, Museums, and Heritage.* Berkeley: University of California Press, 1998.

———. "Erasing the Subject: Franz Boas and the Anthropological Study of Jews in the United States, 1903–1942." Unpublished paper presented to the American Anthropological Association, Philadelphia, 1986.

———. "Objects of Ethnography." In Karp and Lavine, eds., *Exhibiting Cultures,* 386–443.

Krech III, Shepard and Barbara A. Hail, eds. *Collecting Native America, 1870–1960.* Washington, D.C.: Smithsonian Institution Press, 1999.

Krouse, Susan Applegate. "Filming the Vanishing Race." In Taureg and Ruby, eds., *Visual Explorations of the World,* 256–61.

———. "Photographing the Vanishing Race." *Visual Anthropology* 3 (1990): 213–33.

LaCapra, Dominick. *History and Criticism.* Ithaca: Cornell University Press, 1989.

Lant, Antonia. "The Curse of the Pharaoh, or How Cinema Contracted Egyptomania." *October* 59 (Winter 1992): 86–112.

———. "Egypt in Early Cinema." In Roland Cosandey and Francois Albera, eds., *Cinema sans frontiers / Images Across Borders, 1896–1918,* 73–94. Quebec and Lausanne: Nuit Blanche editeur/Payot Lausanne, 1996.

Larkin, Brian. "White Prestige and the Immoral, Subversive Problem of Film: Moral Panic and Colonial Authority." Paper presented to the Sawyer Seminar of the Advanced Study Center, International Institute, University of Michigan, Ann Arbor, Mar. 1997. This paper is drawn from "Uncertain Consequences: The Social and Religious Life of Media in Northern Nigeria" (Ph.D. diss., New York University, 1998).

La Tour, Claire Dupré, André Gaudreault, and Roberta Pearson, eds. *Cinema at the Turn of the Century.* Quebec and Switzerland: Éditions Payot Lausanne/Éditions Nota Bene, 1999.

Laughren Pat and Chris Long. "Australia's First Films (Part 6): Surprising Survivals." *Cinema Papers* 7 (1993): 32–36, 59–60.

Leigh, Michael. "Curiouser and Curiouser." In Murray, ed., *Back of Beyond,* 78–89.

Lippard, Lucy R., ed. *Partial Recall.* New York: New Press, 1992.

Liss, Julia E. "Patterns of Strangeness: Franz Boas, Modernism, and the Origins of Anthropology." In Barkan and Bush, eds., *Prehistories of the Future,* 114–30.

Lomax, Alan, Irmgard Bartenieff, and Forrestine Paulay, "Choreometrics: A Method for the Study of Cross-Cultural Pattern in Film," *Research Films* 6.6 (1969): 505–17.

Lowie, Robert H. *The History of Ethnological Theory.* New York: Holt, Rinehart, and Winston, 1937.

Lund, Karen C. *American Indians in Silent Film*. Washington, D.C.: Library of Congress Catalog (Aug. 1992; updated Apr. 1995).

Lyman, Christopher. *The Vanishing Race and Other Illusions: Photographs of Indians by Edward Curtis*. Washington, D.C.: Smithsonian Institution Press, 1982.

MacCannell, Dean. *The Tourist: A New Theory of the Leisure Class*. New York: Schocken, 1976.

MacDonald, Scott. *Avant-Garde Film Motion Studies*. Cambridge: Cambridge University Press, 1993.

MacDougall, David. "Beyond Observational Cinema." In Hockings, ed., *Principles of Visual Anthropology*, 109–23.

———. "Complicities of Style." In Crawford and Turton, eds., *Film as Ethnography*, 92–98.

———. "Ethnographic Film: Failure and Promise." *Annual Review of Anthropology* 7 (1978): 405–25.

———. *Transcultural Cinema*. Princeton: Princeton University Press, 1998.

———. "Unprivileged Camera Style." *Royal Anthropological Institute Newsletter* 50 (June 1982): 8–10.

———. "Visual Anthropology and the Ways of Knowing." Unpublished paper, 1995.

———. "The Visual in Anthropology." In Banks and Morphy, eds., *Rethinking Visual Anthropology*, 276–95.

———. "Whose Story Is It?" In Lucien Taylor, ed., *Visualizing Theory: Selected Essays from V.A.R., 1990–1994*, 27–36. New York: Routledge, 1994.

Macintyre, Marta and Maureen MacKenzie. "Focal Length as an Analogue of Cultural Distance." In Edwards, ed., *Anthropology and Photography*, 158–64.

Markus, Andrew. *Governing Savages*. Sydney: Allen and Unwin, 1990.

Mast, Gerald, Marshall Cohen, and Leo Braudy, eds. *Film Theory and Criticism*. 4th ed. New York: Oxford University Press, 1992.

Mayne, Judith. "Uncovering the Female Body." In Charles Musser and Jay Leyda, eds., *Before Hollywood: Turn of the Century Film from American Archives*, 63–67. New York: American Federation of the Arts, 1986.

Mead, Margaret. *An Anthropologist at Work*. New York: Avon, 1959.

———. "Visual Anthropology in a Discipline of Words." In Hockings, ed., *Principles of Visual Anthropology*, 3–12.

Meisel, Martin. *Realizations: Narrative, Pictorial, and Theatrical Arts in Nineteenth-Century England*. Princeton: Princeton University Press, 1983.

Mellinger, Wayne and Rodney Beaulieu. "White Fantasies, Black Bodies: Racial Power, Disgust, and Desire in American Popular Culture." *Visual Anthropology* 9.2 (1997): 117–47.

Metz, Christian. *The Imaginary Signifier*. Bloomington: Indiana University Press, 1981.

———. "Photography and Fetish." *October* 34 (1985): 81–90.

Michaels, Eric. "A Primer of Restrictions on Picture-Taking in Traditional Areas of Aboriginal Australia." *Visual Anthropology* 4 (1991): 259–75.

Michaelis, Anthony R. *Research Films in Biology, Anthropology, Psychology, and Medicine.* New York: Academic Press, 1955.

Miller, J. Hillis. *Illustration.* London: Reaktion, 1992.

Miller, Lillian B. and David C. Ward, eds. *New Perspectives on Charles Willson Peale.* Washington, D.C. and Pittsburgh: Smithsonian Institution and University of Pittsburgh Press, 1991.

Miller, R. Berkeley. "Anthropology and Institutionalization: Frederick Starr at the University of Chicago, 1892–1923." *Kroeber Anthropological Society Papers* 51–2 (1978): 49–60.

Mintz, Anne. "That's Edutainment." *Museum News* 73.6 (1994): 32–35.

Mitchell, Timothy. *Colonizing Egypt.* Berkeley: University of California Press, 1991.

———. "The World as Exhibition." *Comparative Studies in Society and History* 31.2 (Apr. 1989): 217–36.

Mitchell, W. J. T., ed. *On Narrative.* Chicago: University of Chicago Press, 1980.

Mitman, Greg. "Cinematic Nature: Hollywood Technology, Popular Culture, and the American Museum of Natural History," *Isis* 84 (1993): 637–61.

———. *Reel Nature: America's Romance with Wildlife on Film.* Cambridge: Harvard University Press, 1999.

Morphy, Howard. "The Interpretation of Ritual: Reflections from Film on Anthropological Practice." *Man* 29.1 (Mar. 1994): 117–46.

———. "The Original Australians and the Evolution of Anthropology." In Morphy and Elizabeth Edwards, eds., *Australia in Oxford,* 48–61. Pitt Rivers Museum University of Oxford Monograph 4 (1988).

Morris, Rosalind C. *New Worlds from Fragments: Film, Ethnography, and the Representation of Northwest Coast Cultures.* Boulder, Colo.: Westview, 1994.

Mottet, Jean. "Aesthetics of Disjunction in the Age of Spectacles and Stereotypes: The Question of Vaudeville." In La Tour, Gaudreault, and Pearson, eds., *Cinema at the Turn of the Century,* 149–72.

Mullaney, Steven. "Strange Things, Gross Terms, Curious Customs: The Rehearsal of Cultures in the Late Renaissance." *Representations* 3 (Summer 1983): 40–67.

Mulvaney. D. J. and J. H. Calaby. *"So Much That Is New"—Baldwin Spencer, 1860–1929: A Biography.* Carlton, Victoria: University of Melbourne Press, 1985.

Mulvaney, John, Howard Morphy, and Alison Petch, eds. *My Dear Spencer: The Letters of F. J. Gillen to Baldwin Spencer.* Melbourne: Hyland House, 1997.

Murray, Scott, ed. *Back of Beyond: Discovering Australian Film and Television.* Sydney: Australian Film Commission, 1988.

Musser, Charles. *Before the Nickelodeon: Edwin S. Porter and the Edison Manufacturing Company*. Berkeley: University of California Press, 1991.

————. *The Emergence of Cinema: The American Screen to 1907*. New York: Scribner's, 1990.

————. "The Travel Genre in 1903–1904: Moving Towards Fictional Narrative." In Elsaesser, ed., *Early Cinema*, 123–31.

Musser, Charles with Carol Nelson. *High-Class Moving Pictures: Lyman H. Howe and the Forgotten Era of Traveling Exhibition, 1880–1920*. Princeton: Princeton University Press, 1991.

Mydin, Iskander. "Historical Images—Changing Audiences." In Edwards, ed., *Anthropology and Photography*, 249–52.

Myers, Fred. "The Politics of Representation: Anthropological Discourse and Australian Aborigines." *American Ethnologist* 13 (1986): 138–53.

Nasaw, David. *Going Out: The Rise and Fall of Public Amusements*. New York: Basic Books, 1993.

Neale, Steve. *Cinema and Technology: Image, Sound, Color*. Bloomington: Indiana University Press, 1985.

Nichols, Bill. *Blurred Boundaries: Questions of Meaning in Contemporary Culture*. Bloomington: Indiana University Press, 1994.

————. *Representing Reality*. Bloomington: Indiana University Press, 1991.

Niver, Kemp R., comp. *Biograph Bulletins, 1896–1908*. Edited by Bebe Bergsten. Los Angeles: Locare Research Group, 1971.

————. *Early Motion Pictures: The Paper Print Collection in the Library of Congress*. Washington, D.C.: LOC, 1985.

Nordström, Alison Devine. "Photography of Samoa: Production, Dissemination, and Use." In Blanton, ed., *Picturing Paradise*, 11–40.

Oettermann, Stephen. *The Panorama: History of a Mass Medium*. New York: Zone Books, 1997.

Orvell, Miles. *The Real Thing: Imitation and Authenticity in American Culture, 1880–1940*. Chapel Hill: University of North Carolina Press, 1989.

Parr, A. E. "Dimensions, Backgrounds, and Uses of Habitat Groups." *The Curator* 4.3 (1961): 199–215.

————. "The Habitat Group." *The Curator* 2.2 (1959): 107–28.

Parry, Ellwood. *The Image of the Indian and the Black Man in American Art, 1590–1900*. New York: Braziller, 1974.

Parssinen, Carol Ann. "Social Explorers and Social Scientists: The Dark Continent of Victorian Ethnology." In Jay Ruby, ed., *A Crack in the Mirror*, 205–17. Philadelphia: University of Pennsylvania Press, 1982.

Pearce, Susan M. *Museums, Objects, and Collections: A Cultural Study*. Leicester, Eng.: Leicester University Press, 1992.

Percy, Walker. "The Loss of the Creature." In Bartholmae and Petrosky, eds., *Ways of Seeing: An Anthology for Writers*, 424–45.

Peterson, Jennifer. " 'Truth Is Stranger Than Fiction': Travelogues from the 1910s in the Nederlands Filmmuseum.' " In Hertogs and de Klerk, eds., *Uncharted Territory*, 75–90.

———. "World Pictures: Travelogue Films and the Lure of the Exotic." Ph.D. diss., University of Chicago, 1999.

———. *World Pictures: Travelogue Films and the Lure of the Exotic*. Durham, N.C.: Duke University Press (forthcoming).

Phelan, Peggy. *Unmarked: The Politics of Performance*. New York: Routledge, 1993.

Pike. Kenneth L. "Language in Relation to a Unified Theory of the Structure of Human Behavior, Part I. II. III." (Preliminary edition). Glendale, Calif.: Summer Institute of Linguistics, 1954–1955–1960.

Pinney, Christopher. "Anthropology and the Colonial Image." In Bayly, ed., *The Raj and the British*, 278–305.

———. "Classification and Fantasy in the Photographic Construction of Caste and Tribe." *Visual Anthropology* 3.2 (1990): 259–88.

———. "Colonial Anthropology in the 'Laboratory of Mankind.' " In Bayly, ed., *The Raj and the British*, 252–63.

———. "The Lexical Spaces of Eye-Spy." In Crawford and Turton, eds., *Film as Ethnography*, 26–49.

———. "The Parallel Histories of Anthropology and Photography." In Edwards, ed., *Anthropology and Photography*, 74–95.

Poignant, Roslyn. "Surveying the Field of View: The Making of the RAI Photographic Collection." In Edwards, ed., *Anthropology and Photography*, 42–73.

Poole, Deborah. *Vision, Race, and Modernity: A Visual Economy of the Andean Image World*. Princeton: Princeton University Press, 1997.

Pratt, Mary Louise. *Imperial Eyes: Travel Writing and Transculturation*. New York: Routledge, 1992.

———. "Scratches on the Face of the Country: Or, What Mr. Barrow Saw in the Land of the Bushmen." *Critical Inquiry* 12.1 (Autumn 1985): 119–43.

Preston, Douglas J. *Dinosaurs in the Attic: An Excursion into the American Museum of Natural History*. New York: St. Martin's, c. 1986.

Pryluck, Calvin. "The Itinerant Movie Show and the Development of the Film Industry." *Journal of the University Film and Video Association* 35.4 (Fall 1983): 11–22.

Pultz, John. *Photography and the Body*. London: Orion, 1995.

Quimby, Ian M. G., ed. *Material Culture and the Study of American Life*. New York: Norton, 1978.

Rabinovitz, Lauren. "Temptations of Pleasure: Nickelodeons, Amusement Parks, and the Sights of Female Sexuality." *Camera Obscura* 23 (May 1990): 71–88.

Renov, Michael ed. *Theorizing Documentary.* New York: Routledge, 1993.

Rexer, Lyle. *The American Museum of Natural History: 125 Years of Expedition and Discovery.* New York: Abrams in association with the AMNH, 1995.

Richards, Thomas. *The Commodity Culture of Victorian England: Advertising and Spectacle, 1851–1914.* Stanford: Stanford University Press, 1990.

Roberts, Lisa C. *From Knowledge to Narrative: Educators and the Changing Museum.* Washington, D.C.: Smithsonian Institution Press, 1997.

Rohner, Ronald P. *The Ethnography of Franz Boas: Letters and Diaries of Franz Boas Written on the Northwest Coast from 1886 to 1931.* Chicago: University of Chicago Press, 1969.

Rollwagen, Jack R. "The Role of Anthropological Theory in 'Ethnographic' Filmmaking." In Rollwagen, ed., *Anthropological Filmmaking,* 287–316. Chur, Switzerland: Harwood Academic, 1988.

Rony, Fatimah Tobing. *The Third Eye: Race, Cinema, and Ethnographic Spectacle.* Durham, N.C.: Duke University Press, 1996.

———. "Those Who Squat and Those Who Sit: The Iconography of Race in the 1895 Films of Felix-Louis Regnault." *Camera Obscura* 28 (May 1992): 263–89.

Rosen, Philip. "Disjunction and Ideology in a Preclassical Film: *A Policeman's Tour of the World.*" *Wide Angle* 12.3 (1990): 20–36.

———. "Document and Documentary: On the Persistence of Historical Concepts." In Renov, ed., *Theorizing Documentary,* 58–89.

Ruby, Jay. "An Early Attempt at Studying Human Behavior with a Camera: Franz Boas and the Kwakuitl — 1930." In Nico C. R. Bogaart and Henk W. E. R. Ketebaar, eds., *Methodology in Anthropological Filmmaking: Papers of the IUAES Intercongress, Amsterdam,* 25–38. Göttingen: Editions Herodot, 1983.

———. "Exposing Yourself: Reflexivity, Anthropology, and Film." *Semiotica* 30.1–2 (1980): 153–79.

———. "Franz Boas and the Early Camera Study of Behavior." *The Kinesis Report* 3.1 (1980): 7–11, 16.

———. "The Image Mirrored: Reflexivity and the Documentary Film." *Journal of the University Film Association* 29.1 (Fall 1997): 3–11.

———. "On the Necessity of Being Painfully Obvious, or the (Mis) Appropriation of the Ethnographic Work." Unpublished MS, 1995.

———. *Picturing Culture: Explorations of Film and Anthropology.* Chicago: Chicago University Press, 2000.

Rundstrom, Don. "Imaging Anthropology." In Rollwagen, ed., *Anthropological Filmmaking,* 317–70.

Russell, Catherine. "Beyond Authenticity: The Discourse of Tourism in Ethnographic and Experimental Film." *Visual Anthropology* 5 (1992): 131–41.

———. *Experimental Ethnography: The Work of Film in the Age of Video.* Durham, N.C.: Duke University Press, 1999.

———. "Playing Primitive: 'In the Land of the Headhunters' and/or 'War Canoes.'" *Visual Anthropology* 8 (1996): 55–77.

Ryan, James R. *Picturing Empire: Photography and the Visualization of the British Empire.* Chicago: University of Chicago Press, 1997.

Rydell, Robert W. *All the World's a Fair: Visions of Empire at American International Expositions, 1876–1916.* Chicago: University of Chicago Press, 1984.

———. "The Culture of Imperial Abundance: World's Fairs in the Making of American Culture." In Bronner, ed., *Consuming Visions,* 191–215.

———. "The World's Columbian Exposition of 1893: Racist Underpinnings of a Utopian Artifact." *Journal of American Culture* 1 (1978): 253–75.

Rydell, Robert W., John E. Findling, and Kimberly D. Pelle, eds. *Fair America: World's Fairs in the United States.* Washington, D.C.: Smithsonian Institution Press, 2000.

Said, Edward. *Culture and Imperialism.* New York: Knopf, 1993.

———. *Orientalism.* New York: Pantheon, 1978.

Salwen, Peter. *Upper West Side Story: A History and Guide.* New York: Abbeville Press, 1989.

Sandberg, Mark B. "Effigy and Narrative: Looking into the Nineteenth-Century Folk Museum." In Charney and Schwartz, eds., *Cinema and the Invention of Modern Life,* 320–61.

Sante, Luc. *Low Life.* New York: Vintage, 1991.

Saunders, John R. "Development of Educational Services, 1869–1956." AMNH *Annual Reports (1955–56),* 11–30.

Scherer, Joanna Cohan. "The Public Faces of Sarah Winnemucca." *Cultural Anthropology* 3.2 (May 1988): 178–204.

———. "You Can't Believe Your Eyes: Inaccuracies in Photographs of North American Indians." *Studies in the Anthropology of Visual Communication* 2.2 (1975): 67–79.

Schildkrout Enid and Curtis A. Keim. *African Reflections: Art From Northeastern Zaire.* Seattle and New York: University of Washington Press and the AMNH, 1990.

Schimmel, Julie. "Inventing the Indian." In Treuttner, ed., *The West as America,* 149–89.

Schivelbusch, Wolfgang. *The Railway Journey: The Industrialization of Time and Space in the 19th Century.* Berkeley: University of California Press, 1986.

Schrire, Carmel. "Native Views of Western Eyes." In Skotnes, ed., *Miscast,* 343–54.

Schwartz, Vanessa R. "Cinematic Spectatorship Before the Apparatus: The Public Taste for Reality in Fin-de-Siècle Paris." In Linda Williams, ed., *Viewing Positions,* 87–113.

———. *Spectacular Realities: Early Mass Culture in Fin-de-Siècle France.* Berkeley: University of California Press, 1998.

Sekula, Allan. "The Body and the Archive." *October* 39 (1986): 1–64.

Sellors, Charles Coleman. *Charles Willson Peale*. New York: Scribner's, 1969.

Sherman, Daniel J. and Irit Rogoff, eds. *Museum Culture: Histories, Discourses, and Spectacles*. Minneapolis: University of Minnesota Press, 1994.

Shohat, Ella. "Gender and the Culture of Empire: Towards a Feminist Ethnography of the Cinema." *Quarterly Review of Film and Video* 13.1–3 (1991): 45–84.

———. "Imagining Terra Incognita: The Disciplinary Gaze of Empire." *Public Culture* 3.2 (Spring 1991): 41–70.

Shohat, Ella and Robert Stam. *Unthinking Eurocentrism: Multiculturalism and the Media*. New York: Routledge, 1994.

Singer, Ben. *Melodrama and Modernity: Early Sensational Cinema and Its Contexts*. New York: Columbia University Press, 2001.

Skotnes, Pippa, ed. *Miscast: Negotiating the Presence of the Bushmen*. Cape Town: University of Cape Town Press, 1996.

Smith, Jaune Quick-To-See. Introduction to *Contemporary Native American Photography*. Washington, D.C.: U.S. Dept. of the Interior and the Indian Arts and Crafts Board, 1984.

Spencer, Frank. "Some Notes on the Attempt to Apply Photography to Anthropometry During the Second Half of the Nineteenth Century." In Edwards, ed., *Anthropology and Photography*, 99–107.

Spindler, Paul. "New Guinea, 1904–1906." *Science and Film* 8.1 (Mar. 1959): 10–14.

Springer, Claudia. "A Short History of Ethnographic Film." *The Independent* (Dec. 1984): 13–18.

Spurr, David. *The Rhetoric of Empire: Colonial Discourse in Journalism, Travel Writing, and Imperial Administration*. Durham, N.C.: Duke University Press, 1993.

Starn, Randolph. "Seeing Culture in a Room for a Renaissance Prince." In Hunt, ed., *New Cultural History*, 205–32.

Steiger, Ricabeth and Martin Taureg. "Sleeping Beauties: On the Use of Ethnographic Photographs [1880–1920]." In Taureg and Ruby, eds., *Visual Explorations of the World*, 316–31.

Stepan, Nancy Leys. "Race and Gender: The Role of Analogy in Science." *Isis* 77 (1986): 261–77.

Sternberger, Dolf. *Panoramas of the Nineteenth Century*. New York: Urizen Books, 1977.

Stewart, Susan. "Death and Life, in that Order, in the Works of Charles Willson Peale." In Elsner and Cardinal, eds., *The Cultures of Collecting*, 204–23.

———. *On Longing: Narratives of the Miniature, the Gigantic, the Souvenir, the Collection*. Baltimore: John Hopkins University Press, 1984.

Stocking, George W., Jr. *After Tylor: British Social Anthropology, 1888–1951*. Madison: University of Wisconsin Press, 1995.

———. "Anthropology as Kulturkampf: Science and Politics in the Career of Franz Boas." In Goldschmidt, ed., *Uses of Anthropology*, 33–50.

———. *The Ethnographer's Magic and Other Essays in the History of Anthropology*. Madison: University of Wisconsin Press, 1992.

———. *Selected Papers from the American Anthropologist*. Washington, D.C.: American Anthropological Association, 1976.

———. "What's in a Name? The Origins of the Royal Anthropological Institute (1837–71)." *Man* 6 (1971): 369–90.

Stocking, George W., Jr., ed. *Colonial Situations: Essays on the Contextualization of Ethnographic Knowledge*. Madison: University of Wisconsin Press, 1991.

———. *Objects and Others: Essays on Museums and Material Culture*. Madison: University of Wisconsin Press, 1985.

Stoller, Paul. *The Cinematic Griot: The Ethnography of Jean Rouch*. Chicago: University of Chicago Press, 1992.

———. *The Taste of Ethnographic Things: The Senses in Anthropology*. Philadelphia: University of Pennsylvania Press, 1989.

Strain, Ellen. "Stereoscopic Visions: Touring the Panama Canal." *Visual Anthropology Review* 12, no. 2 (Fall/Winter 1996–97): 44–58.

Strathern, Margaret. "Out of Context: The Persuasive Fictions of Anthropology." *Current Anthropology* 28.3 (June 1987): 251–81.

Street, Brian. "British Popular Anthropology: Exhibiting and Photographing the Other." In Edwards, ed., *Anthropology and Photography*, 122–31.

Streible, Dan. "Fake Fight Films." In la Tour, Gaudreault, and Pearson, eds., *Cinema at the Turn of the Century*, 63–79.

———. *Fight Pictures: A History of Prizefighting and Early Cinema*. Washington, D.C.: Smithsonian Institution Press (forthcoming, 2002).

———. "Female Spectators and the Corbett-Fitzsimmons Fight Film." In Aaron Baller and Todd Boyd, eds., *Sports, Media, and the Politics of Identity*, 16–47. Bloomington: Indiana University Press, 1997.

———. "A History of the Boxing Film, 1894–1915: Social Control and Reform in the Progressive Era," *Film History* 3.3 (1989): 235–58.

Tagg, John. *The Burden of Representation: Essays on Photographies and Histories*. London: Macmillan, 1988.

Taureg, Martin. "The Development of Standards for Scientific Films in German Ethnography." *Studies in Visual Communication* 9.1 (Winter 1983): 19–29.

Taureg, Martin and Jay Ruby, eds. *Visual Explorations of the World: Selected Papers from the International Conference on Visual Communication*. Aachen, Ger.: Edition Heridot, 1987.

Taylor, Donald. " 'Very Loveable Human Beings': The Photography of Everard im Thurn." In Edwards, ed., *Anthropology and Photography*, 187–92.

Taylor, Lucien. "Iconophobia: How Anthropology Lost It at the Movies." *Transition* 69 (1992): 64–88.

Thomas, Nicholas. *Colonialism's Culture*. Princeton: Princeton University Press, 1994.

———. "Licensed Curiosity: Cook's Pacific Voyages." In Elsner and Cardinal, eds., *The Cultures of Collecting*, 116–36.

Thomson, Rosemarie Garland, ed. *Freakery: Cultural Spectacles of the Extraordinary Body*. New York: New York University Press, 1996.

Tomas, David. "Tools of the Trade: The Production of Ethnographic Observation on the Andaman Islands, 1858–1922." In Stocking, ed., *Colonial Situations*, 76–108.

Toulet, Emmanuelle. "Cinema at the Universal Exposition, Paris, 1900." *Persistence of Vision* 9 (1991): 10–36.

Trachtenberg, Alan. *Reading American Photographs: Images as History, Mathew Brady to Walker Evans*. New York: Hill and Wang, 1989.

Trennert, Robert A., Jr. "A Grand Failure: The Centennial Indian Exhibition of 1876." *Prologue* 6.2 (Summer 1974): 126.

Treuttner, William H., ed. *The West as America: Reinterpreting Images of the Frontier, 1820–1920*. Washington, D.C.: Smithsonian Institution Press, 1991.

Uricchio, William and Roberta E. Pearson. *Reframing Culture: The Case of the Vitagraph Quality Films*. Princeton: Princeton University Press, 1993.

Urry, James. "*Notes and Queries on Anthropology* and the Development of Field Methods in British Anthropology, 1870–1920." *Proceedings of the Royal Anthropological Institute of Great Britain and Northern Ireland* (1972): 45–57.

Vanderwal, Ron, ed. *The Aboriginal Photographs of Baldwin Spencer* (Melbourne: J. Luwey O'Neill on Behalf of the National Museum of Victoria Council, 1982).

Vardac, A. Nicholas. *From Stage to Screen: Theatrical Origins of Early Film — David Garrick to D. W. Griffith*. New York: Da Capo, 1949.

Vaughan, Christopher A. "Ogling Igorots: The Politics and Commerce of Exhibiting Cultural Otherness, 1898–1913." In Thomson, ed., *Freakery*, 219–33.

Vergara, Jr., Benito M. *Displaying Filipinos: Photography and Colonialism in Early Twentieth-Century Philippines*. Quezon City: University of the Philippines Press, 1995.

Vergo, Peter, ed. *The New Museology*. London: Reaktion, 1988.

Warner, Marina. "Waxworks and Wonderlands." In Cook and Wollen, eds., *Visual Display: Culture Beyond Appearances*, 178–201.

Weinberger, Eliot. "The Camera People." *Transition* 55 (1993): 24–54.

Williams, Elizabeth A. *The Physical and the Moral: Anthropology, Physiology, and Philosophical Medicine in France, 1750–1850*. Cambridge: Cambridge University Press, 1994.

Williams, Linda, ed. *Viewing Positions: Ways of Seeing Film*. New Brunswick: Rutgers University Press, 1995.

Wollen, Peter. "Fire and Ice." *Photographies* 4 (Apr. 1984): 16–21.

Wonders, Karen. *Habitat Dioramas: Illusion of Wilderness in Museums of Natural History*. Uppsala: Acta Universitatis Upsaliensis, Figura Nova Series 24, 1993.

———. "The Illusionary Art of Background Painting in Habitat Dioramas." *The Curator* 33.2 (1990): 90–118.

Worth, Sol. "Margaret Mead and the Shift from 'Visual Anthropology' to the 'Anthropology of Visual Communication.'" *Studies in Visual Communication* 6.1 (1980): 15–22. Reprinted in Worth, *Studying Visual Communication*, ed. Larry Gross, 185–99. Philadelphia: University of Pennsylvania Press, 1981.

Zimmermann, Patricia R. "Our Trip to Africa," *Afterimage* 17.8 (Mar. 1990): 3–8.

———. *Reel Families: A Social History of Amateur Film*. Bloomington: Indiana University Press, 1995.

Index